The Signs of Determination

Fachrichtung Angewandte Sprachwissenschaft
sowie Übersetzen und Dolmetschen
der Universität des Saarlandes

Alberto Gil – Johann Haller – Erich Steiner
(Hrsg.)

Sabest

Saarbrücker Beiträge zur Sprach- und Translationswissenschaft

Band 16

PETER LANG
Frankfurt am Main · Berlin · Bern · Bruxelles · New York · Oxford · Wien

Valerio Allegranza

The Signs of Determination

Constraint-Based Modelling Across Languages

PETER LANG
Internationaler Verlag der Wissenschaften

Bibliographic Information published by the Deutsche Nationalbibliothek
The Deutsche Nationalbibliothek lists this publication in the Deutsche Nationalbibliografie; detailed bibliographic data is available in the internet at <http://www.d-nb.de>.

Zugl.: Saarbrücken, Univ., Diss., 2006

Cover illustration by kind permission
of Peggy Daut.

D 291
ISSN 1436-0268
ISBN 978-3-631-56510-0

www.peterlang.de

Contents

Foreword . . . 7

1 Introducing Determination **11**

1.1 Preamble . . . 11

1.2 Empirical coverage: a case study . . . 13

1.2.1 The determiners of English . . . 13

1.2.2 Parts of speech . . . 18

1.2.2.1 Against 'Q(P)' . . . 18

1.2.2.2 Against 'Det' . . . 25

1.3 The NP tradition revisited . . . 32

1.3.1 Determiners, pronouns and 'Ø-nouns' . . . 34

1.3.2 Head hunting: against the DP Hypothesis . . . 45

1.3.3 The case for genitive case . . . 55

1.4 Conclusions . . . 66

2 Meaning and Multilingual Data **71**

2.1 Preamble . . . 71

2.2 Methodology for semantic notions . . . 72

2.2.1 On denotation and reference . . . 72

2.2.2 The interdisciplinary scenario . . . 80

2.3 Insights from a contrastive analysis . . . 86

2.3.1 Articles . . . 87

2.3.1.1 Definite vs. indefinite . . . 87

2.3.1.2 Plural, uncountables, partitive article . . . 93

2.3.2 Demonstratives . . . 96

2.3.3 Possessives . . . 100

2.3.4 Quantitatives . . . 103

2.3.4.1 The lexical field of quantity/amount . . . 103

2.3.4.2 Quantitatives across languages . . . 108

2.3.5 Cardinals . . . 115

2.3.6 Ordinals . . . 121

2.4 Conclusions . . . 123

3 Basic Semantic Modelling **127**
3.1 Preamble 127
3.2 Logical background 130
3.2.1 Logical form and definiteness conditions 130
3.2.2 Generalized Quantifier Theory 141
3.2.2.1 Compositional NP interpretation 141
3.2.2.2 Semantic determiners and related issues 148
3.3 Towards feature-theoretic semantics 154
3.3.1 Quantification and semantics in HPSG 154
3.3.2 Semantic features of determination 164
3.3.2.1 On the range of reference 165
3.3.2.2 Definiteness revisited 172
3.4 Conclusions 180

4 HPSG and the Noun Phrase **183**
4.1 Preamble 183
4.2 From X-bar Theory to HPSG 184
4.2.1 Phrase structure patterns 184
4.2.2 Lexical selection of dependents 195
4.3 A cross-linguistic NP analysis 207
4.3.1 Determiners as specifiers or adjuncts 208
4.3.1.1 On multiple determination 208
4.3.1.2 Lexical selection of heads 217
4.3.2 Plurals between semantics and syntax 227
4.4 Conclusions 239

5 Extended Formal Treatment **245**
5.1 Preamble 245
5.2 The syntactic framework 248
5.2.1 Phrase structure constraints in HPSG 248
5.2.2 Functors for a 'construction theory' 258
5.2.3 The marking system of determination 269
5.3 On the syntax-semantics interface 281
5.3.1 A lexicalist account of quantifier scope 281
5.3.2 The proper treatment of proper names 293
5.3.2.1 Problems with individual terms 293
5.3.2.2 Naming, quantification and indexicality 300
5.4 Conclusions 309

Bibliography **311**

Foreword

"Tu non pensavi ch'io loico fossi!"
DANTE (*Inferno*, XXVII-123)

The following study on **determination** phenomena of the Noun Phrase in some European languages investigates a broad grammatical treatment that covers both syntactic and semantic aspects of relevant linguistic signs. This methodological decision does not question in general the validity of approaches to natural language relying on the 'autonomy of syntax' *à la* Chomsky, given a modular view of grammatical competence. We agree that a reconstruction of purely syntactic facts, which leaves out of consideration what meaning has been expressed, may well be legitimate when one can adequately define the subject of inquiry at such a level of abstraction. However, 'determination' for us is a fundamentally semantic concept (with some pragmatic implications), bearing on issues of definiteness, quantification, etc., and we shall argue at length that there is no adequate syntactic (as well as morphological) definition of a **part of speech** corresponding precisely to the class of expressions known as 'determiners'. These are simply words or phrases expressing a particular typology of semantic information, irrespective of their independently motivated categorization through morpho-syntactic parts of speech that are also available for expressions with a different function.

In a sense, we argue for a revival of the approach to determination matters typical of traditional descriptive grammar and lexicography, contrary to more recent trends in theoretical linguistics, whereby a category Determiner with part-of-speech status is commonly assumed. But the way in which our work develops the revived approach in technical detail is far from being conservative. Compared with the grammatical mainstream following Chomsky's theory (in any of its historical varieties, from early transformational grammar to current 'minimalism'), what characterizes this study from a general meta-theoretic point of view is the formal framework for representing linguistic knowledge: a modern **constraint-based grammar** with a phrase structure backbone and a richly expressive system of features allowing complex values (hence 'feature structures'). On a formalization of that kind, all linguistic objects are defined in a declarative fashion through some pool of logical constraints, combining compatible information without transformations or extrinsic procedures.

Grammars encoded in a suitable declarative formalism have become especially popular for computational linguistics, because of their great flexibility. They straightforwardly apply to linguistic data in models of performance while staying neutral w.r.t. the processing strategies, like **generation** vs. **parsing**, *bottom-up* vs. *top-down*, so as to be integrally reusable in this connection. It is a property that appears theoretically relevant (apart from its practical applications in language technology), insofar as any cognitively realistic grammar should support the human subjects' mastery of the language for both uttering and understanding purposes. Thus, while our work is meant to comply with formal techniques originating from computational linguistics and – particularly in the semantic field – some symbolical languages of logic, the objectives we pursue are empirical (linguistic and cognitive), rather than purely formal (computational or logico-mathematic).

The spirit of the enterprise, as sketched above, has a clear impact on the organization of this volume. The first two chapters offer a relatively informal discussion of empirical bases of our research on determination in English and other European languages, so that insights from descriptive and contrastive linguistics pave the way for adequate assumptions in grammatical theorizing. The linguistic means to express determination are exemplified monolingually in chapter 1, showing how determiners of English can be classified according to a restrictive system of morpho-syntactic categories. Chapter 2 investigates the intuitive cross-linguistic meaning (hence translatable content) of the main kinds of determinative expressions: articles as well as demonstrative, possessive, quantitative, cardinal and ordinal determiners. This is done contrasting data from three **Germanic** languages, namely Danish, English and German, and three **Romance** languages, namely French, Italian and Spanish.

Our presentation becomes gradually more formal in the rest of the volume. In chapter 3, the meaning of determiners is modelled by taking into account Jon Barwise and Robin Cooper's **Generalized Quantifier Theory** and other basic research in logical semantics. Then it is shown how resulting formulae of logic can be recoded as feature structures for the purpose of a constraint-based parallel representation of linguistic expressions and their meaning. Chapter 4 links up determiners with an improved analysis of the Noun Phrase according to 'X-bar syntax' (in Chomskyan terminology) and clarifies their functions as dependents of the nominal head. Technically, both syntactic and semantic aspects of our work are developed in terms of a version of **Head-driven Phrase Structure Grammar** (HPSG), the constraint-based grammatical framework originally proposed by Carl Pollard and Ivan Sag. But whereas these authors treated only the most common cases of determination in English, we extend the system so as to achieve a broad and multilingual coverage of all the abovementioned kinds of determiners with their possible combinations.

In Chapter 5, our HPSG formalization is completed by representing the syntactic trees themselves as complex feature structures, subject to universal principles as well as language-specific constraints like co-occurrence restrictions on multiple determination for the same Noun Phrase. In this connection, the original grammar by Pollard and Sag is revised by formalizing the so-called *specifiers* and *adjuncts* of X-bar theory according to a notion of *functor* which proves ideal for dealing with all sorts of determiners. Finally, the quantification import of determiners but also of self-determining nominal items (in case of proper names, pronouns, etc.) is addressed in relation to the syntax-semantics interface of HPSG, extending and revising its method of 'quantifier storage' so as to achieve radically lexicalist solutions for problems of quantifier scope ambiguity not adequately addressed by previous versions of the framework.

Acknowledgements: This work originates from research that was carried out by the present author (on behalf of Gruppo DIMA, Torino) within a project of the MLAP programme of the European Commission, viz. *Investigation of Linguistic Specifications for Future Industrial Standards*, coordinated by Paul Schmidt (IAI, Saarbrücken). The previous or contemporary participation in other projects, such as *Formal Semantics for Discourse*, coordinated by Frank Van Eynde (University of Leuven), and *COLSIT – Constraint-based Linguistic Specifications for Italian*, coordinated by the author himself, has also partly contributed to the line of research feeding the current volume. All the above projects, together with a few meetings, lectures and publications resulting from them, were extremely useful for interacting with colleagues who commented on work in progress and/or supported it in different ways. At least the following names deserve to be mentioned: Toni Badia, Sergio Balari, Ana-Maria Barbu, Paul Bennett, Peter Blok, Andrea Bolioli, Johan Bos, Luca Dini, Joke Dorrepaal, Jacques Durand, Valerio Fissore, Heleen Hoekstra, Lee Humphreys, Arne Kirchner, Carla Marello, Giampaolo Mazzini, Bice Mortara Garavelli, Klaus Netter, Anne Neville, Cesare Oitana, Nilda Ruimy, Louisa Sadler, Alex Schoenmakers, Jörg Schütz, Harald Trost, Erwin Valentini, Frank Van Eynde, Larisa Zlatic, Franz Zwarts. More specific acknowledgements will be provided in the book, as usual, in the form of references to relevant contributions by some of these colleagues, among others.

The author is grateful to the *Philosophischen Fakultät II* of the University of the Saarland and all those who made it possible for him to submit and defend his work as a PhD dissertation in Applied Linguistics, especially the supervisor Johann Haller, the second reviewer Erich Steiner, and the other examiners, Roland Marti (president), Harald Zimmermann and Dirk Luckhardt. Special thanks also to Paul Schmidt, for much practical help in this enterprise since its inception.

Chapter 1

Introducing Determination

1.1 Preamble

The notion of 'determination' to be investigated in this volume concerns the occurrence (or absence, in 'Ø-determination' conditions) of morpho-syntactic items acting as a particular type of dependents for the nominal head, viz. the **determiners**.[1] Intuitively, determiners as intended here are just adnominal expressions with a relatively uniform semantic function:

> "the function of words and ... phrases which, in general, determine what *kind of reference* a noun phrase has: for example, whether it is definite (like *the*) or indefinite (like *a/an*), partitive (like *some*) or universal (like *all*). Semantically, all noun phrases are determined in some way or other... But some heads are by their very nature self-determining: proper nouns and personal pronouns, for example, are inherently definite... In such cases, then, a noun phrase will not generally contain a separate word with a determinative function."
>
> Quirk et al. (1985: pp. 64-65)

To deal with reference – and the ways of determining it – is not easy, at least because the account tends to vary depending on philosophical views and the system assumed for semantic interpretation. Our book will tackle the issue by drawing on the mainstream of logical and computational semantics, with an eye to cognitive and pragmatic factors as well, but a pre-theoretical understanding of the intended determinative function is provisionally taken for granted so as to focus this introductory chapter on basic morpho-syntactic aspects.

[1] The assumption that the construction combining a determiner and a nominal expression be headed by the latter is traditional, though not uncontroversial: we defer a critical discussion of the opposite view, the so-called 'DP Hypothesis', to § 1.3.2. In the chapters 4-5 we will be more precise about the syntactic relationship linking the two constituents, but for the moment it seems enough to say that the determiner is 'adnominal', i.e. added as dependent of the nominal head. (Cf. the notion of 'adverbial' dependence on a verbal/non-nominal head, § 1.2.2.1 below.)

Section 1.2 exemplifies the pertinent coverage of determination by means of a lexical inventory and classification of English expressions, whose grammatical category is also discussed in terms of the **part of speech** notion. The monolingual 'case study' thus outlined, resorting to minimum formal apparatus at the present stage, is indeed meant to introduce and motivate empirically a clear conceptual model (a 'grid' of classificatory notions) that next chapters will show how to apply to the determination systems of various other European languages. Such a modelling gets extended to the general structure of the Noun Phrase (NP) in section 1.3, before drawing some conclusions in section 1.4.

Although still relatively informal, the discussion of linguistic facts in the current chapter is expected to be consistent with a broad class of formalized systems which can be dubbed **interpreted phrase structure grammars**. Hence a type of grammar where the overall representation of each syntactically well-formed expression of the language, in a given reading, is a phrase structure tree[2] – or equivalent labelled bracketing – whose 'nodes' are paired with corresponding semantic interpretations. As overall representation the resulting tree is grammatically exhaustive and self-contained, not a step in a derivation of "more than one level of syntactically defined structure" (Gazdar et al. 1985: p. 10):

> "we are adopting the view that grammars should be **monostratal**, i.e. referring to only a single [– syntactic –] level of representation. 'Surface structure' is the standard term that comes closest to conveying the properties of this level."

That is, within the proposed framework, all covert syntactic levels like 'deep (or D-) structure' and 'syntax of logical form (LF)', as conceived in Chomsky's line of research[3], are simply ruled out. The phrase structure syntax of our unique level has 'surface' status in the sense of an immediate constituent analysis, preserving the lexical items and linear order of the overt expression.

Modern phrase structure grammars make up for their lack of any transformational derivation of multiple levels by annotating nodes of the surface syntactic tree with a good deal of linguistic information, represented in terms

---

[2]Phrase-structurally, a lexical item is the atomic case of well-formed linguistic expression, its syntactic tree consisting of exactly one 'node'. This fact, obviously, does not make the representation atomic in other respects, since "a lexical entry contains at least four kinds of information: a phonological form, a [morpho-syntactic] category, an indication of any irregular morphology, and a meaning" (Gazdar et al. 1985: p. 34). Gradually richer lexical entries will be outlined as our work proceeds.

[3]See Chomsky (1965; 1981; 1995), for some milestones. (Note that our notion of 'logical form' in chapter 3, unlike his, will not have the status of a syntactic level.)

of **features** with possibly complex values. Even though phonological, morpho-syntactic and semantic features are commonly available in generative grammar at least since Chomsky's (1965) 'standard theory', their great expressive potential has not been fully recognized and exploited until the '80s, with the development of such constraint-based non-transformational theories as GPSG (Generalized Phrase Structure Grammar: Gazdar 1981a; 1982, Gazdar et al. 1985), LFG (Lexical Functional Grammar: Bresnan 1982a) and HPSG (Head-driven Phrase Structure Grammar: Pollard & Sag 1987; 1994). This being the line of research that we also follow, various formal and theoretical aspects of the grammatical systems will be presented in due course by our volume, with special reference to HPSG. Instead of providing now some abstract one-shot overview, which would be superfluous for the experts and likely to baffle the readers that are less familiar with formalization, we have chosen to explain system-internal notions in a piecemeal fashion, as soon as they prove necessary/useful for a complete understanding of the concrete treatment of linguistic phenomena.

1.2 Empirical coverage: a case study

1.2.1 The determiners of English

Empirically, the starting point for defining our coverage of morpho-syntactic expressions of determination can be offered by a 'case study' on data of English, the most widespread language among those to be considered in the book. Drawing on well-known informal descriptions of English – v. especially Quirk et al. (1985: pp. 253-264) – a reasonably comprehensive coverage should take into account at least the following six classes of determiner words:

articles → *the*, *a*(*n*)

demonstratives → *this*, *that*, *these*, *those*

possessives → *my*, *your*, *his*, *her*, *its*, *our*, *their*

quantitatives[4] → the non-numeral determiners of quantity/amount, like *every*, *no*, *some*, *many*, etc.

cardinals → the numerals *one*, *two*, *three*, ...

ordinals → the numerals *first*, *second*, *third*, ... and the ordinals without explicit numeral meaning (e.g. *last*).

[4]The label 'quantitative determiners' – sometimes shortened to 'quantitatives' – refers to the class of words also known as 'quantifiers' or 'indefinites'. In chapter 2 we will make it clear that such other denominations are somewhat misleading, in view of their current technical meaning in modern semantic studies.

We conceive these classes of words as 'paradigmatic kinds' (to be called also 'kinds' *tout court*, when there is no danger of confusion), using the qualification 'paradigmatic' as the opposite of 'syntagmatic' in a broad Saussurian sense: alternative items vs. co-occurring items. (Cf. Saussure 1916: ch. 5 of part 2; Hjelmslev 1943: ch. 11.) In that way, our six kinds of determiners need not form a morphological paradigm proper. For most of them, the key criterion of classification derives from some pre-theoretical semantic notion allowing a certain collection of linguistically expressible alternatives (possibly an infinite series, as in the case of numerals); while in the current chapter we can take for granted an intuitive understanding of the relevant notions, they are to be carefully investigated in chapter 2. On the other hand, semantics aside, the resulting morpho-syntactic coverage deserves a number of comments.

For one thing, according to the same descriptive literature by Quirk et al. that we are assuming, the full coverage of English determination additionally comprises **multipliers** (*double*, *twice*, *three times*, etc.), **fractions** (*one-third*, *two-fifths*, etc.), **wh-determiners** (*whose*, *what*, *whichever*, etc.), as well as items with a more uncertain determinative function (like *such* – cf. Leech & Svartvik 1975: pp. 203, 228; Quirk et al. 1985: pp. 258, 376). We think these further kinds of determiners and their morpho-syntactic and semantic peculiarities can be left out of our present coverage without altering the overall scenario; they are, in principle, compatible with future extensions of the work. Actually, even the six fundamental kinds envisaged above would make the determination coverage too broad for those linguists who deny the status of determiners to some of them. Positions on the issue are very much related to what level of linguistic abstraction one deems appropriate for the 'determiner' concept: in § 1.2.2 we will argue against a common alternative to the view followed by our study.

Five of our six classes of determiners – **articles** being the exception – result from intuitive classificatory notions which may well be extended to items whose distribution is arguably pronominal, rather than adnominal. Those items are, in a sense, 'independent', i.e. they appear to occur instead of the nominal head a corresponding determiner should depend on. In English, identical forms are used both ways in the case of demonstratives, cardinals, ordinals, the possessives *his* and *its* and most quantitatives, whereas 'independent' forms of the other possessives and quantitatives are morpho-phonologically distinct from the corresponding adnominal forms (e.g. *mine* vs. *my*, *everybody* vs. *every*). At any rate, determiners are only adnominal (by definition, according to the concept assumed at the beginning of the chapter), so that a word token literally understood as heading/embodying the pertinent Noun Phrase does not make a determiner. If 'empty elements' (i.e. phonologically unexpressed constituents) with suitable syntactic and semantic properties were postulated, however, the treatment offered for determiners of overt nominal heads could be extended to their 'independent' counterparts as actually adnominal ones: that is, determiners of empty nominal heads (v. Jackendoff 1977: ch. 5, Nerbonne et al. 1989, among others). It is a vexed question we need not settle now, but our preference for pronominal approaches (as in Miller 1991, Kathol 1999) will become clear soon, starting from § 1.2.2.2.

Raising a further issue, we must also consider that many determiner words can be expanded by their own optional dependents with some 'modifying' function, mostly 'degree adverbials' (in a sense to be discussed in § 1.2.2.1). The phrase thus projected inherits the determinative type of its lexical head among other properties; e.g., the phrase *almost twenty* in "*almost twenty* books" is a cardinal determiner on a par with the word *twenty* heading it. That is, even if the paradigmatic classification adopted above for our coverage is lexically based, it need not be restricted to the lexicon. In Saussurian terminology (revived by Pollard & Sag 1987; 1994), it is a typology of 'signs' – the meaningful linguistic units at any rank of structural analysis – covering words and phrases that are in a choice relationship.

By the same token, the possessive kind of English determiners is meant to include both the **possessive words** listed before and distributionally as well as functionally equivalent **Saxon genitive phrases** (like *the teacher's* in "*the teacher's* book"), though the former items do not occur as heads of the latter. This and other problems concerning the structural constituency of more or less complex determinative expressions are indeed addressed in the present volume, but admittedly we do not deal with the complex determiner phrases resulting from two special constructions:

- quantitative comparison, as in "*more than twenty* books" (cf. Pollard & Sag 1994: § 9.4.3, for a tentative analysis of comparative phrases like the italicized one);

- coordination of simple or complex determiners, in examples as varied as "*these and those* books", "*two or three* books", "*most but not all* books", "*Mary's and the teacher's* books", "*at least two but not more than twenty* books", etc.

As comparative and coordinate structures raise notoriously hard construction-specific problems which are well beyond the scope of our current work, they will be mostly neglected henceforth. At any rate, real focus of our research will be the syntactic and semantic contribution of a whole determiner to the Noun Phrase, irrespective of the internal complexity of that determiner in terms of phrase structure (or, when relevant, morphological word structure)[5]. Thus,

[5] Due to affixation and compounding, word structure too can become rather complex in the case of numeral determiners (to be presented in chapter 2).

by default, we shall keep on referring just to 'determiners', 'determination items', 'determinative expressions', etc., so as to neutralize terminologically the distinction between lexical and phrasal units of the kind, whenever the difference remains uninfluential for the argumentation.

At this point of our introductory 'case study' on English determination, taking a step towards the description of determiners as a type of constituent of the NP, we turn to the positions available for them within a **syntagmatic chain**, i.e. according to linear order. Let us first notice that even if the English determiners are normally expected to precede the nominal head, on closer inspection some few exceptions can be found. There are quantitative determiners allowing postnominal uses, like *enough* ("*enough* money" / "money *enough*"), and in the case of *galore* the only possible position is after the noun ("money *galore*"). With a personal pronoun as head, the same position is obligatory for *all* and *both*, as in "they *all*", or "us *both*", etc.[6] One might exclude all postpositive cases from the determination coverage by stipulating that only prenominal expressions be classifiable as determiners, but this would clearly be *ad hoc*, since occurrence after the head does not affect the determinative semantic function. We shall say more about postnominal determiners of English and other languages in chapter 2.

A fundamental syntagmatic aspect which we want to discuss can be called 'multiple determination', being due to the co-occurrence of at least two non-coordinated determiners that depend on (syntactic projections of) the same head noun[7]. Their linear order complies with a generalization presented in the usual descriptive grammar of English by Quirk et al. (1985), a systematic pattern entailing that determiners be distributed into three **positional classes** within the NP. From left to right:

I. **predeterminers** – at the very least, the quantitatives *all* and *both* when they are used before the nominal head, but there are also predeterminers we don't cover, like multipliers and fractions (see above);

II. **central determiners** – articles, demonstratives, possessives, as well as quantitative central determiners (e.g. *some*);

[6]When *all* (or *both*) follows a non-pronominal subject, as in "The students *all* hate syntax", Radford (1997: p. 141) does not assume postpositive determination, but a so-called **floating quantifier** attached to the Verb Phrase (and preceded by an interposing auxiliary in examples like "The villages have *all* been destroyed"). In our view, however, postpositive determination is confirmed for personal pronouns: the adjacent quantitative item can follow them in non-subject positions (v. "John knows them *all*"), where English grammar would forbid the same item to 'float' in case of a non-pronominal NP source. (Cf. Quirk et al. 1985: p. 382.)

[7]The already mentioned case of determiners linked together through coordination is not covered as an instance of 'multiple determination' in our sense.

III. **postdeterminers** – cardinals and ordinals, as well as quantitative postdeterminers (e.g. *few*).

Cf. Quirk et al. (1985: p. 253):

> "The three classes of determiners have been set up on the basis of their position in the noun phrase in relation to each other. Thus we do not find central determiner + predeterminer (* *their all trouble*), or postdeterminer + central determiner + predeterminer (* *five the all boys*), but only the order I + II + III given above: *all their trouble, all the five boys*."

More precisely, predeterminers can precede but cannot follow the determiners of the other classes, postdeterminers can follow but cannot precede the determiners of the other classes, and the relative position of central determiners is derived as a consequence.

Note that the threefold pattern by itself does not rule out the co-occurrence of members of the same positional class, a phenomenon which is actually possible with postdeterminers. As a result, multiple determination cases involving more than three determiners per head noun are found too, although relatively rare. (See chapter 4 below for examples in some languages.) On the other hand, Quirk et al. (1985: p. 254) point out that "central determiners ... are mutually exclusive with each other, i.e. there cannot be more than one" (per head noun); according to **II** above, that one in English must be either an article or an alternative determination item with the same distribution. These determiners are particularly important for NP structure, because of the empirical requirement that NPs headed by singular count nouns – as opposed to plural nouns and 'non-count' nouns – obligatorily take an article or another determiner replacing it (but we refer to the next chapters for extensive discussion of the issue).

Although the determiners' syntagmatic classification is based on the behaviour they show in the event of co-occurence, it leaves them free to (co-)occur or not:

(1) a. *all the five* books

b. *all the* books / *all five* books / *the five* books

c. *all* books / *the* books / *five* books

d. books

As a matter of fact, all the examples in (1) are grammatical as complete NPs and meet the linear order constraints on determination, even if vacuously in some cases. In particular, when none of the three slots is filled – see (1d) – we have a noun phrase with 'Ø-determination' as mentioned at the beginning of the chapter.

It is worth emphasizing that the items *all*, *the* and *five* are referred to respectively as 'predeterminer', 'central determiner' and 'postdeterminer' also in case of examples like (1b)-(1c), i.e. under conditions of partial realization of the pattern exemplified in full by (1a). Certainly, one may wonder to what extent the terminological invariance is just a straightforward convention for classifying empirical items or instead reflects a real invariance in their function across syntactic contexts. At the very least, we are assuming that *all*, *the* and *five* are adnominal dependents with determinative function not only when used alone with the nominal head, as in (1c), but also in all multiple determination examples such as (1a)-(1b)[8], yet their specific way of 'determining' the noun phrase may well partly vary in the two kinds of context. The issue will be addressed in due course by this volume.

1.2.2 Parts of speech

1.2.2.1 Against 'Q(P)'

A crucial point of our case study on English is to show that the class of expressions we call 'determiners' – a notion motivated by functional and semantic affinity as we mentioned – does not correspond to a morpho-syntactic 'part of speech' on a par with Noun, Adjective, Verb, etc. One should not be surprised if determiners were morpho-syntactically heterogeneous like some other class of expressions with a common semantic function, say the restrictive adnominal modifiers, which are projected by various parts of speech. (The domain of entities denoted by the nominal head can be restricted through apt qualifying adjectives, prepositional phrases, relative clauses[9], etc.) Indeed, traditional grammarians and lexicographers have usually regarded the Article as a part of speech in its own right[10], while reckoning the remaining determiners among adjectives or pronouns. Approaches of a different sort are found in contribu-

[8]Chapter 4 will offer evidence in favour of our approach dismissing the hypothesis that sequences like "all the", "all the five", etc. be complex determiner phrases, with a single determiner head expanded by one or more dependents of its own. (Such dependents, given our notion of determiner, would not be determiners in the relevant construction, because they would not bear any dependency relation to the nominal the determination pertains to.)

[9]Opinions about the part of speech projecting relative clauses, or clauses in general, tend to differ; Jackendoff (1977), Gazdar et al. (1985) and Sag (1997), among others, take it to be the Verb. However, what really matters now is just the fact that the three kinds of modifiers we have mentioned are obviously projected by three different parts of speech, despite their common semantic function.

[10]It was already one of the eight classical parts of speech acknowledged by the ancient Greek grammarians (see, e.g., Robins 1967: ch. 2).

tions based on modern generative grammar, where a category Determiner, Det or D, with part-of-speech status, is commonly taken for granted; but a serious drawback is its fairly uncertain coverage, as there appears to be no clear-cut and stable characterization like those of other parts of speech.

For instance, in the pertinent exemplification offered for English by Radford (1981: ch. 2-3) the syntactic determination coverage narrows down compared with ours, because Det covers only articles and adnominal demonstratives and possessives, while a separate category Quantifier or Q is introduced – following Bresnan (1973) – at least for some of the expressions that we would classify as 'quantitative determiners' instead.[11] Apart from terminological issues (see previous note 4), there are difficulties with Det vs. Q qua distinction between parts of speech, in that it seems to be inspired by some intuition concerning absence vs. presence of 'quantificational meaning', contrary to the evidence normally involved in the identification of morpho-syntactic categories: morphological features and, especially, syntactic behaviour based on distributional data (Radford 1997: §§ 2.2-2.3). Such a Det vs. Q distinction, therefore, looks dubious – all the more so, if the related semantic intuition is far from yielding univocal results.

Arguably, all items within the determination coverage of § 1.2.1 above can be credited with quantificational components of meaning, which contribute to determining reference somehow. (It is the approach that will be assumed and extensively discussed in our volume, starting from chapter 2.) Thus, it is difficult to draw well-motivated semantic boundaries for the putative part-of-speech category Q(uantifier). The uncertainty is confirmed by the fact that Q in some treatments subsumes the indefinite article (see May 1977), or the cardinal numerals (an option that was considered by Jackendoff 1977: § 5.5.1), or both (as in Van Eynde 1994: pp. 40-41). Conversely, that category is not adopted at all by Barwise & Cooper (1981) for the syntactic backbone of their uniform quantificational interpretation of noun phrases – a milestone in the study of natural language quantification, to be presented hereafter in chapter 3. Barwise and Cooper stick to the part of speech Det (cf. also section 1.4 below) as the exact grammatical counterpart of their logico-semantic notion of determiners, which covers definite as well as indefinite articles, cardinals and quantitatives and is acknowledged to be extensible to further kinds of determiners.

[11] Radford's well-known textbook presents the state of the art in Chomskyan generative syntax at the beginning of the 80's, but remains an appropriate reference as regards the Det vs. Q distinction, which is still found in later literature on English and other languages (like Italian, v. Graffi 1994: ch. 2). Besides, our work will take into account a more recent textbook by the same author (Radford 1997), where the issue is addressed according to a partly different approach.

If we seek morpho-syntactic evidence for the distinction between Det and Q, there is only one suitable property resulting from Radford's (1981) presentation. The latter category, unlike the former, is meant to project phrasal structure – hence a node QP – in view of possible dependents: expressions of degree as in "*very* few" and "*rather too* many". In the terminology stemming from Chomsky (1965: p. 74), Q(P) would be a 'major category', contrary to a category Det which disallows phrasal projection and consequent attachment sites for dependents, or 'minor category'. Other minor categories, according to Gazdar et al. (1985: p. 25) or P. Bennett (1995: p. 18), are Complementizer (= the category of subordinating *that*, *whether*, etc.) and Conjunction.

A warning is in order here, because some authors are tempted to make the **minor** vs. **major** dichotomy coincide with a different one:

> "the MINOR WORD-CLASSES ... are *closed* in the sense that they cannot normally be extended by creating new members. ... Unlike minor word-classes, major word-classes are 'open' in the sense that they can be indefinitely extended. No one could, for example, make a complete inventory of all the nouns in contemporary English, because new nouns are continually being formed... On the other hand, determiners, pronouns, or conjunctions form a fixed class of words".
>
> Leech & Svartvik (1975: p. 307)

Of course, to rename the closed word-classes 'minor' and the open ones 'major' would be just an innocent (though superfluous) terminological exercise, but an empirical issue arises if the two labels are intended in the independent sense we have introduced before. That is, while there is no doubt about the closed-class status of those categories that lack phrase structure projection, the assumption that only members of open classes project phrase structure cannot be taken for granted and indeed is provably wrong. E.g., pronouns form a closed class, but at the same time their type of category is major, since they occur as head of a Noun Phrase and allow dependents (at least appositive relative clauses), thus implying phrasal projection.

The repertory of closed classes in the English lexicon is fairly well established[12], but in some cases the status of their category is controversial: "In particular, there has been no clear consensus as to whether prepositions are more on a par with minor closed-class elements ... or a major lexical category like nouns, verbs, and adjectives" (Gazdar et al. 1985: p. 131). We opt for the latter position, after Jackendoff (1973; 1977) and Gazdar et al., i.e. the Preposition heads a Prepositional Phrase, embedding some NP (or PP, recursively)

[12] To sum up: auxiliaries (the copula as well as the modal, temporal or aspectual ones); conjunctions and complementizers; determiner words of various kinds (with possible exceptions as in the case of numerals, to be discussed in the next chapters); prepositions; pronouns; in addition, a few words that look more difficult to classify, e.g. the negation *not*.

as complement. Typical modifiers optionally allowed by the construction, e.g. "-ly" adverbs as in "*totally* without shame", "*immediately* before the meeting", could not modify the NP (and its head noun) without the interposing preposition; therefore, they are attached to a prepositional projection and not to a nominal one.

Whereas prepositions are a closed class forming a major part-of-speech category on its own, an open class with the same categorial status may well include some closed class of suitable words as a proper subset. Typical is the case of auxiliaries, which are traditionally seen as a closed subclass within a larger, open class: namely, that of verbs (corresponding to the major category Verb). Likewise, the empirical recognition of adnominal phrases with a quantitative head, possibly modified by degree expressions, need not motivate the new category Q(P), if one can assume that the closed class of quantitative words at issue falls within another, independently available, major category of English. The part of speech **Adjective** – or A, with phrasal projection AP – looks quite appropriate, since the same modifiers are also found with qualifying adjectival heads: "*very* nice", "*rather too* difficult".

It appears that qualifying adjectives/APs in the English NP must be ordered after any determinative expressions (in our sense) may precede the head noun, quantitatives included. This could be seen as distributional evidence for claiming that the two classes of adnominal items belong to different morpho-syntactic categories (Radford 1997: p. 46). But then, the same line of thinking should apply among quantitatives as well, because positionally they are rather heterogenous as previously noticed (v. § 1.2.1). The morpho-syntactic category Quantifier indeed is restricted to our postdeterminer position by Jackendoff (1977: ch. 5), although he acknowledges that only some of the expressions he calls 'semantic quantifiers' belong to it. Those occurring in a previous position he assigns to the morpho-syntactic category of articles and other determiners with the same distribution, which one can simply equate with the Determiner part of speech under discussion here.[13] Jackendoff (1977) does not seem to distinguish between predeterminers and central determiners, but their distributional difference is taken into account in a variant of his system, developed by Coppen (1991), where predeterminers too are assigned to the category QP; this move makes central determiners the only instances of the category Det, which still covers 'semantic quantifiers' with article distribution, however.

The weak points of Jackendoff's approach, or variants thereof, are readily seen. First, the label 'Q(uantifier)' becomes rather misleading insofar as that

[13] Jackendoff's (1977) notational variant of the Det vs. Q distinction is Art [+DET] vs. Q [–DET], where the binary feature DET indicates whether a category is assigned determiner status or not. Confusingly, his 'Art' abbreviates 'Article' but covers also various determiners that are not articles in any traditional sense.

category does not cover all expressions Jackendoff himself considers quantifiers by semantic intuition. Second, also the semantic quantifiers that he classifies distributionally as determiners allow given dependents – v. his example "*almost* every/all" (Jackendoff 1977: p. 165) – and thus project phrase structure, contrary to the requirement for Det identification proposed before[14]. Third, prenominal adjectives co-occurring within the English NP are fairly rigidly ordered according to a semantic classification (Quirk et al. 1985: pp. 1337-1341), so that the alleged distributional evidence for the part of speech 'Q' may well be re-interpreted as evidence for a positionally leftmost and semantically determinative subclass of adjectives. The subclass, envisaged by some authors[15], has much in common with qualifying adjectives apart from its distinctive semantic content (which can be related to that of items with another category, like the quantitative pronouns).

There are also determinative adjectives falling under 'paradigmatic kinds' different from the quantitative one, as indeed a similar analysis of numerals (whose syntactic and semantic implications will be studied in chapter 4) has been advocated by Hoeksema (1983) among others:

> "The treatment given here, which ... recognizes numerals as a subdivision of adjectives[,] ... can handle such expressions as *the first three books*, *John's last two days*, *the almost ninety exceptions* in a natural fashion. ... For *many* and *few* a similar story can be told, and in this case it is even more clear that we have to analyze them as adjectives: they form comparatives and superlatives, they can be modified by degree expressions like *too* or *very* and may take part in the construction *as* ADJ *as* (*as big as*, *as many as*). That cardinal numerals do not have these features is easily explained: they are not vague, and therefore lack these properties, which are typical for vague adjectives."

The line of reasoning emerging from the quotation calls into play an important criterion for the identification of adjectival items. A certain item is legitimately classified as adjective even if it lacks some of the properties associated with typical adjectives, provided the properties the item actually has are sufficient to exclude any other independently motivated part-of-speech category. This argument need not apply to determinative adjectives only, since qualifying adjectives are typically used both attributively (as adnominal modifiers) and

[14]Yet Jackendoff does not acknowledge the requirement. In his view, also those words that do not take any dependent project phrase structure, although vacuously, because he assumes "the most uniform hypothesis" about structural projection, "at the expense of some otherwise superfluous structure" (ibid., p. 36). For an alternative approach to phrase structure projection, cf. our final chapter 5.

[15]See Gazdar (1981b) and, on French, Miller (1991); Gazdar et al. (1985: p. 126) as well mentioned "a limited set of 'quantifying APs' (e.g. *many* and *few*)".

predicatively (as complements of copulative verbs) yet one can also find qualifiers that lack the former property or the latter and nonetheless are standardly considered adjectives (see, e.g., Pollard & Sag 1987: pp. 64-65). Thus it turns out that some quantitative determiners, like *many* and *few*, are not only legitimate candidates for adjectival status, but even more typical members of the category Adjective than several qualifying ones, due to the pertinent morphosyntactic behaviour.

The rejection of the part of speech Q is in keeping with attempts at reducing the possible major categories to a restricted repertory by combination of few **features**. Before we present an empirical proposal, it is worth reminding the reader that features, formally, are pairs of attributes and values (like NUMBER and *singular*, respectively), with the same attribute allowing alternative values (say, *plural* instead of *singular*); sometimes the attribute itself is referred to as the 'feature', if the feature value does not matter for the argumentation. A bundle of (one or more) compatible features, often called 'feature structure', is enclosed between square brackets in the most common notation. There is much more to be said on attributes, values and feature structures, but the cases to be considered now are so simple that some broader discussion (based on Pollard & Sag 1987; 1994) can be postponed to § 1.2.2.2 and other chapters. For the moment, we need just a notion of binary (a.k.a. Boolean) features, whose values '+' and '–' are prefixed to the attribute, following a familiar notational convention.

In Chomskyan syntactic theory (e.g., Chomsky 1981: p. 48, Radford 1981: ch. 3), but also such modern phrase structure grammars as those of Gazdar et al. (1985), Miller (1991) and Netter (1994), the pivotal features for part-of-speech analysis are [+/–N] and [+/–V], yielding four major categories: Noun [+N, –V], Verb [–N, +V], Adjective [+N, +V] and Preposition [–N, –V]. Just to mention a classical example of how to reduce further categories to these four, one can question the adequacy of a separate part of speech Adverb:

> "adverbs are something of an anomaly from a categorial point of view: our Boolean features N and V combine to permit only four categories (noun, verb, preposition, adjective), yet adverbs are clearly not minor categories [[16]] ... This is so because they can be modified, and can head phrases of their own. How, then, can adverbs be fitted into our system? One obvious possibility is that they can be seen as a subclass of one of our already existing categories (just as auxiliaries are a subclass of verbs). The natural candidate is the adjective".
>
> P. Bennett (1995: p. 92)

[16] The cited remark implies that minor categories, unlike major ones, are exempt from decomposition through [+/–N, +/–V], a point to be confirmed in our § 1.2.2.2.

Let's say that at least the adverbs explicitly related to corresponding qualifying adjectives are actually adjectives with adverbial function, hence [+N, +V] like their adnominal correlate. Again some supporting evidence (ibid., pp. 92-93) is that both can be expanded by the same degree modifiers: "*very* careful(ly)", "*rather too* quick(ly)".

The fact that an English adverb stemming from some qualifying adjective is often morphologically marked by the suffix "-ly" need not be interpreted as a change in part of speech[17]. If one defines adverbiality as the function of any item modifying major category constituents other than nouns and their projections (so that 'adverbial' and 'adnominal' are complementary notions), one accounts for the typical distribution of adjectival items adverbialized by "-ly". These, indeed, modify verbs and their projections (clauses included, cf. our previous note 9), adjectival expressions of all sorts (whether adnominal or adverbial) and prepositional phrases (see examples given before) [18]. But modifiers fulfilling the same function may well lack its distinctive morphology, as obviously happens when they do not belong to the category Adjective: so, in "I'll do that (*on*) *Monday*" one finds an example of adverbial NP or PP. Above all, think of the direct adverbial use of qualifying adjectives without adverb-type morphology, as in "I have been working *late*", "We tried *hard*", "He spoke *loud and clear*".[19]

Our study will not explore further the implications of such a way of dispensing with the Adverb part of speech, or any approach implying that the heterogeneous array of words classified as 'adverbs' in traditional grammar and lexicography be re-allocated to different categories, as we have shown for Adjective. We can just cursorily mention the notion of 'intransitive preposition' (cf. Graffi 1994: § 2.2.4); i.e. those cases in which a preposition and an adverb would be homonymous are treated as the same preposition with two readings, a 'transitive' one, calling for a complement of the preposition, and a complementless, hence 'intransitive' one. E.g., *before* is always a preposition, heading an adverbial PP in "John arrived *before* (*the party*)", or an adnominal PP in "the day *before* (*the party*)", even if the complement NP may be missing.

A final comment on the so-called 'degree adverbs' seems appropriate in view of their relevance to determination matters. We have already pointed out that quantitative determiners are a case of heads which can take those degree items as dependents, but the meaning of the two classes of expressions is also related

---

[17]After all, morphological case, marking the grammatical function of nouns in German, Latin, etc., preserves the part of speech Noun.

[18]The adnominal function is possible only for "-ly" words with the homonymous but distinct suffix forming adjectival items from nouns, as in *brotherly* or *monthly*.

[19]This phenomenon tends to be more frequent in informal dialects of English and is simply the rule in German.

because the 'degree' itself appears to be a sort of (non-numerical) quantitative notion. Therefore, it is not surprising that some quantitative items – such as "all", "enough", "little"/"much", "less"/"more" and "least"/"most" – equally have the function of determiner and that of degree modifier (under a number of idiosyncratic restrictions on the range of expressions a particular item is allowed to modify) [20]. This relationship between quantitative determiners and degree adverbs was captured according to Bresnan (1973) by assuming that both belong to her category Quantifier (cf. Radford 1981: ch. 4). However, the same evidence means to us that both are adjectives, with some common quantitative feature and a different (adnominal or adverbial) syntactic function.[21]

1.2.2.2 Against 'Det'

Once the Det vs. Q(P) distinction is dismissed (seeing that the latter does not seem to be a *bona fide* category with part-of-speech status), the question arises as to whether the category Det nonetheless can be maintained by distinguishing it from independently motivated ones, such as A(P) or others. The answer – we believe – is negative, because no generalization would be gained by doing so. Indeed, Det's alleged distinctive feature of being 'minor' (§ 1.2.2.1 above) fails to adequately account for the morpho-syntactic properties of all but one of the kinds of English expressions assigned to that category, say, by Radford (1981). The following discussion will show **articles** are the only items matching the characterization of Determiner as a minor category, which would thereby exclude most items that intuitively are determiners according to their (determinative) semantic function. But clearly, it looks undesirable to make the term 'determiner' ambiguous between a morpho-syntactic part-of-speech notion and a semantically motivated notion and restrict the former to the articles, as these can be simply identified by the traditional part of speech Article.

To substantiate our argumentation, let us consider a type of noun phrase schematically representable as X ___ Y, where some determiner word (in our

[20]For data, we refer to Bresnan (1973), Jackendoff (1977: ch. 6), Gazdar (1981b), Pollard & Sag (1994: § 9.4.3) and other literature. Here we do not discuss the restrictions at issue in English, though we expect them to be simply encodable as lexical features within the 'lexicalist' type of framework to be adopted for the present research (v. chapters 3-5). Moreover, we leave aside the question of those adverbial degree items – including *so* and *as* (in the relevant readings) – which could be claimed to belong to a minor category (Gazdar et al. 1985: p. 122), rather than being adjectival like the others.

[21]It is also worth noting that the adnominal counterpart of a degree adverb need not always be quantitative, as shown by qualifying adjectives whose adverbialized forms allow degree modifier use, like "hard*ly*", "virtual*ly*", "near*ly*", etc.

sense of *determiner*) fills the positional slot '___' within the context consisting of X to the left and Y to the right. We know X can be a degree modifier forming a constituent α with the determiner word, if this is quantitative, e.g.; hence the bracketing $[_{NP}\ [_{\alpha}\ X\ \text{---}\ ]\ Y]$ (for α = AP, under the adjectival account of quantitative determiners). Now, examples like (2) below yield ungrammatical results – conventionally indicated by asterisk marking – when the word in the slot is:

- omitted (thus confirming it was the head modified by X in α, according to a standard test);
- unsuited to the specific X at issue (so that, e.g., *all* cannot go with *very*, and *many* with *almost*);
- replaced by an article.

$$\text{(2)}\quad \text{a.}\ \textit{very} \left\{ \begin{array}{l} \textit{many} \\ *\ \emptyset \\ *\ \textit{all} \\ *\ \textit{the} \end{array} \right\} \text{students}$$

$$\text{b.}\ \textit{almost} \left\{ \begin{array}{l} \textit{all} \\ *\ \emptyset \\ *\ \textit{many} \\ *\ \textit{the} \end{array} \right\} \text{students}$$

In the example, word strings are enough to check (un)grammaticality, whereas other cases require that the intended bracketing be considered too. As a matter of fact, some expressions occurring in our position X are allowed to precede an article, but the article is confirmed to be 'minor' inasmuch as it does not form an extra constituent (= α) with the preceding expression: that is to say, X itself is an immediate constituent of the NP. (For the moment, we avoid a technical discussion of the alternative bracketing $[_{NP}\ X\ [_{\beta}\ \text{---}\ Y]\,]$, where β is some nominal projection.)

Typical NP-initial expressions that one finds before the **indefinite article** are *quite* and *rather*, e.g. in "*quite/rather* a mess". Surely the determiner word could not be omitted here, but an independent motivation prevents us from using this test as we did in (2), cf. $*\ \emptyset$; the ungrammaticality that results from omitting the indefinite article is simply explained because singular count nouns, unlike plural ones etc., are not supposed to head NPs with Ø-determination (see also § 1.2.1 above). Moreover, the real dependency relation established by "quite" or "rather" is elicitable through a paraphrase, exploiting the fact that the expression X at issue can act as degree modifier of adjectives. Since the state of something being quite/rather *a mess* is equally expressed by saying it is quite/rather *messy*, a plausible assumption is that X in the former construction modifies the noun (projection) essentially in the same way as it does with the corresponding adjective in the latter construction.

Very often a suitable adjective A(P) occurs in the Y part of the relevant X__Y noun phrase, so that "*quite/rather* a strong wind" refers to a wind which is quite/rather strong, "*quite/rather* an interesting talk" refers to a talk which is quite/rather interesting, and so on. In short, the two degree modifiers are provided with an adnominal reading semantically consistent with their basic adverbial reading (in the sense of 'adverbial' made clear before in § 1.2.2.1), under the condition that the modified nominal includes some A(P) explicitly or bears an equivalent semantic relation to the degree word. If the explicit A(P) is missing, *quite* can be assigned a qualifying adjectival meaning directly (rather than being just an 'intensifier' as in the other cases) and allows us to paraphrase the NP accordingly.[22]

Turning to NP-initial expressions followed by the **definite article**, consider the X__Y type of NP where "the" fills the positional slot and X is determinative as well, precisely a quantitative predeterminer like "all". Then the bracketing $[_{NP}\ [_{\alpha}$ X __] Y], with X modifying *the* in '__', is ruled out again – at least because determiner status makes "all" adnominal by definition, according to our assumptions on the matter. Distributional evidence already provided by § 1.2.1 (see the NPs in (1)) supports our approach, since the omission test applies successfully to plural examples: "*all* the books" and "*all* Ø books" are both grammatical. The optimally simple way of accounting for this behaviour is to suppose the predeterminer in both cases is assigned the same adnominal reading, with a determinative meaning closely related (though not identical) to that of *every* or *each*. Treating *all* as a modifier of the article in "*all* the books" would result in a loss of generalization, unless one makes the additional stipulation that a phonologically unexpressed constituent with the syntactic and semantic features of an article is equally modified in "*all* Ø books"[23]; chapters 4-5, developing our simpler analysis in technical detail, will show that such unexpressed determiners are unwarranted.

[22]One such meaning corresponds to *remarkable* (or *exceptional*): "quite a/some party", e.g., refers to a/some remarkable (or exceptional) party. The same interpretation works for "quite something" (= something remarkable or exceptional), an example where *quite* can modify nothing but the nominal head, an indefinite pronoun. Another qualifying adjectival meaning of the same word proves equivalent to *complete(-ly)*, *real(-ly)* or *exact(-ly)*: see the already mentioned "quite a mess" (= a real/complete mess), as well as examples with the definite article like "quite the opposite" (= the exact opposite, something completely opposite), "quite the thing to do" (= the real thing to do).

[23]Here and elsewhere the 'Ø' notation allows two interpretations: it may simply mean the complete absence of any constituent which could occur in that position, while in the alternative interpretation 'Ø' indicates the presence of a constituent that is 'empty' w.r.t. phonological form but has syntactic and semantic properties.

To sum up, there are good reasons for denying that articles can be modified.[24] The question now is whether the same negative conclusion holds for the other English words that Radford (1981) assigns to the minor category Determiner, namely (adnominal) **demonstratives** and **possessives**. At first glance, it could seem so, considering that they replace the definite article without affecting our test results as regards candidate elements in the initial X position of an X ___ Y Noun Phrase:

$$\text{(3)} \quad \left\{ \begin{array}{l} \textit{all} \\ *\,\textit{very} \\ *\,\textit{almost} \end{array} \right\} \left\{ \begin{array}{l} \textit{the} \\ \textit{these} \\ \textit{my} \\ \emptyset \end{array} \right\} \text{students}$$

Still, there is a difference from the article, as only the other two kinds of English determiners allow postpositive modification (= $[_{NP}[_{\alpha}$ --- X] Y], adapting our schema accordingly). Possessives can be followed by *own* qua emphatic modifier (optionally modified in turn by *very*), as in: "my (*very*) *own* recipe". A comparable modification by means of postpositive *here* (for *this/these*) or *there* (for *that/those*) is used to emphasize demonstratives, including adnominal ones at least in informal dialects of English[25]; see, e.g., "this *here* boy" / "that *there* boy" (Miller 1991: p. 273). The intuition that the emphatic modifiers depend on the determiner word, and not on the subsequent noun, is confirmed by distributional data, as elicited through the familiar omission test with plural examples:

(4) a. his (own) ideas

b. (* own) ideas

(5) a. these (here) boys

b. (* here) boys

Whatever the part of speech of a demonstrative or possessive word may be, it appears to project phrasal structure, thus being 'major'. Admittedly, the assortment of modifiers depending on these two kinds of determiner is very limited (see above), but other pieces of evidence are available too. In particular, it is not difficult to ascertain which major category looks well-suited for possessive determiners in a language like English. Under the traditional assumption that Saxon genitive phrases are simply NPs marked for genitive

[24] See Van Eynde (1994: § 3.1.1) for a discussion of further data – like negation and comparison tests – that leads to the same conclusions. On the rejection of dependents other than optional modifiers, we refer forward to § 1.3.2.

[25] A corresponding construction of Danish will be touched on in chapter 2.

case[26], a possessive word with the same distribution and function turns out to be a pronoun allowed to replace a non-pronominal NP of that kind. E.g., *his* can occur as determinative expression instead of "the teacher's", just like *he* can occur as subject instead of "the teacher". Concerning morphological information, *my*, *your*, *his*, etc. are "genitive forms of personal pronouns" (Quirk et al. 1985: p. 361), morpho-phonologically related to the nominative or accusative case forms and grammatically marked on a par with them in terms of agreement features (PERSON, NUMBER and, in the 3rd person, GENDER). We see no reason why genitive, unlike the other cases, should alter the part of speech; hence our conclusion that possessive determiner words have the basic morpho-syntactic category of all pronominal forms, which is identified with the major category Noun in a broad sense previously adopted by § 1.2.2.1.

That is, following a feature-theoretic decomposition of major categories, the separate part of speech Pronoun is dispensed with, as the words assigned to it are meant to form a closed subclass of the [+N, −V] words, leaving to other features the task of accounting for differences from the proper names and common nouns. (See, e.g., Radford 1981: ch. 3, P. Bennett 1995: p. 86.) Distributional equivalence to NPs is thus considered crucial, whereas the observation that personal pronouns display morphological distinctions according to first, second and third person does not justify the creation of a separate part of speech. (Agreement data indeed show that the other nominal words do not lack a PERSON feature altogether, but constantly give it the value *3rd.*) Note also that by saying possessive determiner words are **(pro-)nominal**, one does not contradict their **adnominal** function as determiners, because the former status captures a paradigmatic relation between those words and Saxon genitive NPs – namely, they are commutable in determinative position – while the latter status brings about a syntagmatic relation between the determinative expression and the nominal head it depends on.

For demonstrative determiners, a problem arises insofar as English seems to lack enough morphological evidence supporting the identification of their part-of-speech category (cf. § 1.3.1 below). However, there are good syntactic reasons at least for claiming that the category in question should be distinguished from that of articles. As we have mentioned in § 1.2.1, articles are the only determinative words of English without an 'independent' (and arguably pronominal) counterpart, i.e. some identical or morpho-phonologically related form that appears to replace an overt nominal head instead of depending on it. Note the difference from demonstratives in this respect:

[26] Cf. Quirk et al. (1985: p. 326): "We ... see the genitive construction as a noun phrase embedded as a definite determiner within another noun phrase". Readers are referred forward to § 1.3.3 for a critical discussion of alternative approaches.

(6) Mary read $\left\{ \begin{array}{l} \textit{this} \\ \textit{that} \\ *\,\textit{the} \\ *\,\textit{a} \end{array} \right\}$

Granting that the demonstratives in (6) are literally pronouns which make up a full Noun Phrase by themselves – a traditional view now revived by authors like Kathol (1999) – the ungrammaticality of the article forms in the same context "straightforwardly follows from the assumption that for a subset of determiners such as *the*, a corresponding phrasal version does not exist" (ibid.). Within a category system of the type adopted here, the subset can be identified with the class of 'minor determiners' (which narrows down to the articles), so that the existence of pronominal counterparts in the intended sense becomes a distinctive property of those determiner words whose part of speech is a major category.

We can actually make a stronger claim about 'major determiners' thanks to the feature-theoretic analysis already introduced in § 1.2.2.1. Since so far Adjective [+N, +V] and Noun [+N, –V] turn out to be the sole major categories proving relevant for our case study on English determination (because they are required at least by quantitatives and possessives), a plausible generalization suggests itself:

> **Generalization for Major Determiners**
> All determiners belonging to major categories have the feature [+N] and the determiner words of this class are precisely those with (non-determinative) pronominal counterparts.

Being pronouns, which means an instance of [+N, –V], the counterparts of determiners always have the feature [+N] in common with the corresponding determiners, according to our generalization. The fact that there is no such counterpart of articles follows, if the category Article is minor and therefore, by definition, cannot have any feature specific to major categories. And even if the precise part of speech of demonstrative determiners remains to be settled (postponing further discussion to § 1.3.1), the pronominal counterpart phenomenon implies they must be either adjectival or nominal, hence [+N] in any case, complying with the Generalization for Major Determiners.

To conclude with a slightly more formal presentation of the feature-theoretic apparatus concerned, fundamental is a hierarchical structure imposed on the lexicon over and above the collection of separate lexical entries, insofar as these contain information ensuing from a rich system of classification into 'sorts' for the various aspects of linguistic items; see Pollard & Sag (1987; 1994) as well as Carpenter's (1992) feature logic. We assume part-of-speech categories conform to a 'sort hierarchy' such that [+/–N] and [+/–V] are declared appropriate for

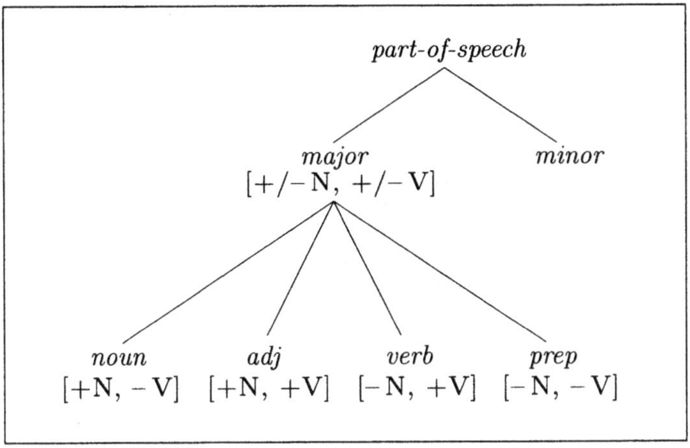

Figure 1.1: Part-of-speech Hierarchy

major categories only, as **Figure 1.1** graphically displays. Sort hierarchies are a formal device – increasingly popular in computational linguistics – whereby information on more general sorts (i.e. hierarchically higher ones) gets inherited and can be made more specific by their subsorts (i.e. lower sorts hierarchically 'dominated' by the former ones). The information is encoded through some **feature structure**, a bundle of appropriate features enclosed between square brackets (as we mentioned in 1.2.2.1), but with "a *sort symbol* that tells what type of object the structure is modelling" (Pollard & Sag 1994: p. 17). In our hierarchy for parts of speech, the feature structure [+N, −V][27], e.g., becomes labelled with the sort *noun*, one of the four alternative subsorts of *major*.

The **Figure 1.1** exemplifies also interactions between inheritance and consistent specification of features, because the subsorts of *major* make more specific the N and V features they inherit from it. Indeed all feature values are sorted as well, so that in the case at issue the attributes get initially declared with underspecified values of Pollard and Sag's sort *boolean* (ibid., p. 396); this we abbreviate '+/−', being equivalent to the disjunction of its two subsorts, '+' and '−'[28]. Each major category constrains N and V, specifying one or the

[27]Or [N *plus*, V *minus*], sticking to Pollard and Sag's attribute-value notation.

[28]That is, our [+/−N, +/−V] corresponds to ([+N] ∨ [−N]) ∧ ([+V] ∨ [−V]), where: ***i)*** '∧' is the logical operator of conjunction implicit in feature structures (e.g., [+N, −V] corresponds to [+N] ∧ [−V], meaning that both features must be satisfied); ***ii)*** '∨' is the logical operator of inclusive disjunction (e.g., [−N] ∨ [+V] means it is enough to satisfy one of the two features and thus captures the three cases allowing adverbial modification in § 1.2.2.1, i.e. [−N, +V], [+N, +V] or [−N, −V]); ***iii)*** the conflict of alternative values for the same attribute makes a disjunction like [+N] ∨ [−N] exclusive, though '∨' in itself is weaker.

other of their *boolean* options. More generally: "If sorts σ_1 and σ_2 bear declarations [F τ_1] and [F τ_2] for the same feature F and σ_2 is a subsort of σ_1, then τ_2 must be a subsort of τ_1" (ibid., p. 395). Although for the moment we use only features with atomic values, such as '+' and '–' or others (e.g. *masculine*, *feminine* and *neuter* for GENDER), considerably more complex values will play an essential role at later stages of our work.

1.3 The NP tradition revisited

To introduce the readers to the coverage and status of determination according to our approach, we have sketched a monolingual case study in the classification of pertinent words or phrases, starting from the assumption that determinative items should be intuitively identified as such on the basis of their semantic function within the Noun Phrase. As far as morpho-syntax is concerned, the conception of determiners and NP structure which underlies this work is deeply rooted in the grammatical (and lexicographic) tradition:

A) The determiners, intended as semantically determinative items, belong to or are projected by various traditional 'parts of speech', like *article*, *adjective*, (*pro-*)*noun*.

B) A construction combining a determiner and a nominal constituent is headed by the latter, which takes the former as dependent.

C) The 'independent' counterparts of (morpho-phonologically related or identical) determiners are literally understood as pronouns heading/embodying the relevant NP.

But admittedly, none of the three points is uncontroversial in the linguistics of today. A fairly large part of the chapter – viz. § 1.2.2 – was indeed devoted to a defense of **A)**, to start with.

All the discussion was about efforts to establish a putative part of speech Determiner by discarding some of the expressions that we classify within the coverage of determination. Linguists in favour of a more restrictive coverage would aim at a morpho-syntactically homogeneous Determiner notion, but on closer inspection their approach(es) proved unsatisfactory. The evidence (as to English, for the moment) appears to support our cross-categorial approach exploiting a typical distinction between linguistic **form** and **function**.[29] The

[29]See Quirk et al. (1985: p. 64): "we need to make terminological distinctions between form and function, so that we can say, for example, that an adjective (formal term) can function either as modifier or as head (functional terms)". Both *form* and *function*, however, are notions relevant to other levels of abstraction besides syntax. Whenever appropriate, we will

determinative function is assigned to items that formally pertain to different parts of speech, in accordance with point **A)** above: it allows us to reconcile the morpho-syntactic heterogeneity of the class of expressions we call 'determiners' with the semantic function they intuitively have in common. By the same token, the determiners of a given formal category (Adjective in the case of quantitatives, e.g.) are distinguished semantically from any non-determinative items may pertain to that category (like qualifying adjectives).

An associated variation to be discussed at times in the book is also the partly language-specific nature of the system which relates morpho-syntactic categorization with semantic contents. Different languages may well draw a boundary between two given categories (or rather, their respective coverages) at different points within the pertinent 'field' of meaning; thus the category/ies of some semantically based paradigmatic kind of determiners need not be the same in all languages. Nevertheless, a large part of the account proposed so far on a monolingual basis will hold for the other languages dealt with in our volume. At the very least, this happens because they are historically related and culturally close to English, but some 'linguistic universals' are likely to matter too: that a language does not include Determiner in its repertory of parts of speech is presumably a universal property on theoretical grounds.

In the current section we are going to informally address another big issue, which will involve more technical developments starting from chapter 4. Namely, how our considerations on the parts of speech in question relate to the other points of the aforementioned conception of determiners and Noun Phrase structure. Up to now, point **B)** in particular was taken for granted by our presentation, consistently with the familiar idea that the syntactic domain where determiners and nominals link up corresponds to the Noun Phrase, the phrasal constituent with the same distribution as a self-contained noun. For instance, both *horses* and *the horses* can occur as subject, direct object, object of a preposition, etc. – cf. "(*the*) *horses* are beautiful", "he likes (*the*) *horses*", "he is looking for (*the*) *horses*" – so that they prove distributionally equivalent, whereas *the* cannot occur alone in the same syntactic slots. According to this standard test, *the horses* is a Noun Phrase headed by *horses* and the fact that the article always requires a nominal 'sister' to combine with plausibly shows that the former item depends on the latter.

A possible counterexample could be provided by expressions which occupy the NP position instead of depending on some nominal, even if their phonological form φ is identical to that of a determiner, like *many*, *some*, *this*, etc.

---

obviously have to consider phonological form too. On the other hand, there is a semantic (as well as pragmatic) sense of function, which proves quite relevant for determination: the sense in which the NP *the book* has a referential function, namely definite reference as indicated by the article.

The pronominal treatment we have summarized in **C)** is traditionally applied in order to solve the problem without any artificial addition or alteration w.r.t. the architecture of NPs. Before saying more on this in §§ 1.3.1-1.3.2, let's see how the same approach naturally extends to items that change φ form when moving from adnominal to 'independent' function.

In English, the paradigm of possessive – i.e. genitive personal – pronouns yields 'independent' forms, suffixing /**n**/ to *my* (hence /**maIn**/ = *mine*) and /**z**/ to the other determinative forms, except for *his* and *its* already ending by sibilant. (Cf. Quirk et al. 1985: § 6.29.) That is, with most possessive words the two functions at issue are overtly distinguished by morpho-phonological variation, but preserve the part of speech, because the determinative forms too are pronouns, for reasons made clear before in § 1.2.2.2. The opposite is true of most quantitative items: *all, many, few*, etc. show the same φ form for both functions, yet their category involves a change insofar as the relevant determiners were argued to be adjectives (in § 1.2.2.1) and have pronouns as form-preserving counterparts. Finally, both part of speech and form φ change if one considers the quantitative determiners *every*, *no*, *some* and *any* (atypical) adjectival items which can be suffixed by "-one", "-body" or "-thing" to yield pronominal counterparts (like *everyone, everybody* or *everything*), though *some* and *any* have form-preserving pronominal counterparts as well.

1.3.1 Determiners, pronouns and 'Ø-nouns'

A theoretical question that was left open since § 1.2.1 is how to defend the pronominal account under **C)** above against a possible alternative whereby what we see as independent counterparts of determiners are the same determiners together with "a phonologically unrealized head, which functions syntactically just as other common nouns" (Nerbonne & Mullen 2000). Then, understanding the 'Ø' notation accordingly (cf. our previous note 23), one can assign the NP *this* a phrase structure like (7a) – as in Nerbonne et al. (1989) – instead of (7b), or equivalent[30].

(7) a. $[_{NP}[_{D}\ \textit{this}\ ]\ [_{N}\ \emptyset\ ]]$
    b. $[_{NP}[_{N}\ \textit{this}\ ]]$

Both treatments have their pros and cons: the a. structure avoids a duplication of parts of speech for *this* and any other pertinent word to be freely used with or without an expressed nominal head, but formally is more complex than b. and requires that empirically dubious entities like the **empty** (=

[30]For $[_{NP}\ \textit{this}]$ qua version of b. without unary branching, v. chapter 5 below.

'Ø') **constituents** be postulated.[31] Their existence could look independently motivated for so-called '*wh*-movement' and other constructions with **gaps**, according to theories in which a 'trace' occupies the gap's place on behalf of the original filler (as in Chomsky 1977, Gazdar 1981a, Gazdar et al. 1985: ch. 7, Pollard & Sag 1994: ch. 4-5). However, such a Ø-constituent representing the phrase-structural location of the gap may well be dispensed with altogether, if the lexical head (e.g. a verb) the trace would depend on is supplied with adequate gap-licensing information. The trace-less treatment has been eventually adopted by Pollard & Sag (1994: ch. 9)[32], supporting the position that empty constituents of any kind can/must be abolished in a grammar where features have sufficient expressive power. This position is also endorsed here and we shall argue for its full linguistic adequacy in capturing generalizations.

We begin by weighing up Nerbonne & Mullen's (2000) claim that there is some syntactic evidence undermining the notion of 'pronominal counterparts' that we have assumed:

> "The main empirical argument supporting our view of these words as determiners stems from their behavior with regard to restrictive relative clauses, and other postnominal modifiers, which differs from that of pronominals, as the following examples [– see (8) –] indicate. ... To consider these words to be pronouns, then, it would appear to be necessary to establish essentially a new class of pronouns".

(8) a. John's paper is nice, but $\left\{\begin{array}{c} \textit{that} \\ *\textit{it} \end{array}\right\}$ *which Peter presented last year* was even better

b. $\left\{\begin{array}{c} \textit{Those} \\ *\textit{They} \end{array}\right\}$ *with long hair* are out of fashion

c. Take $\left\{\begin{array}{c} \textit{any} \\ *\textit{it} \end{array}\right\}$ *you like*

d. He convinced many colleagues, but $\left\{\begin{array}{c} \textit{several} \\ *\textit{they} \end{array}\right\}$ *in Groningen* are sceptical

In (8), the sentences become ungrammatical if the word with uncertain category is replaced by a personal pronoun, so that "the distinctions above follow naturally in an account which postulates a ['Ø'] noun subject to postnominal modification" (ibid.).

---

[31] Both the use of empty constituents and a multiplication of lexical readings can negatively affect efficiency of parsers applying the grammar (cf. Gazdar & Mellish 1989: pp. 151-152, and Markantonatou & Sadler 1998), so that there are anyway computational costs, which our strictly linguistic discussion will not assess.

[32] We refer to Sag (1997) and Ginzburg & Sag (2001) for recent developments.

Now let us reconsider the argument more carefully. The underlying idea is that pronouns should be distributionally equivalent to proper nouns, insofar as the latter make up a complete NP by themselves and indeed reject the same kinds of modifiers as the personal pronouns. A further aspect of the parallelism is that not every modifier is impossible with those nominal items, because both proper names and personal pronouns accept appositive, non-restrictive postnominal modification (cf. "I will meet *Mary/her*, who lives in France"). But, on the other hand, we agree with Kathol (1999) that their common behaviour suggests a semantic (and pragmatic) explanation:

> "The referents of proper names and pronouns are usually fixed by world knowledge or conversational context. Therefore these categories do not typically give rise to a referential domain that a restrictive relative clause [and other similar modifiers] could restrict in a non-vacuous fashion. Hence, it appears that no appeal to syntax is necessary".

The purely interpretative, non-syntactic status of the incompatibility with restrictive modification (and, by the same token, compatibility with the cases of modification not involving restriction) is supported by the fact that personal pronouns may well be restrictively modified in some contexts of use where they receive a special interpretation:[33]

(9) a. You who have already finished may leave the classroom

(said while other students still have to finish their tests)

b. He who comes early will get a table

Concerning the objection that we would need an otherwise unmotivated extra class of pronouns, it is rather misleading. Pronouns can be *tout court* identified with the nominal 'pro-forms': i.e., the closed, grammatically fixed class of those words of nominal category (broadly speaking) which substitute for open-class items of that category so as to preserve the intended effects on reference consistently with the given linguistic or situational context, as in anaphoric and deictic relations. Now, personal pronouns are morphologically as much as semantically a particular case of nominal pro-forms, but the broader class in English covers at least the pro-form *one(s)* as well. This was indeed classified as a pronoun by traditional grammarians and lexicographers, although it does not belong to the paradigm of personal pronouns.[34] It also

[33] Nerbonne & Mullen (2000) dismiss the phenomenon as archaism or literary language (v. "Abandon hope, all ye who enter here"), but Kathol's (1999) examples in (9) show that it is also possible in ordinary modern English.

[34] A pro-form $\mathcal{P}$ can be said to substitute for some lexically contentful expression $\mathcal{E}$ that could have occurred in the place of $\mathcal{P}$, whether a token of $\mathcal{E}$ is actually found in previous discourse or not (cf. Miller 1991: p. 81). The latter option is obviously exemplified by a

differs as for syntactic distribution, which is nonetheless compatible with the more general notion of pronouns, granting that pronominal syntactic behaviour implies distributional equivalence to nouns, yet not necessarily proper names. So, since *one(s)* has the distribution of common nouns, it can take the same dependents (cf. "The blue *one/dress* that Mary bought yesterday").

The determiners' pronominal counterparts, in our view, essentially share with *one(s)* the same status as pro-forms of common nouns. Their syntactic distribution is accordingly similar, thus accounting for those postposed dependents allowed by a common noun but not a proper name or a personal pronoun.[35] In addition, all nominal pro-forms deriving from determiners are 'self-determining' inasmuch as they preserve the determinative value of the originals as part of the resulting semantic content; e.g. a demonstrative pronoun inherits referential definiteness and its particular demonstrative value from the corresponding determiner. That meaningful aspect of determiner-related pronouns makes them less 'semantically unspecified' than *one(s)* out of context and has also an important syntactic correlate: for the pronominal counterpart $\mathcal{P}$ of some determiner $\mathcal{D}$, the interaction of self-determination with the syntactic structure of the NP implies that the determiners allowed to precede $\mathcal{P}$ therein are exactly the same that would precede a nominal projection beginning with $\mathcal{D}$ itself. Then, one can easily predict correct determiner-pronoun combinations like *all these* and *the many*, as well as the ungrammaticality of **the all*, **few these*, etc., by adapting the order constraints that § 1.2.1 stated in terms of pre-, central and post- determiners.

An additional reason that Nerbonne & Mullen (2000) put forward in order to reject a pronominal alternative to the use of 'empty heads' concerns the fact that some pronominal counterparts of adjectival determiners allow degree modifiers that are typical of the corresponding determiners (and adjectives in general): see "*very* few", "*too* many", "*nearly* all", "*hardly* any", etc. Since normal nouns or pronouns do not accept these modifiers[36], the conclusion would be that the modified items are not (pro-)nominal at all, but actually the original determiners acting as dependents of a 'Ø' head noun. The argument is generalized by the same authors to those NPs in which (a lexical item whose form is identical to that of) a qualifying adjective may look like

situation where somebody says "I like the blue *one*" pointing to some dress, when none was mentioned before. Then the parallelism with personal pronouns is evident, since they too allow but don't need an anaphoric antecedent.

[35]On the other hand, common noun distribution will not prevent a pro-form without dependents from occurring as a whole NP, since this is already possible for English common nouns that are 'bare plurals' or 'mass terms' (v. next chapter).

[36]At least in the relevant reading as regards *very*, because the same word can be an adjectival modifier of nouns in such examples as "this *very* room", "the *very* thought", "his *very* life", etc., but the meaning is clearly different.

the head: "Adverbial modification, as in *the desperately poor*, would appear to argue against a simple adjectival nominalization explanation" (ibid.). Once again, Nerbonne & Mullen (2000) rely on an 'empty' head noun instead of considering the overt candidate "a **derived** noun ... that has arisen through a word-formation rule applied to adjectives and/or determiners", because they do not see how to adequately handle the problematic cases of modification in the latter approach.

In our opinion, the problem simply is that Nerbonne and Mullen, or other authors following a similar line of reasoning, are eager to draw syntactic conclusions from phenomena that may well be explained in a more semantically orientied fashion. To this end we shall reconsider the possible degree modifiers of adjectival determiners and take into account distributional differences which are ultimately based on the meaning of the two items to be combined. A first, rough classification of the modifiers at issue would distinguish at least between 'degrees of vagueness' and 'degrees of precision' (or any other equivalent notions, terminology aside), so as to account for the fact that only **inherently vague** adjectives can take degree modifiers of the former kind, like *very* and *too*.[37] By the same token, an adjective expressing some relatively precise concept (including a precise end-point of some vagueness scale) allows modifiers of the latter kind, in order to confirm or decrease its **precision**: see, e.g., "*absolutely/almost* unique", whereas one could not (seriously) say "*very/too* unique". The distinction is also relevant for determinative adjectives, so that typical degree modifiers of vagueness may combine with such vague quantitatives as *few* and *many*, not with quantitatives expressing a precise logical notion (v. the 'universality' of *every* and *all*), nor cardinal numerals; logically or numerically precise determiners are compatible with some degree modifiers of precision, as in "*absolutely/almost* all" and "*exactly/almost* twenty".

Thus, degree modification cannot be merely based on the morpho-syntactic category of the modified head, with its major part of speech. Adjectives, including determinative ones, must be semantically classified in ways that allow the grammatical mechanism of modification (no matter how it works) to discriminate the appropriate degree modifiers from the others. What's more, as also noticed by Jackendoff (1977: p. 164), many degree items "have a wide range of cross-category application", especially those being modifiers of precision (in our sense): e.g., see *almost* modifying a verb in "John *almost* fell" and a preposition in "We pushed John *almost* out of the window". It is clear that the semantic information identifying a head as compatible with a certain kind of modifiers must be carried by any relevant item, irrespective of its

[37]Cf. also Hoeksema's (1983) excerpt which was quoted in our § 1.2.2.1. On the notion of *degree* and a related typology of words in English, we refer the reader to the informal presentation by Leech & Svartvik (1975: §§ 217-226), among others.

part of speech, not only an adjective. But then, instead of taking for granted that the morpho-syntactic category as such is what makes a nominal head incompatible with a degree modifier, we would rather say that the noun or pronoun in question carries semantic information not matching the modifier's requirements.

As things stand, the purported difficulty of the (pro-) nominalization approach disappears, if the word-formation process to be applied will preserve in the (pro-) nominalized output the classificatory value which indicates that input adjectives were compatible with degree modifiers of one kind or another. We consider the output items pronouns when they derive from determinative adjectives (yielding a closed class) and common nouns when they derive from qualifying adjectives (yielding an open class), while their semantic classification remains adjective-like in the intended way: let's say 'attributive' instead of 'substantive', where the latter is not meant as synonymous with 'nominal' but is appropriate for the semantic content typical of the Noun category[38]. It is worth recalling that already the traditional notion of **substantive** was semantically motivated, because of the assumption that nouns and the like would denote so-called 'substances' – in a metaphysical sense – as opposed to their 'attributes' (either qualities or quantities, relations, circumstances, and so on). Since parts of speech in modern linguistics are characterized on purely morpho-syntactic grounds, the traditional terminology may well be revived for a distinct semantic classification, applying *substantive* to typical members of the Noun category, yet not to derived (pro-) nouns with atypical semantic status.

Interestingly, we find also the opposite case of morpho-syntactically adjectival items that are atypical inasmuch as they prove semantically substantive. It is the account we adopt for the adnominal reading of demonstratives, so as to explain their lack of degree modifiers by means of the above-mentioned semantic sensitivity of these dependents. The demonstrative in "*this* book", e.g., is a determinative adjective which preserves the substantive meaning classification of the correspondent pronoun heading/embodying some NP. An alternative treatment could assign the pronouns' part of speech to demonstrative determiners too and thus exploit the alleged incompatibility of the category Noun with degree modifiers, but a consequent problem would be to explain why postpositive dependents of demonstrative pronouns get rejected by the adnominal reading:

(10) a. * [that which Peter presented last year] paper (cf. (8a))

b. * [those with long hair] students (cf. (8b))

[38] Pollard & Sag (1994) use the label *substantive* in yet another, unrelated sense, which we will discuss in chapter 4.

Our adjectival account avoids the problem, insofar as all prenominal adjectives reject the undesired postpositive dependents. In fact relative clauses – an evident instance of syntactically sensitive modifiers – never modify adjectives anyway. As regards prepositional phrases, they may well be included as postposed dependents within adjectival phrases, but there is an asymmetry between prenominal and postnominal A(P)s in this connection: cf. "a *proud* (**of our achievements*) teacher" vs. "a teacher *proud of our achievements*", or "a *polite* (* *in manner*) person" vs. "a person *polite in manner*". Postnominally, an adjective allows attachments of postposed PPs as dependents (with one function or another), whereas the same adjective in prenominal position always rejects them.[39]

Somebody might object that the ban on postpositive dependents is not category-specific, applying to all prenominal modifiers, but such a generalization turns out to be wrong. E.g., PPs too are used for prenominal modification, although not frequently, and the object of the preposition is indeed preserved: v. "the *on board* entertainments", "an *out of the way* cottage". What's more, even prenominal adjectives need not reject all dependents on the right: in particular, *enough* qua degree modifier can follow if the meaning is compatible, as in "a *large enough* street". The substantive meaning of a demonstrative adjective should suffice to avoid that as much as the other degree modifiers, whereas the postposed deictics *here* and *there* are allowed as a marginal dependence phenomenon (mentioned in § 1.2.2.2 above), which presumably bypasses syntactic constraints[40], relying on semantic compatibility only.

In support of a morpho-syntactically nominal alternative to our adjectival solution, perhaps one could try to argue from analogy with the occurrence of some dependent noun before a nominal head consisting of at least another single noun, as exemplified by pairs like *physics student*, *border town*, *country cottage*, *picture gallery*, etc. The point is that in every pair the former item rejects all postpositive dependents which the same noun may accept elsewhere: cf. "a picture (* *of Naomi Campbell*) gallery" vs. "a gallery with pictures *of Naomi Campbell*", or "a border (* *between USA and Mexico*) town" vs. "a town on the border *between USA and Mexico*". But important distributional differences hinder any account of demonstrative determiners as prenominal nouns behaving like those in the construction at issue. Actually, "most lin-

[39]For a review of proposals on how to explain the asymmetry, which is empirically evident, but problematic for theoretical reasons, see Sadler & Arnold (1994).

[40]The distribution of *here* and *there* as regards dependence is cross-categorial: they depend on nouns/pronouns, but also verbs (at any level of clausal projection) or prepositions (as in "from *there*", "up (to) *here*"). If an adnominal demonstrative is adjectival, the fourth major category turns out to be covered too, even though all other adjectives reject the dependence of those deictics for semantic reasons.

guists would ... not regard it as being a syntactic construct at all. Instead, it would be seen as a morphological object, a compound ... that should not be analyzed syntactically" (P. Bennett 1995: p. 28).

The precise status of noun compounding is controversial, since the phenomenon stands somewhere between syntax and morphology (with properties of both), and we will not try to settle the issue. However the neatly syntactic distribution of a demonstrative as 'central determiner' (in the sense we made clear in § 1.2.1) is a completely different matter. The demonstrative replaces the article in its function of completing a Noun Phrase, with fulfilment of the obligatory determination required for singular count number, and can precede quite a variable range of AP modifiers attached to syntactic projections of some simple or compound head noun, as in "*the/this* (second) (very old) (red and blue) (Persian) $[_N$ *(prayer) carpet*]". Then the comparison really relevant here concerns nominal expressions that are central determiners – but they need not respect the ban on postpositive dependents, as shown by examples of Saxon genitive NPs[41], like "*The ambassador from Bulgaria*'s hat was stolen" or "*The candidate I talked to*'s resume was outstanding" (from Pollard & Sag 1987: p. 60).

At first sight, the fact that *this/these* and *that/those* make an overt morphophonological distinction of number, preserving it in adnominal position, might look as a serious problem for our adjectival account, because adjectives in English do not appear to inflect for number. This aspect could arguably favour the alternative proposal that adnominal demonstratives must preserve the part of speech of their 'independent' pronominal counterparts, i.e. Noun, which is regularly associated with the singular/plural distinction. There's more to it than meets the eye, however, if one also considers the covariation in number that is needed between a demonstrative determiner and a head noun, but not when the former item is replaced by a genuine pronoun, viz. some possessive determiner: cf. "*his/their* book(s)", "*this/*these* book", "*these/*this* books". On the other hand, the constraint whereby adjectives have to agree in number (and additional features) with the noun they modify is the rule in languages like German and Italian, so that we can make the plausible hypothesis of some related although much less evident phenomenon showing up in English too.

[41]The comparison with complex Saxon genitive phrases headed by common nouns is appropriate, because we argued that the actual demonstrative pronouns are pro-forms of common nouns, contrary to the standard NP status of personal pronouns (with genitive forms acting as possessive determiners). The degree of acceptability of pertinent examples varies according to their complexity, under pragmatic and stylistic conditions. As Quirk et al. (1985: p. 1345) notice, postmodification by a relative clause within Saxon genitive NPs is restricted to colloquial use: "In normal use, especially in writing, such genitives would be replaced by *of*-constructions: Have you seen *the hat of that man standing at the corner?*", instead of "Have you seen *that man standing at the corner's hat?*".

In this connection, it is important to recognize an abstract notion of agreement features, over and above their empirical realization as an aspect of morpho-phonological form. The difference was touched on by § 1.2.2.2 as regards the PERSON feature, which is involved in subject-verb agreement and consequently assigned to all items belonging to the category Noun, even if phonologically expressed person morphology is confined to a small minority of them, i.e. personal pronouns and the like. By the same token, we can assume that all English adjectives have the NUMBER feature in agreement with the head noun, but qualifying adjectives do not express their singular/plural distinction at the level of morpho-phonological form. (That is, they look akin to such nouns as *sheep*, *species*, *series*, etc., which are available for both singular and plural use without changing form.) Number gets inherently expressed as lexical information by various determiners classified as adjectives in our approach: e.g., *every*, *each* and the cardinal *one* are **singular** on a par with *this* and *that*, whereas *many*, *few* and the cardinals *two*, *three*, *four*, ... are **plural** on a par with *these* and *those*.

To outline in detail the morphological mechanisms presupposed so far is not a task for this study, but some remarks can usefully complete the picture. In essence, we follow quite a simple 'lexicalist' approach to morphology, assuming words – instead of morphemes – as the minimal representation units of the grammar. Hence the grammar of a language is supplied with a lexicon for the set of all words of that language (at a given historical stage) and their lexical entries include grammatical features encoding inflectional and derivational information consistently with the phonological form φ. On the other hand, a morpheme (unless it happens to coincide with a whole word) will not be represented by a separate entry, being only a φ-segment identified across words/entries for its relevance to morphological generalizations. Some kind of 'lexical rules' are the formal tool standardly used to encode the generalizations in question within a word-based framework:

> "Lexical rules ... may be interpreted as rules of inference that derive lexical entries of inflected, derived or compound words from those of simpler words."
>
> Pollard & Sag (1994: p. 37)

Inferences in case of compounding would presumably take the form of a deduction from two premises, corresponding to entries of (simple or compound) words X and Y, whose concatenation becomes a possible compound word XY. There is a clear resemblance with syntax (as we mentioned before), allowing the combination of items to be represented by a tree; e.g.:

(11) $[_N [_N \text{physics}] [_N \text{student}]]$

Yet the outcome is not a phrase but a word structure as in this example of compound noun (from P. Bennett 1995: p. 28), "whether we regard morphological trees as being extensions 'downwards' of syntactic trees, or as constituting a separate structure altogether" (ibid.). Here we can leave compounding aside and abstain from saying more on the issues it raises (like an adequate format of lexical entries), while the different character of lexical rules for affixation must be pointed out.

An inflectional or derivational affix is a morpheme not autonomously represented by any lexical entry according to our grammar design, so that the affix cannot be combined with the stem of a relevant word by means of 'structure-building' rules of the lexicon, comparable to those for compounding[42]. In order to ascertain what kind of rules/inferences must apply, let us first make explicit two distinct technical senses of the layman's **word** notion that is used informally: specific **word form** vs. underlying **lexeme**. E.g. *eat*, *eats*, *eaten*, *eating* and *ate* are word forms of the same lexeme, the verb '(to) eat'. This distinction can be simply captured by representing each word form with a separate lexical entry inclusive of inflection, whereas a lexeme comes down to the disjunction of the lexical entries of all its word forms or, equivalently, is encoded as a single lexical entry whose phonological and morphological values are disjunctive and co-vary (cf. Krieger & Nerbonne 1993). No matter how compact the representation format may be, in case of inflected words a lexeme displaying its whole paradigm of variation is necessarily more complex than the particular forms it subsumes. Then, generalizations about inflection look easier to state directly across word forms, yielding the lexeme in consequence (by disjunction), rather than vice versa.

Within the system proposed by Pollard & Sag (1987: ch. 8) and others, some finite set of lexical entries which represent 'base forms' of words is postulated – hence listed – as primitive, but a larger lexicon is derived applying what generative grammarians call **lexical redundancy rules** (as in Radford 1981: ch. 4)[43]. Any such rule states a mapping $\mathcal{L} \longmapsto \mathcal{L}'$ from input lexical entries (whether primitive or derived via lexical rules) to output lexical entries, so that a lexicon including the entries described by $\mathcal{L}$, the rule's left-hand side, must equally include the corresponding entries described by $\mathcal{L}'$, the rule's right-hand side. If inflectional variation is the 'redundancy' to be inferred from a base

[42] See Van Eynde (1994) for a recent version of the alternative approach, building words as tree structures upon a basic lexicon of morphemes. As he admits, "this approach ... sometimes leads to the postulation of empty elements, such as the zero-affixes in the English verb system" (ibid., p. 221); thus it is inconsistent with our attempt to avoid all empty elements in the tree structures of linguistic expressions.

[43] This notion of rules that avoid 'redundancy' in lexical coding was already employed by Chomsky (1965: § 2.1 of ch. 4), though not for treating morphology.

form qua word form taken as representative of its lexeme[44] (e.g., the infinitive for a verb), the rule will change phonological and morphological aspects of the output entries in accordance with the corresponding inflected forms. The same kind of rules – a.k.a. the 'lexical rules' *tout court*, when those for compounding are neglected – allows further applications, like attaching a derivational affix to a base form so as to yield the base form of a new lexeme.

A possible output of lexical rules which proves useful for derivation without extra affixes, as in most pronominal counterparts of determinative adjectives, just consists of a homophonous version of the input word changing aspects of the entry like its part of speech. Besides the nominalization of qualifying adjectives already mentioned, another category-changing derivation that does not affect phonological form is the nominalization of verbs like *fight*, *love*, *walk*, etc. The case in which a different but morpho-phonologically related word/entry derives from the input is exemplified by a lexical rule forming pronominal counterparts from the determiners *any*, *every*, *no* and *some* via suffixation of "-body", "-one", or "-thing"; we shall call **composite pronouns** the resulting twelve forms. For a comparable phenomenon, consider verb nominalization through suffixes like "-ion", as in "*elect*ion", "*react*ion", etc., or "-ment", as in "*assign*ment", "*invest*ment", etc.

It is worth noticing that suffixes of composite pronouns contribute to the inherent meaning of their respective word forms by encoding a distinction between human beings (or at least 'humanized' ones, e.g. pets) and other entities (typically – but not necessarily – inanimate ones). We find independent motivation for such a semantic opposition in the pronominal field, where it especially applies to the relative pronouns *who* vs. *which*. Yet another instance of the same distinction is entailed by the gender of 3rd-person personal pronouns (including possessives and reflexives), insofar as masculine and feminine can be grouped as subsorts of a 'common' human gender distinguished from neuter.[45] In each case of composite pronoun, the self-determination of this item, which preserves the quantitative import of its adjectival root, combines with the semantic contribution of the suffix, thus quantifying over a domain of entities that essentially equals the denotation of the noun *person*, when the suffix is "-body" or "-one", or the denotation of the noun *thing*, when the suffix is "-thing".

Then one might be tempted to claim that there are no 'composite pronouns' at all, but only an orthographic convention, disguising the syntactic combination of determiners with three nominal heads which are assigned the relevant

[44] In a sense, therefore, the rule states an inference from general to particular.

[45] Some languages (e.g., Danish) actually express morphologically the common gender as such, without distinguishing between masculine and feminine.

denotations[46]. We reject the idea for reasons that Kathol (1999) clarifies as follows:

> "An analysis of this kind ... raises significant questions about semantic compositionality and the proper interplay between syntactic generality and idiosyncracy. In particular, what ensures that it is only in combination with [determiners like] *some* that *body* can (but does not have to) mean 'person'? Moreover, what is the nature of the bonding between *some* and *body* in the idiomatic case ... that prevents any attributive modifiers from intervening between *some* and *body* (cf. *some nice body* vs. *somebody nice*)?"

If that evidence is taken into account, expressions "such as *somebody* are ... NPs without syntactically visible internal organization" (ibid.), a conclusion confirming the soundness of their traditional analysis as a single suitable word, indeed a pronoun. The analysis is also supported by the behaviour of a post-positive modifier, *else*, which applies to the composite forms in question but not to NPs that result syntactically from overt combination of a determiner with a separate head noun; to mean the same when using this syntactic construction, the postdeterminer *other* must be interposed instead. E.g., compare "somebody (vs. *some person) *else*" and "some *other* person".

1.3.2 Head hunting: against the DP Hypothesis

The assumption on how determiner-nominal constructions are headed that was cited in **B)**, at the beginning of section 1.3, has been rejected by Abney (1987) and others in favour of one conventionally known as 'DP Hypothesis' or 'DP Analysis'.[47] The traditional NP characterization of the syntactic domain where determiners and nominals link up, i.e.:

(12) $[_{NP} \ldots X(P) \ldots [_{Nom} \ldots N \ldots]]$

does not hold in the new approach (13), which claims the domain is the phrasal projection of some lexical item X other than the noun N.

(13) $[_{XP} \ldots X \ldots [_{NP} \ldots N \ldots]]$

[46] The convention would be that the given 'determiner + nominal' combination is written as one orthographic word when the determiner is stressed, whereas the words are distinguished also orthographically when the nominal head is stressed. Of course, in the usual approach, the former pronunciation may well be interpreted as stressing the first syllable of a composite pronoun qua actual morpho-syntactic word (following Quirk et al. 1985: pp. 378-379).

[47] The most famous work on the subject is indeed Abney's, but cf. also Szabolsci (1983), Hellan (1986), Hudson (1987; 1990), Hewson (1991), Longobardi (1994), Netter (1994), Radford (1997), Kathol (1999), Nerbonne & Mullen (2000), etc.

In (13), X is typically a determiner with part-of-speech category D, so that the XP domain corresponds to DP; but this is not essential for the 'DP Hypothesis' – despite its name[48] – inasmuch as also categories like Q(uantifier) or A(djective) are allowed to be heads of that phrase, at least according to Abney's version of the theory, thus yielding a QP or AP. At any rate, what used to be an intermediate projection of the noun in the other approach (i.e. Nom in (12)[49]) becomes a full, though determinerless NP, embedded into XP and taken as dependent by the head X.

The opposite conclusions concerning the dependent or head status of a determiner within the construction under consideration raise the issue of which forms of syntactic dependency apply in the two cases. We postpone to chapters 4-5 a more careful discussion of the analysis (12), which would roughly appear to involve some sort of 'adnominal modification' of the head by its determinative dependent[50]. As far as the analysis (13) is concerned, the dependency is basically viewed as a particular instance of '(syntactic) context-sensitive subcategorization', in the sense stemming from Chomsky (1965: § 2.3.4) and technically developed in different ways depending on the grammatical framework to be chosen. By such a subcategorization we mean a subclassification of words that have the same part-of-speech category but can differ in distributional restrictions, because of idiosyncratic lexical information about category and function of the obligatory 'sisters' (if any) making up the syntactic context where the given word is allowed to occur as head. A brief comparison with the subcategorization of verbs in terms of their **complements** (strictly speaking) will clarify this point.

Here are some examples of verbs with different 'subcategorization frames' in English, a language where the head verb occurs before its complements within the Verb Phrase (VP)[51]. The verbs like *put* subcategorize for two sister complements, viz. the direct object NP and a locative PP; those like *devour*

[48] A more general denomination, which does not look confined to the category D(P) proper, would be 'Theory of Functional Heads', as we will explain later on.

[49] Here 'Nom' stands for a possibly complex **Nominal** (see Dowty et al. 1981: p. 212, e.g.); we mean it as a provisional notation for intermediate (not maximal/full) projections of nouns, to be abandoned in the more formal part of our work. Intermediate projections of a determiner are possible too, but now we are neglecting them for simplicity's sake.

[50] However, omission tests contradict the typical optionality of modification when presence of the article or another determiner with the same distribution becomes obligatory because of a count nominal sister in the singular, as already mentioned before. This phenomenon – which calls for special measures in a DP Analysis too (cf. Netter 1994 or Kathol 1999) – is left aside for the moment, but will be treated in the last chapters within our revised version of the traditional NP approach.

[51] Chomsky's original encoding of subcategorization frames included information on linear order too, but the two aspects can be separated as chapter 4 will show. Another issue to be postponed is whether and how also the subject of verbs should be encoded by their frames

subcategorize for the direct object only; and those like *die* do not subcategorize for any complement. At first sight, the frame in the last type of lexical entries "states that *die* occurs before 'nothing' ... but of course this is quite untrue: ... [cf.] *John died on Tuesday*" (P. Bennett 1995: pp. 8-9). If one takes into account that adverbial PPs used as optional modifiers must be distinguished from obligatory complements/objects, the problem disappears: "A temporal adverbial such as *on Tuesday* is not subcategorized by the verb; unlike objects, time adverbials can be added to practically any clause, irrespective of the verb therein" (ibid.). Since the 'nothing' frame of lexical subcategorization – however expressed notationally – concerns complements (in the strict sense), it does not prevent the words it is assigned to from allowing modifiers.

Another problem is raised by verbs like like *eat*, whose direct object NP may well be omitted without making the sentence ungrammatical: cf. *The beast ate* vs. **The beast devoured* (from Gazdar et al. 1985: p. 32). This case seems to contradict the obligatoriness of complements, but a natural solution is to provide *eat* with two different readings, a transitive one, which parallels *devour*, and an intransitive reading without complements, like *die*. That is, the identification of alternative readings makes the direct object obligatory in one and impossible in the other, so that complements are confirmed to be always obligatory in the relevant reading(s) of verbs (see Graffi 1994: p. 51). A compact representation of two or more subcategorization readings in the same lexical entry is nevertheless possible, thanks to formal tools like logical disjunction or the parentheses usually indicating optionality [52].

We will have much more to say on the subcategorization of verbs in chapter 4, but what matters now is the application of similar ideas to determiners. Supporters of a DP Analysis could claim that:

d1. articles as well as the other word forms that are only determinative – v. *every*, *no*, *my*, etc. – always subcategorize for NP, in accordance with (13) above;

d2. those word forms that are 'independent' counterparts of non-identical determiners of type ***d1*** – v. *everybody*, *nothing*, *mine*, etc. – act as determiner-style heads without any subcategorized-for dependent;

---

even though it occurs outside the VP; for the moment, we preserve the original restriction of subcategorization to the lexical head's sisters.

[52] Using a provisional notation, if V: __ NP is the subcategory of *devour*-type verbs, where 'X: __ Y' means 'X occurs before the sister Y', then V: __ (NP) is the subcategory of *eat*-type verbs. Optionality w.r.t. frame elements is not inconsistent with the obligatoriness of complements, but corresponds to disjunction between two cases, the obligatory presence of the parenthesized element and its absence, thus encoding precisely the intended distinction between readings. On the other hand, modification will be accounted for as a different phenomenon, which leaves unaffected the subcategorization frame of the modified head (v. our chapters 4-5).

d3. the word forms with both determinative and 'independent' function – v. *many*, *some*, *this*, etc. – have two subcategorization readings, one of type ***d1*** ('transitive') and the other of type ***d2*** ('intransitive').

In that version of the analysis, if X is the 'independent' counterpart of a determinative word form or reading, X projects the phrase structure $[_{\mathrm{XP}} \ldots \mathrm{X} \ldots]$ (= (13) without embedded NP) as done in our pronominal treatment. However, there is a difference in category labels, because we equate X(P) to N(P), with consequent change from [+N, +V] to [+N, −V] in most cases (as explained before), whereas the alternative approach always preserves the category of the original determiner for its counterpart. This looks like a simplification, presumably allowing a compact lexical representation of the two readings of a 'type ***d3***' form within a single (but somehow disjunctive) entry, so as to dispense with a mapping via form-preserving lexical rule(s).

Even though the DP Hypothesis may be claimed to solve elegantly the problem of seeming head-less NPs phonologically identical to determiners, which is under discussion since § 1.3.1, the solution raises the opposite problem of those phrases with the same distribution that are just "bare nominals" without overt determiners (Radford 1997: p. 153). As far as headedness is concerned, the phenomenon is clearly not problematic for a traditional NP analysis, but has rather complicated consequences for the DP analysis. We shall first consider the approach where phrase structure looks simpler, i.e. the idea that bare nominals are NPs not occurring embedded into a determiner-headed structure, unlike the others. Thus the fact that the domain traditionally known as *noun phrase* would be either a bare nominal NP or an XP of our schema (13) implies a "polycategorial analysis" (Kathol 1999); all the more so because the X in (13) need not be set as 'D(eterminer)' proper, but can range over various suitable parts of speech.

It is readily seen that a polycategorial version of the so-called 'DP' Hypothesis causes the grammar to miss an important generalization (cf. criticism by Payne 1993, Arnold & Sadler 1994, and Netter 1994). Now each of the syntactic slots traditionally captured by 'NP' within the subcategorization frame of lexical entries – hence **subject**, **direct object**, etc. – must be assigned not only that category (owing to bare nominals), but also as many alternatives as the XP in (13) allows. As a result, all the lexical entries of verbs and other words that used to subcategorize for NPs will have to be multiplied or made disjunctive accordingly[53], despite the lack of any empirical motivation in terms of a corresponding subcategorization typology of lexical heads; say, "a division of the set of English verbs into those which select DPs, those which

[53]The disjunction of n subcategorization frames within a single entry is simply a more compact way of encoding the corresponding n non-disjunctive entries.

select QPs and those which select NPs" (Payne 1993). In fact, "there are no two different verbs x and y such that, for example, x only occurs with noun phrases which contain determiners and y only occurs with noun phrases which contain quantifiers" (ibid.).

What's more, the category system envisaged by advocates of polycategoriality *à la* Abney (1987) – and indeed referred to in the above criticism w.r.t. subcategorization frames – typically takes for granted such parts of speech as D(eterminer) and Q(uantifier), whereas they were shown to be untenable, or at least dubious, in our § 1.2.2. The DP Hypothesis does not adequately justify the various part-of-speech categories its polycategorial version allows, nor can it be fully adapted to the category system that was linguistically motivated in the current chapter, especially as regards a separate part of speech for the articles. Of course, one might assume 'Art(icle)' as a possible value for X in (13), yet the question is whether the label is motivated by morpho-syntactic properties setting the articles apart when compared with the other determinative items. Under our system, there is a motivation inasmuch as *article* entails '*minor* determiner', with *minor* meaning 'word that cannot project phrase structure and therefore cannot take any dependent'; in short, articles cannot be heads. But clearly, this is inconsistent with the DP Hypothesis making articles heads.

To avoid engaging in a polycategorial classification of determiner-style heads and their projections, the DP Analysis schema (13) gets instantiated by some authors according to a literal understanding of the 'DP' label. The general idea is to stick to a single part of speech Determiner with full coverage of the X value, so as to achieve the result that all constituents traditionally classified as NPs be converted into DPs (v. Radford 1997: pp. 45-46, 153)[54]. However, this interacts with the problem of bare nominals: whereas they were naturally treated as NPs without determiner, "the uniform DP approach ... has a number of undesirable consequences, for instance the postulation of strange invisible determiners to account for the DP status of unadorned proper names" (Kathol 1999)[55]. It is crucial for the proponents of that version of the DP Hy-

[54]In Radford's work, the old dichotomy Determiner vs. Quantifier as categories with part-of-speech status – cf. our § 1.2.2.1 above – is consequently replaced by a semantic distinction between referential and quantifying members of the category Determiner (according to a referentiality notion that looks restricted to 'definite reference'). Cf. Radford (1997: p. 46): "Quantifying determiners are determiners like *all/some* which denote quantity, and are sometimes said to belong to the subcategory **quantifier**; referential determiners are determiners like *the/this/that/my* which are used to introduce referring expressions".

[55]There are languages allowing overt definite articles to vacuously or redundantly combine with such 'self-determining' definite expressions as the proper names. (See "*el* Juan" in Spanish and "*der* Hans" in German, e.g., as mentioned by Barwise & Cooper 1981.) The overt phenomenon obviously cannot be ignored by an adequate account of natural language

pothesis to show that not all the phonologically 'empty' elements thus implied have vacuous or redundant content like those associated with proper names:

> "an important question to ask about the **empty determiner** analysis of bare nominals is whether it is consistent with ... an **economy principle** ... which prohibits superfluous projections. ... The answer is that it is, by virtue of the fact that the null determiner Ø ... has clear semantic and grammatical properties of its own".
>
> Radford (1997: p. 153)

But contrary to Radford's, our answer is negative, because the account of bare nominals to be provided in the chapters 4-5 will show that any such empty determiner can be dispensed with – both syntactically and semantically – even in cases routinely analyzed by various authors as including it for the completion of NP interpretation [56].

There is yet another line of research to be considered, one whose way of applying the DP Hypothesis tries to remedy some defects that have been criticized so far:

> "In contrast to a pure DP-oriented approach where an obligatory determiner position is postulated as providing the structural head of the phrase, we avoid the necessity of empty determiners. ... In contrast to an approach which treats constructions with and without a determiner as DPs and NPs respectively and accordingly requires disjunctive subcategorizations on the matrix predicate, maximal nominal projections are uniformly assigned the same type".
>
> Netter (1994)

It is noteworthy that the achievements referred to are the same under a traditional assumption of nominal headedness, since this embodies the correct distributional generalization, with the evident result of making the phrasal category of the relevant syntactic domain insensitive to the presence or absence of determiners and to variations in their part of speech. The new variant of the DP Hypothesis is actually 'hybrid' in that it keeps to the assumption that the determiner combining with a nominal sister be the head, but ensures that the phrase resulting from their combination be nonetheless assigned a nominal category.

---

semantics and the syntax-semantics interface, but in no way proves that covert, unexpressed versions of those articles are needed in some language. The systematic postulation of determiners that are not expressed by the speakers would be a spurious generalization, which meets theory-internal demands of a uniform DP Analysis by adding unmotivated complexity to otherwise simpler and self-contained structures.

[56] On the typical case of 'Ø' corresponding to *some* in (non-generic) bare plurals, cf. Link (1987), among others. (See also our chapter 2 below for an introductory discussion of data.)

A particularly clear version of the 'hybrid' approach at issue, taking advantage of the expressive power provided by a 'sort hierarchy' for part-of-speech categories [57], has been developed by Kathol (1999):

> "a rather fine-grained categorial space ... allow[s] for different nominal structures to be headed either by typical nouns or determiners without danger of missing a generalization. For instance, if we assume that rather than picking out a single ... lexical class (i.e. N), *nominal* is the common supertype of a range of categories which (minimally) contains ... nouns and determiners, ... then the parallelism in external distribution is straightforwardly accounted for."

By doing so, he is indeed "dissolving the 'classical' distinction between NP vs. DP in favour of a polycategorial analysis which treats both as subtypes of *nominal*" (ibid.), yet this analysis is not polycategorial at all as regards the determiners themselves. They are said to form the *para-nominal* (sub)category, new class of nominal words to be treated on a par with such standard lexical classes as those of common nouns, proper names and pronouns. Of course, *para-nominal* might be added its own subsorts (instead of being a terminal in the hierarchy), but Kathol's system proves incompatible with the linguistically correct assignment of determiners to parts of speech according to the evidence we offered for English: if most determiners are actually adjectives while the articles form a minor category and the possessive determiner words belong to the paradigm of personal pronouns, no 'para-nominals' exist.

Similar considerations hold for Netter's (1994) work – probably the first and most famous proposal of an 'hybrid' approach to DP Analysis – although the idea of making all determiners (and their projections) nominal is applied by that author in a peculiar fashion. Starting from the usual definition of four major categories in terms of the features [+/–N, +/–V], Netter claims that the same features are also available for so-called 'functional categories', Determiner being a case in point; these are the categories of "heads ... operating in a parasitic manner on the major categories they combine with" (ibid.) [58]. Whereas a word of major category is inherently specified for its part of speech (modulo the appropriate features) in the lexicon, the corresponding information of the other sort of categories follows from a generalization: a functional

[57] We are presupposing the notion of 'sort hierarchy' *à la* Pollard & Sag (1987; 1994) already presented in § 1.2.2.2. (Note that *type* is used as synonymous with *sort* in Kathol's quotations hereafter.)

[58] It should be clear that the *major* vs. *functional* dichotomy in question differs from the *major* vs. *minor* one we have adopted, because his functional categories are heads, while our minor categories (by definition) are not. Then, even if Netter (1994) actually uses also 'minor' as synonymous with 'functional', we will refrain from doing so, to avoid confusion.

word **shares** the part of speech of its subcategorized-for dependent [59], instantiating the N and V features accordingly. Thus, the X category of a determiner qua functional head projecting XP, in (13) above, is [+N, –V] and arises from the nominal sister of the determiner.

Elegant though Netter's (1994) solution may be in a formalization, it retains the substantial linguistic drawback of any 'hybrid' treatment of NPs, ignoring independently motivated categorial differences among determiners because of its undue extension of the nominal coverage, which is required to emulate the effects of nominal headedness. What's more, a typical advantage of the DP Hypothesis as standardly designed disappears, since the new system turns out to raise again the issue of 'empty nouns' to be combined with determiners (as done by Nerbonne & Mullen 2000, among others). The categorial parasitism of functional heads *à la* Netter, in fact, leads to the introduction of an unexpressed dependent N(P) after any item whose functional status of determiner is meant to be preserved when no overt nominal sister occurs. That's a defect for all those who dispute his claim that "empty nouns ... are well-motivated and necessary for anaphoric interpretation" [60] (Netter 1994) and want to dispense with empty constituents altogether.

Further discussion deserves the notion of **functional head** itself, to be examined on more general grounds insofar as other authors (like Abney 1987) have applied it in manners that partly differ yet always extend a head role to categories of words not classified as 'major' by the same authors. Then the DP Hypothesis develops into some broader Theory of Functional Heads, which is expected to be equally relevant for determiners and words playing a parallel syntactic function in the respective structural domains (e.g., a complementizer in the clausal domain). The idea of reusing [+/–N, +/–V] for functional categories is less common, but this proposal has also been made by Radford (1997: p. 69), who adds the feature [+F] in order to distinguish a functional category from the corresponding [–F] (hence major) one. On the other hand, contrary to Netter, he does not mechanically draw the functional category's major-like features from its subcategorized-for dependent, aiming at inherently plausible lexical assignments instead.

Radford's attempt to give a general and intuitive characterization of the *functional* idea must be mentioned to start with. He assumes that the relevant

---

[59] We shall come back to the relevant feature-theoretic notion of 'sharing' from a more general and formal point of view in chapter 3.

[60] Clearly the anaphoric use is quite consistent with a traditional account of the determiners' counterparts as pronominal items on their own, i.e. **C)** at the beginning of section 1.3. The same account is available in Kathol's (1999) system, where "determiners that also double as pronouns such as the demonstrative *that* are lexically underspecified in terms of their nominal subtype" (= *para-nominal* or *pronoun*).

analysis as heads applies precisely to the traditional grammarians' *function words*, i.e. the lexical items distinguished from those known as "*contentives* or *content words*" because the former lack and the latter embody "idiosyncratic descriptive content which varies from one lexical item / word to another" (ibid., p. 45). Given the system of features cited before, contentives are categorially major – and get classified accordingly – but "each ... contentive category has a functional counterpart, so auxiliaries are the functional counterpart of verbs, determiners of adjectives, pronouns of nouns, and particles (e.g. complementizer *for* and infinitival *to*) of prepositions" (ibid., p. 69). Before saying more on the various cases, we wish to observe that the clear semantic basis of such a contentive vs. functional dichotomy does not look really appropriate for establishing the category system of morpho-syntactic parts of speech, unless a correspondence with some independently motivated aspect of grammatical form can be found.

In this connection, Radford suggests that "function words ... serve primarily to carry information about the grammatical properties of expressions within the sentence, for instance information about number, gender, person, case, etc." (ibid., p. 45). Personal pronouns are indeed a relevant class, being function words exhaustively decomposable into the NP's grammatical features mentioned explicitly by the quotation (e.g., *she* just carries information of singular number, feminine gender, 3rd person and nominative case). We can say the meaning of personal pronouns (and the like) is simply the semantic interpretation of that grammatical feature bundle, while their lack of any strictly semantic feature with descriptive status implies they are not 'contentive' (in the intended sense). Another instance of function words characterized by what may be called *grammatical meaning* are auxiliaries with the only task of carrying grammatical features, including tense.[61]

However, we also know of lexical items whose meaning is not of the grammatical sort (= semantic interpretation of grammatical features), but still are classified as function words, in both traditional grammar and Radford's theory. Some have vacuous meaning, being completely void of semantic information (as in the case of Radford's prepositional 'particles'), whereas others have purely logical – e.g. quantificational – meaning specific to individual lexical items, which does not interpret any systematic grammatical property. The logical case is important for our main subject, since various (but not all) determiners are function words of the kind; further examples are the function words ex-

[61] Insofar as the auxiliary is a [–N, +V] function word necessarily combined with a verbal constituent, preserving the same pair of features, this is a case in which the theory of functional heads gives the same result for Netter and Radford. On the contrary, pronouns lacking any subcategorised-for dependent (at least an 'empty' one) from which they would draw their category cannot be functional for Netter.

pressing logical connectives, i.e. negation and the coordinating conjunctions. In sum, it turns out that function words are rather heterogeneous apart from their common lack of descriptive content, the semantic notion to be supported with some properly grammatical criterion.

A criterion hinted at by Netter (1994) is that "functional categories typically form closed classes of elements", yet the two concepts do not have exactly the same coverage, in view of an outstanding counterexample: prepositions form a closed class, but are standardly treated as the major [–N, –V] category. Even if an alternative system with prepositions making up a functional category is conceivable, evidence appears to favour the standard account. Indeed the category of prepositions lacks a property that is said to be congenial to functional heads: "In comparison with major categories, which normally can be subcategorized for all different types of other categories, functional categories are much more selective with respect to the major categories they combine with" (ibid.). So, like verbs, "prepositions allow a range of subcategorization possibilities" (Bennett 1995: p. 75), i.e. they can be transitive or intransitive – as we mentioned in § 1.2.2.1 – and, what's more, take PP or sentential complements (v. "*from* under the table", "*before* the meeting finished").[62]

Moreover, the category Preposition resembles the other major ones insofar as it also includes words that neatly pass the semantic test of **antonymy** (= relation between opposites) applied by Radford (1997: p. 45) to ascertain the presence of descriptive content:

> "if a word has an antonym, it is a contentive... For example, a noun/N such as *loss* has the antonym *gain*; a verb/V such as *rise* has the antonym *fall*; an adjective/A such as *tall* has the antonym *short*; ... and a preposition/P such as *inside* has the antonym *outside*."

Further examples of prepositions forming antonymy-based pairs are *with* vs. *without* (ibid., p. 75), *before* vs. *after*, *up* vs. *down*, *over* vs. *under*, etc. Prepositions that do not seem to have antonyms exist, yet this does not invalidate the positive results of the test, which is meant to check a sufficient but not necessary condition, in the case of prepositions as much as in the others; that is, the test does not tell us whether a word without any antonym is contentive or not.

Antonymy looks interesting for testing determiners too, because it clearly shows that some of them cannot be function words. In particular, *many* vs. *few* (or their noncount, comparative and superlative forms) are antonyms, of the typical type which does not involve logical contradiction but allows intermediate degrees between the two opposites.[63] Therefore such quantitative

[62] See Graffi (1994: pp. 46-47, 187) for the same argumentation applied to Italian.

[63] According to Katz (1972), three different types of antonyms have to be distinguished: those based on a contradiction, e.g. *alive* vs. *dead* (if understood literally); those based on a

determiners prove contentive, a conclusion supported by modern research in quantification pointing out that they do not have purely logical meaning like *every*, *some* or *no*. (See chapters 2-3 below, for details.) In another case of determinative words without logical meaning, viz. the possessive ones, function word status is confirmed, however, because of their grammatical meaning as genitive personal pronouns (cf. our previous discussion). Radford's claim that Determiner is the [+N, +V] category of functional heads, i.e. all determiners act as functional adjectives, gets consequently falsified in two ways[64]: the determiners *many* and *few* are indeed adjectives – as we argued in § 1.2.2.1 – but contentive, not function words, whereas function words of the possessive determiner kind are not adjectives in English, being pronouns.

By way of conclusion, we can say that Radford (1997) has not been successful in the attempt at founding his categories of functional heads on a more traditional notion of function words. Even if one may well endorse some semantic distinction between words that are contentive and words that are not because of purely logical, grammatical or even vacuous meaning, there is no systematic morpho-syntactic motivation for the [+/–F] doubling of categories implied by Radford's theory. It is sufficient to assume that each of the four **major categories** themselves has both contentive members and members that are function words, as a matter of lexical meaning typology only, while function words not classifiable among major ones belong to **minor categories** in the sense we advocated before. Accordingly, determiners do not form the single functional category postulated by Radford but exemplify all our three possible cases: (a) content words of major category, like the adjectives *many* and *few*, (b) function words of major category, like the genitive pronouns with determinative function, and (c) function words of minor category, namely the articles.

1.3.3 The case for genitive case

While the conviction that determiners do not form a single, uniform morpho-syntactic category played a crucial role in our criticism of the DP Hypothesis (v. § 1.3.2), it's only fair to say that not all supporters of some traditional 'NP Analysis' of determiner-nominal constructions would take sides with us as regards the repertory of parts of speech. In particular, we have also departed

gradable opposition, e.g. *big* vs. *little*, a pair we can easily relate to *many* (= a big number) vs. *few* (= a little number); those based on the inversion of a relation, e.g. *buy* vs. *sell*, *husband* vs. *wife*. (Cf. also J. Lyons 1968.)

[64]In addition, the difference such a category Determiner preserves between DP and NP (given the opposite values for the V attribute) leads Radford to the use of empty determiners as previously criticized.

from the presentation of English by Quirk et al. (1985: pp. 42, 67), where Determiner qua part-of-speech category is envisaged despite a notion/coverage of the determinative function closely related to ours. For these authors, "there is rarely a one-to-one match between formal and functional classifications" [65], but when the match obtains "it would be superfluous to introduce two terms for what is effectively the same category" (ibid., p. 64); thus they identify the putative part of speech Determiner with their functionally characterized class of determinative words. Though we don't want to question the right to reuse the same terminological label for a part of speech and a functional class if the two ever match, we deny the empirical adequacy of any claim that a one-to-one match obtains in the field at issue here.

Also Quirk et al. (1985: p. 64) concede that the hypothetical match between a morpho-syntactic part of speech and the functional notion of determiners does not work at least when the determinative expressions are Saxon genitive phrases. If these just consist of a Noun Phrase with genitive case marking (a point already touched on in our § 1.2.2.2 and note 26), we see a clear instance of expression which categorially will not be classified as Determiner by Quirk et al. themselves, though it is functionally a determiner of the same kind as the possessive words *my*, *your*, *his*, etc. Then Quirk and co-workers are compelled to distinguish their category label 'Determiner' from the 'determinative' notion in a way roughly comparable to the traditional dualism between 'Adverb' and 'adverbial': a specific part of speech is introduced for expressions that are characterized by a certain function and, at the same time, don't get classified according to any independently motivated part of speech, unlike other expressions with that function. As we made clear in § 1.2.2.1, the expedient has been abandoned by modern accounts of adverbiality in theoretical linguistics, thanks to a more principled and restrictive category system, and we believe a similar attitude should apply to determination.

Still, the precise grammatical status of genitive case for possessive determination deserves more discussion, because the approach we have informally taken for granted in this connection is not uncontroversial:

> "At first blush, it seems reasonable to specify the possessive pronouns ... as [CASE *gen*], in order to distinguish them from nominative and accusative NPs. However, the question then arises of how to treat non-pronominal possessives ... formed by attaching the clitic *-'s* after a non-pronominal NP".
>
> Pollard & Sag (1987: p. 60)

Consider what happens with such complex examples as *the ambassador from Bulgaria's*, *the candidate I talked to's*:

[65] Now 'function(al)' is again opposed to 'form(al)' as in our § 1.3.1 (cf. note 29), not to 'content(ive)' as in the Theory of Functional Heads we discussed in § 1.3.2.

> "If the Noun Phrase ... unspecified for CASE ... is the head of the possessive phrase, then evidently the latter cannot be [CASE *gen*], for the head noun bears no genitive inflection. Perhaps the right thing to say here is that the clitic *-'s*, not the NP, is the head; in that case, possessive phrases are not really NPs at all." (ibid.)

Pollard and Sag's argument above implies that CASE represents an abstract property of NPs, constraining their syntactic function, and at the same time can correspond to explicit morphological inflection on their lexical heads. So, every NP must have a CASE value in common with its head (according to a feature sharing principle to be presented in chapter 3), but in a language like English that value is morphologically specified for *nominative* or *accusative* provided the NP is headed by (or simply consists of) a suitable pronoun form. We mean the opposition expressed through the forms "I" vs. "me" (and so on), or also "who" vs. "whom", compared with those [+N, −V] heads which can project both nominative and accusative NPs depending on the syntactic function (e.g., the same noun "John" as subject or object). Simple examples of Saxon genitive phrases, with the clitic *-'s* attached to the head noun (as in "John's" or "the teacher's"), might suggest that genitive extends morphological case marking to nominal heads other than pronouns, but the idea looks inconsistent with the more complex examples we have cited.[66]

Hence a very different treatment of the genitive, to be understood as a peculiar syntactic configuration rather than a CASE feature value. As mentioned in the excerpt quoted before, Saxon genitive phrases would be headed by their clitic *-'s*, thus entailing it has the status of a word. The head account of *-'s* can be combined with the 'DP Hypothesis', so as to make this clitic the determiner head of some XP construction (14-i) embedding two Noun Phrases[67]. Alternatively, the *-'s* determiner may well head only the Saxon genitive phrase qua XP-labelled dependent of the subsequent nominal, as done by Pollard & Sag (1994: § 1.8) in their revision (14-ii) of a run-of-the-mill NP Analysis (14-iii).

(14) i. $[_{XP}$ *NP* *'<u>s</u>* NP]
ii. $[_{NP}$ $[_{XP}$ *NP* *'<u>s</u>*] <u>Nom</u>] **(N.B. heads are underlined.)**
iii. $[_{NP}$ $[_{NP}$ <u>*NP*</u> *'s*] <u>Nom</u>]

Even if the type of approach where *-'s* acts as head seems to offer a simple solution for the treatment of Saxon genitive and, in the version (14-ii), is also compatible with our previous defense of the NP Analysis in general[68], we find

[66] Cf. * *the ambassador's from Bulgaria*, * *the candidate's I talked to*.

[67] Therefore (14-i) is an instance of the original (13), § 1.3.2, where *<u>s</u>* is X (typically D) with the left-hand context filled by *NP*. Cf. Drijkoningen (1993) on what a treatment of the kind may imply for the 'theory of movement' within a Chomskyan framework.

[68] That is, (12) in § 1.3.2.

a couple of remarkable difficulties. For one thing, *-'s* is unlikely to be a head because of the distribution of the phrases it would project when they are so-called 'independent' Saxon genitives, occurring in typical NP positions like subject ("*John's* is a good car"), direct object ("I prefer *John's*") and object of a preposition ("that car of *John's*")[69]. Technically, this objection can be avoided by means of empty nominal heads; or, under the DP Hypothesis, optionality of the *-'s* head subcategorization for NP on the right; or just by 'brute force', setting the X of *-'s* to N. But no such way looks appealing to us. The second and crucial evidence against a head role for the genitive *-'s* is due to the fact that it is not added to regular plurals, because they already end in *-s*, and the apostrophe used in written form after them does not make any phonological difference. Therefore *-'s* qua hypothetical determiner should allow a 'Ø' form (subject to the relevant co-occurrence restriction on preceding NPs), i.e. a phonologically empty determiner like others that are adopted in the literature but we are unwilling to accept.

Reverting to an account of the Saxon genitive phrase as NP with a clitic *-'s* restored to the intuitive non-head function of case marker, we have to make sure it is done in a way that actually avoids both defects of the alternative type of approach. A requirement not satisfied by the analysis (14-iii) above, where *-'s* syntactically is still meant as a word, although not a head. (Let's say *-'s* would be assigned to some 'minor category', in our terminology.) That analysis preserves the NP label of a Saxon genitive phrase, but does not solve the problem of NPs already ending in *-s*, unless one postulates a 'Ø' form of the clitic.

Following Zwicky (1987), Miller (1991: § 4.2), P. Bennett (1995: § 8.4), we prefer to consider the clitic *-'s* a so-called 'phrasal affix', a.k.a. 'edge inflection'. That is, a kind of extra inflection affixed to the end of any word form occurring as the (rightmost) edge of a pertinent phrase:

> "Affixes treated in this way ... may exhibit the crucial property of *promiscuous attachment*, that is the possibility of having words of various syntactic categories as their hosts. This is due to the fact that the edges of constituents of a given category XP can often be morphemes of a variety of lexical categories. The English possessive morpheme [*-'s*], for instance, can appear on N, P and V at least... One consequence of postulating inflectional morphemes with promiscuous attachment is that all the words of all the categories to which such items may potentially attach must be inflected for them within the lexicon."
>
> Miller (1991: pp. 110, 113)

[69] Another possible function, that of predicative complement ("The best car is *John's*"), concerns a cross-categorial position compatible with NP. For the notion of *independent genitive*, we refer again to Quirk et al. (1985: § 6.29).

Given the approach to morphology that was exemplified for derivation in § 1.3.1 and equally holds for inflection as we explained (following Pollard & Sag 1987: ch. 8), there is some **lexical rule** applying to a noun, preposition or verb so as to yield the respective *-'s* inflected forms; e.g. *Bulgaria's*, *to's* (for examples like *the candidate I talked to's*) and *talking's* (for examples like *the man who is talking's*, P. Bennett 1995: p. 108). If the input form already ends in *-s*, this ending is not doubled but directly treated as edge inflection w.r.t. the output form.

On the other hand, our repertory of CASE values for English will be completed by *detgen*, abbreviated label representing **determinative genitive** as the case of NPs that are possessive determiners, whether pronominal or Saxon genitive phrases. Note the difference from a *gen* label cited before, but not adopted here: *detgen* – by definition – does not cover all instances of 'genitive case' broadly speaking, as indeed it excludes the **independent genitive** of possessive NPs with any other (= ¬ *detgen*[70]) CASE values. In particular, the non-determinative forms of possessive pronouns consist of morphologically derived 'independent counterparts' of the determinative forms (as previously discussed) and preserve the possessive semantic import that genitive case is traditionally meant to have. Yet the way in which the independent forms are genitive is morphological but not syntactic – in a functional/distributional sense – because they occur in NP positions whose appropriate CASE must be nominative (as in "*Mine* is a good car") or accusative (as in "I prefer *mine*", "this car of *mine*").

To sum up, the system of morphological case – henceforth 'm-case' for the sake of brevity – serves a twofold purpose in English and other languages. It is not sufficient to say that m-case specifies the form of pertinent pronouns so as to encode CASE qua information constraining the syntactic function and distribution of NPs. There is a second task, which is ultimately semantic rather than just syntactic, since genitive morphology – i.e. the particular instance of m-case that may be called 'm-genitive' – marks the presence of **possessive meaning**, irrespective of the syntactic functions of NPs with this meaning.[71] Determinative genitive forms of pronouns specify morphologically their CASE value *detgen* as well as possessive meaning, thus combining the syntactic and semantic tasks of m-case. Once *detgen* ensures that a determinative NP is not

[70]The operator '¬' encodes logical negation.

[71]We postpone to chapter 2 a broad characterization of possessive meaning. As regards the phenomenon of m-case expressing a semantic notion instead of a syntactic function, it is also found in so-called 'ergative languages' (like Avar, Basque, Eskimo, etc.); they mark the semantic role of **agent** for subjects of transitive verbs by means of a special case – known as *ergative* – which differs from the case assigned to the subjects of intransitive verbs, among other NPs.

unspecified for CASE, the grammar cannot wrongly interpret the same NP as somehow ambiguous between alternative options available in the CASE system (nominative/accusative).

The affixal and, more specifically, inflectional status of the 'Saxon clitic' is supported by the fact that *-s* occurs as possessive inflection of various forms stemming from the paradigm of personal pronouns. It has both determinative and independent genitive import for the masculine or neuter third-person singular forms ($his = he + s$, $its = it + s$), whereas it yields the independent genitive from all those determinative forms other than the first-person singular which do not already end in *-s*. Moreover, since head and edge words coincide in a one-word phrase, each possessive pronoun may as well be considered the edge of the minimal NP composed of the pronoun alone, hence an appropriate 'host' for **edge** inflection. That the m-genitive of pronouns need not always be expressed by the inflectional affix *-s* is a matter of morpho-phonological irregularity concerning their closed class of forms; e.g., *my* does not allow segmentation into two morphemes but will be accounted for as a 'frozen' item of the lexicon (i.e. with a primitive lexical entry), just like *I* and *me*.

Thus, what is traditionally known as 'Saxon genitive' turns out to be a generalization of the regular inflection for third-person m-genitive with ambiguously determinative or independent possessive import. As we have seen, the inflectional affix gets generalized to edges that need not be pronouns, from a categorial point of view, nor coincident with the head of the possessive phrase, from a functional point of view. To interpret a Saxon genitive phrase of more than one word, the *-'s* affix on the edge word takes scope backwards over the whole phrase (which is indeed the reason why *-'s* is called 'phrasal affix' too), but then the question of how to define the scope domain arises. We cannot always confine it to the minimal NP whose rightmost edge is *-'s* inflected, viz. *Bulgaria's* in the examples below, or else the only possible reading for (15) would be the absurd b. instead of the correct a. alternative. Yet we cannot say that the scope domain is always the maximal NP whose rightmost edge is *-'s* inflected, or else the only possible reading for (16) would be the absurd a. instead of the correct b. alternative.

(15) The ambassador from Bulgaria's message was published
  a. [THE message OF *the ambassador from Bulgaria*] was published
  b. ?? the ambassador from [THE message OF *Bulgaria*] was published

(16) The message from Bulgaria's ambassador was published
  a. ?? [THE ambassador OF *the message from Bulgaria*] was published
  b. the message from [THE ambassador OF *Bulgaria*] was published

Each of the sentences (15)-(16) gives rise to a surface syntactic scope ambiguity which they resolve in opposite ways as regards semantic (or at least pragmatic) acceptability. For treatments where the Saxon *-'s* is considered a word syntactically (although cliticized at the morpho-phonological level), the ambiguity implies corresponding alternatives w.r.t. attachment of that word. If a compatible NP Analysis applies as schematized in (14-iii) above, the a. reading reflects the attachment of *-'s* to the NP node of the largest possessive phrase that is structurally possible in the sample sentences, while the b. reading corresponds to *-'s* being attached to the NP node of the narrowest possible possessive phrase (= *Bulgaria's*).[72] But by now it should be clear that we adopted a different version of NP Analysis, roughly schematized as follows:

(17) $[_{NP} [_{NP} \ldots$ X-*'s*$]$ <u>Nom</u>$]$

where Saxon genitive inflection occurs on the lexical edge X of the possessive NP.[73] The way of representing scope must consequently change too.

It is worth emphasizing that the *-'s* inflected edge can be located at an arbitrary, potentially unbounded distance from the head of the possessive NP, depending on length and structural complexity of the phrase itself. This phenomenon is not exclusive to *-'s* inflected words, being typically found with so-called '*wh*-words':

> "The word *which* is not the head of the NP *the wording on the covers of which* ... And yet *which* is indubitably responsible for that NP's being a *wh*-phrase, and its consequent ability to appear in the position which it occupies in the example [(18)]. If, as in many analyses, we postulate a WH feature specification on this NP, then we are faced with the problem of relating it to the non-head lexical item that is, in some intuitive sense, responsible for it."
>
> Gazdar et al. (1985: p. 79)

(18) These reports, *the wording on the covers of which* the Commission has censored, are to be destroyed

There are construction-specific differences between the scope potential of *-'s* inflected items and that of *wh*-words[74]; however, the parallelism looks enough

[72] The same structures hold for the variant version (14-ii), apart from the fact that the 'root' of the possessive phrase becomes a DP node projected by *-'s*.

[73] For convenience, in this case we are assuming that the dots used by (17) may stand for possible vertical structure on top of X as much as left-hand context. That is, X-*'s* need not be an **immediate** constituent of the possessive NP including it.

[74] The latter are also allowed to take scope over a PP qua maximal *wh*-phrase, while Saxon genitive phrases must be NPs. Moreover, the pronoun *whose* is a self-contained possessive NP and, at the same time, a *wh*-determiner, which precedes the head of a *wh*-NP and need not be an edge (not even the leftmost edge) of the whole *wh*-phrase. The example "Here is the minister *in the middle of whose sermon* the dog barked" (Pollard & Sag 1994: p. 212) shows a relative clause introduced by a *wh*-PP with a non-edge *whose*.

to maintain that essentially the same kind of treatment applies in both cases (cf. P. Bennett 1995: ch. 8).

Under the system developed in modern phrase structure grammars bearing on our work, like GPSG and HPSG (v. previous section 1.1), the unbounded relation between the highest node marked by some feature $\mathcal{F}$ and the terminal node – a.k.a. 'leaf' of the tree – wherein that feature gets lexically licensed is "simply a global consequence of a linked series of local, mother-daughter feature correspondences. No 'long-distance' statement is involved at all" (Gazdar et al. 1985: p. 138). To achieve the result, there are constraints ensuring that for any specification of $\mathcal{F}$ on a node C_i (= daughter) immediately dominated by the node C_0 (= mother), $\mathcal{F}$ must be identically instantiated on C_0, unless C_i itself is the root node of the whole phrase with $\mathcal{F}$ properties. This feature-passing technique can apply so as to define a *wh*-phrase, e.g. the italicized NP at the beginning of the relative clause in (18) above. Therefore, given a Boolean-valued WH feature for simplicity's sake[75], [+WH] will be the $\mathcal{F}$ specification on C_i that must be passed up to C_0, in any such local pattern, until reaching the root of the whole *wh*-phrase.

For the treatment of Saxon genitive determination as schematized before in (17), some $\mathcal{F}$-type possessive feature to be specified on the NP root node of the phrase in determinative position is meant to record the occurrence of *-'s* inflection (or equivalent) on the rightmost edge of the same NP. To this end, one can use [+POSS] (from Gazdar et al. 1985: p. 149), so that the structural representation (17) allows a restatement through feature annotation:

(19) $[_{\text{NP}}\ \underset{[+\text{POSS}]}{NP}\ \underline{\text{Nom}}]$ (interpreted as 'THE <u>Nom</u> OF *NP*')

Now the scope ambiguity we discussed for sample sentences (15)-(16) depends on how 'high' the [+POSS] specification licensed by the lexical edge goes up their tree. That is, [+POSS] may well stop already at the 'lowest' NP node available, giving rise to the b. reading with *Bulgaria's* as the whole possessive phrase. Alternatively, [+POSS] feature-passing from daughter C_i to mother C_0 continues until another stop on the NP root node of a candidate possessive phrase becomes possible, as in the a. reading.

The proposed method implies that the lexical rule inflecting a word X for the pertinent *-'s* of morpho-phonological form must record grammatical [+POSS] information in the output lexical entry. Yet it will not directly provide X-*'s* with any possessive semantic interpretation: even if [+POSS] appears to contribute to meaning in a way comparable with that of the preposition introducing a possessive PP, one cannot simply interpret the X-*'s* item in

[75] The actual values are likely to be more complex, taking into account differences between *wh*-interrogatives and relative clauses, as proposed by Gazdar et al. (1985: p. 153) or Pollard & Sag (1994: p. 159).

the lexicon as 'OF X' (informal paraphrase). E.g., a lexical interpretation of *Bulgaria's* as 'OF *Bulgaria*' would only capture the narrowest phrasal scope of *-'s*, hence the b. reading in our examples (15) and (16). At least the a. reading of the same examples requires the interpretation of a syntactic phrase rather than a word in itself. (What's more, no possessive 'OF X' interpretation would make sense for the *-'s* inflected form of X words with category Preposition or Verb.) As a generalization, we assume that [+POSS] always contributes the intended OF-component to the interpretation of a whole possessive NP and is 'semantically potent' at its root, which in (19) gets identified by co-occurrence with a nominal heading the construction.[76]

While the OF-component (no matter how it gets expressed) seems to be common to all instances of possessive phrase interpretation, there is an extra semantic component which comes up under the determinative genitive. It is the implicit determination of definiteness for NPs with a [+POSS] *NP* as determiner, i.e. the information that THE displays in our paraphrastic schema 'THE Nom OF *NP*', informally interpreting the construction. (Such a syntax-semantics correspondence was represented in (19) and concretely exemplified through reading paraphrases in (15)-(16).) When possessive phrases are determinative in English, they act as substitute for the definite article which remains unexpressed, so that the implicit THE-component of meaning turns out to be associated with CASE value *detgen*. Indeed, the NP node that in the structural pattern (19) displays a semantically potent specification [+POSS] is constrained to share *detgen* (instead of other CASE values) with the internal lexical head N of the possessive phrase as determiner. Schematically:

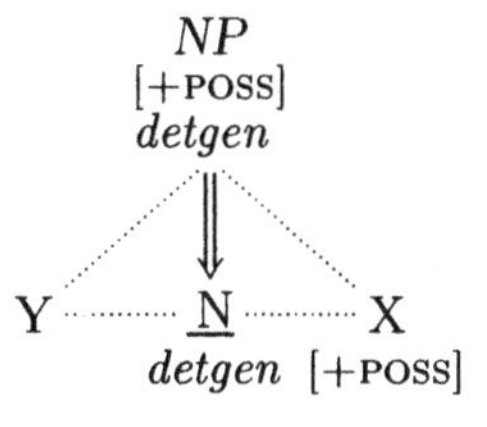

A natural extension of the same approach allows the pattern (19) to be also applied if the determinative NP is a possessive pronoun whose m-case

[76]The notion of *semantically potent* feature specification (by Gazdar et al. 1985: p. 224) concerns those syntactic features that are semantically relevant, raising the "question ... as to where in the tree such features should make their contribution to the interpretation". A construction-based statement, as done for (19), ensures the interpretation of every instance of the syntactic pattern at issue, also including 'nested' constructions where a [+POSS] *NP* works as determiner of another [+POSS] *NP* (cf. Miller 1991: p. 126). Here is a real text sample (from an airline magazine) showing the phenomenon: "Now everyone is buying an apartment in Amsterdam, rather than renting, squatting, or sleeping on *their ex-boyfriend's sister's* floor".

form encodes [CASE *detgen*]. The featurized information [+POSS] makes (19) more general than its predecessor (17) where *-'s* inflection was represented literally, insofar as now we admit alternative concrete realizations of [+POSS] on the lexical edge X at morphological level. To sum up, the [+POSS] morphosyntactic mark of semantic scope records m-genitive information originating from lexical edges with ***(i)*** a Saxon inflection *-'s* or ***(ii)*** an appropriate pronoun form.[77] Option ***(ii)***, clearly, proves relevant for pronouns with determinative genitive case, because an example like **my's* overtly shows that they reject the attachment of inflection ***(i)***. Such a behaviour follows straightforwardly if the correct form *my* is already specified as [+POSS] in its primitive lexical entry, whereas the lexical rule for Saxon *-'s* inflection changes [−POSS] entries into [+POSS] ones and therefore does not apply to *my*.

Another solution, proposed by Kathol (1999), would "assume that the possessive marker [*-'s*] attaches to NPs which must not be headed by a pronoun". At first sight, this constraint has the extra advantage of accounting for the ungrammaticality of examples with the determiner position filled by an *-'s* inflected pronoun whose input form was not possessive, as in **she's coat*, **some's concerns* and **that's consequence*[78]. But the same author acknowledges the generalization is imperfect, owing to "those pronominals that can occur with a possessive marker" (ibid.); see *someone's coat*, *everybody's concerns*, etc. In our system, lexical differences as regards the CASE of [−POSS] pronouns, which is preserved by the attachment of *-'s* inflection changing the original forms into [+POSS] ones, bring about different results of (un)grammaticality for the derived forms.[79]

Composite pronouns (in the sense we mentioned in § 1.3.1) are completely unspecified for CASE in the lexicon, so as to accept any CASE value according to their position within syntactic structure. Then, [CASE *detgen*] too would be theoretically available for the [−POSS] forms *someone*, *everybody*, etc., but the option gets discarded syntactically because they cannot occur in the [+POSS]

[77]Moreover, the generalized version of our pattern should allow a possessive NP to include a modifier – typically *own* – after the *-'s* inflected word (or equivalent). Assuming that the modifier adjoins to a recursive NP[+POSS] node, rightmost edge status nevertheless will hold for the lexical host of m-genitive inflection within the minimal possessive NP. See, for instance, $[_{NP}\,[_{NP}$ *John's/the teacher's/his*] *own*].

[78]With *some* and *that* the problem is raised by the pronominal reading, whereas the adnominal reading in our system is adjectival and consequently excluded from a construction slot reserved for (genitive) NPs.

[79]Note that the value of CASE is also what prevents the 'independent' paradigm of possessive pronouns – *mine*, *yours*, etc. – from occurring in determiner position. The *s*-affixation (or equivalent for *mine*) that these perform on corresponding [+POSS] forms of personal pronouns does not preserve the original value *detgen* and therefore cannot be equated with the Saxon *-'s* inflection attachment, which takes [−POSS] edge words of various categories as input and disregards their CASE (if any).

position where *detgen* works. On the contrary, the same position may well be filled up by the forms *someone's*, *everybody's*, etc., insofar as they combine [+POSS] with *detgen*, while the other possible CASE values are rejected by that syntactic slot. For pronouns like *she*, *some* and *that*, a negative constraint '¬ *detgen*' applies (entailed by the *nominative* of *she*, or else directly encoded in the lexical entries), thus causing the ungrammaticality of **she's*, **some's* and **that's* once these [+POSS] derivatives of the [−POSS] originals are checked as candidate determiners.

Here we will not go deeply into a further issue: how the kind of treatment we have sketched for determinative possessives (whether Saxon genitive phrases or possessive pronouns) can be extended in order to cover also 'independent', non-determinative ones and to what extent the work can be done through the [+/− POSS] feature. Few remarks suffice to show that the phenomenon to deal with is not really uniform, as observed by Miller (1991: pp. 119-120):

> "In the case of the English possessive, it is clear that from a syntactic and semantic point of view, it is necessary to distinguish between standard possessives, locative possessives, and 'double genitives'. I suggest ... that the syntactic features for these items are different."

In particular, the use of some possessive NP as object of the preposition *of* in the so-called **double genitive** construction[80], contrary to other cases of independent possessives, does not correspond to the omission of the Nominal (head) of a contextually equivalent NP with possessive determination. While *Mary's* is elliptical – meaning *Mary's book* – in examples like "This book is good, but *Mary's* was better / I prefer *Mary's*" [81], a double genitive as in "a book *of Mary's* (**book*)" bars that interpretation, i.e. nothing is omitted.

The existence of examples like "a friend *of Mary('s)*" where presence or absence of *-'s* inflection is equally possible without changing meaning confirms that *Mary's* qua object NP of the preposition means the same as non-genitive *Mary*. Possessive marking of the NP in the construction comes down to a sort of morpho-syntactic concord with the m-genitive reading of the preposition *of*. Indeed, it is this reading that expresses what was called 'OF-component'

[80]The traditional term 'double genitive' is consistent with the idea that both *of* and the (Saxon or pronominal) possessive inflection of the NP embody m-genitive case as a cross-categorial property of lexical items.

[81]Given a non-trasformational framework, where deletion operations are impossible, and the ban on empty constituents that we have adopted, an elliptical phrase must be directly generated as it surfaces, without any covert structural additions. It will be up to some semantically relevant feature(s) on the syntactic structure to indicate elliptical status and call for a context-sensitive interpretation recovering the meaning of the missing part, consistently with a general treatment to be designed for the various linguistic phenomena of ellipsis (e.g., verb gapping in coordinations).

of meaning (the only semantic aspect of English possessive relevant for double genitive) and may require 'm-genitive concord' in consequence[82]. Presumably the information on the rightmost edge of double genitives gets encoded by a feature $\mathcal{F}$ whose behaviour is related but not identical to that of [+POSS], since $\mathcal{F}$ does not carry autonomous meaning and must take scope backwards until reaching the possessive preposition. We refer the reader to Miller (1991: § 4.2) for a detailed multi-feature treatment on similar lines, plus some broader discussion of empirical data.

What was said on the notion of genitive case so far looks enough to answer the introductory purpose of the current chapter. In the end, the account we have outlined (drawing on existing technical literature) vindicates an intuition of the 'naive' approach whose alleged inadequacy seemed to motivate the alternative view of Saxon *-'s* as cliticized word. If lexical head and rightmost edge of a Saxon genitive NP coincide, in that there are no dependents after the head (or even no dependents at all, when the NP consists of a single word), a head noun actually turns out to bear genitive inflection on a par with possessive pronouns. But the revised, sophisticated version improves on the 'naive' one through formal techniques available in modern phrase structure grammars, so as to generalize *-'s* inflection for edges separated from the head noun and carry scope information up to the root of the possessive NP.

1.4 Conclusions

That our notion of 'determiners' is essentially motivated in terms of semantic function must be clear by now, but the foregoing introduction to linguistic expressions and mechanisms of determination, exemplified through English data, was focused on some morpho-syntactic aspects. We find no contradiction in this – being hardly controversial that one should systematically link the reconstruction of meaning to an adequate syntax. The problem is to agree on what 'adequate' means here. Much research on grammars specifically designed to be suitable for a logical semantic interpretation, like the framework of Montague Grammar (v. especially Montague 1973), neglects the inherent explanatory value of syntactic generalizations. It is a view reflected by Montague's (1970c) characteristic statement: "I fail to see any great interest in syntax except as a preliminary to semantics", which obviously sounds unacceptable to most linguists, especially the generative grammarians.

[82]Various factors appear to be involved: the function of the *of*-PP as complement or modifier of the noun it depends on, the semantic class of that noun (e.g., *friend* is a relational noun) and the human vs. non-human reference of the object NP.

For the study of determiner-nominal constructions, the NP Analysis that was defended in section 1.3 shows some explanatory power, concerning morpho-syntactic properties of the articles in particular, but would lose it if a single part-of-speech category Determiner were postulated so as to match exactly the determinative semantic function. This point deserves a conclusive discussion, because the over-simplified scenario of syntax-semantics correspondence is quite common in logical semanticists' work on natural language quantification and determiners. Considering how determination expressions may differ in a number of properties which matter for part-of-speech identification, as illustrated before by § 1.2.2, we see that once again a Determiner category label of the grammar has been merely stipulated, in absence of (or even contrary to) empirical evidence. Those who advocate the putative part of speech to ensure a simpler correspondence with relevant semantic aspects should be aware that they commit themselves to rejecting or downgrading important morpho-syntactic differences between types of determiners; enough differences, in fact, to justify the assignment to separate basic categories at the level of parts of speech.

Against our approach one could object that existing dissimilarities are not so crucial, coming down to idiosyncratic behaviour of individual words, without consequences for the system of classification into parts of speech. It is the line of reasoning already exemplified in § 1.3.2, with reference to the lexical subcategorization account of those distributional differences which separate the articles from determiners supplied (also) with an 'intransitive' reading, according to the DP Hypothesis. Apart from all problems that proved inherent to the Hypothesis, a solution at the subcategory level becomes much less convincing once **modification** of determiners is contemplated too. If the article can take dependents, as its alleged subcategorization for NPs would imply, we wonder why the same word disallows any dependence of optional modifiers suitable to determination [83], a restriction that was discussed at length in § 1.2.2. Such a departure from the ordinary behaviour of determiners cannot be due to the 'subcategorization frame', since this, by definition, does not predict modifiers (cf. chapter 3 below for a general presentation of the matter).

Some attempt to motivate the alleged idiosyncratic behaviour of the articles if they are assigned to a broader part of speech Determiner (or similar) could

---

[83] We mean 'genuine', empirically evident modifiers that determiners allow irrespective of the linguist's view as regards the DP vs. NP controversy and not cases of modification that merely follow from the decision of altering the assignment of head role within the phrase. E.g., appositive relative clauses (or perhaps all relative clauses, if one agrees with Kathol 1999) are NP-level modifiers under the traditional NP analysis, but a change of category from NP to DP would make them modifiers of any determiner – even an article – projecting the node they attach to.

try to exploit semantic rather than syntactic peculiarities. In § 1.3.1 we noted that modifiers are indeed sensitive to the meaning of the head constituent they modify, thus proving rejectable on semantic grounds. By the same token, a lexical item arguably incompatible with meaning requirements of all modifiers need not be syntactically 'minor', because one might propose to consider it just a semantically anomalous member of the most plausible major category. To check this proposal on the articles, their semantic import must be accurately investigated, a task the present work will carry out in due course – especially in the chapters 2-3 – without finding any independent evidence for the claim that the meaning of articles rejects all modifiers. We leave the burden of proof to those who believe the claim is correct.

Moreover, attempts at reducing the articles to anomalous members of some major, structure-projecting category appear heuristically weaker than an alternative whereby the alleged anomaly is explained away as a principled diversity from the other determiners. In the treatment we have sketched for English, adopting the category system of **Figure 1.1** and the Generalization for Major Determiners (v. § 1.2.2.2) on top of the traditional type of NP analysis which was condensed into the assumptions **A)-B)-C)** of section 1.3, a single morphosyntactic property – the *minor* category status – brings about two fundamental differences that set articles apart:

- since a minor category does not project phrase structure, no modifier or other dependent is allowed by the articles;
- only major categories undergo decomposition through [+/–N, +/–V], so that the articles are excluded from the ([+N]) determiners that have counterparts with pronominal function.

Altogether this model looks more explanatory than two heterogeneous stipulations of idiosyncratic lexical behaviour, one concerning just the articles' lack of any modifier, the other their putative subcategorization for an obligatory NP sister (given the DP Hypothesis).

Various questions remain to be answered, of course. As regards the general architecture of our category system, there is not a complete repertory of minor parts of speech, following from some principled criterion that we can borrow in a way comparable to the standard analysis for major ones. The gap should not come as a surprise, since the systematic study of any 'minor category/ies' notion was mostly neglected in the literature. A notable exception is the line of research addressed by Van Eynde in papers advocating essentially a one-to-one correspondence between major and minor categories (cf. Van Eynde 1994, 1998b, 2004). His system differs from Radford's (1997) – already reviewed in § 1.3.2 – because the counterpart that a major category is meant to have is not a category of functional heads, but one of minor words, which cannot be heads. Technically, Van Eynde assumes a sort *category* with subsorts *major* vs. *minor*[84], combining the distinction with each part of speech (from a relatively traditional repertory), so as to yield a major category and a minor category accordingly. E.g., the part of speech Preposition would allow both major and minor prepositions, hence prepositions acting as heads vs. others attached to non-prepositional projections (two options respectively called 'endocentric' and 'exocentric' by Bresnan 1982c).

Although Van Eynde's approach summarized above might be appealing in view of its formal elegance, problems of empirical application discourage us from adopting it. In our opinion, it is rather difficult to find convincing cases of minor words that can be assigned to a part of speech independently needed for major category items. Without entering into a detailed critical discussion which would go much beyond the intended scope of the present volume, few remarks on the only minor words responsible for determination – the articles – should suffice. Originally, Van Eynde (1994: § 3.1.1) treated the definite article as minor member of a part of speech Determiner (with the demonstratives as major members) and the indefinite article as minor member of a part of speech Quantifier (with other 'quantifier' words as major members). In later work by the same author, however, "the determiners ... are classified as adjectives, ... the articles as minor adjectives" (Van Eynde 1998a), whereas his most recent proposal – for Dutch, at least – is that articles can be also considered reduced forms of pronouns on morphological grounds (cf. Van Eynde 2006)[85]. We see such a categorial instability as a demonstration of the empirical difficulty that was mentioned and we are not convinced by any of the proposed classifications of articles.

The very idea of organizing the minor category range on the analogy of the major (although not necessarily in an identical way as done by Van Eynde) can actually prove misleading. In a system like ours, where the *major* part-of-speech repertory just follows from [+/–N, +/–V], the lack of those features for *minor* may well mean the sort is terminal within the hierarchy, hence a 'part of speech' in itself. The resulting system will consist of exactly five part-of-speech categories: Noun, Verb, Adjective, Preposition and Minor, the first four being predicted by *major* feature declarations, as usual, whereas the part of speech

[84]The *category* sort, which stems from Pollard & Sag (1994: p. 18), is distinguished from the *part-of-speech* sort (or equivalent), but empirically there would be no difference if Van Eynde's major/minor distinction were declared as a binary feature for *part-of-speech* and inherited by every part of speech within the hierarchy.

[85]Actually, in the last paper we could not find an explicit reference to the *major* vs. *minor* distinction within the category system, but in other recent work by the same author the phonological reduction of major pronouns is associated with morpho-syntactic minor status: "the full forms are major since they can head a branching NP whereas the reduced forms are minor since they lack this property" (Van Eynde 2004).

Minor (with its characteristic syntactic behaviour) corresponds to absence of the pertinent features. Like all parts of speech, Minor is lexically subclassified according to the different restrictions its members must obey as regards the combination with some adjacent constituent, even if this plays the head role instead of being a complement. Thus, what traditionally used to be parts of speech with a common 'minor behaviour' become instances of Minor selecting different head projections[86] – e.g., articles combine with nominals (for determination purposes), complementizers with verbal projections (at the sentence level) and coordinating conjunctions with any major category (cf. Gazdar et al. 1985: ch. 8, on coordination matters).

We shall again touch on the advisability of a single part-of-speech category Minor when the monolingual angle adopted so far will be complemented with a contrastive approach in chapter 2. More generally, the next chapter will point out data and phenomena to be considered when the notion and treatment of determination we originally exemplified for English must be adapted for other languages. On the theoretical side, a fundamental objective is meant to remain constant throughout our book: how the semantic function of determiners can be adequately modelled without postulating a corresponding morpho-syntactic category Determiner. In particular, even if Jon Barwise and Robin Cooper were mentioned in § 1.2.2.1 as a case of logical semanticists exploiting it for the sake of syntax-semantics correspondence, that category does not appear to be an essential aspect of their work on quantification:

> "we use 'determiner' to refer to a wide class of syntactic elements which also include what are sometimes called predeterminers, postdeterminers, numerals, etc. A more detailed investigation may well show that some of these finer distinctions are necessary."
>
> Barwise & Cooper (1981)

Among other things, our volume will indeed discuss how to integrate a version of Barwise and Cooper's logical semantics into a grammatically adequate account of determination, such that the "finer distinctions" in question are dealt with for various European languages.

[86]We refer forward to chapters 4-5 for a general picture of the combinatorial properties of head-selecting dependents, e.g. modifiers.

Chapter 2

Meaning and Multilingual Data

2.1 Preamble

Chapter 1 considered morpho-syntactic data from a single sample language, English, but the rest of our book and especially the present chapter will look at determination in a multilingual perspective, contrasting Germanic and Romance languages. This implies some notion of "cross-linguistic comparability" (roughly in the sense of Croft 1990: § 1.3)[1]; hence a research strategy eliciting the common intuitive content which makes it possible to identify equivalent expressions across languages, despite their differences in phonological, morphological and syntactic form. Drawing on a concept typical of **contrastive linguistics** (v. James 1980, Krzeszowski 1984, Chesterman 1991), let's say we have to outline the *tertium comparationis* relevant for any two languages to be compared here:

> "the notion of the *tertium comparationis* ... is defined in contrastive analysis as a shared common denominator in terms of which the comparison can be carried out. Without such a third term there can be no motivation for a contrastive analysis at all, for one does not set out to compare entities that have absolutely nothing in common. ... The kind of *tertium comparationis* used will depend on the nature of each analysis. Contrastive analysis in fact makes use of various types of third term, some based on formal correspondence, others on semantic equivalence".
>
> Chesterman (1991: pp. 162-163)

In our case, both methods of comparison will come into play for the contrastive analysis of multilingual determination data in section 2.3, the bulk of

[1] Croft's presentation of the subject (following work by Greenberg, Comrie, Keenan, etc.) concerns typological studies on very large collections of the world's languages, but some methodological aspects – like his emphasis on a "semantic heuristics" (ibid.) – look quite well-suited for contrastive linguistics in general.

this chapter, by using an empirical, largely pre-theoretical system of double classification that was applied to English determiners (cf. chapter 1). On the one hand, we assume six classes of alternative items ('paradigmatic kinds') mostly motivated by semantic intuition; on the other hand, we will also take into account a syntagmatic classification of the same items as 'predeterminers', 'central determiners' and 'postdeterminers', allowing a simple comparison of the surface syntactic form of languages in terms of co-occurrence and linear order. Yet the readers should not be surprised by the prevalence of semantic (and, to some extent, pragmatic) considerations in our contrastive exercise, since determiners were primarily characterized as expressions with a certain semantic function.

We can say that the main theoretical concern of this chapter is a basic dimension of the speakers' conceptual system whereby contents to be expressed and communicated are modelled across languages. In any natural language there are nominal expressions, which ultimately serve the purpose of referring to (real or imaginary, concrete or abstract) world entities, so that one equally finds a number of adnominal dependents that determine the possible typology of reference – i.e., the different 'ways of referring' – to be conventionally associated with the resulting Noun Phrases. It is indeed the class of adnominal items we have called *determiners* since the very beginning (following Quirk et al. 1985, above all); thus, differences in their determinative function/meaning, by definition, relate to referential differences at the NP level and should be accounted for accordingly. To this end, we deem it important to devote the whole section 2.2 to a preliminary methodological discussion concerning fundamental semantic notions like 'reference' and others, before engaging in the (multilingual) empirical survey planned for 2.3. The chapter's conclusions will be summarized in section 2.4.

2.2 Methodology for semantic notions

2.2.1 On denotation and reference

Following the mainstream of semantic research carried out in the 20th century by logicians and formally minded philosophers and linguists[2], we can start with a standard distinction between:

(*i*) The **meaning**, or **sense**, associated with some expression of language L by linguistic conventions of the community that knows/speaks L. It is a notion

[2]See, e.g., Chierchia (1997: pp. 23-24) for a presentation of the terminological pairs in **(*i*)-(*ii*)**. Another distinction of the kind is Rudolf Carnap's one between **intension** and **extension**, whose technical use within the semantics of Montague Grammar (v. Montague 1974, Dowty et al. 1981) will be touched on in chapter 3.

of 'meaning' strictly speaking, a.k.a. 'conventional meaning' or '(purely) linguistic meaning', which need not exhaust the global amount of information conveyed by uttering the given expression (or 'meaning' broadly speaking, cf. Chierchia 1997: § 5.0).

(ii) The **denotation**, or **reference**, which results from applying ***(i)*** to the extralinguistic world, according to the context.

To sum up, "a meaning of an expression is something that determines, for any time, place and possible situation, the denotation of the expression in that time, place and situation" (Dowty et al. 1981: p. 145). Logical semantic studies have shown how to treat denotations as extralinguistic entities defined within a world model M interpreting L, in such a way that the denotation of a given expression need not be assigned once and for all, but can vary depending on M and its 'indices' of possible state of the world and context setting (see especially Montague 1974). Without going into technical details, our discussion now is just meant to address preliminary – conceptual and methodological – issues arising from terminology.

While the terms 'meaning' and 'sense' are mostly interchangeable for our purposes[3], we intend to question the *prima facie* equivalence of 'denotation' and 'reference' in ***(ii)***. For one thing, this second terminological pair appears to reflect the existence of different approaches to a basic issue in semantics, "how language connects with the world" (cf. Dowty et al. 1981: p. 5). There is a very traditional way of understanding (20) below that takes for granted an objective correspondence relationship between linguistic expressions and extralinguistic entities:

(20) *the expression denotes the entity* **a** (*in context C*)

i.e. expressions themselves have some denotation (by virtue of their meaning as applied in a given context). An alternative line of thought – which can be typically traced back to Strawson's (1950) article "On referring", a reply to Russell's (1905) article "On denoting" – replaces (20) with (21a) and understands the latter just as an abbreviation of (21b), the more careful theoretical statement (v. Searle 1969: § 2.3).

(21) a. *the expression refers to the entity* **a** (*in context C*)

b. *the speaker refers to the entity* **a** *by uttering the expression* (*in context C*)

[3]By saying this we do not want to exclude plausible ways of drawing a conceptual distinction between the two terms. In particular, following ordinary usage, it is natural to reserve 'sense' for each of the alternative meanings (= readings) of an ambiguous linguistic expression, whereas one can also refer to the whole set of alternatives as '*the* (multiple) meaning' of the expression.

Thus, in the approach (21), it is the speaker's action that associates expressions with their referents (in accordance with linguistic meaning and the context), i.e. referring is a 'speech act'.

Given the purpose and scope of our book, we can only cursorily deal with notions of Speech Act Theory (SAT) following Austin (1962) and Searle (1969). Much SAT work concerns the 'illocutionary act' of stating, asking, ordering, promising, etc. by uttering a full sentence, but acts like referring are typically performed by means of sentence-internal expressions to make explicit which 'propositional content' is specifically stated, asked, ordered, promised, etc.[4] Propositional content is systematically related to the conventional meaning worded in a sentence and applied/disambiguated in context, so that clearly there is an overlapping of pertinent aspects of SAT and the traditional research field of (denotational) semantics. However, the precise character of such an interdisciplinary connection is not easy to define and various methodological issues arise.

At first sight, it would be tempting to deny empirical relevance to the above contrast between (20) and (21) and reduce all to a matter of philosophical views, under the assumption that the notions of 'denotation' and SAT 'reference' be at least equivalent for the assignment of extralinguistic entities. (In both cases, the same expressions would be assigned the same entities, even if these are said to be *denoted by the expressions* in one approach and *referred to by the speaker* in the other.) But the assumption is inadequate, as shown by an argument to be worked out soon. The discussion will lead us to the alternative position that Robin Cooper (1983: p. 22) summarizes as follows:

> "It is important to draw a distinction between denotation and reference. People can refer to objects in the world by using expressions of natural language. If somebody refers to John by saying *John*, they are talking about John. The denotations of natural language expressions are objects (possibly of quite an abstract nature – certain kinds of complicated [model-theoretic] functions, for example) which we assign to them in order to be able to define the truth-conditions of a sentence in terms of the denotations of its syntactic subconstituents. We will see that the denotation of an expression and the object which a person uttering that expression refers to need not be the same."

For an example of the empirical evidence that bears on the matter, consider the existence of intuitive co-reference relations between a Noun Phrase

[4]Cf. Searle (1968): "for example, the proposition that I will leave may be a common content of different utterances with different illocutionary forces, for I can threaten, warn, state, predict, or promise that I will leave. ... We need to distinguish the illocutionary act from the propositional act". In his SAT, referring is indeed treated as a type of 'propositional' speech act (see Searle 1969: §§2.1-2.4).

introduced by the indefinite article and an anaphoric (i.e. 'backward pointing') pronoun, as in the following discourse segment:

(22) Yesterday $Mary_1$ bought $a\ book_2$. Now she_1 is reading it_2.

Both the NPs with index 2 refer to the same book that Mary bought yesterday, just like the two NPs with index 1 refer to Mary. That is, besides proper names, also such indefinite NPs as *a book* in (22) are uttered by the speaker in order to introduce what Karttunen (1969) called a 'discourse referent', an entity which is thus made available for co-reference in discourse. Nevertheless, not an indefinite NP, but only a proper name – or equivalent – can be assigned the intended referent as denotation under a semantic interpretation modelled on First Order Logic (FOL):

> "a sentence like *a woman loves Bill* ... is true just in case some woman is in the set of individuals that love Bill (i.e. is a member of the denotation of the verb-phrase *loves Bill*). But how do we know which woman to choose as the denotation of *a woman*? Suppose, for example, we choose some woman who does not love Bill. Would the sentence have to be false on that understanding even if there were another woman who did love Bill? The problem is that the sentence is true just in case we can find *any* woman who is a member of the set. The sentence does not limit us to the choice of one particular woman."
>
> Robin Cooper (1983: pp. 22-23)

Interpretation issues of that sort are faced differently, depending on whether one sticks to FOL or adopts a higher-order treatment in the wake of Montague (1974) and Barwise & Cooper (1981). First-order approaches do not assign a denotation to the indefinite NP as a whole, simply because the semantic interpretation of the sentence S where the NP occurs applies to a logical (FOL) 'translation' of S that includes no interpretable expression corresponding to the whole NP. A sample NP-VP sentence like Cooper's, i.e. (23a), would result in "a formula which contains a logical connective [= conjunction] and three instances of a variable having no direct counterparts in the English sentence" (Dowty et al. 1981: p. 67); see (23b).[5]

[5] Here a semi-formal (but fully equivalent) paraphrase is provisionally resorted to instead of the FOL notation proper, so as to facilitate comparison with the ordinary English sentence. Another formal representation with the same expressive power from a logical standpoint, though exploiting a bidimensional 'box' notation, is Kamp's (1981) original version of Discourse Representation Structure (DRS). However, later versions of DRS (v. Kamp & Reyle 1993) have been enriched with logical tools that make it more powerful than FOL, in order to overcome the semantic inadequacy of any first-order treatment of natural language (a topic which we will revert to in chapter 3).

(23) a. $[_S [_{NP}$ a woman$] [_{VP}$ loves Bill$]]$
b. *for at least one* x: woman(x) *and* loves(x,Bill)

Contrary to such a lack of exact correspondence between natural language syntax and logical representation of meaning, the other line of research strives to provide every well-formed expression of English (or any other natural language) with some denotation:

> "The recursive clauses of the semantics will then specify how complex expressions receive a denotation in the model on the basis of the denotations of their component expressions."
>
> Gazdar et al. (1985: p. 7)

By doing so, the denotational reconstruction of linguistic meaning will satisfy "a principle of compositionality, attributed to Frege, which requires that the meaning of a complex expression should be a function of the meaning of its component parts" (ibid., p. 8). Compositional approaches, to be presented at length in subsequent chapters, "motivate quite complex and abstract denotations for noun phrases but we do not mean to say that these denotations are also the reference of the noun phrase" (Robin Cooper 1983: p. 22). Summing up the argument outlined so far, reference and denotation are actually not equivalent as regards the assignment of extralinguistic entities, a proof being offered by NPs that get intuitively associated with an individual referent but lack denotation, in a FOL-style account, or have a higher-order denotation [6], in a compositional account.

Further evidence in favour of the cited distinction between reference and denotation stems from the compositionality-related fact that one can devise denotations for any class of expressions, even those utterly unfit for referential use: the connectives are a typical case. Indeed, next to the meaningful, denotative expressions, logicians traditionally envisaged so-called *syncategorematic expressions* – "to which no meaning at all is ascribed in isolation, but which may combine with one or more meaningful expressions to form a meaningful expression" (Church 1951). A syncategorematic treatment can be avoided and the otherwise exceptional items recognized to be meaningful in accordance with a denotational reconstruction of meaning, if we assume they denote functions from (n-tuples of) denotations to denotations; e.g., functions from truth value pairs to truth values in the case of binary connectives between sentences, since sentences are standardly assigned a value *true* or *false* as denotation (following

[6] The entities which variables range over and predicates take as arguments are only individuals in first-order languages, yet also sets of individuals in second-order languages, sets of sets of individuals in third-order languages, and so on, according to Type Theory in the logicians' sense. (See, e.g., Dowty et al. 1981: ch. 4.)

Frege 1892). But truth functions and values obviously are not referred to in the sense intended here, inasmuch as they are not meant as referents by the speaker (at least when the relevant utterance does not include the word *truth*, or similar).

To circumscribe more precisely the reference notion, an intuitive reading of 'to refer' available in ordinary language can be elaborated on as was done by Strawson (1950; 1952: § 5.5), Alston (1964: ch. 2) and Searle (1969: § 2.3). The act of referring to some entity **a** (or a range of entities – v. our § 2.3.4.1 below) by means of an apt expression, uttered as part of a sentence S, makes it explicit that *the speaker is using* S *to say something about* **a**. What the speaker says of the referent(s) in question is the content of a 'propositional' speech act of **predication** (in Searle's 1969 terminology), a.k.a. **ascription** (a term often found in Strawson's work). Just a simple example: by uttering "Bill snores", the individual named "Bill" is referred to through the subject NP and the property of snoring is ascribed to that referent through the verbal predicate. Even if "snores", in a FOL-style model-theoretic interpretation, will be assigned the (contextually relevant) set of those who snore as its denotation, whoever utters our sample sentence is saying something about Bill, not about that set or the corresponding, defining property, which are consequently not referred to.

The same line of reasoning extends to n-ary predications, e.g. the act ascribing the binary relation of loving to the referent of "a woman" (qua lover) and the referent of "Bill" (qua beloved) in the case of (23a). But admittedly, the boundaries between referential and non-referential parts of an utterance need not always be so easy to define as in the simplest examples of the kind. In particular, one has to clarify the SAT status of syntactically predicative complements with NP category, like *a woman* in "Mary is *a woman*". Though NPs are precisely the class of expressions which the referential function (in the sense of 'function' as action potential) typically pertains to, their occurrence in predicative complement position is expected to prevent referentiality, according to Searle (ibid.), Karttunen (1969), Chesterman (1991) and others. That is, the semantic contribution of the NP in these cases would come down to a property ascribed to the subject by means of predication (i.e. the content of the ascriptive/predicative act), just like what happens with an adjectival predicative complement in such examples as "Mary is *beautiful*".

The seemingly plausible assumption of 'non-referentiality' for predicative NPs, however, has the undesirable consequence of implying that an article introducing them should differ semantically from the same word introducing referential NPs. Since the article of a non-referential NP does not have the function of determining reference, it needs some reading other than that of *determiner* in our sense. Also the related distinction between definiteness and indefiniteness is affected, insofar as its standard characterization on the basis of definite vs. indefinite reference (cf. § 2.3.1 below) becomes inapplicable at least for the corresponding article forms in predicative NPs. A reasonable alternative to all of this may well recognize that the complement NP in "Mary is *a woman*" is traditionally said to be predicative just because it occurs within the syntactic predicate (VP) of a copular clause, whose semantically predicative – i.e. ascriptive – part must be reduced to the copula alone, adopting a referential interpretation for the complement. It is essentially what logical treatments do (ever since Frege 1892) when a predicative complement NP is definite, e.g. as in "Varenne is *the horse which arrived first*", so that the sentence is meant to state the identity between referent of the subject and referent of the complement.

An approach preserving the ordinary interpretation of determiners for NPs in predicative complement position can equally apply to the indefinite cases, as suggested by Montague (1970b): "the 'is' of such formulas as 'v_0 is a horse' may be identified with the 'is' of identity, and the indefinite singular term 'a horse' treated, as usual, existentially". That is, if we add the identity predicate to our previous semi-formal notation, where *for at least one* x (or, *there is at least one* x *such that*) paraphrases a so-called 'existential quantifier', the example "Mary is a woman" will allow the FOL-style translation (24a), which is logically equivalent to (24b).

(24) a. *for at least one* x: woman(x) *and* Mary$=x$

b. woman(Mary)

Given the simplicity of (24b), it is not surprising that this was often adopted as direct logical translation of the English sentence, skipping the step (24a). But theoretically, the more elaborate analysis proves rewarding insofar as it contributes to a uniform semantic treatment of NPs and their determiners, which can be worked out in a compositional fashion (once FOL is superseded by a higher-order denotational interpretation as mentioned before) and must be linked up with an appropriate typology of reference.[7]

[7]By adopting the position that also predicative complement NPs are referential, we do not deny various peculiarities in their semantic behaviour. So, they appear to allow only a rather limited choice of the determiners available for NPs in general, as noticed by Pollard & Sag (1994: p. 360) in relation to such examples as "John is *a/the/*every/*each* Republican", "Kim, Sandy and Dana are *the/three/*few/*most/*all* Republicans". Restrictions on the reference types compatible with the syntactic function of predicative complement, then, are necessary and must also explain its lack of 'specific' reading for indefinites: e.g., "Every salesclerk was *a woman*" cannot concern a specific woman that every salesclerk was, whereas "Every salesclerk met *a woman*" can – but need not – concern a specific woman that every salesclerk met. (Chapter 3 will take into account standard logical correlations between the specific vs. non-specific reference distinction and quantifier scope.)

Thus our research will be based on the working hypothesis that all items already classified as **determiners** according to the coverage of chapter 1 have indeed the semantic function motivating that name – the function of determining the type of reference – in every NP where they occur, irrespective of the syntactic function of the NP itself, whether subject, object, (syntactically) predicative complement, etc. Different 'ways of referring' are possible for the speaker depending on which determiner is chosen, because a determiner encodes abstract reference-related information, like the constraint that the type of reference be definite. This gets substantiated in context, consistently with descriptive information also conveyed by the NP, so as to yield token reference: say, a particular individual identifiable by the audience, like the one referred to with "*the* horse which arrived first". (See Hawkins 1978, for comparable ideas about the definiteness vs. indefiniteness distinction in a speech-act theoretic perspective.)

A major question that the proposed approach must answer is how to account for the linguistic meaning of a determiner qua expression which must contribute to the referential information conveyed by the NP but normally is not referential in itself.[8] In one solution, no meaning would be assigned to the determiner in isolation, inasmuch as it is dealt with in a 'syncategorematic' way (according to the logicians' notion touched on before). The contribution of a given determinative item could be directly formulated as part of a semantic rule interpreting the construction that results from attachment of the item, but then such a treatment should stipulate as many different rules of the kind as there are determiners in the language (fragment) under consideration. The multiplication effect is only tolerable for quite a limited coverage, as in a 'first-order' logical language (formalizing an equivalent fragment of natural language), where operators of universal quantification, existential quantification and definite description – if descriptive 'individual terms' are allowed – would respectively correspond to the meaning of *every*, *a(n)/some* and *the*.[9] It becomes completely inacceptable if one aims at treating the broad repertory of determiners available in a natural language like English, in compliance with our coverage.

[8]Possessive determiners are exceptional because they have their own reference, in addition to the usual function of determining reference for the broader NP that embeds them. Their referential status is particularly evident in languages where the possessive determiners are genitive pronouns or non-pronominal NPs, as we discussed for English in chapter 1. The semantics of possessive determination will be addressed in detail by § 2.3.3.

[9]What's more, any of the two sorts of quantification can be defined by means of the other and negation, while the individual (-denoting) terms with descriptive content are made unnecessary by Russell's (1905) analysis of definite descriptions. Thus FOL languages avoid the pertinent multiplication effect if they adopt a single quantification operator, at the cost of more complex and convoluted formulae.

A linguistically adequate account is possible if determination words are acknowledged as inherently meaningful expressions, recording their semantic interpretation in the lexicon. We have mentioned that what used to be considered syncategorematic expressions can alternatively receive a denotation, although a rather abstract one. Well-established versions of the compositional semantic approach to natural language – as in Barwise & Cooper (1981) [10] – assume that a determiner denotes some function (in the mathematical sense) yielding the denotation of the resulting NP from the denotation of the nominal head the determiner combines with. The interpretation of the construction is consequently achieved through an operation of functional application which generalizes over the various determiners, without multiplying semantic rules. This is the kind of treatment that we shall present more technically starting from chapter 3.

2.2.2 The interdisciplinary scenario

All the evidence we offered in § 2.2.1 implies that **denotation** and **reference** should be seen as related but distinct subjects of inquiry, emerging at different levels of abstraction, not philosophically incompatible accounts of the same ('real world') entities. A semanticist may well apply denotational interpretation techniques without taking them for a metaphysical account of how natural language connects with the world. Cognitions, intentions and actions of the discourse participants mediate between the two sides of the language-world connection, as speech-act theorists and cognitive scientists stressed, but the direct correspondence of linguistic expressions to extralinguistic entities in logical semantic models is a methodological idealization, whereby the purely linguistic aspect of meaning, the 'conventional meaning' of sentences, can be formally computed from lexicon and syntax.

On the other hand, there are factors contributing to 'meaning in a broad sense' as the global communicative information of a discourse – speech acts, implicit meaning due to 'conversational implicatures' (Grice 1967), etc. – which are allocated to **pragmatics**, qua complementary discipline, by advocates of logical semantics like Dowty et al. (1981: p. 138), Gazdar et al. (1985: p. 7) and Chierchia (1997: p. 169). We accept this move as a legitimate instance of the standard methodology that enables some branch of science to capture an otherwise hidden regularity by abstracting away from various factors found in raw empirical data, provided one can expect the neglected aspects to be appropriately dealt with elsewhere, from a different angle. However, at least

[10]But see also some revisions that Dowty et al. (1981: ch. 7) and Gazdar et al. (1985: ch. 9), among others, have introduced in Montague's (1973) original system as regards the treatment of determiners.

in the long run, it is also common scientific practice for the complementary research programmes to strive to converge on an interdisciplinary integration of results achieved under the original division of scientific labour, so as to counterbalance their inherent limitations and allow controlled ways of relaxing their theory-internal idealization of data. The convergence in the case at issue here should lead to an integrated account of linguistic form, meaning and use, making explicit the links between pragmatics and semantics in a narrow sense, or 'denotational semantics'.

Some remarks on the terminology are in order at this point. We do not attach too much importance to the conventional labels identifying the two main "subcomponents" of "the theory of meaning", as Gazdar et al. (1985: p. 7) phrase it. By labelling *semantics* the global meaning theory, subdivided into pragmatics and denotational semantics, the attribute *denotational* (or equivalent) would be needed for the relevant subcomponent so as to make duly explicit which branch of semantics is intended. The attribute, to be sure, becomes redundant if semantics is defined *à la* Morris (1938) as the study of the relationship between the expressions and the entities they denote, pragmatics being the study of the relationship between the expressions and their users/contexts. (His picture was completed by the study of the relationship between the expressions themselves, called 'syntax' broadly speaking.)

Furthermore, it's only fair to say that divergent opinions on the appropriate usage of the label *pragmatics* too are found in linguistic sciences. Given the context-sensitivity of denotations (a fact that will be considered more carefully in chapter 5), denotational semantics calls into play 'pragmatic' aspects whose systematic logical study was started by Richard Montague and his school. He thought that "pragmatics should at least initially follow the lead of semantics, which is primarily concerned with the notion of truth (in a model, or under an interpretation), and hence concern itself also with truth – but with respect ... to a context of use" (Montague 1968). By doing so, the coverage of pragmatic research narrows down in the extreme, excluding speech acts as well as other traditional areas of the discipline; the terminological unnaturalness of this choice has been typically countered by the opposite decision of those authors who "reserve the term *pragmatics* for the study of ... problems [which] may involve quite a different methodology from that of formal semantics" (Dowty et al. 1981: p. 138). Since the latter usage "seems to be more in accord with that of linguists" (ibid.), it sounds preferable, especially when the distinction between subcomponents of the global meaning theory matters instead of their interconnections.

Interconnections between complementary disciplines, however, are precisely what one needs when dealing with such a complex, two-sided topic as reference. Pragmatic conditions on the successful performance of the acts of reference are indeed a proper subject for Speech Act Theory [11], but at the same time, the extralinguistic entities a speaker refers to must satisfy semantic conditions encoded by the conventional linguistic meaning of the referential expressions (s)he utters. In chapter 3, we will show how referents can be systematically related to the higher-order denotations that a compositional semantics of the kind we mentioned in § 2.2.1 assigns to the respective NPs. For the moment, suffice it to recognize reference as an evident instance of the partial overlap that an interdisciplinary account of meaning must establish between the fields of semantics (in the narrow, denotational sense) and pragmatics (in a broad sense, not just Montague's).

Our study of the meaning of determiners assumes the reference/denotation dualism and can accordingly be organized into two major steps. A first step is taken below in section 2.3, where the 'paradigmatic kinds' of determinative items will be characterized in terms of the type of reference they determine for their NP. We defer to other chapters the second step of our work, addressing the logical representation as well as denotational interpretation of determiners and NP structure within a formal framework. The reasons for exploiting the proposed conceptual distinction so as to proceed in a two-step fashion, instead of involving also denotational semantics from the start, are a matter of expository convenience and simplicity. If denotational interpretation is based on compositional methods (as we will eventually do to some extent), the computation of denotations for complex expressions reflects their syntactic structure, which must be adequately specified; but that would mean to anticipate formal technicalities of the grammatical system we want to carefully motivate and develop in the rest of this volume. Now we prefer to keep the exposition relatively informal or, at most, semi-formal, in order to make it more accessible to readers with different sorts of background and interests.

The contrastive analysis in section 2.3 will remain closer to a 'functional', pragmatics-oriented spirit like much literature in the field (cf. some references in section 2.1 above), but there is nonetheless a distinguishing mark that sets our approach apart. The present work is animated by the conviction that a speech-act view of reference does not prevent some formalization of its contents in accordance with the achievements of mainstream Logical Semantics, while pragmaticians and 'functionalists' have often adopted the opposite position, sticking to Strawson's (1950) slogan: "ordinary language has no exact logic".

[11] Most contributions to SAT are actually focussed on the pragmatic conditions that define illocutionary acts, neglecting any type of 'propositional act' in the sense of note 4 above; Searle (1969) is a notable exception, even if his version of reference conditions (based on Searle 1958) lays itself open to criticism (cf. Kripke 1972). Another problem with classical SAT is the lack of formality, yet see Vanderveken (1990; 1991) and Ginzburg & Sag (2001) for recent trends towards formalization.

In particular, Chesterman (1981: pp. 188-189) – within the framework of a contrastive analysis of determiners – claims that "reference is not a clear-cut concept" but "a slippery term", whereby "the cut-off point between the two poles, ... 'referential' and 'non-referential', would be difficult to place with any precision".

Chesterman is specifically concerned with the study of the ways in which the concept of definiteness is realized by means of articles in English, as opposed to Finnish, a language without articles, but his approach entails broader considerations (ibid.):

> "The paradigm case of reference is definite concrete singular count ..., for it is here that the original deictic sense of the word – 'pointing' – is at its clearest. Hence the traditional focus on singular definite descriptions, and also on proper names. However, when we move into indefinites, ... mass and plural nouns, the term 'reference' is less clear. ... If definite singular reference is the prototypical case, then 'referentiality' seems to diffuse outwards from this core along not one but several parameters."

That is, some reference types look more 'prototypical' than others [12], raising a question of **vagueness** that we would like to settle at the methodological level before relying on such concepts for our survey of determination.

Let us adopt a distinction between two main aspects of conceptual vagueness, following Alston (1964: ch. 6). On the one hand, a given concept P can be vague for reasons of degree, insofar as its criterion of application depends on some dimension of continuous variation [13] – a so called 'continuum' – where no precise border is established between what is P and what is not P. We shall touch on an instance of this kind of vagueness in § 2.3.4.1, when discussing a quantitative degree item like *many*: if the underlying dimension of variation concerns the context-dependent standard that a set must exceed for its members to be many, the lack of any precise border within the continuum at issue is shown by the existence of marginal (utterly non-prototypical) cases where

[12] On this sense of 'prototypical' or, roughly, 'stereotypical', see Marconi's (1997) discussion of how "a prototype [*à la* Rosch (1973)] became something like the psychologist's stereotype, whereas stereotypes [*à la* Putnam (1975)] were the philosopher's prototypes, and frames [*à la* Minsky (1975)] were the computer scientist's way of representing either" (p. 26). But what matters here is simply the fact that *reference* does not look so different from more mundane concepts, which have traditionally undergone that sort of analyses: "some items (the 'good examples') were more easily identified as falling under a concept than others (the 'poor examples'). Thus ... the mental representation of the concept *bird* is 'closer' to a robin than to an ostrich. A robin was perceived as a more 'birdish' bird than an ostrich or ... closer to the *prototype* of a bird" (Marconi 1997: p. 23).

[13] Infinitesimal values, however, need not be involved, because a certain dimension of variation may well be perceived as continuous (for the purpose of ordinary language concepts) even if it is not mathematically/physically continuous strictly speaking.

one cannot say whether the quantitative condition is satisfied or not. On the other hand, consider some concept P whose criterion of application combines the conditions P_1, P_2, ... P_n, in such a way that ***i)*** the prototypical case of P is defined as their overall conjunction, but ***ii)*** there are also instances of the same concept P that satisfy only partial combinations of those conditions (e.g., cases in which P_1 is satisfied while P_2 is not); vagueness arises insofar as ***iii)*** some of the possible partial combinations show indeterminacy as to whether they provide instances of P or not. It is essentially this combinatory kind of vagueness that seems to affect the *reference* concept (under conditions like *definite*, *singular*, *count*, etc.) according to Chesterman's excerpt quoted above.

Throughout our work, we assume a vagueness-free account of natural language semantics, making appeal to a methodologically legitimate abstraction that is expected to be counterbalanced somehow by complementary studies [14]. Especially the vagueness of degree looks relatively easy to accommodate in a semantically interpreted grammatical system with some 'open parameters', corresponding in each case to a dimension of variation whose values depend on extralinguistic factors outside the system itself. To be sure, the issues raised by the concept of *reference* are more complex, because of its twofold status as meaning of the corresponding word(s) in the given object-language(s) and theoretical construct defined at the metalanguage level, yet the only aspect concerning us here is the latter. What we need is not a piece of lexicographic knowledge about the noun "reference", the verb "to refer", etc. (or equivalent translations in other languages), preserving their vague usage in common parlance, but a reasonably precise theory of the relevant phenomenon/behaviour that has come to be known as **reference** in the philosophical and linguistic tradition.

To stipulate a technical sense of some existing word, overcoming the semantic vagueness that the ordinary meaning shows, is standard practice when the word is adopted as theoretical term in a scientific discipline. By the same token, one can counter Chesterman's (or other authors') objections to the intuitive vagueness of the reference notion through a theory of reference where the vagueness disappears. Some proposals have simply chosen to confine the theoretical concept to the above case ***i)***. This, i.e. the prototypical core of the intuitive concept, essentially comes down to definite reference to single individuals, yet the problem is that such a restrictive stipulation makes it difficult

[14] A future integration of interdisciplinary results, which remains highly speculative at present, could exploit empirical/experimental studies in lexical vagueness stemming from psycholinguistics (Rosch 1973) and sociolinguistics (Labov 1973); on the formal side, tools like Zadeh's (1965) 'fuzzy sets' (v. also Zimmerman 1985), or a 'three-valued' logical semantics applied to vagueness by Kamp (1975).

or impossible for the theory to capture important generalizations, like those concerning co-reference (as briefly presented in the previous § 2.2.1 and also § 2.3.1.1 below). Our position resembles all approaches to reference that relax some condition or other among the prototypical ones [15], but the general point of the current section is methodological: instead of isolating ***i)***, the core, to the exclusion of everything else, we allow our theoretical concept to cover less typical cases as well, i.e. ***ii)*** in terms of our foregoing discussion, provided the theory solves related problems of indeterminacy in the sense of ***iii)***.

As a result of the proposed methodology, the theoretical *reference* concept can show reasonably clear-cut boundaries while keeping an internally 'graded' structure with prototypical core. The vagueness of boundaries – or any other form of *continuum* – and that pattern of internal organization are logically independent properties, even though they happen to be frequently associated in words/readings of ordinary language. Drawing on a distinction which was put forward in dialectology and sociolinguistics, especially by Stehl (1988), we could say our view of reference implies some notion of *gradatum*, i.e. variation with discrete gradations and borders, as opposed to *continuum*; cf. Labov's (1973) rich typology of 'categorization borders' too. Terminology aside, it is possible to recognize something similar in taxonomies of natural sciences: e.g., most mammals have also such other typical properties as being viviparous and placental, but monotremes (like the platypus) lack both, laying eggs instead, and for this and further reasons (beaked mouth, etc.) they look akin to birds to some degree, without losing the mammals' distinguishing feature of breast-feeding their young.[16]

An exhaustive study of the internal structure of the 'graded' reference concept assumed here goes well beyond the scope of our volume, so that we will keep the present work within limits that should not be mistaken for intended theoretical restrictions. As mentioned by Chesterman (1991) in the excerpt we cited before, there are several parameters of variation w.r.t. reference: one reflects the interpretation of *singular* vs. *plural* plus *count* vs. *mass* distinctions. Corresponding types of entities undergoing reference are obviously taken into account in our analysis, but this 'ontological' parameter will not be explored in all respects. We shall basically confine our research to countable – singular or plural – referents, building on a classical domain of individuals, while un-

[15] Though a review of the literature on such a broad subject would take us too far afield, we wish to recall at least the discourse referents introduced by indefinites according to the approaches by Karttunen (1969), Kamp (1981) and Heim (1982).

[16] Example inspired by an e-mail message that Carl Pollard sent to the HPSG List (1 May 2001). Eco (1997: § 4.5) reports the 'case history' of the platypus as regards its originally controversial classification in zoology, with some interesting epistemological and semiotic implications.

countable, 'mass'-type entities (or any other possible referents with puzzling ontological status) will be mostly neglected apart from few observations to be made in § 2.3.1.2. After all, focus of our research is not reference as such, but its linguistic determination by some adnominal dependents, i.e. *determiners* in the terminology we adopted generalizing over a wide variety of relevant kinds of items[17]. Resulting differences in the referential function of NPs will be introduced on the basis of empirical data by section 2.3 and briefly summarized at the end by section 2.4.

2.3 Insights from a contrastive analysis

Although the theoretical kernel of the approach to be followed here is expected to have more general value, in the concrete our contrastive analysis deals with data from Germanic or Romance. Six languages will be considered in particular, including English again, but also – in alphabetic order – Danish, French, German, Italian and Spanish. Their coverage equally comprises the six kinds of determiners envisaged by chapter 1: articles, demonstratives, possessives, quantitatives, cardinals and ordinals; thus, each of the following subsections 2.3.1-2.3.6 will be reserved for one of these ('paradigmatic') kinds. Since an important goal of the multilingual survey that we have planned is to get some semantic substance out of our contrastive exercise, the discussion of data in every subsection will be introduced by a presentation of selected theoretical matters, characterizing the type of determinative meaning and function for the corresponding kind of expressions.

To keep the survey within realistic limits of space and time, it seems enough for us to exemplify and discuss substantial evidence from the various languages without providing any exhaustive inventory of the respective determination systems – especially as regards morphological paradigms and phonological details. By default, the determiners of richly inflected languages will be just mentioned through their standard 'citation forms' (e.g., masculine singular)

[17]Interestingly, one can partly relate our approach to that of Zelinsky-Wibbelt (1988), despite her terminological choice of distinguishing 'determiners' in a narrow sense from so-called 'quantifiers': "We ... describe determiners and quantifiers by one integral system ... for the following reason: although both determiners and quantifiers have characteristic functions, they have others in common, so that a borderline is very difficult to draw. Moreover, this is not necessary, as it is more natural and possible in a differentiation that yields more than two types to have a spectrum of types with determiners constituting one pole and quantifiers the other pole of the spectrum, and other types which resemble the one or the other more or less in between". In the present work, the 'spectrum of types' she is concerned with turns out to be the internally graded structure of the *determiners* concept which we extend to cover all of her 'integral system', ranging between two 'poles' to be identified with the paradigmatic kinds of *articles* and *quantitatives* (in our terminology).

unless other forms prove more interesting for our exemplification. The morpho-syntactic status of determiners (adapting to languages other than English the category system we proposed in chapter 1) and their interactions with various aspects of NP structure (also involving 'agreement' facts) are only cursorily touched on for the moment, but more will be said in the rest of the volume. Now some classification in terms of 'predeterminers', 'central determiners' and 'postdeterminers' can normally suffice for an informal analysis.

2.3.1 Articles

2.3.1.1 Definite vs. indefinite

Whereas the terminology used for the other kinds of determiners sounds vaguely inspired by their semantic function, *article* is the traditional morpho-syntactic label of a 'minor' part of speech (cf. chapter 1 above). This and equivalent labels in different languages (like *artículo* in Spanish, *Artikel* in German, etc.) derive from the Latin *articulus* – literally, 'small joint' – and ultimately from the Greek *arthron*, whose part-of-speech sense was introduced by the ancient grammarians to cover inflected words of closed classes (see Robins 1967: ch. 2). However, one can hardly deny that articles too have some typical semantic function, which Quirk et al. (1985: p. 255), among others, summarize by saying that "the articles ... solely contribute definite or indefinite status to the nouns they determine". The point deserves some discussion.

To start with, one could question the adequacy of a two-value opposition at the semantic level and observe that the articles can express a third value, **generic**, neutralizing the distinction between definite and indefinite. At first sight, the idea is supported by such sentences as "*The lion* is a ferocious beast" and "*A lion* is a ferocious beast", which look equivalent under the generic interpretation, concerning the whole class of possible lions without contextual restrictions. A more careful investigation, though, shows definite and indefinite article are not interchangeable with respect to different sorts of predicates implying or allowing a generic interpretation, e.g. 'kind predicates' like *extinct* in (25a), 'collective predicates' like *gather* in (26a) and even 'dynamic predicates' like *reach* in (27a). See Gerstner-Link & Krifka (1993) for these – and other – data, which are not specific to English, being preserved by translation into different languages, e.g. Italian as shown by the corresponding b. sentences.

(25) a. $\left\{ \begin{array}{c} \textit{The} \\ \neq \textit{A} \end{array} \right\}$ *lion* is extinct

b. $\left\{ \begin{array}{c} \textit{Il} \\ \neq \textit{Un} \end{array} \right\}$ *leone* è estinto

(26) a. $\left\{ \begin{array}{l} \textit{The} \\ \neq \textit{An} \end{array} \right\}$ *antelope* gathers near waterholes

b. $\left\{ \begin{array}{l} \textit{La} \\ \neq \textit{Una} \end{array} \right\}$ *antilope* si raduna vicino agli stagni

(27) a. $\left\{ \begin{array}{l} \textit{The} \\ \neq \textit{A} \end{array} \right\}$ *rat* reached Australia in 1770

b. $\left\{ \begin{array}{l} \textit{Il} \\ \neq \textit{Un} \end{array} \right\}$ *ratto* ha raggiunto l'Australia nel 1770

We have used '≠' to indicate that the acceptable interpretation of the sample sentences with indefinite article is different from the generic interpretation of the respective sentences with definite article. In (27), of course, one may well interpret *A rat* non-generically, as referring to an individual rat, and all our indefinite NPs allow the interpretation called 'taxonomic' by Gerstner-Link and Krifka, which can be made explicit by adding an expression like *kind of*: "*An antelope* (i.e. *a kind of antelope*) gathers near waterholes, the Impala". Taxonomic NPs do express some sort of genericity, but this concerns just a subclass (even though a contextually unrestricted, taxonomically motivated one) and not the whole class in question, so that the resulting sentences are not equivalent to the generic sentences with definite article.

A plausible conclusion emerging from our discussion is the lack of motivation for a three-way semantic system where genericity would be on a par with definiteness and indefiniteness and distinct from both. Following Gerstner-Link & Krifka (1993), we assume that genericity is actually an heterogeneous notion, "a kind of family resemblance at best", which "has to be dissociated into two separate concepts, namely D[efinite]-genericity ... and I[ndefinite]-genericity" (ibid.), with quite a few differences. Since the opposition between definite and indefinite holds for generic interpretations too and gets neutralized in a limited range of contexts, it is the essential aspect we want to focus on now, starting from the standard case of contextually restricted, non-generic interpretations. Our aim is to briefly sketch the referential conditions of (in)definiteness in a rather informal fashion, while remaining provisionally agnostic as regards their 'level of semantic abstraction' and thus the extent to which they affect truth conditions, over and above pragmatic considerations. We postpone to next chapters the clarification of this vexed issue, a more formal presentation of related logical matters, as well as further remarks taking into account also generic interpretations.

First and foremost, definite reference is typical of **proper names**, which are interpreted by conventionally associating them with individual entities. A certain person, pet, town, firm, etc. can be referred to through the associated name, in contexts where that individual is relevant while no namesake is.

Generalizing, the definiteness of a given NP is a constraint of 'existence and uniqueness': it implies that one and only one referent, existing in an adequately restricted context[18], satisfies some requirement appropriate for the NP's own referential interpretation, like being named *John* when the NP is "John". For a so-called 'definite description' – NP in the singular introduced by the **definite article** – the referent is meant to be the contextually unique individual that satisfies the property expressed by the NP itself as descriptive condition. E.g., "*the* book that Mary bought" describes an x with the property of being a book that Mary bought, just like "*a* book that Mary bought", but, by definiteness, the former NP requires that one and only one such x exists in the context.

Indeed a corresponding NP with **indefinite article** replacing the definite article conveys a weaker type of reference, indefinite existential reference, which does not enforce the uniqueness constraint. So, a context C is appropriate for uttering the sentence "*a book that Mary bought* is on the table", say, even if the description that the subject NP offers is satisfied in C by more than one possible referent x (inasmuch as several books that Mary bought exist in C); the sentence is true when at least one such x has the predicated property of being on the table. Since the status of indefiniteness tends to vary according to what is meant by 'reference' theory-internally, another possible way of seeing these facts would confine the 'reference' notion to definiteness and deny that indefiniteness be referential at all. But ever since § 2.2.1, we have made clear that the view adopted here is supported by the discourse phenomenon whereby an indefinite NP turns out to have the same intended referent as an anaphoric definite NP. The latter can be a pronoun (v. our previous example (22)), or a definite description as in:

(28) Yesterday Mary bought *a book*. Now *the book* is on the table

Both italicized NPs refer to a specific book that Mary bought yesterday, but in the first sentence the object in question is referred to for the first time, as just one of the existing books, whereas in the second sentence the same referent is taken for granted and presented as the only book relevant to the context (restrictions) resulting from the utterance of the previous sentence.

The basic values and constraints of the (in)definiteness meaning system – which in § 2.3.1.2 will be extended to plural and non-count NPs – are very

[18]This results from previous discourse (if any), pertinent bits of world knowledge, and the situation of utterance (speaker, hearer, etc.). Of course, due to contexts of fiction, belief, etc., the 'existence in context' need not be existence in the real world and one can technically relativize it to a 'possible world' (among other so-called *contextual coordinates* in the sense of Lewis 1970; v. also Dowty et al. 1981: pp. 136-137). For various versions of the existence and uniqueness conditions of definiteness, cf. Russell (1905), Strawson (1950), Searle (1969), Sharvy (1980), Barwise & Cooper (1981), Barwise & Perry (1983), Robin Cooper (1991), as well as the detailed discussion to be provided in our chapter 3.

general, presumably universal, but languages differ in the ways the system can manifest itself by morpho-syntactic means. For one thing, the article is not an indispensable component of natural language grammars, inasmuch as many of the world's languages lack it altogether, nor does it always make a separate word, as often the element with article function comes down to an affix/clitic, bound up with the noun or some other lexical 'host' at the morphological level. Statistically, we are told by typological studies, "about a quarter of the world's languages have article words and about another quarter or perhaps a little less have bound articles" (Plank & Moravcsik 1996).

Those linguists who see articles as atypical members of a 'part of speech' independently motivated for *major* words like adjectives or pronouns (an idea we criticized in chapter 1) could claim their approach "provides a better understanding of why there are languages without articles, such as Latin and most of the Slavonic languages. What these languages lack is not an entire syntactic category, but just a reduced counterpart for ... demonstrative and/or quantifying determiners" of the same languages, Van Eynde (2006) says. However, the non-universality of articles may well be viewed as confirming the solution suggested at the end of our previous chapter: articles, together with all other items that have the distinctive distributional property of being syntactically 'minor', belong to a single part-of-speech category Minor. Then a language without articles does not lack "an entire syntactic category", insofar as there are words – complementizers, coordinating conjunctions – instantiating Minor in that language. By the same token, "also languages ... in which coordinate constructions appear without overt conjunction morphemes like English *and*" (Gazdar et al. 1985: p. 179) can turn out to preserve the Minor category for other reasons, whereas no assignment of coordinating conjunctions to any of the four categories containing *major* items (N, V, A or P) looks plausible.

A caveat should be useful here. The notion of *parts of speech* in traditional grammar was a mix of syntactic, morphological and even semantic criteria, due to their convergence in 'prototypical' cases of category assignment. But the problem is that criteria for defining grammatical concepts may diverge in a number of 'peripheral' – yet not negligible – cases, just like what happens with other concepts organized in terms of **prototypes**. Thus, the linguists' opinions may also diverge, depending on the kind of criteria to be considered theoretically crucial for categorization in order to avoid the trivial conclusion that the concepts are just too vague (see § 2.2.2 above for a related discussion). Leaving semantic criteria aside as marginal for grammatical categories, the question is whether a classification into parts of speech must be ultimately based on morphological properties of inflection and derivation or syntactic properties concerning distributional behaviour. It is the latter position that we intend to adopt consistently, since the classification itself aims at being a basis for syntactic projections of phrase structure, though morphology confirms distributional evidence in particular cases but not in others[19].

As regards our determination coverage, in all the six languages concerned there are article words expressing the (in)definiteness system with equivalent syntactic distribution, despite considerable language-specific differences at the morphological level. It's indeed a distribution severely restricted by the *minor* property, which prevents occurrence in any syntactic position where a phrasal constituent is required. (Like the Noun Phrase, whose position can be filled by pronouns but not articles, even if, in some cases, the two kinds of items are morpho-phonologically related up to homonymy, for historical reasons.) Other positional restrictions arise from the article's function as a determiner: being a central determiner, in multiple determination it follows predeterminers and precedes postdeterminers; moreover, it does not co-occur with other central determiners depending on (projections of) the same head noun, because the determiners belonging to this positional class are mutually exclusive with each other. Such constraints, which were mentioned for English in chapter 1, are not just monolingual, but also apply to the rest of the languages we cover.

The point is confirmed by the Danish article system, notwithstanding its peculiarity. In Danish, postpositive forms of the definite article occur bound up with the head noun – e.g., see (29b) below – but just when there is no preceding central determiner, postdeterminer or qualifying adjective. The typical prenominal position of central determiners, which is the only possible for the indefinite article use as in (29a), is required for alternative forms of the definite article, used when other adnominal expressions interpose before the noun as in (29c).

(29) a. *et* (store) hus, *en* (svag) mand
'a (big) house', 'a (weak) man'

b. hus*et*, mand*en*, dreng*ene*
'house+the', 'man+the', 'boys+the'

c. *det* **store** hus, *den* **tredje** mand, *de* **mange** drenge
'the big house', 'the third man', 'the many boys'

Being in mutual exclusion with all the central determiners of Danish (such as demonstratives, possessives, etc., besides the prenominal articles), the postpositive article too can be considered a central determiner. In fact its central determiner status is compatible with previous occurrence of a predeterminer, e.g. as shown by "**alle** dreng*ene*" ('all boys+the' = all the boys).

[19] As a striking example, the inflectional variation of personal pronouns makes them morphologically very different from uninflected proper nouns, but the two classes of words have the same syntactic distribution and therefore belong to the same part of speech ('Noun').

The grammatical status of the postpositive article in Danish is not obvious. It looks as if *definiteness* were "expressed inflectionally" on the nouns – yet "this is sometimes seen as an example of cliticization rather than inflection" (P. Bennett 1993). We need not settle the issue here, also considering that the difference may become rather fuzzy in the light of lexicalist approaches to Romance pronoun cliticization (v. Miller & Sag 1995, Monachesi 1996; 1998, and Abeillé et al. 1998), which treat the clitic itself as an additional affix of its host, not as a morpho-syntactically separate word. Likewise, by applying the affixation technique we have presented in chapter 1, a **lexical rule** could be stated for Danish in the format $\mathcal{L} \longmapsto \mathcal{L}'$, taking the lexical entry of an article-less noun form as input $\mathcal{L}$ and yielding the respective output entry $\mathcal{L}'$ inclusive of affixed article. The study of cliticization in the world's languages, however, has pointed out the existence of various kinds of clitics with partly different properties (cf. Miller 1991: § 4.1, for a review of literature), so that a more careful analysis of the Danish phenomenon might support an alternative treatment.

A straightforward way of accounting for our previous conclusion that the postpositive article forms have the **central determiner** status of any article word is possible, if those forms are cliticized at the morpho-phonological level while preserving morpho-syntactic properties of words. That is, all articles of Danish are *minor* words syntactically attached to the NP node and mutually exclusive with each other (and central determiners in general); but morpho-phonologically 'free', non-clitic articles appear before the nominal head they combine with, as usual, whereas postpositive ones are 'bound' with the head qua lexical host. The fact that simultaneously the same constituent has to be lexical host of cliticization and the Nominal combining with the article under the NP node (v. our NP analysis in chapter 1) explains why the Nominal must consist of the head noun alone. Since items with predeterminer distribution can precede the co-occurring article irrespective of its position w.r.t. the head, they are the only prenominal dependents whose attachment is allowed in the construction via a recursive NP node (according to a treatment that chapters 4-5 will also motivate for other languages of our coverage). Schematically:

(30) $[_{\text{NP}}$ **alle** $[_{\text{NP}}\,[_{\text{Nom}}$ drenge $]$+*ne* $]\,]$

The analysis that we have cursorily sketched requires formal development in terms of an adequate syntax-morphology (plus phonology) interface, while weighing the pros and cons of alternative treatments of cliticization for various languages[20], but all of this is not work we can carry out in the present book.

[20]A lexical rule of affixation, licensing a feature of 'definiteness concord', could be the best solution for the postpositive form of Swedish, which co-occurs with the prenominal definite article in case of some interposing expression X; hence the pattern 'Art_{DEF} X N+$\mathit{affix}_{\text{DEF}}$'.

Suffice it to notice that in the set of languages we consider, only the Danish postpositive article is preceded by the head noun, but there are cases of articles undergoing a comparable process of fusion with a preceding preposition. See, e.g., *à* + *le* → *au* ('to the') in French, *su* + *il* → *sul* ('on the') in Italian, *de* + *el* → *del* ('of the') in Spanish. The result is a so-called 'contracted preposition', normally preserving syntactic and semantic properties of both components. An interesting semantic phenomenon discussed by Bosch & Geurts (1990) is due to the optionality of the same process in German: "For some prepositions and articles (in fact whenever phonology permits), German offers the choice between cliticizing the article to the preposition or not... Semantically, ... contraction of a preposition and an article is possible if a role is at issue, but not if specific reference is involved". In the example (31), which means that Helma took her poodle *to the* vet, the expression *zu dem* (as opposed to the contracted form *zum*) "would only be used if an anaphoric reference to a particular vet was intended" (ibid.).

(31) Helma brachte ihren Pudel $\left\{ \begin{array}{c} \textit{zum} \\ \textit{zu dem} \end{array} \right\}$ Tierarzt

2.3.1.2 Plural, uncountables, partitive article

While articles are available in any language we cover, the problem is that their distribution proves partly language-specific, because a given NP with article in one language may well translate (as) an articleless NP of another language. The contrastive part of the following discussion will focus on mismatches of that kind systematically arising from NPs headed by a plural count noun or a non-count noun.

As a first approximation, just like the singular number of count nominals is used for reference to individuals (whether one individual or more, as in cases of indefinite singular reference where various possible referents are available in the same context), the plural is used for reference to sets of individuals.[21] What matters now is that plural reference too can be definite or indefinite, applying criteria essentially equivalent to those of singular reference, but shifted from the level of individuals to the higher level of sets. Thus, a plural NP introduced by the definite article refers to the set whose members are all and only the contextually existent individuals that satisfy the descriptive conditions expressed by the NP – like being books that Mary bought, in the case of *the books that Mary bought*. This 'maximal' set of individuals with the desired

[21] This, in the wake of M. Bennett (1974), Hoeksema (1983) and others, seems the most straightforward approach, although alternatives have also been proposed. We shall have more to say on the issue in chapters 3-4, within a broader discussion of plurality and how it interacts with quantification.

properties is contextually unique by definition, accounting for the uniqueness requirement of definiteness. As usual, indefiniteness drops the requirement, so that also non-maximal sets of the relevant kind are allowed as possible referents in the plural. It is precisely the morpho-syntactic way of indicating plural indefiniteness that turns out to be a systematic source of cross-linguistic mismatches.

Among our sample languages, Spanish alone is actually provided with a plural form of the indefinite article, derived from the singular one by adding plural inflection: cf. "*un* hombre" (= a man) and "*unos* hombres" (= some men). In French, the so-called **partitive article** (whose forms result from a peculiar morphological process to be presented soon) is the marker of indefiniteness with a plural or non-count noun, so as to fill corresponding gaps in the distribution of the indefinite article proper. Hence the difference from a language like English, which in the same contexts allows Ø-determination, yielding a 'bare nominal' NP, or alternatively translates the French partitive article as the quantitative determiner *some* (v. also § 2.3.4 below). Compare the following sentences:

(32) a. J'ai vu $\left\{\begin{array}{c} \textit{des} \\ *\emptyset \end{array}\right\}$ hérons sur la rive

b. I've seen $\left\{\begin{array}{c} \textit{some} \\ \emptyset \end{array}\right\}$ herons on the shore

(33) a. Je voudrais $\left\{\begin{array}{c} \textit{du} \\ *\emptyset \end{array}\right\}$ thé

b. I would like $\left\{\begin{array}{c} \textit{some} \\ \emptyset \end{array}\right\}$ tea

As the examples (32)-(33) show, there is a parallelism between plural and non-count nominals with respect to the pertinent determination strategies in the two languages (and other languages behaving alike). This is not surprising, insofar as one can argue for some parallelism at the semantic/referential level as well.

Although the meaning of uncountables is quite a hard issue, treated in many different ways in the literature[22], a common pre-theoretical intuition would at least suggest that non-count reference has to do with some 'mass' or psychologically 'mass-like' aggregate, which is not (presented as) a single individual or a countable set of individuals, but can be divided into arbitrary portions with the same mass properties as the undivided whole. For instance, by dividing a (not too small) mass of water one gets smaller masses of water,

[22] See a broad review of proposals in Pelletier & Schubert (1989).

and the process can be iterated – down to the smallest particles of water [23]. Here we see an obvious difference from the reference to a single individual: if a certain car is referred to and we split the referent, we don't get smaller cars but a number of heterogeneous pieces (engine, wheels, seats, etc). On the contrary, a plural referent seems to share some division properties of masses: if a set of cars is referred to and we divide it into subsets, each of these parts is again a set of cars, like the undivided whole, and the process can be iterated – down to the minimal subsets, with just one car each. By the same token, the (non-) maximal set notion we applied to (in)definite plural reference lends itself to be adapted to the mass case, so that definiteness and indefiniteness respectively indicate reference to the maximal amount of a mass and to possibly smaller portions of that stuff, under usual contextual restrictions.

Concerning the morpho-syntactic manifestation of semantic values, one has to consider that the 'semantic number' offered as a three-way distinction between singular count reference, non-count reference and plural reference is expressed through the singular vs. plural dichotomy of morphological number available in all languages we deal with. As a rule, plural morphology is reserved for plural reference, so that both singular count reference and mass, non-count reference pertain to singular qua 'unmarked' value of morphological number (cf. Croft 1990: pp. 64-94, for criteria of 'markedness' in linguistic typologies). Plurality and uncountability, therefore, are differently expressed at least by morphological number, whereas their semantic similarity motivates the same determination strategies for expressing indefiniteness as previously mentioned: ***i)*** 'Ø-determination' – unless language-specific constraints rule it out, as in the examples (32a) and (33a) above – or ***ii)*** a suitable central determiner distinct from the indefinite singular article proper.

The **partitive article**, which instantiates ***ii)*** in French, combines/merges the preposition form *de* (typical of partitive constructions) with some form of the definite article, as regards morpho-phonological processes, but distri-

[23]Modern physical science would identify them with the molecules, which are not mass-like (in the intended sense) since they break down into hydrogen and oxygen atoms, not further water particles. The semantic relevance of such physical notions is questionable, though, also considering that the ordinary meaning of a word like "water" is much older than modern science. On the other hand, the idea of an intuitive lower bound for mass concepts actually stems from common human experience, inasmuch as the process of dividing masses without scientific tools cannot continue for ever but must stop at some point, when the particles one gets are too small to handle; these are the smallest water particles, as far as the ordinary, pre-scientific concept of water is concerned. Furthermore, Pelletier & Schubert (1989) notice that the 'minimal portions' of various non-count, mass-like concepts like *forniture* are actually macroscopic objects: think of single pieces of forniture such as a table, a chair, etc. It should be clear that uncountability does not merely reflect some physical property of entities, but is first and foremost a matter of how they are conceptualized by the speakers (cf. Zelinsky-Wibbelt 1988).

butionally, functionally and semantically results in a central determiner like the other articles.[24] This must be distinguished from the homonym Preposition + Article (with or without contraction in the sense already made clear by § 2.3.1.1); thus *de l'/la*, *des* and *du* are accordingly ambiguous out of context. An interesting issue, known to traditional grammarians under the heading 'cacophony rule', is raised by the cases in which some NP introduced by the partitive article should occur as object of the preposition *de*: the concatenation turns out to be impossible, therefore French too in that syntactic context appears to make use of Ø-determination to indicate indefiniteness. Cf. below the examples with mandatory omission of the partitive article forms in (34a), meaning "He is speaking *of* bread/flour/breads", and those with contracted prepositions in (34b), meaning "He is speaking *of* **the** bread/flour/breads" (Miller 1991: § 4.4.4).

(34) a. Il parle $\left\{\begin{array}{l} \textit{de} \ (*\ \textit{du}) \text{ pain} \\ \textit{de} \ (*\ \textit{de la}) \text{ farine} \\ \textit{de} \ (*\ \textit{des}) \text{ pains} \end{array}\right\}$

b. Il parle $\left\{\begin{array}{l} \textit{du} \text{ pain} \\ \textit{de la} \text{ farine} \\ \textit{des} \text{ pains} \end{array}\right\}$

2.3.2 Demonstratives

The label *demonstrative* derives from the Latin verb (*de*)*monstrare*, meaning 'to show' or 'to point (out)' as an act of reference to a given entity located within the situation of utterance. Indeed the deictic purport of determinative or pronominal words classified under this label is typically made clear by ostensive gestures accompanying the utterance of the pertinent NP. On the other hand, demonstratives are closely related to the definite article, which originated from them in Romance and Germanic languages alike (and in German is still homonymous to the demonstrative *der*, *die*, *das*). The evolution resulted in an article as versatile determiner of definiteness, without pragmatic constraints specifically associated with demonstratives.

Before presenting the pragmatic constraints, we want to emphasize that also demonstratives yield definite reference and therefore impose a uniqueness requirement as already discussed for the definite article (in § 2.3.1). In this connection, consider the following remarks, criticizing a notion of non-uniqueness found in unpublished work by Hans Kamp:

[24] Another language showing a partitive article like that of French is Italian, but note that also 'Ø-determination' can indicate plural or non-count indefiniteness in Italian, under various syntactic, semantic and stylistic constraints (v. Renzi 1988).

> "Kamp notes that a demonstrative *this/that* α carries an implicature [= nonliteral meaning implied by the speaker] that there is more than one object satisfying α... Kamp gives as evidence for his non-uniqueness assumption examples like *that pope*, which is odd or at least highly marked. However, there are clear cases of descriptions with a single satisfying object which combine easily with the demonstrative *that*, e.g. *that small planet beyond Uranus*, or *that woman who sold me the book on Situation Semantics*... Actually, there are cases where a strong non-uniqueness presupposition or implicature is carried by a demonstrative phrase, i.e. cases with contrastive stress on the demonstrative... However, the presupposition goes with the stress here, and is not a specific property of the demonstrative."
>
> Pinkal (1986)

The point is that such a presupposition of non-uniqueness, whenever appropriate for intonational and contextual reasons, concerns the descriptive content α expressed by the rest of the NP, whereas a further, deictic constraint – call it δ – is added by the demonstrative and must be taken into account with α for the uniqueness requirement of definiteness in our sense. E.g., by uttering the NP "that book" the speaker may or may not imply that there is more than one book in the situation, but in any case the utterance enforces the requirement that a unique referent must satify both the condition α of being a book and the demonstrative constraint δ, possibly made explicit by some gesture. So, think of a situation where several books exist and "that book" is uttered by somebody pointing to a table: by definiteness, just one of the books is expected to be on the table, or at least, in case of several books being placed there, just one of them is expected to be within reach of the speaker's ostensive gesture.[25]

Concerning the linguistic contents of our 'δ constraint', we see that the demonstratives available in the languages to be dealt with here can combine the definiteness of the NP, referring to x, with two deictic distinctions: x's distance or proximity relatively to the speaker and, in case of distance from the speaker, x's distance or proximity relatively to the hearer.[26] When both δ distinctions are instantiated lexically in a language, a three-term system is offered, as in Spanish:

---

[25]Note that Pinkal (1986) acknowledges Kamp to accept an equivalent version of uniqueness as regards the deictic use of demonstratives and simply disagrees on the alleged non-uniqueness to be associated with the condition α alone.

[26]Distance and proximity are meant as spatial concepts in the first place, but they may well be extended to the temporal dimension. Cf. Pinkal's examples "Do you remember *that* professor with the old Mercedes?" and "Do you remember the professor with *that* old Mercedes?" (ibid.), where *that* focusses a referent (professor or car) belonging to the shared past of speaker and hearer and therefore presented as equally far away in time from both.

- *este*, with δ = proximity to the speaker;
- *ese*, with δ = proximity to the hearer but distance from the speaker;
- *aquel*, with δ = distance from both speaker and hearer.

The same kind of system was found in ancient Latin (*hic*/*iste*/*ille*), but many languages, following an historical trend of linguistic evolution (Milewski 1970), instantiate only the speaker-oriented distinction as a two-term system (e.g. *this*/*that*). In Italian, the reduction of a three-term system (*questo*/*codesto*/*quello*) to a two-term one (*questo*/*quello*) has mostly taken place, yet the former survives in very formal – especially bureaucratic – written language, and colloquially in Tuscany.

An extreme case is French, where the demonstrative determiners (*ce* and its variant forms) are completely unspecified as to the intended deictic value.[27] If somebody wants to make explicit the proximity to or distance from the speaker, a postpositive deictic particle *ci* (= here) or *là* (= there) has to be added to the NP introduced by the ambiguous demonstrative:

(35) *ce* garçon$\left(\text{-}\left\{\begin{array}{c} ci \\ là \end{array}\right\}\right)$
'this/that boy (here/there)'

Likewise, in German the deictic items *hier*, *dort* and *da* are added in order to disambiguate or emphasize the intended interpretation of the demonstrative *dieser*, which is used to mean either 'this' or 'that' (unlike *jener*, exclusively used for distant referents). In Danish, another language with deictically ambiguous demonstratives[28], disambiguating deictics can also occur prenominally as modifiers of the demonstrative determiner: see "*dette her* hus" (= this here house), compared with "*dette* hus *her*" (= this house here). As we mentioned in chapter 1, the corresponding modification of English demonstrative determiners is marginally possible for reasons of emphasis. In French, the deictic particle is obligatorily attached to the pronominal counterparts of determinative demonstratives, as in *ceci*, unless the pronoun is added a relative clause

[27] Another phenomenon neutralizing the proximity/distance contrast is noticed in English by Leech & Svartvik (1975: p. 58), as regards the use of demonstratives shifted from deixis to anaphora broadly speaking: "*This* and *that* can replace each other with no difference of meaning in back-pointing" (ibid.). Here is an example (classifiable as 'text reference' in the terminology of Halliday & Hasan 1976: pp. 66-67): "I tried to open the door, but *this*/*that* was a mistake".

[28] This, in principle, is true of *denne*, *dette*, *disse*; however, especially in spoken language, one finds an unambiguously 'distant' use of the demonstrative forms *den*, *det*, *de*, which are distinguished by their stress from the prenominal forms of the definite article discussed in § 2.3.1.1 above. (For a descriptive introduction to the related aspects of Danish determination, v. Jansen 1978: pp. 22-24, 42-43.)

("*ce* que vous voulez") or a suitable PP ("*ceux* de Marie") or – less acceptably – some adjectival expression (cf. Miller 1991: § 3.4).

It's hardly surprising that the deictic items co-occurring with demonstratives in the ways described above can emphasize and, in case, disambiguate the demonstrative meaning of the construction, because they are semantically very close to the corresponding determiners or pronouns. Indeed also the words *here* and *there* (or their equivalent in other languages) respectively indicate proximity to and distance from the speaker, which explains the co-occurrence restrictions in "this (α) *here* / **there*" and "that (α) *there* / **here*". We assume that the same deictic constraint δ of demonstratives is at work, but words like *here* and *there* express spatial concepts, applying δ to locations instead of referents. A word of the kind has the meaning schematically represented by the joint conditions $\delta(l)$ and $Loc(\_\_\_, l)$, where the slot '___' must be filled by something situated in a location l satisfying the relevant deictic condition of proximity/distance. Our notation roughly formalizes standard lexicographic paraphases of *here*/*there* such as 'in (or at) *this*/*that* place', since *Loc* corresponds to the locative preposition, δ encodes the relevant aspect of *this*/*that* and l stands for the 'place'. The content that fills the slot depends on the head thus modified: if the locative deictic is used as modifier of a nominal or demonstrative head, one gets the result $Loc(x, l)$, where x stands for the referent of the NP.[29] Then the information $\delta(x)$, which demonstratives directly express in virtue of their determinative or referential function, follows by inference from $\delta(l)$ and $Loc(x, l)$, under 'common sense knowledge' postulates about the spatial properties of entities in a location.

Turning to the syntagmatic distribution of demonstrative determination items, they occur instead of the article in the languages we deal with, being prenominal central determiners:

(36) a. (*those) the interesting books
b. (*the) those interesting books

This contrasts sharply with such other languages of Europe as Greek, Hungarian, Maltese and Romanian, whose demonstrative determiners can or must co-occur with the definite article, in prenominal or postnominal position; see Kolliakou (1996), Plank & Moravcsik (1996) and Barbu (1999). However, a postnominal demonstrative is exceptionally possible in a Spanish noun phrase introduced by the definite article (thus making the demonstrative a postdeterminer), so as to achieve a particular emphasis, somewhat derogative:

[29]The same semantic schema applies to adverbial uses strictly speaking. Its slot in that case gets filled by relevant content of the clause (projected by the verb) modified by *here* or *there*; for instance, an event e in the sense of Event Semantics (Davidson 1967), yielding $Loc(e, l)$.

(37) el señor ese
'the gentleman THAT' (= that fellow)

2.3.3 Possessives

The notion of 'possessive' in itself is clearly quite broad and applies not only to determiners of the pertinent kind (determinative Saxon genitive phrases included), but also to non-determinative expressions with possessive meaning. Since determinative items in our sense are a particular class of adnominal dependents, let us start from an informal semantic characterization of possessive constructions within the Noun Phrase. All these constructions associate the reference of an embedded expression with the reference of the whole NP – i.e. the 'possessor' x_1 with the 'possessed' x_2 – according to some relevant relation, inferred from the context or lexicalized by the nominal head. Any such relation can be considered an instantiation of the abstract hyperonym $Poss(x_1,x_2)$, which covers cases as varied as x_1 being owner of x_2 in a legal sense, x_1 including the part x_2, x_1 being author of x_2, x_1 being a relative of x_2, x_1 taking or undergoing the action x_2, etc.[30]

Given the class of NP-internal constructions with some $Poss(x_1,x_2)$ purport as sketched so far, the possessive item proper is meant to be the embedded expression referred to x_1, whose morpho-phonological form can or must display genitive marking (under language-specific conditions). Our general criterion of adnominal dependence applies qua necessary requirement to ascertain whether some **possessive** – in the sense we have made clear – fulfils a **determinative** function as well. The criterion excludes those occurrences of the possessive that do not depend on the nominal referred to the possessed x_2, but are typically taken as complement by an interposed head, like the preposition in "a book [$_{PP}$ of *Mary's/hers*]" [31]. That such an 'independent' possessive in the English construction has the ordinary distribution and function of a non-determinative NP is plausibly proved by examples like "a friend of *Mary('s)*", where the Saxon genitive marking can be omitted without changing meaning (cf. Bennett 1995: p. 107, as well as some discussion in our first chapter).[32]

[30]For more discussion (from various angles) as regards possessive meaning and the morphosyntactic strategies expressing it in the world's languages, see Seiler (1983), Haiman (1985: pp. 130-136), Lyons (1986), Nichols (1988), Cinque (1991: ch. 6), Pollard & Sag (1994: §§ 1.8, 9.4.5) and others.

[31]Or, by the same token, the copula in "the book [$_{VP}$ is *Mary's/hers*]", though irrelevance to determination in this case is shown *a fortiori* by the clause-level (not NP-internal) scope of the 'Poss relation' between the book and Mary/her.

[32]To make the possessive complement of a preposition artificially adnominal by postulating some empty nominal head, then, would be completely unmotivated and a source of useless complications. Nor would it change our conclusion concerning non-determinative status of

Now, being adnominal is necessary but not sufficient for a possessive to serve as determiner. Its determinative status is ultimately a matter of semantic function, characterizing the referential type of the whole NP referred to the possessed x_2. In our set of sample languages we find two different (but compatible) ways in which the possessive meaning of the adnominal expression can combine with a determinative function: (i) possessive determiners as **definiteness markers** make the x_2-referring NP definite; (ii) possessive determiners as **para-demonstratives** set the NP reference x_2 in a 'pragmatic space' that pertains to the x_1 they exclusively determine through the information of one of the three grammatical persons, hence *the speaker*, *the hearer*, or some *third element* of the situational or linguistic context. That is, type (i) items take on the definite article function and type (ii) items make a determinative use of personal deixis (or co-reference, when the third-person reference is recovered from linguistic context). The latter determinative function is called 'para-demonstrative' as it parallels the deictically based component $\delta(x)$ of demonstrative determination in the general case, with δ meaning: 'near to *the speaker* / *the hearer* [vs. the speaker] / *neither*' (v. § 2.3.2 above). We shall have more to say on the formal status of *Poss* and δ in chapter 3.

As regards constraints on morpho-syntactic realization, property (i) causes a possessive expression to occur instead of the definite article and (ii) is an inherent property of the possessive determiner words. The two properties may well coexist in the same determiner word – a definiteness-marking and para-demonstrative possessive – as shown in English and various other languages (but not all; see some examples afterwards). However, we warn the reader not to confuse the definiteness mentioned in this connection ('property (i)') with the fact that para-demonstratives are also definite as far as their own reference to the possessor is concerned. While the former aspect implies marking for definiteness the NP in which the possessive serves as determiner, the possessive itself is a referential expression characterized by the definiteness of personal deixis, just like personal pronouns without determinative function.

On the other hand, if a possessive lacks both properties (i)-(ii), we will not consider it a determiner at all. The requirement that a possessive determiner be definiteness-marking and/or para-demonstrative offers an additional criterion to ascertain the presence of determinative function, subject to our previous criterion of adnominal dependence. Indeed, adnominal possessives too may well be devoid of determinative function, because of plainly semantic reasons. In English, for instance, one finds so-called 'descriptive genitives' (Quirk et al. 1985: §§ 5.122, 17.110) fulfiling some non-determinative function of adnominal

---

the same possessive for the $Poss(x_1,x_2)$ construction in question, because the item would depend on its empty sister and not on the precedent noun (just like *Mary's/her* in "this picture of *Mary's/her* dog" obviously depends on "dog", not "picture").

modifiers, as done by the italicized expressions in "the ten *farmer's* wives" (= the ten wives whose respective husband is a farmer) or "a *girls'* school" (= a school for girls). Their descriptive lexical content lacks any para-demonstrative value – cf. (ii) above – and the fact that they modify the nominal head without influencing definiteness shows their irrelevance to determination according to part (i) of the criterion. By the same token, Saxon genitives replacing the article in a given NP do act as (central) determiners, because they always make that NP referentially definite, irrespective of their own internal determination; e.g., "*some students'* idea" is definite though *some* is indefinite.

In German, a comparable distinction can be made between postnominal NPs in the genitive case and Saxon genitives:

(38) a. das Buch *Karls*
'the book [of] Karl's'

b. *Karls* Buch
'Karl's book'

The former genitive phrases are not mutually exclusive with the article and do not affect the definiteness or indefiniteness of the resulting NP referred to the possessed x_2, whereas the latter are definiteness-marking central determiners like the equivalent English expressions. In German, however, the Saxon genitive does not allow all the expressive options of the English construction, which just adds genitive case to a possibly quite complex NP; cf. "*someone else's* car", "*the two other teachers'* room", "*a man of distinction's* influence", "*the woman over there's* dress", "*an hour and a half's* discussion", etc. On the contrary, contemporary German, especially in spoken usage, tends to keep the Saxon genitive phrase as short as possible, most instances being one-word long, normally proper names as in (38b) above (v. also Winhart 1997). A slightly more complex phrase as in "*meines Onkels* Haus" (= *my uncle's* house) would sound as an obsolete literary expression, to be replaced by "das Haus *meines Onkels*" (= the house [*of*] *my uncle's*), with postnominal genitive.[33]

By way of conclusion we offer some remarks on the syntactic distribution of possessive determiner words. They are central determiners or postdeterminers, depending on the languages:

(39) a. (*the) my book

b. (*my) the book

[33] Alternatevely, one can resort to a prepositional phrase, as in "das Haus *von meinem Onkel*" (= the house *of my uncle* $_{\text{DATIVE}}$). Likewise, languages where the NPs other than pronouns lack any explicit case marking (v. French, Italian and Spanish) translate non-pronominal genitive phrases as corresponding PPs, whose embedded possessive NP is not determinative according to our criteria.

(40) a. (*le) mon livre

b. (*mon) le livre

(41) a. il mio libro

b. (*mio) il libro

In English and French, as (39) and (40) show, the relevant determiners are distributionally alternative to the article, hence central. In Italian, postdeterminer status is revealed by the fact that (41a), the equivalent of (39a) and (40a) when the possessive co-occurs with the article, is grammatical (while (41b) in the same conditions remains as ungrammatical as (39b) and (40b)). The distributional difference corresponds to a semantic difference, because all possessive determiner words are para-demonstrative (type (ii)) but only those occurring as central determiners of some NP mark it for definiteness (type (i)). On the contrary, Italian possessive postdetermination is referentially compatible with all sorts of preceding determiners: cf. "questo/ogni/un/nessun/... *mio* libro" (= this/every/a/no/... book [*of*] *mine*). Note also that the possessive postdeterminers in Italian can follow the noun (v. "il libro *mio*") and this is their only position in Spanish. The Spanish system is quite interesting, since it makes available two alternative paradigms of para-demonstrative possessive determiners:

- *mi*, *tu*, *su*, ... are central determiners and accordingly marking for definiteness, v. "*mi* casa" (= *my* house);
- *mío*, *tuyo*, *suyo*, ..., when used adnominally, are postnominal postdeterminers not affecting (in)definiteness, v. "aquellos/unos amigos *tuyos*" (= those/some friends [*of*] *yours*).

2.3.4 Quantitatives

2.3.4.1 The lexical field of quantity/amount

Our way of labelling the determiners to be treated hereafter (as well as their 'pronominal counterparts' in the sense introduced by chapter 1) is reminiscent of Quirk et al. (1985: p. 258), e.g., when they mention "the 'quantitative' determiners *every*, (*n*)*either*, *each*, *some*, *any*, *no*, *enough*", etc. However, the same authors – like many others – make more frequent use of different labels, which we find less appropriate: "indefinites" (ibid., p. 377) and "quantifiers" (pp. 262-264). So, let us start from some preliminary comments motivating our terminological preference; we will then move on to a broader theoretical discussion this kind of determiners warrants because of its complexity.

The term traditionally employed in descriptive linguistics by grammarians and lexicographers, namely *indefinites*, is not well chosen for a class of expressions that don't all share indefiniteness, according to the 'existential' notion of indefinite reference we have adopted in § 2.2.1 and § 2.3.1; there are quantitative determiners indicating other sorts of NP reference, as our discussion will make clear. Furthermore, the same class does not include at least one obvious case of indefiniteness, the indefinite article. Turning to *quantifiers*, that term was originally inspired by the logical operators which roughly correspond to "every" and "some": **universal quantifier** (= '$\forall$') and **existential quantifier** (= '$\exists$'), respectively. Although their notions are quite relevant to the quantitative kind of determiners, we are not going to identify this with the quantifiers of natural language, as it is arguable that one or the other of the two basic operators (possibly negated) represents some meaning component of any determiner. Above all, the linguists' use of the denomination *quantifiers* for a class of adnominal dependents (and alleged part of speech, according to the approach we have already criticized in chapter 1) does not reflect an important development of contemporary semantic research: the whole NP rather than the determiner alone should be treated as quantifier (in the 'generalized' sense stemming from Barwise & Cooper 1981). Since next chapter we will revert to the issue and see how quantification as a mechanism for NP interpretation uniformly applies to NPs with or without determiners of any kind.

Having discarded the most common terminological alternatives, it is up to us to make a notion of **quantitative** determiners clear. The items of this class, intuitively, "specify the range of reference of a noun [phrase] ... by indicating quantity" (Leech & Svartvik 1975: p. 225). A similar constraint results from numeral information in the case of cardinals (v. § 2.3.5 below), but the meaning of non-numeral quantitatives is defined within a characteristic 'lexical field' (to be presented soon) which relates items by entailment, contradiction and scalarity. Consistently with its non-numerical essence, the quantitative concept in question applies to uncountable reference too and therefore allows various quantitative determiners to combine with mass nouns and the like. In English, such words as *all*, *some*, *no*, *more*, etc. are used for both 'count' and 'non-count' determination purposes; one finds also quantitative word forms that are reserved for the former or the latter use but belong to pairs with a common core meaning, e.g. *many/much* and *few/little*. Admittedly, henceforth we will only occasionally touch on uncountables (cf. § 2.3.1.2 above for a brief introductory discussion of the difficult semantic issues specifically raised by them), while our work will focus on count readings and forms.

The following presentation concerns the overall 'lexical field' formed by quantitative determiners and schematized in **Figure 2.1** with English examples (but the approach will be extended to multilingual data in § 2.3.4.2). Our

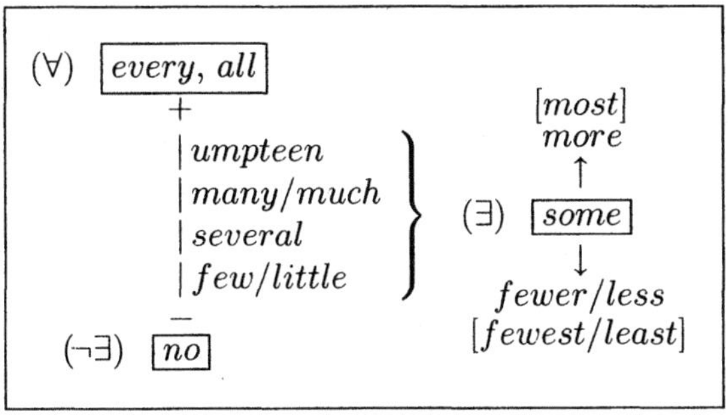

Figure 2.1: English quantitative determiners

figure reflects the subclassification of quantitatives according to three main types of 'range of reference' which we identify by logical symbols: (∀) **universal reference**, (∃) **existential reference** and (¬∃) **negated existential reference**. Framed words are prototypical instances of the corresponding subclasses; in particular, we place (∃) *some* in a side position and make it embrace further words by a curly bracket, in order to show that various degrees of non-null quantity/amount can be lexicalized by determinative items entailing *some*.[34] The outcome of specifying different lexical degrees of ∃-determination is indeed "a scale moving from the inclusive words at the top, to the negative words at the bottom" (Leech & Svartvik 1975: p. 51), so as to bridge the opposite (= '+' and '−') polarities of ∀-determination and ¬∃-determination. Comparative determiners are other words implying the scale, inasmuch as they increase (= '↑') or decrease (= '↓') a quantity/amount implicitly located on it[35]; the related superlative forms (to be discussed on contrastive grounds in § 2.3.4.2) have been added nearby between square brackets.

We leave to our next chapters the task of integrating formally the above triadic distinction (∀, ∃ and ¬∃) into a more general framework of reference, which covers also topics already touched on in § 2.3.1, like definiteness vs. indefiniteness and the interpretation of plural grammatical number. Now we content ourselves with a simple set-theoretic way of treating the determinative

[34]Cf. also § 2.3.4.2 below for other quantitative degrees, expressed through syntactic modification of the basic lexical items we are treating.

[35]Note that we consider only cases in which a comparative determiner is used without making explicit the relevant 'term of comparison' by means of a *than*-type expression, because the specific grammatical issues of comparative constructions are not addressed in the present volume. Therefore, here we cover sample NPs like "*more* students" (where the increase in the number of students must be calculated by comparison with some set of students provided by the context), but not "*more than twenty* students" or "*more* students *than professors*".

value of (count) quantitative words and their position on the relative scale.[36] If D is the contextually given domain of individuals satisfying the descriptive conditions expressed by the nominal sister of some quantitative determiner **Q**, the range of reference that **Q** allows is a subset R_{Q} of D:

- $R_{\mathsf{Q}}=D$ (the whole D as a subset of itself) in case of $\forall$-determination,
- a non-empty subset $R_{\mathsf{Q}}\neq\emptyset$ in case of $\exists$-determination,
- the empty subset $R_{\mathsf{Q}}=\emptyset$ in case of $\neg\exists$-determination (thus forming a contradictory pair with $\exists$-determination).

The 'scalar' aspect of the lexical field in question is accounted for as follows: if $R_{\mathsf{Q}'}$ and $R_{\mathsf{Q}''}$ are possible subsets of the same domain D, where $\mathbf{Q}'$ and $\mathbf{Q}''$ are quantitative item values such that $\mathbf{Q}'$ occurs higher than $\mathbf{Q}''$ on the scale of quantity/amount, the number of elements – a.k.a. **cardinality** – of the former subset exceeds or equals that of the latter. That is:

$$\text{Card}(R_{\mathsf{Q}'}) \geq \text{Card}(R_{\mathsf{Q}''}).$$

In ordinary contexts with a non-empty D, $\emptyset$ qua $\neg\exists$-determined range of reference becomes a proper (i.e. identity-excluding) subset of any other range of reference. It is also worth noticing that the existential quantitatives need not always be applicable to a given domain, as the corresponding range of reference is not a possible subset of every domain. When D is empty, indeed, $\exists$-determination is ruled out by definition, while $\neg\exists$- and $\forall$-determination remain possible in appropriate contexts (yielding $R_{\mathsf{Q}}=D=\emptyset$) as shown by the following examples:

(42) a. Yes, *no friend of Mary* came to the party; unsurprisingly, because nobody is friend to Mary.

(where $D=$ the set of Mary's friends)

b. What a fast examination session! We have already considered *all candidates*, as there were no candidates at all.

(where $D=$ the set of candidates)

A less marginal case of inapplicability of $\exists$-determination to a given domain arises when the determiner is *many* and the domain does not have many elements. That is, we need some D with a sufficient number of elements in order

[36] We refer to Pelletier & Schubert (1989) for a review of different proposals on how to extend some set-theoretic treatment to 'non-count' quantities/amounts as well. For remarks on a notion of 'smallest particles' or 'minimal portions' that could bear on the issue, see our previous note 23, § 2.3.1.2.

to state the relationship (43), where $\mathbf{Q}'$ is *all* (or equivalent), $\mathbf{Q}''$ is *many* and $\text{Card}(R_{\mathbf{Q}''})$ exceeds the $\mathcal{K}_m$ value of maximal cardinality allowed by the context for sets whose elements are not many.

(43) $\text{Card}(D) = \text{Card}(R_{\mathbf{Q}'}) \geq \text{Card}(R_{\mathbf{Q}''}) > \mathcal{K}_m$

The context-dependent standard that a given set must compare with for its elements to be many (or few, enough, etc.[37]) is normally vague, allowing also situations in which it is impossible to say whether the elements are many or not. We acknowledge the problem but leave it aside, following Barwise & Cooper (1981): "a theory of vagueness like that given by Kamp (1975) for other kinds of basic expressions could be superimposed on our theory. We do not do this here, to keep things manageable". On the other hand, there are some quantitative items associated with an utterly precise numerical constraint on the cardinality of the relevant D, inasmuch as they are only applicable to a domain with exactly two elements. Such a phenomenon, which is reminiscent of the **dual** grammatical number found in languages like ancient Greek and Anglo-Saxon, results in the following subsystem of the English quantitative lexical field: ($\forall$) *both* as dual determiner of universal reference; ($\exists$) *either*, in the sense of 'one and/or the other', as dual determiner of existential reference; ($\neg\exists$) *neither* as dual determiner of negated existential reference. (Cf. also Horn 1989: pp. 220-224.)

Finally, our sample presentation of English quantitative determiners is completed by a brief review of their distributional syntactic properties. The items belonging to a certain (paradigmatic) kind of determiners in a given language may differ from each other as regards syntagmatic behaviour, being distributed to different **positional classes** (= pre-, central and post- determiners), and this possibility is largely exploited by quantitatives. Quantitative items of $\forall$-determination are central determiners, like *each*, or predeterminers, like *all* (and the dual *both*), when used before the nominal head. Other quantitative central determiners express $\exists$-determination, like *some* (and the dual *either*), or $\neg\exists$-determination, like *no* (and the dual *neither*). Context-sensitive quantitative degrees of $\exists$-determination are lexicalized by postdeterminers, like *few*, and again by central determiners, like *enough*. The determiners *enough* and *galore* are respectively allowed and obliged to follow the nominal head, as already noticed in chapter 1; nevertheless, they can be confirmed in the central determiner class, since their occurrence in postnominal position appears to be incompatible with any other determiner depending on (projections of) the same head.

[37]There are various items whose meaning implies a quantitative standard established by the context. In the case of *few*/*little*, the standard has a 'negative bias'; for *enough*, *galore* and *sufficient*, it is a quantity/amount assumed as adequate to meet a need or purpose.

2.3.4.2 Quantitatives across languages

The basic semantic system of quantitative determination we sketched in § 2.3.4.1 holds cross-linguistically, but is lexicalized to a different extent depending on the languages. Apart from obvious differences as regards the phonologic expression of some quantitative concept, in a given language there may well be no single determiner word directly expressing that concept. In this connection, it is important to distinguish 'lexical gaps' that are just language-specific from those reflecting general restrictions on the system.

One such restriction applies because the triadic distinction between universal, existential and negated existential reference (see **Figure 2.1** in § 2.3.4.1 above) can be viewed as a subconfiguration of Aristotle's Square of Opposition, which is completed by a fourth corner: ($\neg\forall$) **negated universal reference.**[38] However, as Horn (1989: § 4.5) noticed, "not all four corners of the Square are equal under the law of natural language", because it turns out that "no one-word lexical items with or without negative morphology are available to express ... the negation of a universal" – not only in English, but cross-linguistically. Any determiner with the intended meaning is a phrase built up by explicit negative modification of some head determiner of universal reference, as in English "*not* every/all". The three-cornered lexical field we have adopted is supported by the systematic lack of an autonomous lexicalization for the $\neg\forall$-determination value, while lexicalization of the $\neg\exists$-determination value (as in *no* and *neither*) is common to all languages we deal with.

We have observed that the contribution of negation to quantitative determination can be expressed by an explicit syntactic modifier, as in the case of negated universal reference, or directly incorporated by a lexical determiner (whether the determiner's negative component is only semantic or also distinguished in the morpho-phonological form of the word), as in the case of negated existential reference. Similarly, the two options are found for modifications affecting a quantitative item that conveys other aspects of meaning besides its main ($\forall$ or $\exists$ or $\neg\exists$) type of 'range of reference': see the modification system that **multal** quantitatives, like *many*, and **paucal** ones, like *few*, allow because they "are gradable, and can be accompanied by degree adverbs such as *very*, *too*, *so*, *as*", etc. (Quirk et al. 1985: p. 385). Without indulging in

[38] In essence, Aristotle distinguished four ways of quantifying a statement 'N is P' where N is nominal and P predicative: in the top corners, '*every* N is P' and '*no* N is P' (= *every* N is *not* P); in the bottom corners, '*some* N is P' and '*not every* N is P' (= *some* N is *not* P). According to Aristotelian logic, each statement in one of the top corners of this square entails the statement in the bottom corner on the same – left or right – side of the square, i.e. the universal entails the particular; but modern logic shows that such inferences and others allowed by the original interpretation of the square hold only if one excludes the empty set as possible denotation of N (v. Strawson 1952: ch. 6; Kneale & Kneale 1962: ch. 2).

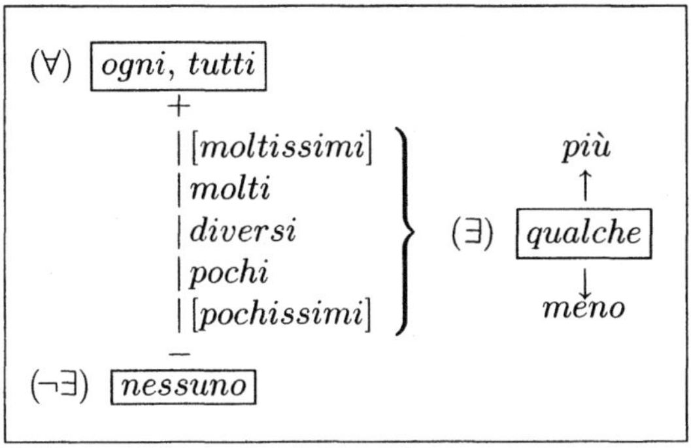

Figure 2.2: Italian quantitative determiners

a long digression about the interesting semantic issue, suffice it to say that *very* makes the relevant standard on the quantitative scale increase towards the positive polarity, when modifying *many/much*, or towards the negative polarity, when modifying *few/little*, whereas *too* indicates the inadequacy of a quantity/amount because this exceeds or falls short of some *enough*-type standard (in the sense of our previous note 37). Once again, the alternative to explicit syntactic modifiers is to include the modifying semantic value directly as component of a lexical determiner: cf. *very many* and its one-word equivalent *umpteen* (in informal English).

Incorporation of a *very*-type value into Italian words is expressed by the so-called 'absolute superlative degree' of adjectival inflection. Neglecting morphophonological details, it is instructive to compare the resulting lexical field of Italian quantitatives with that of English. In Italian, as shown by **Figure 2.2** (which is restricted to count items for convenience), the word forms we put between square brackets are related to the adjacent ∃-determiners on the scale, the counterparts of *many* and *few*, by adding superlative inflection to the multal or paucal root, with a *very*-type effect. Hence *molti* (= many) → [*moltissimi*] (= very many), *pochi* (= few) → [*pochissimi*] (= very few). On the other hand, Italian morphology does not distinguish the superlative degree of comparison, typically expressed in English by the ending "-(e)st" (with possible allomorphism) as in *more* → [*most*], *fewer* → [*fewest*] and *less* → [*least*]; cf. **Figure 2.1**, § 2.3.4.1 above.

The superlative comparison meaning of the multal determiner *most* is rendered in Italian by expressions like ***(i)*** "più di metà" or ***(ii)*** "la maggioranza" – which literally translate ***(i)*** "more than half" and ***(ii)*** "the majority" [39] – fol-

[39] These are equivalent in the pertinent sense of *majority*, inasmuch as we consider an absolute and precise – not vague – majority; cf. what we said on vagueness in § 2.3.4.1.

lowed by a partitive PP. In construction ***(i)***, explicit quantitative comparison combines with a fraction [40], two phenomena that are not part of our present grammatical coverage (as already declared in chapter 1), nonetheless the semantics involved is fairly clear. According to van Eijck & Alshawi (1992), for semantic representation purposes "a reduction of superlative to comparative can be performed by expressing the superlative in terms of ... *more*" and indeed the approximation of the meaning of *most* by resort to *more than half* is standard in logical semantics (v. Barwise & Cooper 1981). Within the conceptual framework that we sketched in § 2.3.4.1, a multal determiner **Q** expressing superlative comparison makes the cardinality of $R_{\mathbf{Q}}$, the corresponding 'range of reference', greater than half the cardinality of the relevant domain D which includes $R_{\mathbf{Q}}$:

$$\mathrm{Card}(R_{\mathbf{Q}}) > \tfrac{1}{2}\,\mathrm{Card}(D).$$ [41]

Thus, *most students* refers to more than half the students forming the domain in question.

Let's now move on to ***(ii)***, the paraphrase/translation of "most" in terms of "majority", or equivalent. The relevant sense is **absolute majority** (as we mentioned in note 39), but the approach may well be generalized to cases of **relative majority**. One will simply apply some context-dependent criterion to partition a domain D into mutually exclusive subsets with different cardinality: the largest of them is the majority, though a relative majority when the division results in more than two subsets. Such a generalization enables us to account for the paucal superlative form "fewest", which is not equivalent to "less than half". Accordingly, a literal translation of the latter would not express the meaning of the former in Italian, a sample language where *fewest*

[40]Fractions, as understood here, are a semantically characterized 'paradigmatic kind' of items, including *half* (or equivalent words in other languages) because of its fractionary meaning: $\frac{1}{2}$. The numerator of this fraction, however, can be (and often is) omitted, contrary to the most typical morpho-syntactic structure of fractionary items (e.g. "a/one third", "two thirds").

[41]Unsurprisingly, the meaning of the other multal determiners too can be traced back to the relation 'greater (or, informally, *more*) than', according to a schema $\mathrm{Card}(R_{\mathbf{Q}}) > \mathcal{K}_x$. This is quite evident when **Q** has comparative degree, $\mathcal{K}_x$ being the cardinality of the set identified by some explicit or implicit 'term of comparison' (see our previous note 35 on that notion). Furthermore, in the formula (43) of § 2.3.4.1, the range of reference enforced by *many* has been represented through the inequality $\mathrm{Card}(R_{\mathbf{Q}}) > \mathcal{K}_m$, where $\mathcal{K}_x = \mathcal{K}_m$ is the maximal cardinality that the context allows in case of a set whose elements are not many. Also the fact that the $\mathcal{K}_x$ value of *most* or equivalent expressions is established in proportion to the domain D (because $\mathcal{K}_x = \frac{1}{2}\,\mathrm{Card}(D)$) does not look so exceptional if one takes into account proportional uses of *many*, which can – but need not – be made explicit by a suitable modifier as in "*relatively* many". Under the intended interpretation, the standard that a range-of-reference set must exceed for its elements to be many is not independent of the cardinality of the superset D: it is actually established as $\mathcal{K}_m = \frac{a}{b}\,\mathrm{Card}(D)$, where the a and b values of the fraction depend on the context.

is rendered by literally translating expressions like "the *smallest number* of". Cf. the following English sentence and its Italian translation:

(44) a. The *fewest* publications were submitted to the board by the third candidate

b. Il *minor numero* di pubblicazioni fu sottoposto alla commissione dal terzo candidato

The paucal superlative of comparison indicates that the NP refers to the smallest of the subsets resulting from a suitable partition of D, e.g. sets of publications associated with the respective (three or more) candidates in the situation described by (44).

An interesting issue concerns the grammatical pattern exemplified above by construction ***(ii)*** and its paucal counterpart. According to Quirk et al. (1985: p. 264), there is "a large open class of ... quantifiers which function semantically like the closed-class quantifiers, but most of which consist of a noun of quantity (*lot*, *deal*, *amount*, etc.) followed by *of*". Apart from the uncertain status of the label 'quantifier' (as already discussed in § 2.3.4.1), the syntactic pattern of the resulting constructions is controversial. Here is again a quotation from Quirk et al. (ibid.):

> "Although the quantity nouns *lot*, *deal*, etc. look like the head of a noun phrase, there are grounds for arguing that the whole expression (*a lot of*, *a good deal of*, etc.) functions as a determiner. Notably, the verb regularly has number concord with the second noun, rather than the first, as in:
> { *Lots of food* was on the table.
> { = There was *lots of food* on the table."

On the other hand, number is ultimately a semantic matter and agreement mismatches by-passing morpho-syntactic dependency relations are independently motivated for cases of 'notional concord' like (45), so it is far from clear that the phenomenon mentioned in the quotation justifies a syntactically eccentric (and, in our view, *ad hoc*) structure with a preposition not heading a PP.

(45) a. The $\text{government}_{sing.}$ $\text{have}_{plur.}$ broken all $\text{their}_{plur.}$ promises

(more typical of British English than of American)

b. The hash $\text{browns}_{plur.}$ at table fourteen $\text{is}_{sing.}$ getting angry

(said by a waiter referring to somebody who ordered hash browns)

There are various versions of the hypothetical structure $[_{\text{NP}} \ldots \mathbf{Q}\ \textit{of} \ldots \text{N} \ldots]$ with the second noun N (and not the quantitative noun **Q**) heading the whole construction. In the approach suggested by the quotation from Quirk et al. (but see also Chomsky 1970), *of* is part of a complex determiner including

Q, whereas a common alternative involves attaching the preposition to the subsequent nominal expression (cf. Jackendoff 1977: ch. 5, Barwise & Cooper 1981 and – on comparable constructions of French – Miller 1991: § 2.2.4). At any rate, the morpho-syntactic status of such a prepositional item without the normal property of projecting a PP is so uncertain that some authors reject the traditional classification as word belonging to the category P: e.g., Jackendoff (1977: p. 108) claims that "*of* is a transformationally inserted grammatical formative" and Miller (1991: p. 40) treats its French equivalent *de* as "prefixal inflection". To avoid blurring word boundaries in that way, the lack of phrase structure projection could be motivated through some treatment of *of* (or equivalent) as a 'minor word' on a par with articles, conjunctions, etc. But the existence of unquestionable cases of prepositions belonging to a major category was pointed out in our first chapter, so that one would be forced to postulate an additional, morpho-syntactically distinct class of minor prepositions. (It is essentially the kind of treatment developed by Van Eynde 1994; 2004, as well as Badia 1998.)

The most plausible approach to such constructions as "*lots* of ___", "the *majority* of ___", "a (small/large) *number/amount/set/group* of ___", etc. recognizes the quantitative or, also, collective noun as head of the whole NP and "of" as head of a PP. This preposition establishes a semantic relation between the preceding noun and the object of the preposition itself, an embedded NP. For partitives proper, the complement NP is a definite pronoun (*us*, *these*, etc.) or requires a definite determiner, as in "a group of *the/those/my* students", whereas the parallel construction with a bare indefinite object and accordingly unlike sense, as in "a group of students", is known as pseudo-partitive (cf. Jackendoff 1977: § 5.4). At any rate, the semantics of a relevant nominal head **Q** combined with the PP yields the same quantification result one gets by corresponding determination, and can trigger notional concord [42]. Syntactic dependencies, though, are different: contrary to the determiner in "*most/many* students", the **Q** noun – or any projection thereof – in "the *majority* of the students" or "a *lot* of students" does not depend syntactically on "students", so it is not a determiner according to our characterization of determiners as a type of adnominal dependents.

The same conclusion holds for quantitative pronouns followed by a partitive PP, even if they are formally identical to determiners, as in "*all* of ___", "*most* of ___", "*many* of ___", "*some* of ___", etc.[43] Like Jackendoff (1977: § 5.3.2),

[42] On a partially semantic account of agreement phenomena, to be taken up in our chapter 3, see Pollard & Sag (1994: ch. 2); cf. Wechsler & Zlatić (2003) for recent developments.

[43] As noticed by Jackendoff (1977: pp. 106-107), English determiners whose counterparts can take a partitive PP are also cardinals ("*one/two/three/...* of ___"), ordinals ("the *first/second/third/...* of ___") and, to a limited extent, demonstratives ("*those* of ___").

one could treat the **Q** item as a determiner (in our sense) by postulating an unexpressed, 'empty' nominal head, but nonetheless **Q** would not depend on the overt nominal head in the complement of the preposition; both the quantitative determiner and the PP would be dependents of the 'empty head'. Consistently with our favourite approach in this connection, whose basic ideas were outlined in chapter 1, we will rather adopt a pronominal treatment, so that the **Q** pronoun qua head projects the whole NP and takes the PP as dependent. On the semantic side, the intended partitive value of the '**Q** + PP' construction implies that the set which **Q** quantifies over be identified in terms of definite reference through the object of the preposition. Hence the need for some definite determiner introducing the embedded NP ("all/most/many/... of *the* students"), unless this NP is a suitable pronoun ("all/most/many/... of *us*"), as mentioned before.

In French, various English determiners that lexicalize quantitative degrees are typically translated as **Q** items followed by "de" (= of): see "*beaucoup* (= many/much) de ___", "*peu* (= few/little) de ___", "*plus* (= more) de ___", "*moins* (= fewer/less) de ___", "*assez* (= enough) de ___". The construction is also used for quantitative degrees that in English are not expressed by any single word but require explicit syntactic modification: "*trop* (= too many/much) de ___" and "*autant* (= as many/much, or so many/much) de ___" [44]. Above all, a difference from the '**Q** + PP' construction of English (and other languages) arises because that one needs a definite object for the preposition, whereas *de* in the cases at issue precedes a bare indefinite nominal, the result being the semantic equivalent of English NPs that combine a determiner and a nominal head, without any interposing preposition. Semantically, "beaucoup de fautes" is indeed equivalent to "many (*of) mistakes", not "many of the mistakes".

Since the existence of determiners built up from the preposition form *de* and another morpho-phonological component is witnessed in French by the partitive article (cf. § 2.3.1.2 above), we may wonder whether a comparable phenomenon comes into play now too. Thus the semantic equivalence of "many mistakes" and "beaucoup de fautes" would follow from an identical syntactic structure, one which combines a determiner – the morphologically complex expression *beaucoup de* in French – with a nominal head. Tempting though this hypothesis may seem, it is provably wrong in the light of data like the following:

(46) a. Beaucoup *de* garçons de Paris et *de* filles de Bordeaux
'Many OF boys from Paris and OF girls from Bordeaux'
(= Many boys from Paris and girls from Bordeaux)

[44] In Italian, the respective degrees are lexicalized as determiners by *troppo* and *altrettanto* (or their variant forms), not followed by any preposition.

b. Beaucoup *de* ces garçons
'Many of these/those boys'

In (46a), the repetition of *de* at the beginning of both conjuncts shows that the preposition called for by *beaucoup* is morpho-syntactically separate from it, like any other word; the most natural and straight-forward way of treating such examples is again a **Q** + PP analysis, with the whole PP resulting from the conjunction of PPs headed by *de*.[45] Further evidence supporting our analysis stems from (46b) because the meaning and the structure displayed by this second kind of French data look exactly the same as in the English partitive construction, implying *de* is not a negligible morpho-phonological detail of the **Q** item, but a prepositional head that can express partitive meaning (cf. the previous discussion). If *beaucoup* and the other **Q** items of French behaving alike are provided with a pronominal reading that takes some *de*-PP as dependent, as motivated by partitive data, there is no need for putative determiners like *beaucoup de*: nothing prevents the same pronoun (reading) from taking a *de*-PP of the **pseudo-partitive** kind, in the sense originally introduced for cases depending on a quantitative noun.[46]

To sum up, French shows quite a peculiar language-specific way of instantiating the semantic field of quantity/amount, inasmuch as the lexicalization of ∃-degrees as determiners is mostly limited to items that are uncommitted or intermediate with regard to the multal vs. paucal opposition, like *quelque(s)* (= some), *plusieurs* (= several), and few others. Multal and paucal degrees corresponding to 'lexical gaps' of the determination system get lexicalized as the pronominal counterparts of adverbs like *beaucoup*, *peu*, etc. (see above). Exploiting the approach of the first chapter, we may well assume that the morpho-syntactic category of quantitative adverbs is Adjective in French too and then their difference from English ones comes down to the lack of adnominal function. This is compensated by the use of pronominal counterparts, since French lets them take both partitive and pseudo-partitive *de*-PPs, as we mentioned. It is the semantics of the '**Q** + PP' construction that will ensure cross-linguistic equivalence to NPs combining a suitable determiner and a nominal head, in English or other languages that cannot use pronouns with a pseudo-partitive PP.

[45] Coordination data like (46a) do not falsify those approaches in which a non-head (affixal or minor) preposition form is attached to the right as we have seen before. (Miller 1991: p. 275, e.g., deals with the example by coordinating two NPs case-marked by *de*.) In that way, however, the anomalous status of *de* lacks the independent motivation that one could adduce, by analogy with the partitive article, under the hypothesis of a morphologically complex determiner including the *de* form as component.

[46] Although the use of pseudo-partitives with a quantitative noun was previously exemplified for English alone, there are also French examples, like "un groupe de maisons" (= a group of houses), "un tas de choses" (= a lot of things), etc.

2.3.5 Cardinals

Traditionally, two parallel series of numerals, the **cardinals** (*one*, *two*, *three*, *four*, ...) and the **ordinals** (*first*, *second*, *third*, *fourth*, ...), are distinguished in linguistic studies. The same coverage is adopted for the purposes of the present work (cf. our first chapter), yet a natural language like English offers other related numeral expressions, which deserve to be mentioned here. From a cardinal numeral *n*, as a rule, English grammar derives the *nth* ordinal, but also the multiplier *n times* and fractions with that cardinal qua numerator or a form of the derived ordinal (mostly pluralized) qua denominator. E.g., given *four* as the value of *n*, one gets *fourth*, *four times*, *four fifths*, etc., *one fourth*, *two fourths*, etc. For some derived numerals (of low numbers), an original item is lexicalized though it is not a regular result of the pertinent affixation or compounding processes: v. *first/second/third*, *once/twice*, *half*. The various numeral expressions of English are determiners when they occur as adnominal dependents, conforming to our characterization of the determinative function, but the distribution of cardinal and ordinal determiners differs from that of related multipliers and fractions. Normally, the former are postdeterminers and the latter predeterminers, cf. (47) and (48) respectively.

(47) a. (the) *three* students
b. a/the *third* attempt

(48) a. *three times* this amount
b. *one-third* the time

The following multilingual survey will deal with cardinals and, in § 2.3.6, ordinals, ignoring multipliers and fractions (but few remarks on the expression of fractionary meaning were provided in § 2.3.4.2 and notes 40, 41). We begin by discussing the particular status of the first cardinal (i.e. the numeral that expresses number 1), because this in various languages is phonologically identical to the indefinite article and syntagmatically tends to behave like it as far as the determinative function is concerned, acting as central determiner. On the contrary, English has two distinct forms, the cardinal *one* and the article *a*(*n*), and the former may sometimes follow the definite article, as in "the *one* book I like best", so that a postdeterminer classification appears adequate (cf. Quirk et al. 1985: § 5.21). As a rule of thumb, the main criteria for appropriate usage of the two English forms can be taken into account and adapted for the distinction between corresponding readings of their uniform translation in another language.

First, whereas *a*(*n*) occurs only as dependent of an explicit nominal head, the distribution of *one* is also pronominal. (Not all occurrences of *one* heading/

replacing a noun phrase are numeral – see, e.g., "the *one* I have" or "*one* must be careful about *one*'s investments" – but for the present purposes we neglect a discussion on the matter.) Given the Generalization for Major Determiners which we stated in chapter 1, it is clear that the numeral has 'major' categorial status, contrary to the article. By the same token, the article reading must be excluded for the pronominal occurrences of any form that looks ambiguous between indefinite article and first cardinal in some language.

The second criterion to be considered, like the others that will follow, allows us to discriminate between the readings of adnominal occurrences: exploiting again the major vs. minor distinction, we are able to predict that the numeral can take modifiers, unlike the article. This prediction is borne out by English examples, as in (49a) (from Van Eynde 1994: p. 41), which sounds fine with *one* but ungrammatical or at least quite anomalous with *a*[47]. Likewise, only the numeral reading of the corresponding Italian form (ambiguous in isolation) is compatible with the modifier in translation (49b).

(49) a. There is *exactly* $\left\{\begin{array}{c} \textit{one} \\ ?{*}\,\textit{a} \end{array}\right\}$ car in the whole street

b. C'è *esattamente una* automobile in tutta la strada

Third criterion: since the article is a central determiner, only *one* or the numeral reading of an ambiguous form in another language can (occasionally) exploit the postdeterminer status typical of numerals, so as to follow a central determiner. We have already exemplified the phenomenon for 'the *one* N'-NPs in English, but a similar behaviour is found in German, a language with the ambiguous form. E.g., (50) shows the first cardinal (and not the homonymous article) preceded by a demonstrative central determiner.

(50) Ich habe nur dies *eine* Exemplar
'I have only this one (= single) sample'

Fourth criterion: *one* occurs in contrast with plural cardinals, in various contexts involving coordination ("*one* or *two* friends", "the *thousand* and *one* nights") or other correlation patterns ("*one* man in a *thousand*", "*one* time out of *three*"). For some constructions, the plural cardinal can be replaced by

[47] Of course, one can always come across some dubious example. For instance, "There is not a single car in the whole street" is a fully grammatical and acceptable sentence where negation concerns the number of cars (= not even one), so that somebody could claim that *not* modifies the indefinite article modified by *single*. It is not a necessary conclusion, though, because the same semantic effect may well be achieved if *single* modifies the head noun – as in the NP "single individuals" – and negation the whole NP introduced by the article. (This, indeed, is an option available for the scope of *not*, as one can see from examples of contrast like "not a car, but a track", "not the students, but the professors", "not Mary, but Bill", etc., showing that the nominal is in the focus of negation, not the article.)

a non-numeral quantitative, as in "John has *one* secretary now, whereas he used to have *three/many*". A related case is the use of *one* in contrast with *(an)other*, because this special ordinal (v. § 2.3.6 below) implicitly conveys the numeral information that a second element in some set is referred to: "I've been busy with *one* thing or *another*", "*One* man went this way, the *other* that", "We overtook *one* car after *another* / the *other*" (Quirk et al. 1985: § 6.54). There are counterparts of all the above types of correlative construction in the languages with ambiguous form, whose numeral reading can be selected according to the same criterion. Interestingly, Italian allows the first cardinal to follow the definite article (cf. our third criterion) only in contexts of the *one* ... *other* type: e.g., "l'*una* cosa non esclude l'*altra*" (= the one thing does not exclude the other), "nell'*un* caso e nell'*altro*" (= in the one case and in the other).

The fifth and last criterion we want to mention acknowledges that *one* is also used as "the stressed equivalent of the indefinite article" (Quirk et al. 1985: p. 386) in contexts where previous criteria do not apply. That is, while the discussion so far has pointed out a range of constructions in which the article cannot replace the numeral, now we are concerned with cases of distributional equivalence between the two: e.g., nothing in the sentence "I would like *one* photocopy of this article" would prevent *a* from occurring instead of *one* (cf. Quirk et al. 1985: p. 261). In such English examples, the use of the numeral form provides the only linguistic indication of the speaker's intention of stressing cardinality information[48]. A corresponding version of essentially the same criterion, for languages with homonymous article and numeral, is to apply optional phonetic stress on the word, drawing the hearer's attention to the latter reading; see, in Italian, "Avevo ordinato $\textbf{una}_{str.}$ birra!" (= I ordered [only] *one* beer!). This phenomenon is particularly systematic in Danish, where the relevant stress, typically involving longer vowels and glottal stop, can be indicated by the orthography (Bredsdorff 1956: p. 77):

> "In 'een' [= $\text{one}_{masc./fem.}$[49]] and 'eet' [= $\text{one}_{neut.}$] the double vowels are used to distinguish the numeral form from the indefinite article, 'en' and 'et'. In cases where the numeral cannot be mistaken for the indefinite article a single *e* is sufficient, e.g. 'en og firs' [= one and eighty, eighty-one]."

Unlike the first cardinal, the others, the plural ones, are unproblematically identified in terms of morpho-phonological form in any language we deal with.

[48]Choice of the stressed form "one" is not due to mere emphasis, because the indefinite article has its own emphatic forms, the /eI/ and /æn/ pronunciations of "a" and "an", respectively.

[49]In Danish there is a morphological distinction between *common* gender (= semantically masculine or feminine) and *neuter*.

Nonetheless we find it useful to continue our discussion of this class of numerals in a comparative fashion, drawing an analogy between them and the class of 'quantitative' items in our sense. Both kinds of items show a scalar organization, whose basic requirement was sketched for the scale of quantity/amount in § 2.3.4.1 above: if two items which determine possible 'ranges of reference', i.e. subsets of a given domain D, are ordered according to the pertinent scale, the range of reference determined by the item that occurs higher on the scale has greater (or, at the very least, not smaller) cardinality than the other. The numeral version of the scalar system adds the further constraint $\mathrm{Card}(R_{\mathsf{N+1}}) = \mathrm{Card}(R_{\mathsf{N}}) + 1$ for every pair of adjacent items (in top-down order) on the scale; e.g., when the pair is <*five*, *four*>, the respective cardinalities are indeed 5=4+1 and 4.

Not only the looser way of constraining scalarity, but also the classification into three main types of range of reference, $\forall$ (universal), $\exists$ (existential) and $\neg\exists$ (negated existential), makes a quantitative 'lexical field' much more general than the series of cardinals (cf. § 2.3.4.1 again). Any cardinal numeral used as the sole determinative dependent of a nominal head is existential, so that the range of reference thus determined is a non-empty set of n elements (according to the value n of the numeral) and need not coincide with the relevant domain D from which the range of reference gets selected. (By means of the NP "*three* students", e.g., one may well refer to n=3 out of $m \geq 3$ relevant students.) This allows us to distinguish the cardinals proper from quantitatives that enforce a numerically precise cardinality constraint (unlike most other items that belong to the same class). In particular, the cardinality $=2$ constraint of 'dual' quantitatives is imposed on the domain D and not directly on their range of reference, or else a $\neg\exists$-type dual like *neither* would be impossible; it is the $\forall$-type status of *both*, as well as *beide* in German, *(entr)ambos* in Spanish, etc., that causes the subset concerned by reference to coincide with the binary domain (i.e. $R_{\mathsf{Q}}=D=\{\mathbf{a}_1, \mathbf{a}_2\}$).

Whereas the scale of quantitatives is a closed system, bounded by the opposite $\forall/\neg\exists$ polarities, the scale of cardinals begins with a word for '1' [50], but is open in that it grows infinitely in the other direction. To the extent that

[50] Indeed, in our view, the cardinal scale does not begin with a word expressing number 0, which is the cardinality of the empty set and therefore negates existential reference. Looking at English, we see that any such word "is replaced, in general use, by the negative determiner *no* or the pronoun *none*" (Leech & Svartvik 1975: p. 254). The rare occurrences of *zero* as a determiner in non-mathematical examples (like "This job has *zero* interest") are explained by classifying it as a $\neg\exists$-type quantitative, in fact a marginal stylistic variant of *no*. After all, $\neg\exists$-determination is simply another case of numerically precise quantitative notion that has to be distinguished from the one of cardinal determiners, as we have already done in the case of duals. The only sense in which *zero*, *naught* and the like are 'numerals' is that of being proper names of number 0, a sense irrelevant to determination.

infinite is (rarely) used as a determiner in expressions of non-mathematical discourse like "*infinite* times", one might consider it as the upper bound of the cardinal series, but the maths reflected by the speakers' numeral system in ordinary language is too simple to account for that. In terms of the relevant constraint stated above, there is obviously no numeral N that licenses <*infinite*, N> as a pair of adjacent items on the scale, whose ranges of reference would be infinite and finite, respectively, but with the cardinality of the former just adding +1 to the cardinality of the latter. Since *infinite* satisfies only the looser, 'quantitative'-style condition that the number it expresses be greater than the cardinality of any finite range of reference, to classify it as a cardinal determiner would interrupt the continuity of the cardinal series. As a matter of fact, it simply appears to have the linguistic status of a vague multal item, related to *many*, *umpteen*, or similar; this is confermed by the occurrence of its adverbial form as modifier in "*infinitely* many".

We can treat the infiniteness of the numeral series as a particular instance of the classical problem of showing how a language "makes infinite use of finite means" (cf. Chomsky 1965: Preface). Since the finiteness of human mind would not allow the speaker to memorize an infinite number of arbitrarily different lexical items, just few words are taken as primitives of the numeral system, and all the other elements of the series are derived by some generative mechanisms of language. Concretely, these can be morphological mechanisms of affixation and compounding whereby complex words derive from simpler ones, but also coordination, which is typical of syntax and, what's more, falls outside our grammatical coverage (v. chapter 1 above). Note that the same language can behave quite differently in different parts of its numeral system: the English system makes extensive use of compounding (as in *twenty-four*, compound of *twenty* and *four*), yet the cardinals from 13 to 19 add the derivational affix "-teen" to the corresponding primitive numeral (as in *six* → *sixteen*). Moreover, the extent to which a certain mechanism applies may vary depending on the language: in English, coordination is not used until *a/one hundred and one*, while Spanish normally resorts to it instead of compounding, starting from *diez y seis* ('ten and six' = 16).

Other differences between languages are found in their way of expressing multiples of ten from 20 to 90. Many modern languages derive the relevant numerals consistently with the decimal system, insofar as the corresponding word of the primitive series – from 2 to 9 – is added some derivational affix that practically means 'multiplied by 10'.[51] However, numeral items of certain languages turn out to reflect a numeration system having a base other than

[51] This morphological process can be blurred by allomorphism phenomena, but a sample language where it mostly takes place in a transparent fashion is German, which uses the suffix "-zig", as in *neun* (= 9) → *neunzig* (= 90).

ten. Such differences arose in ancient cultures because of the different ways of counting with reference to parts of the body: from binary systems, originally motivated by parts of the body forming pairs (like eyes, hands, arms, etc.), to decimal systems based on the 10 fingers of two hands, or vigesimal systems based on the 20 digits of hands and feet taken together (v. Milewski 1970). Among the languages we cover, Danish and French show residuals of a vigesimal system in the numerals expressing some multiples of 10 as multiples of 20, e.g. *quatre-vingt* ('four[-times]-twenty' = 80) in French. Especially remarkable is the Danish method with fractionary multipliers:

> "The numeral 'halvtreds' [= 50] is an abbreviated form of 'halvtredsindstyve', which literally means 'half third (i.e. $2\frac{1}{2}$) times ... twenty'. Similarly 'tres(indstyve)' [= 60] has the original meaning of 'three times twenty'; 'halvfjerds(indstyve)' [= 70] means 'half fourth (i.e. $3\frac{1}{2}$) times twenty'; 'firs(indstyve)' [= 80] means 'four times twenty'; and 'halvfems (indstyve)' [= 90] means 'half fifth (i.e. $4\frac{1}{2}$) times twenty'. The short forms of the cardinals given in the list above ... are generally used, but it is possible (e.g. for special emphasis) to use the long forms".
>
> Bredsdorff (1956: p. 77)

A further way of expressing numbers that is available in natural languages resorts to some lexically and morphologically primitive noun with the same numerical meaning as one of the items of the ordinary cardinal series, whether primitive or derived. Sample English nouns of the kind are *couple*/*pair* (i.e. *two*), *dozen* (i.e. *twelve*), *gross* (i.e. *twelve dozens*) and *myriad* (i.e. *ten thousand*), but potentially the class is open: a neologism, coined by the American mathematician E. Kasner and accepted by dictionaries, is *googol*, which stands for the number represented as 1 followed by 100 zeros (= 10^{100}). Drawing on Jackendoff (1977: § 5.5), we call the words in question 'seminumerals' when they require a preceding article or other determiner, combine with a subsequent nominal without any interposing preposition and appear with invariably singular morphology (irrespective of the number of the whole construction); e.g., "a/two *dozen* eggs". The same nouns of English, however, fulfil standard agreement in an alternative reading, which is often used in the plural without preceding determiner and only combines with a subsequent nominal through the preposition "of"; e.g., "*dozens* of eggs".

The latter reading bears a close resemblance to the case of those quantitative or collective ('group'-type) nouns we have touched on in § 2.3.4.2, so that similar conclusions plausibly apply here, making a noun like *dozens* the head **Q** of the resulting noun phrase **Q** + PP. The status of the seminumeral reading is less clear and we leave the problem open for research extending the framework to be detailed in the next chapters. Now we content ourselves with the remark that also some items which are an integral part of the cardinal series show the two types of morpho-syntactic behaviour in English, as noticed by Jackendoff (1977: p. 131): "Though *hundred*, *thousand* and *million* are seminumerals, *hundreds*, *thousands* and *millions* are group nouns; thus we have the contrast of *six million men* ... vs. the somewhat fusty *six millions of men*" (or, to be sure, the numerically imprecise but linguistically standard *millions of men*).

2.3.6 Ordinals

Finally, let us turn to the notion of 'ordinal'. A numeral of this kind is simply an item whose numerical value indicates the corresponding position in a sequence, formed by ordering the elements of the domain under consideration. Often the context is the main or only source of information allowing one to infer an extralinguistic criterion which the ordering is based on. Yet there are NPs making the criterion explicit at least in part by means of some descriptive expression – like the PP in "the *second* student **on the right**", the relative clause in "the *first* person **who comes along**", or the superlative qualifying adjective in "the *third* **oldest** building" (cf. van Eijck & Alshawi 1992).

As we have mentioned in § 2.3.5, a strict parallelism exists between the two series of numerals, because:

- "ordinal numerals have a one-for-one relation with the cardinals: *first/one*, *second/two*, *third/three*, *fourth/four*, *twentieth/twenty*, etc." (Quirk et al. 1985: p. 262);
- normally the former derive from the latter by affixation (of "-th" in English, "-ième" in French, "-(s)te" in German, "-esimo" in Italian, and so on).

However, the class of ordinals is broader than the strictly numeral series: "'general ordinals' ... like *next*, *last*, *past*, *(an)other* ... resemble the ordinal numerals grammatically and semantically" (ibid.) and therefore are grouped with them here. The repertory of general ordinals is quite heterogeneous, but we can make sense out of it by thinking in terms of the ordinal counterpart of relevant 'quantitatives' (rather than cardinals). In few examples, like *umpteen* → *umpteenth* or the Italian *infinito/i* → *infinitesimo/i*, such a relationship is made explicit by the morpho-phonological form, deriving a 'multal' ordinal from the corresponding quantitative item through the same suffix used for numeral ordinals.[52]

[52] On the multal quantitative status of (the expressions of) infinity in ordinary language, see § 2.3.5 above. Note also that a peculiar example of ordinal with the ending of numeral ones, but not corresponding to any cardinal or quantitative, is offered by *nth* and its translations *(é)nième* in French, *x-te* in German, *enésimo* in Spanish, etc. At least in some languages, the pertinent word has also a non-mathematical use as general ordinal with multal meaning, roughly equivalent to *umpteenth*. See in Italian, e.g., "Te lo dico per l'*ennesima* volta" (literally: I tell you for the 'nth' [= umpteenth] time).

Another sort of correspondence, involving parallelism instead of derivation, emerges at the morpho-phonological level in English because of the superlative ending "-st" shared by the pairs *fewest/most* and *first/last*. Each pair indicates the extremes of a sequence, which in the case of the former pair is based on decreasing/increasing cardinality of subsets obtained as we mentioned in § 2.3.4.2. Indeed the first numeral ordinal has also a 'general ordinal' value, symmetric to that of *last*: they can be seen as opposite superlatives of the relevant type of order (just like *fewest* and *most* are opposite superlatives of quantity, *worst* and *best* opposite superlatives of quality, *smallest* and *biggest* opposite superlatives of size, etc.). The symmetry is confirmed by the numeral-like function that *last*, or its equivalent in other languages, is assigned as the beginning of an ordinal series in reverse order. The items of the series mean 'N*th* from the end', for any intended value N, and in fact can be expressed by a corresponding syntactic paraphrase, but there is also a (normally rather small) number of words derived from the 'first from the end' one. E.g., *avant-dernier* (= penultimate, literally 'before-last') in French, *antepenúltimo* (= third last, literally 'before-penultimate') in Spanish, *viertletzt* (literally 'fourth-last') in German, etc.

Since the notion of superlative equally bears on quantitatives and general ordinals, one may wonder whether the same happens to the non-superlative notion of comparison. In § 2.3.4, such paucal/multal comparatives as *fewer/more* were assumed to decrease/increase some implicit set-cardinality value to be located on the quantitative scale. It is readily seen that corresponding ordinals should decrease/increase the implicit (value N of the N*th*) position of some element to be located according to the sequence concerned: general ordinals like *previous/next* or *precedent/subsequent* (and their translations in other languages) do fulfil exactly that function. Moreover, the pair *former/latter*, morpho-phonologically marked by the comparative ending "-er", is available in English when positional comparison focuses on an ordered domain with two elements only. Thus the ordinals *former* and *latter* are also 'duals' (rather than numerals strictly speaking), in the sense we made clear for *both*-type quantitatives in § 2.3.4.1 (cf. § 2.3.5 too).

Even languages that lack peculiar words with 'dual' meaning may well enforce an ordered-pair restriction on the domain, in contexts of contrast between the first cardinal and the ordinal translating *other* [53], used together with the definite article in the singular. An alternative definite determiner (like the possessive in "her *other* sister", e.g.) can replace the definite article and preserve the effect of dual restriction, which disappears when the 'other'-type word is used in the plural or with determiners devoid of definiteness. One such deter-

[53] A particularly interesting case is the Danish ordinal *anden* (or *andet*, neutral form), which means 'second' as numeral and 'other' as general, non-numeral item.

miner is indeed the indefinite article, yet English in the same case resorts to the form *another*: "although spelt as a single word, [it] is to be considered a fusion of the two words *an* and *other*" (Quirk et al. 1985: p. 389). So, *another* takes up central determiner position by replacing the article, contrary to ordinal postdeterminers (the norm already exemplified in (47b), § 2.3.5). Spanish ones occur also after the head noun: "los números *primeros*" (= the prime numbers), "tu tío *segundo*" (= your great-uncle, literally 'second uncle'), "página *tercera*" (= third page), etc.

2.4 Conclusions

It is time to gather up the threads of our fairly detailed presentation of the different kinds of expressions with determinative function. A concise overview w.r.t. some (cross-linguistic) meaning components, which emerge from the empirical study carried out so far, is meant to pave the way for a comprehensive theoretical schema to be developed in the next chapters.

From the standpoint adopted here, it is essential that a theoretical reconstruction of determinative meaning specifies how different types of reference thus determined are encoded through the linguistic content of words with a related function. Following a common idea of modern grammarians, we shall assume that information on word meaning is provided in the lexical entries of the grammatical system by means of features, formally analogous to the phonologic and morpho-syntactic features in the same entries. (The notion of 'feature' was presented by chapter 1, in connection with the decomposition of morpho-syntactic parts of speech.) Features encoding a semantic concept like [+/–ABSTRACT], [+/–ANIMATE], [+/–HUMAN], etc., were originally introduced into the 'standard' version of generative grammar (Chomsky 1965) with a view to impose 'selectional restrictions' on the subcategorization frames of lexical heads, but the need to featurize also information of the sort our study deals with has been acknowledged at times. Chomsky (1975), e.g., proposed a tentative feature [+/– DEFINITE], "which determines the set that is the subject of predication, i.e., either the full set denoted or a subset of it" (ibid.); this interpretation of the definiteness feature, in our opinion, is oversimplified, but bears a clear resemblance to the one we will employ.

In particular, we intend to preserve a discrete (rather than vague or fuzzy) opposition between [+DEFINITE] and [– DEFINITE], contrary to Chesterman's (1991: p. 182) claim that "definiteness is ultimately not a binary phenomenon at all, but a scalar one":

(51)	**most indefinite**	$\emptyset_{\text{ind.}}$	*some*	*a*	*the*	$\emptyset_{\text{def.}}$	**most definite**
		(0)	(0.2)	(0.4)	(0.8)	(1)	

Let us have a look at (51), his scale of increasing definiteness for the English article system, where the five forms considered are the articles proper – viz. *a* and *the* – or can be used to fill gaps in their distribution. The latter case covers *some*, which substitutes for the indefinite article with mass and plural nouns, and two different senses of 'Ø-determination' [54]: the indefinite sense (= $Ø_{ind.}$), with essentially the same function as mass or plural *some*, and the definite (= $Ø_{def.}$), corresponding to the lack of article with proper names. The most controversial part of Chesterman's treatment is actually his decision to replace a binary feature of definiteness with one whose additional values are decimals, ranging from 0 (= '–') to 1 (= '+') qua extremes, so that the assignment of values interpreted as degrees of definiteness on the scale (51) prevents a clear-cut division between indefinite and definite forms (ibid., § 9.3.3).

Such a reinterpretation of (in)definiteness resorts to utterly artificial assignments of decimal values in order to achieve some fuzziness effect that does not look motivated by the linguistic data at issue [55], because Chesterman is just confusing what we would classify as an instance of *gradatum* with one of *continuum* (cf. § 2.2.2 above for the distinction). It can be hardly questioned that a clear-cut boundary separating the indefinite forms from the definite ones, in (51), is intuitively located between *a* and *the*, while allowing the identification of different degrees of definiteness or indefiniteness on two separate scales. Thus, even if we may well accept that some uses of *the* – say, in case of plural NPs – are considered less prototypically definite than a proper name without article, this does not mean that the definite article is also indefinite to a degree and, by the same token, only slightly more definite than the indefinite article. Here we treat definiteness and indefiniteness as two well-distinguished concepts, under the system we started sketching in § 2.3.1, and we assume that also the internal gradations of each concept can be traced back to such basically discrete conditions as presence of a determiner vs. Ø-determination, singular vs. plural, or similar.

How to reconcile distinctions between discrete concepts with the 'scalar' semantic organization of some lexical field is a question that appears especially relevant for the *quantitative* kind of determiners, in the sense previously made clear in § 2.3.4.1. As we discussed therein, the lexical field of those items can be ordered in terms of a scale where various degrees of 'non-null quantity' occur between two extremes, the maximally positive and negative polarities of the

[54] Respectively called 'zero' and 'null' by Chesterman (1991), but we prefer to elaborate on our 'Ø' notation.

[55] Chesterman himself seems to be partly aware of the problem: "Of course, we so far lack empirical evidence for the actual numerical values of ... degree, and it is likely that these values themselves are intrinsically imprecise. Fuzziness ... does no more than (temporarily) postpone the introduction of non-fuzzy arbitrariness one stage deeper" (ibid., p. 196).

scale, respectively corresponding to 'total quantity' and 'null quantity'. Yet this scalar aspect does not prevent us from setting clear-cut boundaries at least for the three general concepts thus identified, inasmuch as they allow definition on a logical basis, yielding a triadic typology of reference: universality ($= \forall$), existentiality ($= \exists$) and negated existential ($= \neg\exists$). Even if we acknowledged that quantitative items may have vague meaning as shown by *many*, *few*, etc., the resulting continuum, being confined to degrees of non-null quantity, is internal to the existential part of the scale, without affecting its conceptual separation from the other two parts (i.e. the extremes).

Leaving aside a more formal modelling of the whole system at least for the moment, a strong point of our few, basic notions of reference determination is that they have quite far-reaching linguistic coverage. On the one end, the importance of a feature allowing us to specify lexical items w.r.t. definiteness (or the opposite) should be evident, in view of several kinds of determiners and 'self-determining' nominals to be marked as [+DEFINITE]: besides the definite article, demonstratives, (definite) possessives and personal pronouns, as well as proper names. On the other hand, we can readily see that at least $\exists$, among the types introduced for quantitative items, proves relevant to further kinds of expressions: cardinal numerals (previously discussed in § 2.3.5) and, moreover, the indefinite article, or the corresponding reading of 'Ø-determination' (i.e. '$\emptyset_{\text{ind.}}$' in (51) above) with plural and non-count common nouns.

What makes the quantitative determiners unique, compared with any other paradigmatic kind of determination, is the fact that they are reciprocally related and distinguished in such a way as to form a lexical field covering all the three 'logical' types $\forall$, $\exists$ and $\neg\exists$. Indeed, it instantiates these by few words that are pure, prototypical expressions of each given type, as in the case of *every*, *some* or *no*, even if the same field includes also items conveying additional quantitative information, like the duality restriction of *both*, *either* and *neither*, or the multal/paucal degrees expressed by *many*/*few*. The difference from cardinals (as the semantically closest kind of other determiners) was already made clear in § 2.3.5: any such numeral adds a cardinality constraint to the basic type of reference associated with the NP, which is existential 'by default' when there are no co-occurring determiners of a different kind [56]. Of course, at least the case of cardinals shows that in a general account of determiners our basic binary system must be added features with infinitely possible semantic values (e.g. lists), a point to be addressed in the next chapters by upgrading the formalism to adequately expressive feature structures.

[56] In examples like "*all* seven books" and "*no* seven books" the type of reference, which becomes respectively universal and negated existential, is contributed by the first determiner of the NP and not by the numeral, whose existential import can be overridden according to a mechanism that chapter 4 will touch on.

Chapter 3

Basic Semantic Modelling

3.1 Preamble

A common approach to the representation of meaning in modern linguistics, ever since pioneering work by Katz & Fodor (1963), Katz & Postal (1964) and Chomsky (1965), is to integrate some sort of **semantic component** into the grammar of a natural language (in a broad sense of 'grammar' stemming from Chomsky's theory). The real nature and organization of that component, the representations it is meant to deliver and their connection with other aspects of the grammatical description of natural language sentences, however, have always been highly controversial. Here we will not try to summarize a debate which went on for several decades – involving linguists, psychologists, philosophers, logicians and computer scientists – and is still lively, but we can derive from it a few methodological points, to be taken into account in the developments of our work starting from the present chapter.

For one thing, we expect a semantic theory to establish close links with the overt grammatical form of linguistic expressions in order to be cognitively realistic, as Jackendoff (1983: § 1.5) has stressed:

> "Under the reasonable hypothesis that language serves the purpose of transmitting information, it would be perverse not to take as a working assumption that language is a relatively efficient and accurate encoding of the information it conveys. To give up this assumption is to refuse to look for systematicity in the relationship between syntax and semantics. A theory's deviation from efficient encoding must be rigorously justified, for what appears to be an irregular relationship between syntax and semantics may turn out merely to be a bad theory of one or the other."

More specifically, we think that an optimal implementation of such a methodological position becomes feasible if some version of **compositionality** (in the sense already introduced by chapter 2) is applied for the task of 'translating' surface phrase structures into corresponding semantic representations. In the abstract, the semantic component of a grammatical system of the kind we have in mind "is plausibly viewed as a function which, given a local subtree where translations are associated with the daughter nodes, yields ... a translation associated with the mother" (Gazdar et al. 1985: p. 208).

It clearly follows that compositionality for us is a structural constraint, the semantic correspondent of an 'immediate constituent analysis' as reflected by syntactic rules – or structurally equivalent principles – of a phrase structure grammar, inasmuch as these can only concern a mother-daughter (i.e. strictly 'local') subtree pattern. Hence the definition of *interpreted phrase structure grammars* which we adopted since the beginning of chapter 1. Other versions of compositionality are possible, whereby rule-to-rule correspondences between syntax and semantics apply even if the former does not just stick to phrase structure constraints (as it may involve some sort of transformational rules *à la* Montague 1973) [1]. But the approach we have chosen is consistent with our grammatical views and, in addition, proves more liberal than the alternative, because a compositional interpretation via structural patterns of trees makes the semantic component of the grammar compatible with whatever syntactic rules (or principles) may be designed to generate the same trees, thus enhancing modularity.

There is another peculiarity in the specific compositional technique that we intend to adopt. Although compositionality could be literally worked out in terms of a translation procedure between two different formal languages for syntax and semantics (as done by many authors), we deem it quite appealing to achieve equivalent results by means of a uniform notation encoding syntactic, semantic and further linguistic information. Grammatical systems like ours identify the relevant tool with a formalism of 'features': attribute-value pairs arising from the analysis of lexical entries as well as nodes of phrase structure trees. Apart from formal aspects of the feature notion (an issue to be treated in this chapter by adding more technical details to what was said in the previous part of the book), it is worth pointing out the linguistic status of represention where morpho-syntactic and semantic features get associated.

[1] The rule-based type of compositionality coincides with the structural, pattern-based type when each syntactic rule taken as input for semantic correspondence describes precisely a mother-daughter subtree pattern. It is a case that might look ideal for interpreted phrase structure grammar, since the system could be provided with "pairs consisting of (a) a phrase structure rule and (b) a semantic rule which specifies how the constituent analyzed by (a) is to be translated" (Gazdar et al. 1985: p. 206). However, that technique – adopted by Gazdar (1982), e.g. – does not work in case of modern systems of phrase structure grammar where a considerable part of the morpho-syntactic information found in trees and required for semantic interpretation (= 'translation') is not specified by phrase structure rules, since it follows from general principles of feature percolation, linear order, etc., as our chapters 4-5 will show. The resulting subtree patterns are indeed what must be looked at.

The idea, loosely borrowed from Saussure (1916: ch. 1 of part 1) by Pollard & Sag (1987; 1994), is that of a **sign** as linguistic unit in which both the expression/form (= Saussure's *signifiant*) and its content/meaning (= Saussure's *signifié*) are simultaneously encoded and accessible, at any rak of structural analysis.

Whereas Saussure said little about the meaning of signs, apart from the remark that it would be some sort of mental concept, Pollard & Sag (1987: p. 82) argue that "even if we think that signs are associated with concepts, we cannot give a truly semantic account of language unless we relate those concepts to something external". Consequently, an adequate 'sign-based' framework should be grounded on the logical tradition of semantic studies, which goes with the distinction between two main types or aspects of meaning, the denotational (hence truth-conditional) and the pragmatic, as we have made clear in chapter 2. In a way reminiscent of Morris' (1938) semiotic theory [2], the 'sign' unit can be organized in terms of a triadic relation linking the linguistic expression to its denotational meaning and a context of use. To some extent, the present chapter will have to consider both aspects of sign interpretation (and their connections).

Thus the starting point for section 3.2 is a thorough discussion of the distinction between truth conditions and pragmatic factors in a fundamental case of reference determination, viz. definiteness as conveyed through the singular definite article (but the approach will be extended to plural definiteness, in § 3.3.2.2). Our related presentation of logical background, whose knowledge proves relevant for grasping an adequate compositional interpretation of the Noun Phrase, is completed by introducing selected aspects of **Generalized Quantifier Theory**, in the sense of Barwise & Cooper (1981), among others. To incorporate the resulting treatment of determination, the semantic representations that a grammar assigns to natural language expressions must be equivalent to model-theoretically interpreted formulae of a suitable language of logic. But then we need to make a feature notation equally expressive, since we have opted for grammatical systems where features provide the semantic representation which annotates a tree node (in parallel to morpho-syntactic information). Feature-theoretic semantics indeed is the main subject of section 3.3, drawing on the **Head-driven Phrase Structure Grammar** (HPSG) by Pollard & Sag (1994), a 'sign-based' framework that looks well-suited at least for our representational purposes. The chapter, as usual, ends with a section of conclusions (namely 3.4).

[2] There is a terminological difference insofar as Morris called *sign* the expression alone and *semiosis* its relation to (the aspects of) meaning, while we follow Pollard & Sag (1987; 1994), who extend the Saussurian, relational sense of *sign*.

3.2 Logical background

3.2.1 Logical form and definiteness conditions

In First Order Logic (FOL) approaches to natural language semantics stemming from the seminal work by G. Frege, B. Russell, A. Tarski and others, quantifiers are variable-binding operators ('$\forall x$', '$\exists y$', etc.) that can be taken to correspond to quantitative determiners like *every* and *some*, but prefixed to a formula qua counterpart of a whole clause. Quantifiers of the kind go with a view of quantified NPs in natural language as expressions whose overt grammatical form is 'logically misleading', in that it can disguise a considerably dissimilar (aspect of the) **logical form** on which the denotational semantic interpretation is based. Hence the need for some non-compositional conversion from the grammatical form of relevant sentences to the associated logical form, the result being represented by 'logical translations' in traditional FOL style. E.g., compare the syntactically rather uniform subject-predicate constructions (52) of English with their respective FOL translations[3], which in the quantified cases (53b)-(53d) involve quantifier-prefixing, variable-binding and the introduction of propositional connectives.

(52) a. $[_S [_{NP}$ John$] [_{VP}$ walks$]]$

b. $[_S [_{NP}$ *every* man$] [_{VP}$ walks$]]$

c. $[_S [_{NP}$ *a/some* man$] [_{VP}$ walks$]]$

d. $[_S [_{NP}$ *no* man$] [_{VP}$ walks$]]$

(53) a. walks(John)

b. $\forall x\,[\text{man}(x) \supset \text{walks}(x)]$

c. $\exists x\,[\text{man}(x) \wedge \text{walks}(x)]$

d. $\neg\exists x\,[\text{man}(x) \wedge \text{walks}(x)]$

Under this system, whereas a proper name is readily interpreted as 'individual(-denoting) term' filling an argument position of a given predicate (as

[3]Actually, English words are kept for convenience as non-logical constants (i.e. the type of expressions whose denotation depends on the models/worlds/contexts of the interpretation but is constant in each given model/world/context). We do adopt a run-of-the-mill logical notation for variables (i.e. the type of expressions whose denotation systematically varies by ranging over the 'universe of discourse') and the items that can be treated as 'syncategorematic expressions' (in the sense already mentioned in chapter 2) or equivalenty as logical constants (i.e. the type of expressions whose denotation is defined in the same general way across models/worlds/contexts). More readable semi-formal paraphrases could be obtained by replacing '$\forall$' with *for every*, '$\exists$' with *for at least one*, '$\neg$' with *not*, '$\supset$' with *only if* (= *if ... then*) and '$\wedge$' with *and*.

done by *John* in (53a))[4], any NP that cannot be assigned a denotation of the individual type is assumed to contribute separate quantificational and predicative contents to the overall interpretation of the clause, without translating as a whole denotation-bearing expression. However, it is not always clear which of the two treatments must apply, because of the existence of NPs in the singular introduced by the definite article, the so-called **definite descriptions**: they appear to have the same referential function as proper names, picking up a definite individual, but structurally combine a determiner with a possibly complex nominal just like the quantified NPs. In Russell's (1905) pioneering approach, a quantificational analysis was intended to capture the definiteness import of such descriptions, at the cost of a rather convoluted logical form. The logical form Russell assigned to the sample sentence "[*the* king of France] is bald", where the subject is a definite description, can be made explicit by the following FOL formula:

(54) $\exists x\, [\text{king}(x, \text{France}) \wedge \forall y\, [\text{king}(y, \text{France}) \supset y = x] \wedge \text{bald}(x)]$

The logical pattern shown by (54) meets the definiteness notion we introduced in chapter 2, insofar as it encodes an 'existential' condition (i.e. there is at least one king of France in the relevant context) and a 'uniqueness' condition (i.e. there is not more than one king of F. in the relevant context)[5], besides the main predication (i.e. the individual satisfying both conditions is bald). By the same token, it accounts for the difference from a corresponding case with the indefinite article or *some*, since the logical form of "[*a*/*some* king of France] is bald" would simply lack the uniqueness condition (= the second conjunct in (54)); cf. (53c) above for an example of that kind. It is also worth saying that Russell did not question the right of using a more compact notation, closer to the overt grammatical form of the English sentence, like (55) below (see, e.g., Martin 1987: § 8.1.3). But (55), in a Russellian analysis, is just shorthand for (54), and thus the expression '$\imath x \mid \text{king}(x, \text{France})$' (to be read: 'the one and only x such that x is king of France') does not receive any semantic interpretation of its own.

(55) $\text{bald}\,(\imath x \mid \text{king}(x, \text{France}))$

On the other hand, Russell's critics raised the issue of the empirical, linguistic inadequacy of his treatment and challenged the assumption that the conditions of definiteness be analytically encoded in the logical form (or, more radically, the assumption that any logical form disguised by the overt grammatical form exist at all). The Russellian analysis was especially criticized by

[4] The logicians' predicate-argument notation is meant to reflect functional application, an idea that will deserve further discussion in § 3.2.2.

[5] As a matter of fact, the (sub)formula '$\forall y\, [\text{king}(y, \text{France}) \supset y = x]$' is logically equivalent to '$\neg\exists y\, [\text{king}(y, \text{France}) \wedge \neg\, y = x]$', but spares us the use of negation.

Strawson (1950) because it predicts that a natural language sentence with an 'improper' definite description, i.e. one whose existential or uniqueness conditions are false, is also false (as an obvious consequence of the truth-functional interpretation of conjunction, given (54) above). The prediction clashes with the speakers' intuition that such a sentence is simply judged inappropriate for evaluation of truth and falsity. Strawson's alternative was to claim that the two conditions are not stated or entailed, but presupposed, resorting to a notion of 'presupposition' originally introduced by Frege (1892). In his philosophical remarks on natural language, Frege indeed noticed the existential condition associated with definite descriptions, conceiving it as the presupposition that a definite description must have a denotation (on a par with a corresponding proper name) for a sentence which includes that expression to be true-or-false. Strawson (1950) applied a similar approach to both conditions of the Russellian analysis, in the context of a pragmatic theory of reference.

Also the analysis *à la* Frege-Strawson can be developed into a logical treatment, in such a way that expressions like '$[\iota x \mid \text{king}(x, \text{France})]$' are recasted as genuine individual terms in argument position and get assigned a denotation accordingly. Thus, the denotation of our sample description would be: (i) the only individual **a** whose assignment to x satisfies the embedded formula 'king(x,France)', or (ii) undefined otherwise[6]. At the level of sentences/ formulae in which a description occurs, it is possible to handle formally the truth-value gap resulting from presupposition failure, in case (ii), by means of some three-valued logic or so-called 'supervaluation' techniques (*à la* Van Fraassen 1968); see Martin (1987: § 8.1), for an introductory presentation.

However, a characterization of **presupposition** as purely logico-semantic relationship[7] does not seem to adequately account for the negation of sentences that convey presuppositions (as already noted by Atlas 1977, Levinson

[6]An alternative solution, also stemming from Frege's work, is to assume that all the 'improper' definite descriptions are assigned the same arbitrary denotation, chosen so as to be outside the extension of every predicate (apart perhaps from '='); the standard evaluation of predicate-argument formulae then obtains, yielding *false* for any improper description a predicate applies to. (Cf. Martin 1987: § 8.1.2.) It is worth noticing that this solution was proposed by Frege for the artificial languages of logic, not as an account of the actual behaviour of corresponding natural language expressions. In fact, it is not different from Russell's analysis as far as the dependence of truth-conditions on definiteness conditions is concerned (failure of the latter resulting in falsity in both cases), and therefore does not comply with Strawson's criticism. On the other hand, Russell's analysis has the clear advantage of avoiding the *ad hoc*, philosophically and linguistically counter-intuitive postulation of an arbitrary denotation.

[7]The relationship between two propositions P and Q such that "P presupposes Q iff: whenever P is true or false, Q is true" (Martin 1987: p. 265). But note that the term 'presupposition' commonly stands for both this relationship and the presupposed proposition Q.

1983, van der Sandt 1988 and Blok 1993). Under typical assumptions about the truth-value gap or 'third value' due to presupposition failure – "an infection that corrupts the whole if any part is affected", as Martin (1987: p. 227) puts it – (56b) below would become neither-true-nor-false on a par with the component sentence (56a), but this is not in accordance with the linguistic intuitions. In case there is no king of France, (56a) in isolation is felt inappropriate for the evaluation of truth and falsity, while sentences like (56b) are accepted as appropriate and true by many speakers.[8]

(56) a. The king of France is not bald

b. The king of F. is not bald, because there is no king of F.

(said in reply to somebody's claim that the king of F. is bald)

Similar considerations apply to "The king of France does not exist", which is uncontroversially appropriate and (at present) true, not a self-contradictory sentence both presupposing and denying existence of the king of France.

Now, it would be an implausible solution to assume that negation in natural language is ambiguous between two negation operators, one which preserves the lack of truth-or-falsity and the other which turns such a 'third value' into *false*. The assumption that natural language negation is lexically ambiguous in the way required does not appear to have any independent motivation. By contrast, no doubling of negation operators (nor corresponding lexical ambiguity) is required in Russell's analysis, because the logical form of sentences with definite descriptions allows different options as far as the scope of negation is concerned. That is, **narrow scope** as in:

(57) $\exists x\,[\text{king}(x, \text{France}) \wedge \forall y\,[\text{king}(y, \text{France}) \supset y = x] \wedge \neg\xi(x)]$

vs. **wide scope** as in:

(58) $\neg\exists x\,[\text{king}(x, \text{France}) \wedge \forall y\,[\text{king}(y, \text{France}) \supset y = x] \wedge \xi(x)]$

Intuitions of the speakers are thereby captured if we assume that an ordinary preference for narrow scope negation – corresponding to the interpretation (57) of (56a), given *bald* as ξ – will be overriden in contexts which make it clear that wide scope negation is meant instead. (The preference could be taken to follow from 'conversational maxims' like those proposed by Grice 1967.) Then (58) turns out to be the intended interpretation of (56a) in a (56b) context, or the only acceptable interpretation of "The king of France does not exist", given a semantically redundant 'existence predicate' as ξ (Kamp & Reyle 1993:

[8] Here is a perfectly natural example with a slightly more complex interplay of negation and definiteness: "Mary didn't have lunch with the king of France, because France doesn't have a king".

pp. 250-1; but cf. Dowty et al. 1981: pp. 129-130, for an alternative). The discarded interpretations would indeed result in contradictions.

Moreover, the remark that truth and falsity judgements look inapplicable in case of presupposition failure need not be accounted for by the literal lack of standard semantic values. In pragmatic approaches to the presupposition notion (such as Stalnaker 1970; 1974, Gazdar 1979, Blok 1993), the falsity of some presupposition associated with a sentence simply makes the latter inappropriate, whether *true* or *false*. One may well accept that the sentence be false (in the abstract sense of 'non-correspondence with the facts') as Russell claimed, although the speakers will not overtly judge it in that way, because of the pragmatic inappropriateness overriding an evaluation of truth/falsity irrelevant for language use. This solution has the advantage that the denotational semantics remains unaffected by the non-trivial (and mostly undesired) consequences of any purely logico-semantic account of presuppositions. We mean rejection of standardly valid entailment relations (in three-valued logic), or non-truthfunctionality of propositional connectives (with so-called 'supervaluations'), referring again to Martin's (1987) textbook for technicalities.

Of course, a pragmatic treatment of presuppositions must be able to explain why their failure causes the inappropriateness in question, but the explanation is readily derived from Speech Act Theory. As a first approximation, the requirement that all the presuppositions associated with a sentence need fulfilment can be considered an additional **felicity condition** on the overall speech act performed by uttering the sentence[9]. A more accurate account, drawing on Searle (1969) as we have mentioned in chapter 2, would distinguish between 'illocutionary' and 'propositional' components of that speech act, the latter components being the acts of reference and predication whereby the speaker expresses the propositional content to be asserted (or asked, ordered, etc., in case of a non-declarative sentence). Successful performance of these propositional acts is a necessary (though not sufficient) condition for the felicity of the whole and, in its turn, can be made conditional upon fulfilment of presuppositions. Thus the presupposition of existence and uniqueness associated with a definite description which is uttered in order to perform some act of reference must be fulfilled for that act to be successful.

The most straightforward way of defending a Russellian analysis, by the light of pragmatics, would assume that the two presupposed conditions of definiteness are part of the logical form of the sentence where a definite description occurs, provided the distinction between what is presupposed and what is explicitly expressed – and asserted, if declarative – can be indicated somehow. A

[9]The notion of 'felicity (conditions)' in Speech Act Theory originates from Austin (1962). It is understood that a sentence cannot be felt appropriate in the context of use if the speech act thereby performed proves infelicitous, i.e. not successful.

proposal of the kind was put forward by Grice (1967: ch. 4-5), whose variant analysis of "the king of France is bald" roughly sounds like "there is at least one king of France and there is not more than one king of F. and (*assertion:*) whoever is king of F. is bald", allowing formalization as follows.

(59) $\exists x\,[\text{king}(x, \text{France}) \wedge \forall y\,[\text{king}(y, \text{France}) \supset y = x]\,] \;\wedge$
$\vdash \forall z\,[\text{king}(z, \text{France}) \supset \text{bald}(z)]$

The formula (59) is just meant to recode Russell's original (54), but:

- what used to be the **open formula** 'bald(x)' (with a free variable 'x' to be bound in a broader context) becomes a **closed formula** (with variable binding internal to the formula itself), which can be independently expressed as true or false [10];

- the presupposed definiteness conditions have been separated from the asserted proposition by means of a conventional device, the symbol '$\vdash$' in our sample notation.

Looking at the negative aspects of (59) qua analysis of "the king of France is bald", however, we see that the logical form of such a simple sentence has been made even more complex than before and mixes the standard FOL notation with an extra device like '$\vdash$' (or similar), whose logical status seems dubious or redundant [11]. Furthermore, the inclusion of a presuppositional part makes logical form sensitive to "the 'projection problem' for presuppositions, that is, the problem of stating the conditions under which the presuppositions of components of utterances are either inherited or discarded by successively larger components of utterances" (Pollard & Sag 1994: p. 334). In order to treat some presupposition that gets discarded when the expression $\mathcal{E}$ conventionally associated with it occurs in the broader context of $\mathcal{U}$, a suitable text

[10] Cf. Dowty et al. (1981): "it is usually said that formulas with free variables cannot be either true or false as they stand because the variables themselves do not denote any particular individuals, hence the formulas make no real assertion until the variables have been quantified" (p. 57). To be precise, the denotations of free variables and open formulae (i.e. the respective individuals and truth-values) are relative to an **assignment** (of values to the variables of the logical language), so that they vary accordingly and should not be confused with actual denotations staying constant in each given model/world/context (ibid., pp. 56-66).

[11] This assertion (or 'judgement') symbol, originally introduced by Frege (1879) as part of his *Begriffsschrift*, was denied logical significance by Wittgenstein (1921: § 4.442; 1953: § 22). For a pragmatic device '$\vdash$' not belonging to the logical formula as such, but superimposed on it to introduce the propositional content that undergoes assertion or, more generally, an 'illocutionary act' – on a par with '?' and '!' – cf. Searle (1969: § 2.4). However, the same pragmatic use is compatible with a trivial logico-semantic interpretation (also mentioned by Ajdukiewicz 1935): the unary propositional connective that simply preserves the truth-values of the embedded formula, instead of inverting them as negation ('$\neg$') does.

utterance, $\mathcal{E}$ could be claimed to be ambiguous between two readings, one with presupposition and one without, determining alternative logical forms accordingly. The $\mathcal{U}$ (con)text at issue would reject the former reading, so as to keep only the presupposition-free logical form as desired, but then some 'preference' machinery should ensure that the opposite choice is made by default whenever $\mathcal{E}$ turns out to occur in an ordinary, presupposition-preserving (con)text. The task of formally defining that mechanism does not look trivial and, at any rate, the processing of sentences would be loaded by additional indeterminism resulting from the putative ambiguities.[12]

To avoid these drawbacks, a more radical revision of Russell's analysis is called for, resorting to a system like that of Karttunen (1973) or Karttunen & Peters (1979), which "associates two propositions with a sentence. One is the proposition that it expresses and the other is the proposition that it presupposes or, using the term that they adopt from Grice, conventionally implicates" [13] (Robin Cooper 1983: p. 152). Despite various technical differences, also Gazdar (1979), Heim (1983) and Pollard & Sag (1994: § 8.4.1) have opted for related approaches, which share the idea of an additional proposition to be presupposed in the contexts where the sentence it is conventionally associated with gets uttered. In our case, splitting Grice's previous version (59) as a first approximation, the usual sample sentence with definite description could be assigned the pair (60) qua 'semantic representation' (broadly speaking), where a. – the logical form – encodes what is expressed, or 'propositional content', and b. the associated presupposition.

(60) a. $\forall x\,[\mathrm{king}(x, \mathrm{France}) \supset \mathrm{bald}(x)]$

b. $\exists x\,[\mathrm{king}(x, \mathrm{France}) \wedge \forall y\,[\mathrm{king}(y, \mathrm{France}) \supset y = x]\,]$

The approach exemplified in (60) may as well be dubbed 'pragmatically revised Russellian analysis'. Indeed Russell's original assumption that a definite description plays some quantificational (rather than argumental, individual-denoting) role is preserved, while adopting a revised logical form much simpler than its predecessors, (54) and (59), as definiteness conditions are pragmatic presuppositions divided from it. By the same token, our account of truth-conditions is related but not identical to Russell's: in both, the proposition

[12] Another possible way of addressing the same problem could claim that $\mathcal{E}$ in isolation has only the reading with presupposition, although the corresponding piece of logical form is dropped in a presupposition-free $\mathcal{U}$ (con)text embedding $\mathcal{E}$. Ambiguity would then be avoided at the cost of considerably increasing non-compositionality on the syntax-semantics interface for logical form.

[13] Grice's (1967) characterization of what he calls *conventional implicatures* (as distinguished from 'conversational' ones following from general principles of discourse) shows they are pragmatic presuppositions conventionally conveyed by specific words or constructions.

represented by the logical form is always true-or-false in accordance with two-valued (standard) logic, but the value assigned if a definite description proves 'improper' differs, depending on the versions of the analysis. In his original version, as we mentioned, the falsification of at least one of the definiteness conditions makes the overall proposition false too by conjunction. The revised logical form (60a), on the contrary, turns out to be (trivially) true when there is no king of France, given the truth-table for the '$\supset$' connective; yet there are no consequences for the speakers' judgements, as the corresponding presupposition failure anyway yields pragmatic inappropriateness overriding every concern for truth/falsity.[14]

Actually, two different kinds of objections to the utterance of "The king of France is bald" appear to be legitimate in case there is no such king. The replier may want to point out the inappropriateness of that utterance by means of apt expressions:

(61) { *What do you mean by that?* / *That sounds strange to me.* / *Don't talk nonsense!* } There is no king of France.

The other option consists of expressions more or less overtly negating truth, even if the communication goal remains the same and requires the usual explanation by the replier:

(62) { *What you said is false,* / *That's not true,* / *No, you are wrong,* } because there is no king of France.

The latter way of objecting shifts negation to a **metalinguistic** level, where the presupposition of "The king of France is bald" becomes accessible and can be denied instead of the propositional content. To show how the desired result is achieved, let us consider the following method of evaluating the Semantic Representation (SR) which encompasses both propositions.

Our idea is that judgments of truth or falsity are primarily applied to the whole SR; that is, when the propositional content is associated with a presupposition, there is a joint evaluation of the pair, as if the two propositions

[14]That is, the only cases of the truth-table that prove relevant for the speakers' explicit evaluation of truth/falsity are those in which the lefthand formula (= A) is true, but they are exactly the cases in common with conjunction. Compare:

A	B	$A \wedge B$	$A \supset B$
true	**true**	**true**	**true**
true	***false***	***false***	***false***
false	true	false	true
false	false	false	true

were in conjunction. Still, the SR evaluation is normally equivalent to the evaluation of the propositional content alone, not only in absence of any presupposition 'conventionally implicated' by words or constructions, but also in all ordinary contexts where the associated presupposition is satisfied. Indeed, given a true proposition as presupposed part of the SR, the truth or falsity of the whole SR pair exclusively depends on the other preposition, the expressed part. In case of falsified presupposition, however, the situation is reversed: the truth-functional evaluation of SR yields the same value – **false** – as the presupposition evaluation, due to the truth-table for conjunction, and that's the only value the replier's truth-judgements can make explicit. Since pragmatic inappropriateness affects the proposition expressed, the truth or falsity of this part of SR is irrelevant and consequently ignored by the replier.

Corresponding evaluation results could also be achieved with Grice's logical form inclusive of a presuppositional part (as in (59) above), but we already explained the reasons for making logical form separate from presuppositions. Note that the lack of a conjunction connective to be interpreted, in our 'SR pair' treatment, does not prevent the joint evaluation of the two components as a pragmatic matter, a 'rule of language use' that encompasses their purely semantic, model-theoretic interpretation and adds on to it. Furthermore, in logic there is a clear-cut distinction between an **object language** whose formulae are to be interpreted and the **metalanguage** in which the model-theoretic interpretation gets described, so that the consequences of applying a similar approach to natural languages must be taken into account. Even if only sentences of a single natural language – say, English – are considered[15], it seems clear that some linguistic expressions can be semantically classified as being metalinguistic, i.e. part of a fragment of natural language used as the metalanguage for another fragment. That's indeed the status of English expressions whereby truth-judgements are made explicit, e.g. those cited before in (62).

Likewise, a sentence of the form:

(63) *It is not true that* the king of France is bald

(or equivalent: "*It is false that...*", "*It is not the case that...*") expresses metalinguistic negation and therefore its logical level is not the same as that of the embedded sentence. If p is the propositional content of "the king of France is bald", the status of negation in (63) would not be correctly represented by $\neg p$, understood as formula of the same logical language which p belongs to. Instead, (63) involves quotation within another logical language acting as metalanguage, where metalinguistic negation applies not only to the propositional

[15] Obviously, the *object language* vs. *metalanguage* distinction becomes evident when two different natural languages are involved, e.g. when an English sentence is commented on in French, or vice versa.

content, but to the whole SR, inclusive of presupposition. Hence the pragmatic ambiguity of (63) out of context, since an utterer may want to deny either the propositional content, when the presupposition is true, or the presupposition itself, as our previous discussion has made clear.[16] To complete this picture in a consistent way, though, we have also to show that such a simple sentence as "The king of France is *not* bald", despite its lack of explicit metalinguistic expressions, allows essentially the same sort of pragmatic ambiguity rather than a structural ambiguity in the scope of negation.

We are obviously aware that negation can be ambiguous in scope, e.g. *not* modifies syntactically (the clauses projected by) the modal or the embedded verb of "He may *not* speak about it" (v. Gazdar et al. 1982, Van Eynde 1998, among others). As regards logical ambiguities arising from an interaction with quantifier scope, there are examples like:

(64) Bill didn't see a misprint

a. $\exists x\,[\text{misprint}(x) \wedge \neg\,\text{saw}(\text{Bill}, x)]$

b. $\neg\,\exists x\,[\text{misprint}(x) \wedge \text{saw}(\text{Bill}, x)]$

whose two interpretations have been paraphrased by Karttunen (1969) as 'Bill didn't see a *certain* misprint' (= 64a) and 'Bill didn't see a *single* (i.e. any) misprint' (= 64b).[17] But negation does not give rise to scope ambiguities in such examples with quantified subjects as the a. of (65)-(66); they have no alternative reading meaning the same as the corresponding b. example of wide-scope negation (cf. Lasnik 1972, Hornstein 1984) and therefore preserve surface scope in logical form.

(65) a. Every king of France is not bald

b. Not every king of France is bald

(66) a. A/Some king of France is not bald

b. No king of France is bald

Since the only difference between the a. sentences and "The king of France is not bald" is made by the definite article, which has quantificational status on a par with the other determiners in all versions of the Russellian approach, it seems plausible to generalize unambiguous negation to the case with definite description.

[16] Semi-formally, one could represent (63) as: '*p and q*' *is false*, a metalinguistic statement entailing the truth of '$\neg\,[p \wedge q]$', which is equivalent to '$[\neg p] \vee [\neg q]$'. That is, the inference yields an alternative (= disjunction) between our two cases of negation, for the propositional content p or the presupposition q.

[17] That is, *certain* and *single* (in the relevant readings) could be added to (64) in order to disambiguate the scope of the indefinite NP as wide (= wider than negation scope) and narrow (= narrower than negation scope), respectively.

The consequence for our ('pragmatically revised') version of the Russellian analysis is that "The king of France is not bald" gets the same logical form as the universally quantified sentence (65a):

(67) $\forall x\,[\text{king}(x, \text{France}) \supset \neg\, \text{bald}(x)]$

while their full meaning differs because of a separate, presupposed proposition showing the definiteness conditions conventionally associated with "the" (the (60b) that we have provided before). Now, let us consider a context where the existential condition is falsified, i.e. there is no king of France. If we are dealing with some ordinary context, in which the presupposition is expected to hold, inappropriateness results, ovverriding the evaluation of (67) as trivially true[18]. On the other hand, that truth-value becomes relevant for the special kind of context in which the speaker cancels the presupposition (and thus restores appropriateness and the evaluation of truth/falsity) by adding "because there is no king of France", or equivalent. That is, the resulting sentence – repeated below as (68a) – essentially says that "The king of France is not bald" is true just because the pertinent A condition in the $A \supset B$ body of (67) is false.

(68) a. The king of F. is not bald, because there is no king of F.

b. ?? The king of F. is bald, because there is no king of F.

The question raised by this simple account is why a presupposition-canceling (con)text of the "because there is no..." kind, or equivalent, proves exclusively appropriate for cases where predication is negated – v. *not bald* in (68a) – and not for the corresponding cases with positive predication. Nothing in our argument so far, apart from stipulation, would prevent acceptance of the odd (68b) too, as a sentence saying that "The king of France is bald" is true just because the pertinent A condition in the $A \supset B$ body of its logical form (= (60a) above) is false. Then a few remarks on the actual role of negation in canceling presuppositions are called for.

That an intervening expression $\mathcal{E}$ of a certain type – some predicate or connective – can block inheritance of presuppositions from another expression, which $\mathcal{E}$ combines with, is standardly acknowledged in the research work on the 'projection problem', since Karttunen (1973) and Karttunen & Peters (1979). Three kinds of $\mathcal{E}$ combining with a clause are distinguished according to how the presupposition(s) coming from the embedded clause get affected: predicates preserving the presupposition(s), like *know*, *realize*, etc., are called 'holes'; predicates blocking presupposition inheritance[19], like *say*, *believe*, etc.,

[18] Since there is no king of France, '$\text{king}(x, \text{France})$' is false and so the truth-table of the conditional makes '$[\text{king}(x, \text{France}) \supset \neg\, \text{bald}(x)]$' true, for every assignment of an individual to the variable.

[19] Because they cancel or, sometimes, partly alter what is presupposed. (Cf. also Pollard & Sag 1994: § 8.4.1.)

are called 'plugs'; expressions that behave like plugs under particular conditions, or else like holes, are called 'filters', binary connectives being the typical case. E.g., (69) does not inherit the presupposition of the verb *stop* from "John has stopped beating his donkey", because the connective *if ... then* is a filter and the same proposition that would be presupposed is overtly expressed by "John used to beat his donkey" qua condition in the *if*-clause of the sentence.

(69) If John used to beat his donkey, then John has stopped beating his donkey

Likewise, "If there is a king of France, then the king of France is bald" does not presuppose that there is a king of France.

Negated predicates – i.e., the result of applying (the unary connective of) negation to an input predicate[20] – are arguably a case of expression $\mathcal{E}$ acting as filter for some presupposition introduced by the NP that $\mathcal{E}$ combines with. A filter and not a total 'plug', since the presupposition-canceling effect is only achieved under particular conditions, through an explicit statement of the intended cancellation, like "because there is no...", as we have shown before. Such a filtering status thus predicts the ordinary presupposition-preserving behaviour of negation (the filter comes down to a 'hole' by default), as well as the opposite situation in which an apt statement is not sufficient to cancel a presupposition inasmuch as the presupposition-bearing clause lacks negation: see our previous example (68b). We will have more to say on related matters in § 3.2.2.2, but we believe our discussion has already provided enough evidence that the contribution of a definite description to logical form proper is simply like that of a corresponding quantified NP, indeed the same as universal quantification.

3.2.2 Generalized Quantifier Theory

3.2.2.1 Compositional NP interpretation

Ever since Montague's (1973) 'Proper Treatment of Quantification' (PTQ), an important line of research in logical semantics for natural languages has strived to apply some version of compositionality as an alternative to the traditional assumption that overt grammatical form be logically misleading. Exploiting the fact that artificial languages of logic conform to compositionality, a compositional interpretation for (an infinite fragment of) the natural language L can be induced by its translation into a suitable logical language L′, provided that the translation too is made up compositionally. In a nutshell, every well-formed L-expression α translates as some well-formed L′-expression τ, whose

[20]This is not FOL negation, but see § 3.2.2 for complex predicates allowing '$\neg$'.

model-theoretical interpretation is *ipso facto* passed on to the former expression, and the way α is constructed from its syntactic components (if any) systematically dictates how the translation τ is constructed from the translations of α's components.[21] All of this contrasts sharply with treatments that are not subject to the same kind of constraint: they exploit the derivation of logical forms/translations to bridge a non-compositional gap between the overt grammatical form and the desired model-theoretic interpretation of L-sentences, while neglecting to assign any logical translation to several other types of well-formed L-expressions.

The intermediate step of translation into a logical language is not strictly necessary in a compositional approach, since one could directly assign every L-expression α the same model-theoretic interpretation of its logical translation τ. In particular, the Intensional Logic adopted by Montague for the PTQ fragment of English (and standardly applied for subsequent research work in related systems) "is not a level of linguistic description and it does not make theoretical claims of its own", but "could in principle be replaced by a direct mapping from expressions of English to denotations in a model" (Gazdar et al. 1985: p. 9); "the intensional logic translations ... are only a convenient way of making these denotations explicit" (ibid., p. 10).[22] Nevertheless, in our view, the logical form relations that underlie sentence meaning in natural language (such as predication, logical scope, variable-binding) should be reconstructed unambiguously by supplying the grammar with a cognitively motivated level of logic-style representation, even though there are no differences from a direct model-theoretic interpretation as far as the assignment of denotations is concerned. Hence the notion of a **compositional logical form**, which we will assume to be pivotal for the semantic representation system the human mind applies when processing linguistic data and drawing inferences from them.

Now, the proposed methodology implies we must leave FOL and adopt a **higher-order** notion of 'quantifier' – fit for the interpretation of the whole Noun Phrase – to achieve a compositional and uniform treatment (as well as a broader coverage of data) of natural language quantification, as occasionally noted in previous chapters. Reworking Montague's PTQ in accordance with

[21] What is meant by 'syntactic components' of an expression may vary depending on the grammatical framework. In our case, they are the 'immediate constituents' of the expression analysed in terms of surface-syntactic phrase structure, as we have made clear since chapter 1. This is a departure from Montague's approach, which allowed transformation-like, non-concatenative string operations in syntax, but v. also Gazdar et al. (1985) for a grammatical framework applying Montagovian semantics under the syntactic restriction that we are assuming.

[22] Cf. Dowty et al. (1981: pp. 110, 263-264) for essentially the same methodological remarks. (The option of a direct, translation-free model-theoretic treatment is exemplified in Lewis 1970, Montague 1970b and Robin Cooper 1983, *inter alia*.)

the branch of logic known as *Generalized Quantifier Theory* (GQT), Barwise & Cooper (1981) have proposed the following correspondences for NPs that combine a determiner and a possibly complex nominal as immediate constituents:

natural language	GQT
noun phrase	generalized quantifier
syntactic determiner	semantic determiner
nominal (head)	restriction

The three GQT notions in the table, which we will discuss hereafter in turn, are ambiguously used to indicate both the **logical language translation** of a natural language expression and its **model-theoretic denotation**. Under the most common model-theoretic interpretations, a 'generalized quantifier' in the denotational sense is a set of properties, where a property can be represented ***i)*** by the set of individuals making up the property's extension in (a model that reflects) some fixed world/context, or ***ii)*** intensionally as a function from possible worlds/contexts to extensions, given a Montague-style formalization of Carnap's (1947) *extension* vs. *intension* dichotomy. We shall have a little more to say about intensional versions in chapter 5, but the view of generalized quantifiers as **sets** – or 'families'[23] – **of sets**, applied by Barwise & Cooper (1981), looks enough for our present purposes.

Traditional FOL quantifiers can be reformulated as a particular case of (expressions denoting) generalized quantifiers:

> "Quantifiers are used to assert that a set has some property. $\exists x\, \varphi(x)$ asserts that the set of things which satisfy $\varphi(x)$ ... is a nonempty set. That is, the set of individuals having property φ contains at least one member. $\forall x\, \varphi(x)$ asserts that the set contains all individuals. ... It is clear that a quantifier ... combined with some sets ... will produce the value 'true' and when combined with others it will produce the value 'false'. In order to capture this idea formally, quantifiers are taken to denote the family of sets for which they yield the value 'true'."
>
> Barwise & Cooper (1981)

Thus, quantifiers which used to be binding operators in a 'first-order' language, i.e. a logical language such that **individuals** are the only type of entity variables get assigned and predicates take as arguments, become predicates of sets, upgrading the language to the second order (or higher up) in the logical hierarchy (cf. Dowty et al. 1981: ch. 4). Straightforward is the conversion from

[23]On this terminology, cf. Bach (1989: p. 51): "Sometimes, writers prefer to say *families* of sets to make clear that they are presupposing a system that avoids paradoxes that arise when we talk too freely about sets of sets, but ... just say 'sets of sets' for the sake of simplicity and uniformity".

the (classes of) FOL formulae mentioned in the above quotation to a corresponding GQT apparatus, where suitable predicates – '$\forall^*$' or '$\exists^*$', in (70) – replace the original FOL quantifiers. The binding of the variable in the GQT formulae is due to the 'λ' operator[24], which builds up a **set**(-denoting) **term** taken as argument of those predicates (v. Dowty et al. 1981: pp. 98-102).[25]

(70) $\Sigma^*(\lambda x\colon \varphi(x))$ if Σ is '$\forall$' or '$\exists$'

However, there would be no serious reasons for such a change in quantification techniques if it were nothing but a recoding of the FOL formulae. A great asset of GQT is the fact that one can leave FOL for a system making available infinitely many possible quantifiers, inasmuch as a generalized quantifier need not be primitive: indeed it normally combines a '(semantic) determiner' with a 'restriction', in the sense illustrated by our previous table of correspondences to natural language expressions. Model-theoretically, any determiner of GQT is a function that yields a generalized quantifier Q from its restriction A, a subset of the 'universe of discourse' U adopted in the given model. Intuitively, the domain of individuals over which the quantification takes place gets restricted to A qua denotation of some set term, instead of being necessarily identical to U as in FOL. Since set terms can be arbitrarily complex depending on the embedded formula they derive from, there are infinitely many such terms and, in consequence, infinitely many generalized quantifiers restricted by them.

Here is the informal statement of simple cases of NP interpretation conceived according to the generalized theory:

> "*every man* is interpreted as denoting the set of all properties which every man has; *the king* as denoting the set of all properties such that there is a unique entity which is a king and he has those properties; *a fish* as denoting the set of all properties which some fish has (the union af all the properties of all the fish there are)."
>
> Partee (1976)

Bearing in mind that properties in the present treatment are intended extensionally (so that possession of a property comes down to membership in the property's extension set), the quoted excerpt implies that *every man*, relative to a given world/context, denotes the set of all sets which include the set of men. (Likewise, *the king* denotes the set of all sets which include the unary set of kings, but we shall come back to the GQT treatment of *the* in § 3.2.2.2.) As regards existential quantification, it follows that *a* (or *some*) *fish* denotes the set of all sets whose intersections with the set of fish are not empty.

[24]Equivalently, Barwise & Cooper (1981) write '$\widehat{x}$' instead of 'λx'.

[25]Since a set term has the same type of denotation as a one-place predicate of individuals, it could also take an (individual term as) argument to form a formula.

The coverage of other cases is quite straightforward too. Negated existential quantification, hence the meaning of *no*, could be obtained by applying (external) negation to the corresponding positive case, as usual, but equivalent is the result achieved by a semantic determiner yielding a generalized quantifier that denotes the set of all sets whose intersections with the restriction are empty. Moreover, a GQT mechanism of NP interpretation goes much beyond the explicit occurrence of determiner words, and can be extended – at least for uniformity's sake – to NPs with Ø-determination (like bare plurals, see chapters 4-5 below). Thus "Montague [1973] treated proper names such as *John* as denoting not an individual, John, but the set of John's properties. This move assimilates names to the same logical type as quantified noun phrases such as *every man*" (Dowty et al. 1981: p. 184).

By means of GQT, we finally assign logical translations in a compositional and uniform fashion to the sentences (71) = (52), § 3.2.1 above:

(71) a. $[_{S}\,[_{NP}\,\text{John}]\,[_{VP}\,\text{walks}]]$
b. $[_{S}\,[_{NP}\,\textit{every}\ \text{man}]\,[_{VP}\,\text{walks}]]$
c. $[_{S}\,[_{NP}\,\textit{a/some}\ \text{man}]\,[_{VP}\,\text{walks}]]$
d. $[_{S}\,[_{NP}\,\textit{no}\ \text{man}]\,[_{VP}\,\text{walks}]]$

(72) a. $\text{John}^{*}(\lambda x\colon \text{walks}(x))$
b. $\forall\,(\lambda x\colon \text{man}(x))\,(\lambda x\colon \text{walks}(x))$
c. $\exists\,(\lambda x\colon \text{man}(x))\,(\lambda x\colon \text{walks}(x))$
d. $\neg\exists\,(\lambda x\colon \text{man}(x))\,(\lambda x\colon \text{walks}(x))$

All of the (72) are formulae $Q(\xi)$, where a generalized quantifier Q is the predicate and a set term ξ fills the argument position; at least in the cases (72b)-(72d), Q is a complex expression $\Sigma(\zeta)$ such that a set term ζ fills the argument position of a semantic determiner Σ. We have kept the usual notations of universal and (also negated) existential operators for convenience, even though their status is changed shifting from FOL to GQT, as should be clear by now. In (72a), the notation of 'John^{*}' stands for a predicate denoting the set of all sets John belongs to, but Barwise & Cooper (1981) argue that one need not introduce that item as a primitive of their logical language. It may well be an abbreviation of '$\forall\,(\lambda x\colon x = \text{John})$', or equivalent, i.e. a $\Sigma(\zeta)$ expression denoting the set of all sets which include the restriction set whose only element is John[26]. In the same spirit, one can get rid of '$\forall^{*}$' and '$\exists^{*}$' as

[26]The logical language being unambiguous, there is exactly one individual that the individual term 'John' is assigned as denotation; then the intended restriction follows. Of course, the name *John* in natural language is not unambiguous out of context, but it has to be unambiguously used under pragmatic constraints like those of definite descriptions (cf. chapter 5 below for further discussion).

primitives (introduced before in (70)) by applying the corresponding Σ to a restriction that coincides with the whole universe U.[27]

How to relate the GQT system of denotations to truth-conditions is readily explicated: "to evaluate a sentence consisting of a subject NP and a VP ... we check whether the VP-denotation is a member of the NP-denotation. If yes, the sentence is true, if no, it is false" (Robin Cooper 1983: p. 25). E.g., (the formula (72b) translating) "*every* man walks" is true just in case the set of walkers denoted by (the set term translating) the VP is one of the sets that include the set of men, these sets being the members of the denotation of (the generalized quantifier expression translating) the NP. The same semantic relationship, as we will show in a moment, can be modelled by **functional application** of the NP-interpretation to the VP-interpretation:

(73) $S' = f(NP', VP') = NP'(VP')$ *where* $[_{S}$NP VP$]$

(Conventionally, the interpretations, or their representations through logical translations, are indicated in the compositional schema (73) by prime-bearing versions of the category labels of the morpho-syntactic expressions concerned, following Gazdar et al. 1985: ch. 5.)

Let us introduce the notion of a function corresponding to the extension of a predicate of individuals: "Sets of individuals are in a one-to-one correspondence with functions that map individuals to 0 [= false] or 1 [= true]... It is very convenient to follow Montague in the common mathematical practise of not distinguishing between the two isomorphic sorts of objects ... and to consider an object sometimes as a set, sometimes as a certain ... *characteristic function* ... saying 'true' or 'false' to each individual" (Dowty et al. 1981: p. 26). This explains why the logical type of the expressions denoting a set of individuals (whether one-place predicates or set terms) is $<e, t>$ in Montague's notation, where e and t are mnemonic for 'elementary entity' – i.e. individual – and 'truth value', respectively, and their ordered pair is meant to display the function's input-output. Since the characteristic function of a set of entities other than individuals is envisaged too, one can equate a generalized quantifier (denotation) to the characteristic function of the intended set of sets. That function applies to the set denoted by the term ξ in argument position and yields the truth-value for the resulting $Q(\xi)$ proposition accordingly; hence the logical type of a generalized quantifier expression Q is $<<e, t>, t>$. By the same token, the logical type of a determiner forming generalized quantifiers from restriction set terms is $<<e, t>, <<e, t>, t>>$.

[27] Barwise & Cooper (1981) denote U with a logical constant, the predicate true of every member of U across models, but "it can be simulated by any formula which is satisfied by every object, e.g. by the formula $x = x$" (Kamp & Reyle 1993: p. 251). The starred versions of '$\forall$' and '$\exists$', thus, become abbreviations of '$\forall(\lambda x{:}\, x = x)$' and '$\exists(\lambda x{:}\, x = x)$', respectively.

The GQT treatment can be extended to increasingly complex cases, in the first place those combining a transitive verb with an object NP to form the VP, like:

(74) $[_S\, [_{NP}\, every$ pilot$]\, [_{VP}$ admires $[_{NP}\, some$ hostess$]]]$

a. $\forall\,(\lambda x\colon \text{pilot}(x))\,(\lambda x\colon \exists\,(\lambda y\colon \text{hostess}(y))\,(\lambda y\colon \text{admires}(x,y)))$

b. $\exists\,(\lambda y\colon \text{hostess}(y))\,(\lambda y\colon \forall\,(\lambda x\colon \text{pilot}(x))\,(\lambda x\colon \text{admires}(x,y)))$

Two possible S-interpretations are found here, due to an ambiguity in logical scope of the indefinite. In the narrow-scope reading (74a), the combination of verb and NP resembles the NP-VP one of examples with a mono-argumental intransitive verb, in that the object NP too is translated as a generalized quantifier applied to a set term which translates the verb. The term in question, namely '$\lambda y\colon \text{admires}(x,y)$', denotes the set of those individuals that x admires, where the variable corresponding to the subject is left free so as to be available for the expected binding at the VP level. Indeed, the subject NP translation is applied to the VP translation as before, but now the latter is a more complex set term derived from the quantified formula in which the translations of object NP and transitive verb are combined. There is, then, a difference in compositional interpretation (= semantic function f) between (73), which is simply an instance of functional application as mentioned above, and (75), which involves λ-binding of the 'subject variable' on top of that.[28]

(75) $\text{VP}' = f(\text{V}', \text{NP}') = \lambda x\colon \text{NP}'(\text{V}'_x)$ *where* $[_{VP}\, \text{V NP}]$

The other possible option of λ-binding for our two-place predicate, yielding '$\lambda x\colon \text{admires}(x,y)$', is exploited by the interpretation (74b), paraphrasable as "There is an hostess that every pilot admires". The new translation of the verb denotes the set of those individuals that admire y, where the variable corresponding to the object NP is left free so as to be available for subsequent binding. Thus, the quantifier that translates the object NP can take wide scope by applying to a set term binding y, derived from the quantified formula in which the translations of subject NP and transitive verb are combined. Elegant though such a formalization of the reading in question may look for logical purposes, it involves a violation of compositionality as far as the syntax-semantics interface for natural language is concerned, since the wide-scope quantifier occurs in a position of logical form which is not the one that the

[28]Notational details aside, the schema (75) comes from Barwise & Cooper (1981) and calls for the same warning: "There would be a closer correspondence between the structure of this kind of phrase and its translation if we were to adopt Montague's treatment in PTQ of intensional verbs like *seek*. Under his treatment the translation would be $\text{V}'(^\wedge Q)$ where '$^\wedge$' is an intensional operator. We avoid this here because we are not presently concerned with the semantics of intensional contexts" (ibid.).

surface syntactic structure of (74) would predict. The sentence seems to have a single *compositional logical form* strictly speaking, viz. (74a), so that the problem of how to make also (74b) fit the compositionality programme arises and has been variously tackled in the literature, but we postpone a discussion to chapter 5.

3.2.2.2 Semantic determiners and related issues

Hitherto we have just considered one reason for the infinitely many possible quantifiers of GQT – the fact that they are restricted – but another reason is the unlimited availability of possible determiners. An obvious proof is offered by the cardinal numerals, because they are infinite in number and can be interpreted as GQT determiners of an existential kind, imposing the relevant cardinality condition on the intersections between the restriction set and the sets that belong to the denotation of the resulting quantifier/NP. E.g., "*three* fish" can be taken to denote the set of all sets whose intersections with A, the set of fish, have at least three members. (Or exactly three members, in another conceivable interpretation of *three*; see Barwise & Cooper 1981 for both interpretations.)

Aiming at a syntax-semantics interface based on compositionality, the GQT treatment of cardinals is linguistically very appealing, even though it is not strictly necessary for the semantic coverage of natural language sentences. All cardinal determiners occurring in them might as well be paraphrased by means of FOL expressions in formulae that are logically equivalent to the pertinent GQT formulae (so as to get the same truth-values in the same circumstances), despite their structural differences. Cf. the (partial) formulae (76), where a. shows a generalized quantifier translating "*three* fish", while b. makes use of FOL only but is logically equivalent. A FOL version of '$\underset{3}{\exists}$' could be defined too, licensing c. as a mere abbreviation of the more complex logical form displayed by the previous FOL formula; v. Quine (1959: § 39).

(76) a. $\underset{3}{\exists}\,(\lambda x\text{: fish}(x))\,(...)$

b. $\exists x\,\exists y\,\exists z\,[x \neq y \neq z \wedge \text{fish}(x) \wedge \text{fish}(y) \wedge \text{fish}(z) \wedge ...]$

c. $\underset{3}{\exists} x\,[\text{fish}(x) \wedge ...]$

So, in order to prove that GQT has greater expressive power than FOL as regards truth-conditions and thus yields a broader semantic coverage of natural language, one must consider determiners that are not first-order definable:

> "The transformations employed in standard logic to handle 'every' and 'some' depend on the fact that any statement about every P or some P is logically equivalent to a statement about everything or something; for

example, 'Some P is Q' is equivalent to 'Something is P and Q'. What Barwise and Cooper show is that there is no such transformation for determiners like 'most' or 'more than half'. That is, statements about most P's or more than half P's cannot be rephrased as statements about most things or more than half of all things."

Moore (1981)

The point is that the problematic determiners compare the cardinalities of two sets – an operation which is consistent with what was assumed in chapter 2, but calls for **second-order** expressive power.[29] Hence the impossibility of any FOL translation for a sentence like *most men walk*: its meaning is reflected by the GQT translation (77), interpreting the semantic determiner 'Most' so as to yield the set of all sets whose intersections with the given set of men are greater than (approximately) half of that restriction.

(77) Most $(\lambda x\colon \mathrm{man}(x))\,(\lambda x\colon \mathrm{walks}(x))$

Of equal importance is the idea that the denotation of some GQT determiner may well depend on the models/worlds/contexts, so that the item at issue need not be a **logical constant** (contrary to first-order definable determiners such as '$\forall$', '$\exists$', '$\underset{3}{\exists}$', etc., whose interpretation stays constant across all models/worlds/contexts; cf. our previous note 3). Even neglecting problems of vagueness, as done throughout this book, it is clear that 'multal' quantitative determiners, like *many*, and 'paucal' ones, like *few*, are semantically context-sensitive. (Again, the fact was mentioned in chapter 2.) Also *most* involves actually the same phenomenon, as soon as one leaves those prototypical cases in which it is sufficient to equate the relevant ratio to 'more than half'. There are situations in which the speaker would be reluctant to apply *most* unless the ratio were much more than half – and obviously the sense of 'much' is context-sensitive. Denotational interpretation can be made dependent on the context through model-theoretic techniques that are of general interest to the semanticists, being required by various other types of expressions besides determiners.

Next to the distinction between 'logical' and 'non-logical' determiners (depending on the respective kind of constants), GQT since Barwise & Cooper (1981) provides other formal criteria for classifying determinative items as well

[29] See Landman (1991: pp. 28-29): "Most *A*s are *B*s means that the cardinality of the set $\lambda x\colon [A(x) \wedge B(x)]$ is greater than the cardinality of $\lambda x\colon [A(x) \wedge \neg B(x)]$. Since in second order logic we can quantify over properties and relations, we can express that there is [such] a relation between two properties" (to be represented by the corresponding extension sets). Generalized quantifiers being predicates of sets, GQT consists of a suitable fragment of second order logic, though "one that ... keep[s] the formal definition [of *most*, etc.] as part of the metalanguage, ... without bringing all the problems of set theory into the syntax and semantics of the logic *per se*" (Barwise & Cooper 1981).

as the resulting quantifiers. Here we content ourselves with touching on the criterion of **monotonicity**, which will prove useful in § 3.3.2.1. For any set X belonging to a generalized quantifier Q, Q is 'upward monotone' (= 'monotone increasing') when all sets including X as a subset belong to the quantifier; alternatively, Q is 'downward monotone' (= 'monotone decreasing') when all the subsets of X belong to the quantifier. The same terminological pair is also applied to those determiners which always yield quantifiers with the corresponding monotonicity property.[30] Clear examples of upward monotone determiners are *a/some*, *many* and *every/all*, as shown by the fact that (78a) becomes logically valid if one of them occurs in both Σ positions of such a sentence pattern; note that the VP *left the party early* (but the same would hold for *left the party and went home*, etc.) denotes a subset of the denotation of the second VP.

(78) a. If Σ girl(s) *left the party early*, then Σ girl(s) *left the party*.

b. If Σ girl(s) *left the party*, then Σ girl(s) *left the party early*.

By exchanging the VPs we get (78b), which is not valid unless the Σ positions are filled by a downward monotone determiner, resulting from negation of an upward monotone one[31], as in the case of *no* (qua lexicalized negation of 'some'), '*not* many' and '*not* every/all'. It has been noted that downward (contrary to upward) monotonicity allows so-called **negative polarity items** such as *ever* in (79a), German *ein Deut* in (79b) and Italian *muovere un dito* in (79c).[32]

(79) a. $\left\{\begin{array}{c}\text{No}\\ *\,\text{Some}\end{array}\right\}$ student would *ever* say that

b. Es interessierte $\left\{\begin{array}{c}\text{keinen}\\ *\,\text{einen}\end{array}\right\}$ *einen Deut*
'It interests nobody (vs. ∗ somebody) a farthing'

c. $\left\{\begin{array}{c}\text{Non}\\ *\,\emptyset\end{array}\right\}$ piú di 2 uomini *mossero un dito* per aiutarla
'Not (vs. ∗ Ø) more than 2 men lifted a finger to help her'

[30] In this succint presentation we do not consider another sense of 'monotonicity' which can concern determiners, but on the basis of their restriction set, viz. the property Barwise & Cooper (1981) call 'persistence'. (Cf. van Eijck 1988.)

[31] For expository convenience, we present negation as directly operating on the semantic determiners, whereas Barwise & Cooper (1981) apply it at the quantifier level: '$\neg Q$' denotes the set of all subsets of the universe of discourse that do not belong to the denotation of the generalized quantifier expression Q.

[32] See, e.g., van Eijck (1988) and Bach (1989: pp. 62-64) for introductions.

Examples like the last one illustrate also the case of an expression that reverses monotonicity by setting an upper bound to cardinality. Thus, complex determiners of the form *not more than n* (with a quantitative comparison construction), or – equivalently – *at most n*, are downward monotone and negate the respective cardinals *at least n*+1, which are upward monotone instead.

Finally, the meaning and presupposition of a very important determinative word of natural language, the definite article[33], remains to be discussed here in the perspective of GQT. Barwise & Cooper's (1981) view on the matter lies between the analysis *à la* Frege-Strawson with individual terms qua arguments and a 'pragmatically revised' Russellian analysis (drawing some terminology and notions from our § 3.2.1 above). As in the former analysis, an 'improper' definite description is not assigned any denotation, so that a sentence/formula in which the expression occurs is made neither-true-nor-false by failure of a presupposed condition of definiteness. Still, definite descriptions get uniformly treated as generalized quantifiers like all NPs. A special manner of universal quantification is introduced, because "**the** *A*" denotes the set of all sets which include the restriction *A* (hence the interpretation so far is like that of "**every** *A*"), but just in case *A* has **exactly one element**, or else the denotation is undefined (i.e. "**the** *A*" will not denote anything at all). This may well look appealing as a synthesis of two major trends in the logical analysis of definite descriptions, yet it does not consider that there are good reasons for rejecting the account of presupposition failure with a truth-value gap or 'third value', as we argued in § 3.2.1.

Moreover, a straightforward alternative becomes available in GQT if we recode our version of Russell's FOL analysis accordingly. (Instead one could recode his original or other variants thereof[34], but the pertinent drawbacks we pointed out in that connection would be inherited too.) Keeping a simplified treatment of the name *France*, for the moment, the semantic representation pair (60) which was assigned to the example "The king of France is bald" can be converted into:

(80) a. $\forall\,(\lambda x\colon \text{king}(x, \text{France}))\,(\lambda x\colon \text{bald}(x))$

b. $\exists^{*}\lambda x\colon [\text{king}(x, \text{France}) \wedge \forall^{*}\lambda y\colon [\text{king}(y, \text{France}) \supset y = x]\,]$

---

[33] As usual in the current section 3.2, we consider only the singular interpretation of the article and postpone a treatment of plural definites to § 3.3.2.2.

[34] By literally recoding Russell's logical form plus uniqueness condition, as in:

$$\exists\,(\lambda x\colon [\psi(x) \wedge \forall\,(\lambda y\colon \psi(y))(\lambda y\colon y = x)\,])(\lambda x\colon \varphi(x))$$

where the restriction set which '∃' applies to is unary at most, the NP denotation is the possibly empty set of all sets whose intersections with the unary set at issue are not empty. In the empty case (i.e. if one of the conjunct conditions is falsified), no set belongs to the NP denotation and the whole formula is false. Alternatively, a determiner **the** can be defined so as to entail uniqueness with the same results.

A presupposition (80b), or equivalent [35], makes all the difference from "Every king of France is bald", (80a) being the common logical form (for the propositional content) of both sentences. When such a 'pragmatically revised Russellian analysis', previously worked out on a FOL basis, gets upgraded to GQT in the way shown by (80), the old logical forms change into more compositional ones which preserve the results already achieved as regards truth-conditions [36]. At the same time, GQT itself becomes simpler, conforming to standard two-valued logic and getting rid of **the** as a special kind of semantic determiner with presupposition conditions built into its denotational interpretation.

It is evident that in our system the definite article's semantic contribution as a morpho-syntactic determiner is not exhausted by the semantic determiner of GQT thus expressed, viz. '∀'. While the latter, denotationally, leads from a set to a generalized quantifier Q characterized as we know, the meaning of the definite article too can be seen as a function, but one that yields a **pair** whose elements are the same Q and the relevant presupposition(s) [37]. In the terminology introduced before, this pair of abstract entities – or rather, the pair of logical expressions representing them – is a Semantic Representation (SR) at the level of NP interpretation (just like (80) was a sample SR at the sentence interpretation level) and one may call it 'quantifier-SR', for the sake of brevity. Formal properties ascribed to the quantifiers with a special **the**-type semantic determiner by Barwise & Cooper (1981) are simply traced back to corresponding quantifiers with '∀' (as in the case of upward monotonicity, which definiteness inherits from universality), or linked to the framework of quantifier-SRs.

Let us investigate the property of being **self-dual**. The so-called 'logical dual' of a quantifier Q [38], in GQT, is the quantifier Q' such that $Q' = \neg Q \neg$,

---

[35] For convenience, omitting parentheses that indicate application of the second-order predicates, we have just substituted '$\exists^* \lambda x$:' and '$\forall^* \lambda y$:' for the respective FOL operators '$\exists x$' and '$\forall y$' (cf. § 3.2.2 above). We can be content with a minimal change like this since presuppositions are non-compositional anyway, but a shorter yet logically equivalent formulation will be introduced by § 3.3.2.2.

[36] In particular, the conditional connective of a universally quantified FOL formula corresponds to set inclusion in the interpretation of the generalized quantifier with determiner '∀' employed by a corresponding GQT formula. E.g., the latter formula is made trivially true when the quantifier gets restricted to the empty set, because this is included by any set and then the quantifier denotation turns out to be the set of all subsets of the universe of discourse (v. Barwise & Cooper 1981).

[37] The pair interpreting "The king of France", say, can be obtained from (80) by limiting the a. part to the generalized quantifier; the b. part remains the same.

[38] Readers are warned that such a logical sense of *dual* (originally applied to the connectives of conjunction and disjunction, cf. Quine 1959: § 11) is not related with the sense usually intended by grammarians and lexicographers, which concerns a word (form) indicating that exactly two entities are referred to.

and vice versa; when $Q = Q'$, a quantifier is also self-dual, i.e. the dual of itself. A typical case of duality pattern for distinct quantifiers with the same restriction is '$\forall(\lambda x{:}\, \varphi(x))$' = '$\neg\exists(\lambda x{:}\, \varphi(x))\neg$' (or, in the GQT recoding of FOL quantifiers, '$\forall^*$' = '$\neg\exists^*\neg$'), and vice versa. Concerning self-duality, Barwise & Cooper (1981) make it clear that the quantifiers their **the**-type semantic determiner yields are self-dual, but the same property holds for any compatible quantifier whose restriction set has one and only one element. (E.g., if this element is John, by denying that John is not bald we just affirm that John is bald.) Therefore, self-dual quantifiers can equally result from '$\forall$' because of a suitable input set, depending on the context, and the only difference of the special determiner is its lack of denotational output whenever the restriction does not contextually meet the definiteness requirements. The effect of discarding all contexts which violate definiteness is achieved through a separate pragmatic presupposition in the approach adopted here, so that our definite article meaning enforces self-duality for any resulting $\forall$-quantifier associated with the (supposedly) truthful presupposition at quantifier-SR level.

Now consider an elegant consequence of self-duality: if $Q = \neg Q \neg$, then $\neg Q = \not\neg\not\neg Q\neg = Q\neg$; that is, "we can push negations back and forth across self-dual quantifiers. Hence there is no need to use any syntactic construction to show that negation has wide scope over quantification when the quantifier is self-dual" (Barwise & Cooper 1981). This logical fact explains the seeming ambiguity of negation over definite NPs, in a way that is consistent with our assumption of unambiguously narrow scope for VP negation in pertinent clauses (v. § 3.2.1 above). We will simply translate them as '$Q\neg\xi$' formulae, since in Barwise & Cooper's GQT system, if ξ is a set term (i.e. complex predicate), '$\neg\xi$' equally is, the latter being equivalent to '$\lambda x{:}\, \neg\xi(x)$'.

Interestingly, the logical notion of negated predicate can be associated with a pragmatic aspect, following ideas that § 3.2.1 sketched starting from FOL. In our GQT-based version, the universal quantifier interpreting an 'improper' definite description is restricted to the empty domain by a falsified existential presupposition. Although this fact would normally cause inappropriateness, a 'projection' process in the sense of Karttunen (1973) and Karttunen & Peters (1979) need not pass the presupposition formula up to sentence level from the NP. In particular, a negated predicate applying to the description at issue acts as 'filter' which may cancel the presupposition under appropriate contextual conditions. We already know the role of overt expressions like a "because there is no..." clause, but a more accurate account of that phenomenon should show how it relates to the discourse level too.

For one thing, we note that there are cases in which the analysis of a multi-sentential discourse is required in order to link up at a distance the source of a presupposition with the expression canceling it. E.g.:

(81) *The king of France* is not bald. Nor has he a thick head of hair, for that matter. The point is that *there is no king of France.*

It might look as if this (con)textual flexibility were very different from what happens when 'filtering' – in absence of negation – is an effect of some binary connective joining the respective clauses from which a presupposition and the expression canceling it derive (as in the example (69) cited by § 3.2.1). But research on presupposition projection has pointed out that the filtering conditions for binary connectives must be relaxed, insofar as the presupposition pertaining to one of the two clauses can also be canceled by inference from the other clause and a set of background assumptions, either implicit or expressed in preceding discourse/text. While referring to the literature (like Karttunen's original work) for discussion of relevant examples with connectives, we may well conclude that negation is not alone in allowing (con)textual flexibility for the purpose of filtering.

Furthermore, a discourse-level account of presupposition-canceling uses of negation is called into play by their frequent association with a peculiar type of conversational move (v. Blok 1993: § 3.3.5). As we saw before, some speaker A utters a sentence that carries a certain presupposition and the conversation partner B replies by uttering a corresponding sentence with negation, whose purpose is (*i*) the **refutation** of A's presupposition, as opposed to (*ii*) ordinary presupposition-preserving disagreement about A's assertion. Compare:

A: The king of France is bald.

B: The king of France is not bald, because $\left\{\begin{array}{l}(i)\text{ there is no king of France.}\\(ii)\text{ he has a thick head of hair.}\end{array}\right\}$

But it would be wrong to believe that a dialogue of the kind is strictly necessary for negation to cancel presuppositions. The following sounds like a perfectly acceptable opening for such a monologic text as the speech by some barrister before the court: "I will provide evidence for the defense of my client here. First of all, let me make it clear that *the murderer of Mr. Smith* is not in this room, because *nobody murdered Mr. Smith.* It was just an accident, as I'm going to show you".

3.3 Towards feature-theoretic semantics

3.3.1 Quantification and semantics in HPSG

Generalized Quantifier Theory has made it possible for semanticists to start the systematic study of determiners and NPs, leading to new insights into their logical properties and the formulation of related linguistic universals (v.

Barwise & Cooper 1981, Zwarts 1983, Gärdenfors 1987, as well as more recent literature; for a first introduction, Bach 1989). Still, what actually matters to our work, beyond any research on model-theoretic issues as such, is a GQT-like account of quantification w.r.t. the syntax-semantics interface of grammatical systems, especially the Head-driven Phrase Structure Grammar by Pollard & Sag (1987; 1994) we cited at the beginning of the current chapter. In HPSG, the essentials of generalized quantification are retained, though adapted to the framework of **Situation Theory** (Barwise & Perry 1983), whose ontological postulate of 'realistic' intensional objects implies a major departure from the approach of Montague (1974) and all the others who decompose intensions as functions from possible worlds/contexts to extensions.

A systematic discussion of the situation-theoretic variety of logical semantics, a.k.a. *situation semantics*, falls outside the scope of the present work. Occasionally, without indulging in technical details, we shall mention some basic differences from a traditional modeltheoretic treatment, which looks sufficient to interpret the relevant grammatical fragment in ways provably adequate for our purposes. In particular, the main improvements on unrestricted first-order quantification that are emphasized by Pollard and Sag, in an informal sketch of their logical language for translating the semantic representations of HPSG, need not require any situation-theoretic interpretation:

> "the variables over which we quantify are always *restricted*: instead of 'for every x, x howls', we have 'for every cat x, x howls'. ... And second, in addition to the determiners 'exists' and 'forall' countenanced by first-order logic, we have a full range of **generalized** determiners, such as 'most', 'no', 'exactly three', 'more-than-two-but-less-than-seven', etc."
>
> Pollard & Sag (1987: p. 89)

These two, in essence, correspond to distinguishing characteristics of GQT as such and are perfectly captured by the extensional interpretation we presented in § 3.2.2. Thus, at least for methodological convenience, our touchstone in model-theoretic matters may well remain Barwise & Cooper's (1981) version of generalized quantifiers, rather than one of its situation-based or, anyway, intensional variants (but pragmatic aspects of intensionality will be eventually considered in chapter 5).

Technically, the restriction of a generalized quantifier Q and the expression which Q applies to are 'set terms' in Barwise and Cooper's GQT language, as highlighted by § 3.2.2.1 above. However, we could re-interpret in equivalent ways also a notation like the one Pollard & Sag (1987: ch. 4; 1994: ch. 8) have adopted for HPSG purposes: i.e., Q combines a determiner with a restricted variable of the form $x_i | \psi$ and takes some φ as external scope, where ψ and φ are formulae. In (82)-(85), for example, the HPSG-style logical translations a., under our intended extensional interpretation, are the exact equivalent of the corresponding formulae b. in GQT notation:

(82) a. $(\forall x|\,\mathrm{man}(x))\,\mathrm{walks}(x)$

b. $\forall\,(\lambda x\!: \mathrm{man}(x))\,(\lambda x\!: \mathrm{walks}(x))$

(83) a. $(\exists\,x|\,\mathrm{man}(x))\,\mathrm{walks}(x)$

b. $\exists\,(\lambda x\!: \mathrm{man}(x))\,(\lambda x\!: \mathrm{walks}(x))$

(84) a. $\neg(\exists\,x|\,\mathrm{man}(x))\,\mathrm{walks}(x)$

b. $\neg\exists\,(\lambda x\!: \mathrm{man}(x))\,(\lambda x\!: \mathrm{walks}(x))$

(85) a. $(\mathrm{Most}\,x|\,\mathrm{man}(x))\,\mathrm{walks}(x)$

b. $\mathrm{Most}\,(\lambda x\!: \mathrm{man}(x))\,(\lambda x\!: \mathrm{walks}(x))$

A brief comparison will be enough to make the point intuitively clear even if we do not give a formal proof of equivalence.

For one thing, the domain of individuals which a restricted variable ranges over is a subset of (and need not coincide with) U, i.e. the whole **universe of discourse**[39]; the domain thereby selected corresponds to the restriction set of GQT. Thus, if a formula ψ with one or more free occurrences of the i-th variable, x_i, is apposed to it as done through the '|' notation[40], the members of x_i's domain are all and only those cases of individual **a** that would make ψ true, should **a** be the value of x_i in a given assignment. From the same formula, in GQT, a set term is derived by means of the 'λ' operator (or equivalent), so as to assume the restriction set itself as denotation, whereas the restricted variable is an 'individual term' which denotes any single member of that set in turn (depending on the assignment of values). Finally, a quantified formula $Q\varphi$ without set terms is true *iff* the scope formula φ is true for as many assignments of x_i's domain members as the determiner of Q prescribes: e.g., all such assignments, in the case of '$\forall$'; at least one of them, in the case of '$\exists$'; most of them, in the case of 'Most' (whatever it may mean contextually,

[39]Cf. Church (1951), who argued for such a revision of Frege's original concept of unrestricted variables. (A semantic analysis of English sentences that informally applies restricted variables is found in Chomsky 1976, among others.)

[40]That is, the formula is apposed to the occurrence of x_i adjacent to the determiner of the binding quantifier, yet the resulting restriction equally affects the value assignments for all the subsequent occurrences of that variable under the same binding. (The definition of variable-binding is understood so as to cover also the occurrences within the binding quantifier itself, besides those within its external scope.) Formally, distinct occurrences are identified as occurrences of the same variable because they have the same numerical index, so that when we mention the 'i-th variable', or 'x_i', we mean (any occurrence of) the variable indexed with the number i; for example: x_4, with i=4. The logicians in fact envisage infinitely many variables: x_1, x_2, x_3, ... (or equivalent), even though few shorthands without index – like 'x', 'y' and 'z' – usually suffice for sample formulae.

according to a previous discussion in § 3.2.2.2). This technique, which could be modelled on GQT to yield the same coverage of determiners, is basically a standard definition of truth-conditions *à la* Tarski (1936) but adapted for restricted quantification, thanks to the assumption that the only legitimate assignments are those which make the restriction formula ψ true.[41]

To sum up, one possible way to ensure equivalence to mainstream GQT would be a direct interpretation of Pollard & Sag's logical language according to extensional counterparts of the situation-theoretic objects/constructs they have assumed (somewhat informally)[42]. Instead of engaging in such a logical exercise, we prefer an easy solution with a view to reconcile the HPSG-oriented notation without λ-binders, which is 'light', very readable, and Barwise and Cooper's original semantic modelling of GQT, which appears to have several advantages of formal simplicity for the purpose of providing intuitive denotations suited to the interpretation of linguistic expressions. There is in fact another, much more straightforward way of equating the respective notations of the sample a. and b. above (in (82)-(85)): one can just consider the former an abbreviation of the latter, essentially as suggested by Allegranza & Mazzini (2000: pp. 230-231).

To clarify a related matter, note that the resort to independent λ-binders for building the set terms of restriction and external scope, in mainstream GQT, allows **alphabetic variants** in accordance with a principle of 'λ-languages' (cf. Dowty et al. 1981: p. 111, for instance). That is, since variable-binding is strictly internal to a set term, the interpretation of a quantified formula would not change if each of its two set terms were built by binding a different variable, so as to yield:

(86) $\forall\,(\lambda x\colon \text{man}(x))\,(\lambda y\colon \text{walks}(y))$

instead of (82b) above. Such variants make sense (and can be exploited) from a logical point of view, but we must avoid that they become a source of over-generation for the grammar. The result is easily ensured by stipulating that a quantifier Q in logical translations of linguistic expressions always applies to a set term that λ-binds the same variable as Q's restriction set term. If this is done, however, the information about the variable bound by the external

[41]In Heim (1982: ch. 2), Allegranza (1986) and, informally, Diesing (1992: pp. 7-8, 137), related approaches to restricted quantification based on a 'tarskian' system are proposed for the interpretation of May's (1977) Logical Form within the grammatical framework of Extended Standard Theory and Government-Binding Theory (v. Chomsky 1975; 1976; 1981). Other treatments assuming the framework essentially conform to some GQT system with set terms (e.g., May 1985: pp. 7-8, or Chierchia 1997: §§ 2.2-2.4, 7.1).

[42]The precise situation-theoretic status of their quantification machinery is not so clear from a formal point of view, in light of the critical discussion by Richard Cooper (1990: pp. 125-126, 170) pointing out differences from more 'orthodox' systems of Situation Semantics.

set term can already be derived from the other set term, so that Pollard and Sag's alternative notation for quantified formulae works as an abbreviating convention which eliminates the redundancy from the GQT notation.

Technicalities aside, the idea that some notation lends itself to be reinterpreted for different versions of logical semantics is not without precedent in the research on natural language meaning. It is time to consider the same issue according to the actual grammatical format of semantic representations in HPSG, since so far we have only presented their logical translations under notational conventions of GQT (also including Pollard and Sag's variant version thereof). Essentially, one needs **recursive feature structures**, extending the formalism adopted by our previous chapters in such a way that the value of a feature may well be another feature structure instead of being atomic. Hence what Fenstad et al. (1987: p. 21) have called *situation schemata*:

> "attribute-value pairs where the attributes name things which situations are analyzed in terms of, i.e. RELation, ARGument, POLarity, LOCation, etc. The values are either atoms, which stand for relations, individuals and properties, or situation schemata".

By taking an explicit step towards the **open-ended status** of interpretation, Fenstad et al. present their 'schemata' (or indeed any equivalent notation) as suited but not necessarily committed to the modelling of situation-theoretic objects/constructs:

> "Situation schemata can be adapted to various kinds of semantic interpretations; we could interpret in some system of higher order intensional logic as in the Montague tradition ..., or we could give some kind of operational interpretation in a suitable programming language".
>
> (ibid., pp. 3-6)

These remarks are perfectly in line with the liberal policy in model-theoretic matters which we would like to adopt here.

In current HPSG terminology, a semantic pattern comparable to situation schemata is known as '(parameterized) state of affairs', a label usually abbreviated by writing initials only:

> "A (p)soa is represented by a feature structure that specifies a relation (for us the value of the RELATION ... attribute) together with values for the (argument) roles of that relation (for us, represented by the other attributes [of the same feature structure]). In situation theory, a soa also specifies a polarity (either 1 [=positive] or 0 [=negative]), but since we will not be concerned with the analysis of negation, we suppress the POLARITY attribute, which can always be assumed to have the value 1."
>
> Pollard & Sag (1994: p. 25)

A more recent variation on the same representational scheme exploits the formal device of 'sort hierarchies' available within HPSG (and already introduced in our chapter 1), so as to dispense with the RELATION attribute and represent the possible relations as subsorts of *quantifier-free*(=*qf*)*psoa* (Pollard & Sag 1994: p. 338). Here are both versions of attribute-value matrices, encoding relevant examples, with boxed numerals (a.k.a. 'tags' in HPSG terminology) that stand for unspecified values:

(87) a.
$$ {}_{\textit{qfpsoa}}\begin{bmatrix} \text{RELATION } \textit{book} \\ \text{INSTANCE } \boxed{1} \end{bmatrix} \quad \text{or:} \quad {}_{\textit{book}}\begin{bmatrix} \text{INSTANCE } \boxed{1} \end{bmatrix} $$

b.
$$ {}_{\textit{qfpsoa}}\begin{bmatrix} \text{RELATION } \textit{eat} \\ \text{AGENT } \boxed{1} \\ \text{THEME } \boxed{2} \end{bmatrix} \quad \text{or:} \quad {}_{\textit{eat}}\begin{bmatrix} \text{AGENT } \boxed{1} \\ \text{THEME } \boxed{2} \end{bmatrix} $$

c.
$$ {}_{\textit{qfpsoa}}\begin{bmatrix} \text{RELATION } \textit{give} \\ \text{AGENT } \boxed{1} \\ \text{THEME } \boxed{2} \\ \text{GOAL } \boxed{3} \end{bmatrix} \quad \text{or:} \quad {}_{\textit{give}}\begin{bmatrix} \text{AGENT } \boxed{1} \\ \text{THEME } \boxed{2} \\ \text{GOAL } \boxed{3} \end{bmatrix} $$

Representations like the (87), roughly, correspond to atomic formulae of various traditional languages of logic, but "keywords instead of ... argument position in the formula are used to distinguish the roles of a relation" (Pollard & Sag 1987: pp. 88-89). The unique argument in (87a), e.g., plays the role of being an INSTANCE of *book*, an object which is assigned that property or 'unary relation'.[43] Cases of relation with greater 'arity' are treated in (87b)-(87c), as also suggested by Richard Cooper (1990: pp. 121, 131), Allegranza & Mazzini (2000: pp. 232-233) and others, importing such attributes as AGENT, THEME and GOAL from the theory of Thematic ('Θ-') Roles in the sense of Jackendoff (1972: §§ 2.1-2.2), which is quite familiar to generative linguists[44]. It is only fair to say that this approach to argument roles is considered problematic by Pollard & Sag (1987: p. 85): since "no consensus has emerged as to just what ... [Θ-]roles there are" for general purposes, they prefer to assume that "each

[43] See, again, Pollard & Sag (1987): "It is a fundamental fact about relations that they vary as to the number of things that can participate in them. For each relation, that characteristic number is called the *arity* of the relation. Thus we classify relations as *unary* (arity one), *binary* (arity two), *ternary* (arity three), etc. ... Unary relations are usually called *properties*. ... As a matter of convenience, we will usually call the role in sortal properties the *instance* role" (pp. 84-86).

[44] Cf. related research in model-theoretic semantics (by Chierchia 1985, Dowty 1989, Parsons 1995), as well as other systems of argument roles proposed in theoretical linguistics (v. especially Halliday 1967/68, Fillmore 1968, Anderson 1986) or computational linguistics (e.g. Steiner et al. 1988, Badia & Colominas 1998).

relation is equipped with its own inventory of roles". By doing so, however, one fails to express intuitively plausible generalizations across relations, e.g. the agentive argument notion shared by *eat* and *give* cannot be captured because the subjects of the two (active) verbs get interpreted as an EATER and a GIVER, respectively.

Whether Pollard and Sag's scepticism about Θ-roles is really justified is not a question that will preoccupy us here. We can easily evade it by using 'logical style' abbreviations like *eat*($\boxed{1}$,$\boxed{2}$) and *give*($\boxed{1}$,$\boxed{2}$,$\boxed{3}$), where the attributes are omitted and we assume standard conventions identifying arguments by their position (subject first, etc.), while the readers remain free to imagine their preferred keywords for argument roles.[45] Here we are actually interested in the values which can specify the (kind of) entity/construct playing the role represented by a given feature: Pollard & Sag (1994: p. 397) "assume that for each subsort of *qfpsoa*, the only sorts of values that are available for these features are either *ref* or *psoa*". The latter – a type of feature structure that will be discussed in chapter 5 – encompasses a 'qfpsoa' and therefore yields recursion when used in argument position, but additionally can introduce quantificational information, so that this broader notion of 'psoa' is meant as *possibly quantified parameterized state of affairs* by Pollard & Sag (1994: p. 320). In compliance with our methodological decision to focus on extensionality, we will neglect the case of *psoa* filling an argumental slot of some suitable relation (*believe*, *try*, *want*, etc.), because it requires intensional interpretation; cf. Pollard & Sag (1987: pp. 88-90).

Let us then consider the other sort of values combining with attributes of argument roles, namely the subsort *ref(erential)* of *index*, "the HPSG analog of a reference marker in discourse representation theory (DRT: Kamp 1981) or of a parameter introduced by an NP use in situation semantics" (Pollard & Sag 1994: p. 24)[46]. Assuming the alternative subsorts of *index* concern only expletive, pleonastic uses of pronouns, like *it* in "*it* is raining" and *there* in "*there* is something wrong", *referential* indices (broadly speaking[47]) are the ones which receive a semantic interpretation (ibid., p. 249):

---

[45]Our abbreviated notation neutralizes also the technical difference between *qfpsoa* structures with the RELATION attribute and corresponding ones without it.

[46]The analogy between HPSG indices and situation-theoretic parameters indeed explains in which sense a 'psoa' is said to be *parameterized*: because "certain of its argument roles – its *parameters* – have not yet been anchored to determinate objects" (Pollard & Sag 1987: p. 91). Cf. also Richard Cooper (1990: p. 122).

[47]Note that the *ref* indices of Pollard & Sag (1994) are also used for **quantification** in general, so that the referentiality notion thereby conveyed is not confined to definite and/or individual reference, but in practice gets extended as we argued in chapter 2. (We will have more to say on the topic in § 3.3.2.1.)

> "The semantic import of indices ... is simply this: if an NP is referential (or quantificational), then any NP coindexed with it must have the same reference (or covary over the same domain of quantification)."

The indices, in a sense, are comparable to variables of logical languages, but additionally include **agreement** features of NUMBER, PERSON and GENDER, which can be assimilated with a system for classifying variables into different 'referential sorts'; variables over individuals vs. variables over 'plural entities', e.g., as regards NUMBER. The fact that in HPSG such features are internal to indices implies that coindexed elements – i.e. elements sharing their index – always agree.[48]

From a grammatical point of view, the indices of HPSG are roughly like those of Chomsky's (1981; 1986) Government-Binding theory:

> "In both theories they are entities associated with NP tokens; in both theories two distinct NP tokens are 'coindexed' under certain conditions (e.g. if they are in ... an antecedent-pronoun relationship) and ... constrained to have non-identical indices ... under certain other conditions. ... The chief difference in the two approaches is that GB theory treats indices as rather mysterious abstract syntactic objects. In HPSG, by contrast, indices are essentially semantic in nature: they are components of semantic descriptions".
>
> Pollard & Sag (1987: p. 105)

Whereas NP indices in Chomsky's GB-style syntax are just numerical subscripts added to the 'NP' category label of relevant phrase tokens, HPSG keeps the corresponding notation (with subscript tags) as an abbreviating convention, but in actual feature structures spells out the contribution of indices to a semantic representation taken as value of the attribute CONTENT. The abbreviation '$NP_{\boxed{i}}$', where i is any positive integer, technically stands for some noun phrase whose CONTENT value of sort *nominal-object* introduces the index $\boxed{i}$ (v. Pollard & Sag 1994: p. 28).

The so-called 'nominal object', a semantic construct characteristic of nouns and their projections according to Pollard & Sag (1994), is represented by a feature structure with the attributes INDEX, which takes as value the index $\boxed{i}$ of

[48]Therefore, the linguist is provided with a clear test for deciding whether some candidate feature occurs within the indices. The values of CASE, e.g., need not agree in such coindexed pairs as a pronoun and its antecedent, although there are phenomena of 'case concord' between noun and determiner/adjective in German; hence the conclusion that these phenomena are purely morpho-syntactic and CASE is not an attribute of indices. As Pollard & Sag (1994: Ch. 2) discuss in detail, the broad area of agreement or concord shows a semiotically 'hybrid' nature, involving syntactic, semantic and pragmatic considerations, in ways that are often largely language-specific.

the NP$_{\boxed{i}}$ at issue, and RESTR(ICTION), which expresses a semantic restriction on that index. The resulting feature specifications respectively correspond to the i-th variable and the restriction formula making up the logical translation $x_i|\,\varphi$ (or, in mainstream GQT notation, $\lambda x_i\!:\varphi$) of the nominal object itself. As for the information that a nominal object can provide through the feature RESTR, it is represented by a **set** of *psoa* objects, "written as a list of feature structure descriptions between curly brackets", wherein "the order of elements ... is not significant" (Pollard & Sag 1987: p. 47)[49]. See a very simple – and notationally simplified – example as part of (88), the *npro* (= *nonpronoun*)[50] value of CONTENT assigned to the common noun "book" in the singular. (Of course, a set value for RESTR is not motivated by one-word items, but more complex nominals use it to collect psoas from both the head noun and modifiers like adjectives, relative clauses, etc., as chapter 4 will show.)

(88)
$$_{npro}\begin{bmatrix} \text{INDEX } \boxed{1}\ _{ref}\begin{bmatrix} \text{PERSON } \textit{3rd} \\ \text{NUMBER } \textit{sing} \\ \text{GENDER } \textit{neut} \end{bmatrix} \\ \text{RESTR } \left\{ \textit{book}(\boxed{1}) \right\} \end{bmatrix}$$

In this structure, the set description contains a single *psoa*, which concerns the unary relation *book* (cf. (87a) above) and logically corresponds to the atomic formula 'book(x_1)', with an occurrence of the same variable that is restricted by apposition of the formula in '$x_1|\,$book(x_1)'.[51]

---

[49]The peculiar status of set values in feature-theoretic systems should not be obscured by the fact that a feature structure too may look like a kind of unordered set. Just to show the simplest case of feature structure commutation, $[f,\ f']$ is the same as $[f',\ f]$, but f and f' are single features (i.e. attribute-value pairs), whereas the elements of a *set* in the sense of HPSG are feature structures. Moreover, each feature structure must be internally consistent, in a way that is not required at the level of a set of feature structures. E.g., there cannot be any feature structure [+N, −N], because of the contradictory values for the same attribute, but a set {[+N], [−N]} is possible.

[50]A subsort of *nominal-object*; the alternative to *nonpronoun* is, unsurprisingly, the subsort *pronoun*, which we leave aside for the moment.

[51]The value of RESTR should translate as a conjunctive formula $\wedge\{\varphi_1, \varphi_2, \ldots \varphi_n\}$ where each φ_k is a formula translating one of the n elements of the RESTR set, for $1 \leq k \leq n$. This notation, prefixing the relevant connective to a nonempty set of formulae, is inspired by versions of Situation Semantics (v. Pollard & Sag 1987: pp. 88-89, Richard Cooper 1990: p. 125), but also a traditional Boolean interpretation of connectives can be generalized to the n-ary case, e.g. as standardly done for the corresponding 'logical gates' of digital circuits in electronics. Even if common applications of the idea assume $n \geq 2$ conjuncts, nothing prevents us from adding the trivial (truth-value preserving) case with $n = 1$, so that (88) now translates more precisely as '$x_1|\wedge\{$book(x_1)$\}$', equivalent to '$x_1|\,$book(x_1)'.

The property of feature structures which HPSG applies here, in order to warrant that two (or more) value positions in a given attribute-value matrix share the very same value, is known as **token identity**, or indeed 'structure sharing' (see Pollard & Sag 1987: p. 31; 1994: p. 19). The relevant kind of identity, which is indicated by multiple occurrences of the same tag (possibly prefixed to information specifying the shared value at least in part), must be distinguished from the mere **type identity** of values that look identical even if they are reciprocally independent (i.e. distinct 'tokens' in the intended sense) [52]. Since in our example (88) the value of INDEX and (the value of any attribute representing) the argument of *book* are equally tagged as [1], they are token-identical; therefore, the very same index (with all its agreement features) is shared by the two value positions. This is also the relation established – at a distance in some sentence/discourse – by two or more NPs coindexed through their value of INDEX, whereas other NPs may well have type-identical indices without the token-identity that coindexation requires. (E.g., both "a book" and "the table" have an index of type $_{ref}$[PERSON *3rd*, NUMBER *sing*, GENDER *neut*] although they cannot share it, due to their disjoint reference.)

We finally turn to quantificational information. Neglecting earlier versions of HPSG [53], Pollard & Sag (1994: §§ 1.7, 8.2) assume that determiner words like "every", "few", "some", "the", etc., are lexically assigned a generalized quantifier representation which is expected to incorporate the semantic contribution of the adjacent nominal head as an effect of determiner-nominal combination. So, an attribute DET(ERMINER), whose possible values are such 'semantic determiner' labels as *forall* (i.e. '∀'), *exists* (i.e. '∃'), *few*, *most* and others, is introduced to get a feature structure of sort *quant(ifier)*, where the 'nominal object' of the corresponding NP is embedded as value of the attribute RESTIND (= RESTRICTED-INDEX). This treatment exploits the underspecification, or partiality, of linguistic descriptions in the HPSG formalism: out of context, the *quant* information in the lexical entry of a determination item fully specifies the value of DET (according to the meaning of that word) but not the value of RESTIND, which is up to the semantic content of the adjacent nominal head to instantiate.

See in (89) below – slightly simplified as usual – the *quant*-sorted structure a. and the equivalent logical translation b. for the sample NP "some book". Accordingly, the semantic contribution of "some" alone, represented by an

[52] There is some danger of terminological confusion, inasmuch as the notions of 'occurrence' and 'token' of a variable are normally intended as synonymic in logical studies. If the variable is an index of HPSG, however, there can be distinct occurrences of a token $x^{\tau}{}_{i}$, where the superscript τ shows the type with agreement information (even though we usually neglect it in logical translations) and the subscript i is used to distinguish tokens of the same type.

[53] Cf. Pollard & Sag (1987: pp. 106-107), Richard Cooper (1991: pp. 179-183).

attribute-value matrix (90a) with unspecified value $\boxed{2}$, can be equated to the class of those generalized quantifiers which satisfy the pattern (90b), for any set term (= '$x_i|\psi$') translating the RESTIND value. It is clearly tantamount to saying that the semantic representation assigned to the syntactic determiner works as a function yielding fully specified generalized quantifiers from input restrictions, essentially like a GQT semantic determiner.

(89) a.

$$_{quant}\begin{bmatrix} \text{DET } \exists \\ \text{RESTIND} \quad _{npro}\begin{bmatrix} \text{INDEX } \boxed{1} \ _{ref}\begin{bmatrix} \text{PERSON } \textit{3rd} \\ \text{NUMBER } \textit{sing} \\ \text{GENDER } \textit{neut} \end{bmatrix} \\ \text{RESTR} \left\{ \textit{book}(\boxed{1}) \right\} \end{bmatrix} \end{bmatrix}$$

b. $(\exists x_1 | \text{book}(x_1))$

(90) a.

$$_{quant}\begin{bmatrix} \text{DET } \exists \\ \text{RESTIND } \boxed{2} \end{bmatrix}$$

b. $(\exists x_i | \psi)$

The resulting quantifier, i.e. (89a) in our example, will be passed up to the NP node, and further on, for sentence-level interpretation represented by a quantified case of *psoa* (in the sense mentioned before). We postpone to chapter 5 the discussion of techniques applied in HPSG to transmit the quantifier and ultimately give it correct scope within the semantic representation of the whole sentence.

3.3.2 Semantic features of determination

Apart from pertinent constraints on agreement features, like NUMBER (e.g., "a" calls for *singular*, "three" for *plural*), within the original HPSG presented above by § 3.3.1 the particular semantic contribution of a given determiner compared with others comes down to some atomic value of DET in most cases. Pollard & Sag (1994: § 1.8) just envisage an exception for English possessives to be analyzed through the same DET value of the definite article and a RESTR-embedded relation *poss*($\boxed{1}$,$\boxed{2}$) between the 'possessor' $\boxed{1}$ and the 'possessed' $\boxed{2}$ (essentially as we have anticipated in chapter 2). But in general their approach will be revised here so as to decompose every case of 'semantic determiner' in terms of complex feature structures, reflecting regularities and generalizations across determinative items. There are alternative ways of carrying out such a decomposition (cf. van Eijck & Alshawi 1992), yet the one we begin to sketch

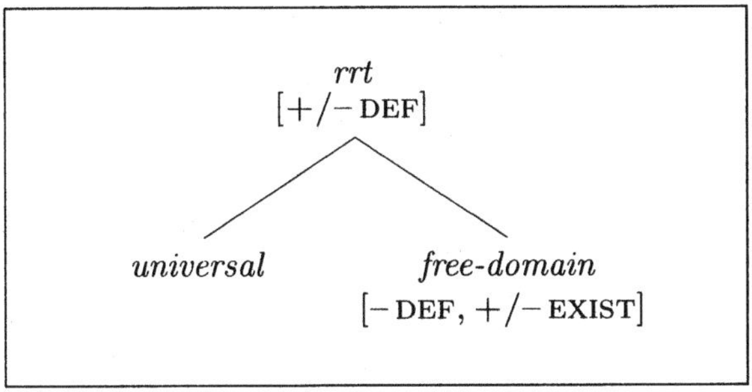

Figure 3.1: RRT Hierarchy

below aims at complementing (our HPSG version of) GQT with pragmatic notions of 'reference' and 'presupposition' which have been argued for in chapter 2 and section 3.2, respectively.

3.3.2.1 On the range of reference

A central role will be played here by the typology of information whose distinctions, conveyed by means of suitable words in natural languages, concern what we call *range of reference*. Hence the abbreviation 'RRT' = **Range of Reference Typology**, to be used from now on. Such a 'range' notion is a set-theoretic constraint on reference which was first introduced to account for the contribution of quantitative determiners in chapter 2, but proves relevant to determiners of any kind, as well as self-determining nominals (proper names, pronouns, bare plurals). For our version of HPSG, the same reference options presented in the above chapter are encoded through the simple 'sort hierarchy' of **Figure 3.1**. We would like to briefly comment on this classificatory schema of RRT from a content viewpoint, whereas notions of the purely formal apparatus that gets thereby applied (viz. sort hierarchies with feature declarations) should be already familiar since our chapter 1.

The hierarchy root, identified by the sort label *rrt*, introduces the declaration of a Boolean feature [+/− DEF(INITE)] and is the mother of two subsorts: *universal* and *free-domain*. A feature co-occurrence restriction is enforced on *free-domain* by restricting it to the '−' value of DEF while introducing another Boolean feature, [+/− EXIST(ENTIAL)], declared at the same node. Neglecting [+/− DEF] temporarily, the referential import of our labels is defined as in (91) so as to yield the three main options of reference (determination), namely:

a. **universal reference**
b′. **existential reference**
b″. **negated existential reference**.

They correspond to the logicians' $\forall$, $\exists$ and $\neg\exists$, respectively, and we shall use the logical symbols accordingly as shorthand for their RRT counterparts.

(91) **RRT Interpretation Criteria**
For a referential expression typed as Σ in terms of RRT hierarchy, if D is the contextually given domain of entities satisfying the descriptive content of that expression, the speaker can assume at least one set R_Σ as range of reference over D, under the following constraints conveyed by Σ:

a. *universal* is interpreted as $R_\Sigma = D$;

b. *free-domain* is interpreted as $R_\Sigma \subseteq D$, with

b′. [+EXIST] interpreted as $R_\Sigma \neq \emptyset$;

b″. [−EXIST] interpreted as $\neg R_\Sigma \neq \emptyset$, i.e. $R_\Sigma = \emptyset$.

Note that the tree in **Figure 3.1** does not include a distinct node (with sort label) for every fully specified feature. It could have been otherwise, e.g. the two feature specifications [+EXIST] and [−EXIST] might be assigned to subsorts of *free-domain*. However, the resulting tree would just display more redundantly the same information that follows from declaration of [+/−EXIST] for the *free-domain* sort. The further subsort distinction could be required to add features and co-occurrence restrictions not envisaged by the current RRT hierarchy, as in the case of a cardinality feature being declared as exclusively associated with [+EXIST]. This restriction turns out to be empirically wrong, though, in view of examples like "*all* (*the*) seven books" or "*no* seven books", where the cardinality information expressed by the numeral combines with an instance of universal or negated existential reference. Cardinal numerals have inherent existential force just in case they are not preceded by any other determiner; hence the need for a modular treatment making cardinality information independent of RRT features as chapter 4 will show.

In a possible different version of the RRT hierarchy, universality might be recoded on a parallel with existentiality, thus specifying a distinction between [+UNIVERSAL] and [−UNIVERSAL] (plus consequent sorts and feature declarations). The result would include the 'fourth corner' of a Square of Opposition like Aristotle's: **negated universal reference**, interpreting [−UNIVERSAL] as $\neg R_\Sigma = D$, i.e. $R_\Sigma \neq D$, while the (91a) interpretation of our *universal* sort would be assigned to [+UNIVERSAL]. But in chapter 2 we already argued for a 'three-cornered subconfiguration' of the Square in natural language lexica, taking into account Horn's (1989: § 4.5) observation that $\neg\forall$-type meaning (unlike $\neg\exists$-type meaning) cannot be expressed by one word alone, but always needs syntactically explicit negation, as in "*not* every/all". Then we assume a set-up that determines $\neg\forall$ reference by combining some independently motivated treatment of general negation (whatever this may mean depending on the framework) and our notion of ∀ or *universal* as a primitive of the system, whereas the ¬∃ reference option follows from the binary status of the feature EXIST under our interpretation[54].

The labels *universal* and EXIST, which appear on opposite branches of the RRT sort hierarchy, have reciprocally 'free' interpretations as regards logical entailments, because in both cases the interpretation of one does not entail the other, or its sheer negation. With English sample items, in particular, neither "every/all" entails "some" nor "some" entails "*not* every/all", contrary to what was claimed by a number of authors[55]. Universal-type reference to the Ø set, for one thing, is consistent with modern logic and proves empirically possible at least in marginal contexts (as we noticed in chapter 2 and – for definite NPs – section 3.2), though a strong pragmatic expectation of non-empty domain applies to the D of (91) in ordinary usage.

Even more evident is the defeasible status of the expectation that not all the domain D be referred to when using an item which determines existential reference. As discussed in detail by Horn (1989: ch. 4), there is a 'conversational implicature' in the sense of Grice (1964) – roughly, a pragmatic inference of implicit information, based on rules of conversation – and the speaker can override it scot-free in appropriate contexts: (92), say, looks fully acceptable and would yield a contradiction if *some* were replaced with *not all.*

(92) *Some* policemen are available in case of need, $\left\{ \begin{array}{c} \text{even} \\ \text{perhaps} \end{array} \right\}$ all

Then the interpretation of *free-domain* was formulated in (91b) by means of '⊆', the relation 'is a subset of' compatible with identity, instead of '⊂', the relation 'is a proper subset of', which would imply ¬∀ reference. (The RRT interpretation of ¬∀ mentioned before, $R_\Sigma \neq D$, is equivalent to $R_\Sigma \subset D$, since all elements of R_Σ must come from the given domain D in any case.)

Our next step is to clarify how the **RRT Interpretation Criteria** fit the uniform quantificational approach to NP interpretation which was outlined in section 3.2, building on mainstream GQT. For one thing, the quantification at issue gets restricted to the same domain we are assuming in (91), insofar as D

[54]It is a linguistic assumption (with possible implications for cognitive patterns) and not a matter of logical necessity, to be sure, because one might as well define ¬∃-determination by combining general negation and (our counterpart of) '∃', as usually done in FOL. But note that '∃' too would be dispensable in FOL, being defined as the **logical dual** of '∀', and nevertheless is retained by most logicians, at least for reasons of simplicity and naturalness. Moreover, a primitive semantic determiner corresponding to *no* is also assumed in GQT (Barwise & Cooper 1981).

[55]The former claim underlies the Aristotelian version of a Square of Opposition, as we observed cursorily in chapter 2, while Horn (1989: § 4.2) ascribes the latter claim to the philosopher W. Hamilton and the linguist O. Jespersen (but cf. also Hawkins 1978: p. 187, for a similar interpretation of the indefinite article).

coincides with the 'restriction set' denoted by the set term of GQT quantifier expressions, or equivalently, by its HPSG representation of sort *nominal-object* (see § 3.3.1 above). In typical cases of explicit determination, D is indeed the set of contextually available individuals that satisfy the descriptive conditions expressed by the nominal the determiner combines with, whereas RRT options for the resulting NP depend on the determiner. However, our work will also show that HPSG lends itself to extend the semantic treatment to less transparent forms, including determinerless NPs, even if they do not distinguish morpho-syntactically between a part of the NP with determinative function and a part denoting the quantification domain.[56]

Irrespective of the morpho-syntactic expression of RRT options, the proposed feature structure interpretation can be proved to supply usual GQT denotations for the NP. To this end, we have to take into account a logical constraint Barwise & Cooper (1981) imposed on the generalized quantifier Q as denoted set of sets, by saying that Q **lives on** its own restriction set, a.k.a. quantification domain. The 'lives on (D)' property means that for any set X of elements of the universe of discourse, $X \in Q$ iff $[X \cap D] \in Q$, where '$\in$' and '$\cap$' are set-theoretic operators of membership and intersection, respectively. (In practice, the part of X that is outside D is irrelevant for evaluating Q.) Different quantifiers result from a given domain through different ways of living on it, whose prototypical cases expressed by determiner words form the same triad that was identified by familiar logical symbols since chapter 2. Hence the intersection $X \cap D$ must equal: ***(i)*** D itself, so that $D \subseteq X$, in case of $\forall$-determination; ***(ii)*** a non-empty subset of D, in case of $\exists$-determination; ***(iii)*** the empty set, in case of $\neg\exists$-determination. Given our interpretation of the RRT Hierarchy, ***(i)***-***(iii)*** clearly match the three reference options of (91), as indicated by the corresponding logical symbols used as abbreviations.

We are actually in a position to formulate this overall 'conversion rule' for deriving NP denotations *à la* GQT from the range-of-reference sets allowed by the RRT Interpretation Criteria:

(93) **Conversion from RRT to GQT**
Let Q be an upward or downward monotone quantifier denoted by a given NP, such that Q lives on the domain D. For every R_Σ which is a possible range of reference over D according to the typing Σ of that NP, Q is the set of all sets X whose intersection with D

- includes R_Σ, i.e. $R_\Sigma \subseteq [X \cap D]$, when Q is upward monotone,
- or is included by R_Σ, i.e. $[X \cap D] \subseteq R_\Sigma$, when Q is downward monotone.

[56] Of course, the morpho-syntactic distinction could be artificially restored by postulating some '(phonologically) empty constituent' to fulfil one function or the other, but that kind of approach was already criticized in chapter 1.

The distinction w.r.t. $\subseteq$ depends on the determiner yielding a quantifier with a certain monotonicity property (a notion explained before by § 3.2.2.2), but gets neutralized in the two 'extreme' cases (91a) / ***(i)*** and (91b″) / ***(iii)***, because they reduce inclusion to identity. That is, all sets X belonging to Q share the same $R_\Sigma = [X \cap D]$ when the NP's typing Σ allows only one possible range of reference per domain D: either D itself, which is the maximal subset of D that $[X \cap D]$ can include, in accordance with upward monotonicity, or the empty set, which is the minimal subset of D that can include $[X \cap D]$, in accordance with downward monotonicity. The remaining case (91b′) / ***(ii)***, instead, is also known as **indefinite** because of its greater indeterminacy in setting the range of reference, a point that we are going to expand on henceforth.

Since [+EXIST] in itself imposes on R_Σ the sole constraint of being non-empty (i.e., '$\exists$' informally means *at least one*), the range-of-reference sets thus allowed over a certain domain D are in fact all the subsets of D apart from $\emptyset$, the empty set. It is consequently necessary to distinguish between a **possible** range of reference as allowed by Σ for D and the **intended** range of reference in a given context. The distinction, neutralized by $\forall$ and $\neg\exists$ (qua options of Σ whereby the intended range of reference obviously coincides with the only possible one), causes the 'indefiniteness' of existential determination/reference. To what extent a particular set can be identified as intended range of reference among various alternatives that are abstractly possible, given an indefinite NP with relevant D, is a matter of context in which the NP occurs; reinterpreting a traditional notion accordingly (as in Karttunen 1969), let's say the same NP can be used with different degrees of 'specificity'. Occasionally, we shall touch on factors of linguistic and extralinguistic context which bear on the process of set selection making indefinite reference more or less specific, like the content of predication, the scope of such expressions as quantifiers, negation, modals, etc., the presence of anaphoric or deictic references, and the speaker's world knowledge, even if we cannot examine their contribution in detail.

Let us turn to the lexical realization of indefiniteness in natural languages of our coverage. In chapter 2, *some* was considered the prototypical instance of $\exists$-determination entailed by all the determinative items that express degrees of non-null quantity in English. It is tantamount to saying that the semantic determiner '$\exists$' captures precisely the count interpretation of the determiner word *some*, which in RRT terms would then allow any non-empty subset of D as possible range of reference. This claim lays itself open to criticism, insofar as the semantic relevance of grammatical number looks neglected: traditional grammarians and lexicographers of English have often described the singular count use of *some* as a distinguished lexical reading of the determiner, roughly meaning 'an unspecified single individual', while a complementary reading in the plural would be restricted to sets of at least 2 elements. What's more, the semantic distinction correlates with partly different phonetic forms, since the singular count *some* must be stressed, contrary to the form in the plural (or singular uncountable, which we don't treat [57]). Nevertheless, even if lexically distinct readings or forms are assumed for the English word, at a certain level of abstraction we deem it legitimate and useful to integrate the corresponding interpretations into an overall one with *some* just meaning '∃' altogether, also because there are languages where a sheer lexicalization of existential meaning without extra constraints of number is available.

E.g., the existential determiner *qualche* in Italian is grammatically singular, but compatible with a range of reference containing several individuals at the same time, as in the following context:

(94) Maria porterà *qualche* amico$_{sing.}$: per lo meno Giovanni, Luigi e Piero
'Maria will bring some friend[s]: at least Giovanni, Luigi and Piero'

If one wants to morpho-syntactically constrain *qualche* so as to exclude multiple reference of the kind, the indefinite article must be added; thus, "*un* qualche amico" has to be referred to an unspecified single friend, just like "some friend" in English, and would not be appropriately used in a (94)-type context. On the other hand, the complementary constraint on cardinality can be enforced in Italian by opting for an alternative word, the plural existential *alcuni* qua exact equivalent of *some* in the plural. Extending to these items a quantitative schema chapter 2 applied to 'multal' determiners, namely $\mathrm{Card}(R_\Sigma) > \mathcal{K}_x$, the cardinality value $\mathcal{K}_x$ that a set is expected to exceed in order to satisfy the requirement for plural existential reference is simply 1, instead of a vague context-dependent standard as in the case of *many*, or Italian *molti*, etc.

To sum up, the overall meaning of *some* may as well be represented by the constraint $\mathrm{Card}(R_\Sigma) \geq 1$, which is the exact equivalent of $R_\Sigma \neq \emptyset$ but encoded through cardinality. A singular vs. plural distinction of count readings for *some* corresponds to the respective cases ($= 1$ and > 1) ensuing from the cardinality constraint. That the distinction does not follow from a general interpretation of grammatical number, but has lexical status on a par with the idiosyncratic constraints of 'multal' quantitatives or similar, is shown by determiners in the singular whose range of reference is not restricted to cardinality $= 1$; e.g. Italian *qualche* and, moreover, universal determiners like *every*, or Italian *ogni*, etc. Anyhow, it is clear that an adequate way of encoding cardinality constraints must supplement the prototypical 'triad' of reference (determination) within our system of semantic representations.

For the moment, we focus on empirical evidence concerning cardinality of ∃-type semantic determiners in mainstream GQT. Obviously fundamental is

[57] But cf. chapter 2, where we argued that somehow uncountables can be semantically related to plural meaning.

the case of cardinal numerals, which in chapter 2 were assumed to express an utterly precise numerical constraint in such a way that any range of reference thus determined has to be a non-empty set of n elements, where n is the value of the numeral. It might seem that this proposal captures only a derivative reading/use of cardinals, the one Barwise & Cooper (1981) made explicit as 'exactly n' and then defined by conjunction of 'at least n' and 'at most n'[58]; since the latter, in its turn, corresponds to the negation of 'at least $n+1$', the basic reading/use of a cardinal like *three* can be reduced to 'at least *three*' $= \exists_3$, as we reported in § 3.2.2.2. (Note also that the conjunction of 'at least n' and 'at most n' neutralizes their opposite monotonicity, explaining why 'exactly n' is neither upward nor downward monotone.)

Still, the criticism does not really apply to the present approach, because we do not claim that a numeral n means 'exactly n' as far as truth-conditions are concerned. Here a precise cardinality constraint is imposed on the range of reference, not the intersection set $[X \cap D]$, which preserves the same truth-conditions as in the case of 'at least n'. The result follows from the conversion into upward monotone quantifiers – as per (93) above – given that a range of reference R_Σ with exactly n elements may well be a **proper** subset of $[X \cap D]$; i.e., the set X belonging to the quantifier Q in question is allowed to contain more than n elements of D[59]. A nice consequence of this method is that the speaker can appropriately refer to a precise number of pertinent individuals with property/ies P, even in contexts in which there is a greater number of individuals that are P and the speaker does not (intend to) deny that.

E.g., by uttering a discourse like:

(95) At the end of the lesson, *three girls* were leaving the classroom. John decided to follow *them* among the crowd.

one neither says nor implies (in any sense of 'implying') that those were the only three girls leaving the classroom at the end of the lesson.[60] There might

[58]Like negation (to be interpreted by GQT as we mentioned in note 31), binary connectives apply to quantifiers, although we find it convenient to think in terms of conjunction of determiners when their quantifiers share the same restriction. For a quantifier expression formed by **conjunction**, the denotation is the intersection of the denotations of the two component expressions; in case of **disjunction**, it is the union.

[59]Readers acquainted with GQT may have noticed that in (93) our range-of-reference set plays a role very similar to what Barwise & Cooper (1981) dubbed '**witness set** for the quantifier', meaning any subset of D that is also an element of Q qua set of sets. A difference arises when some precise cardinality costraint n implies that only those witness sets whose cardinality is n be accepted as possible range of reference according to RRT.

[60]That is, the situation of (95) is not one where the speaker means 'there are exactly three girls ...', whether the 'at most' component of 'exactly' mentioned before belongs to the conventional meaning expressed or results from a purely pragmatic inference – a.k.a. conversational implicature – *à la* Grice (1964) and Horn (1989).

be other girls among the crowd, so that '$\underset{3}{\exists}$' yields the right truth-conditions, but exactly three girls are referred to – also anaphorically, through the pronoun – and John is meant to follow them, not any random group of possibly more than three girls behaving in the way described by the text. Interestingly, the same line of reasoning applies to other indefinite determiners, especially the indefinite article. If (95) is revised so as to replace *three girls* with *a girl* and adapt agreement and anaphora accordingly, one gets a completely analogous situation. There may well be more than one girl in the crowd which leaves the classroom, so that '$\exists$' yields the right truth-conditions, but exactly one girl is referred to with *a girl* and justifies the subsequent use of the co-referential anaphoric pronoun *her*.

As we mentioned in chapter 2, some notion of 'discourse referents' applied by much research in discourse semantics (ever since Karttunen 1969) is clearly involved here, while fully preserving the compositional set-up of mainstream GQT. We will not explore in detail the implications for a theory of anaphoric relations within discourse (or, in general, beyond quantifier scope boundaries), but what one can foresee appears to be in line with remarks on the subject by Pollard & Sag (1994: p. 328):

> "The analysis of quantification we have sketched ... treats indefinite NPs in terms of existential quantifiers rather than **reference markers** of the sort proposed within discourse representation theory (Kamp 1981) or file change semantics (Heim 1982). Instead, ... our treatment would have to rely either on an 'E-type' analysis of pronoun interpretations (Evans 1977; 1980, Heim 1990) or else on a 'dynamic' approach to the interpretation of the appropriate existential quantifier (Groenendijk & Stokhof 1990; 1991)".[61]

Especially the Evans-type view of anaphoric pronouns as somehow 'disguised' definite descriptions lends itself to a straightforward reformulation according to our proposals. But before saying anything on such possible developments based on the import of definiteness, we must revisit this in the light of RRT.

3.3.2.2 Definiteness revisited

To complete our general survey of the RRT Hierarchy displayed by **Figure 3.1** above, let us explicitly link it up with the HPSG representation of quantifiers in terms of feature structures. The point of contact obviously is the feature DET by Pollard & Sag (1994), whose atomic values *forall*, *exists*, etc. can be superseded by slightly more structured, yet corresponding representations of

[61]See also Van Eynde & Allegranza (1995) for articles with introductory presentations of various systems cited in the quotation.

sort *rrt* (instead of *semdet*), namely those we have been discussing in § 3.3.2.1. Pollard & Sag's original feature declaration (ibid., p. 399) is simply revised as:

(96)
$$_{quant}\begin{bmatrix}\text{DET } \textit{rrt} \\ \text{RESTIND } \textit{nom-object}\end{bmatrix}$$

Thus one should preferably understand the familiar label DET as abbreviating DETERMINATION-RANGE, rather than DETERMINER (cf. Pollard & Sag 1987: p. 106; 1994: pp. 47, 432), also considering that its values in this version are not meant to exhaust the semantic contribution of determiners. (E.g., cardinality constraints are not included; the issue of how to introduce them within the HPSG representations will be discussed in chapter 4.)

A theory-internal difference in the information to be encoded through DET values follows from the variant of GQT we have motivated in § 3.2.2.2. That is, Pollard & Sag (1994: § 1.8) envisage a DET value *the* and therefore seem to share Barwise & Cooper's (1981) idea of a special semantic determiner of GQT for the definite article (at least in the singular), whereas we decompose the same meaning into two parts: the ordinary ∀, which would be represented by *forall* in Pollard and Sag's original HPSG and becomes *univ(ersal)* for us, and definiteness information proper. Following a somewhat traditional proposal from grammatical work in the field, we have resorted to the [+/− DEF(INITE)] feature that was vindicated by chapter 2 and can be revisited with a view to embody the account of definiteness already presented extensively in the current chapter by section 3.2.

Since definiteness in our approach is an extra constraint to be distinguished from any 'semantic determiner' in a strict GQT sense, the display of [+DEF] information by some fully specified object of sort *quant* makes this the HPSG counterpart of what was called a 'quantifier-SR' in our § 3.2.2.2, i.e. the representation of a generalized quantifier together with a relevant presupposition. E.g., (97) is meant as feature structure (with familiar abbreviations) encoding the same information provided by the pair of logical expressions (98) [62], viz. the quantifier-SR translating the NP "the book".

(97)
$$_{quant}\begin{bmatrix}\text{DET } \forall\begin{bmatrix}\text{+DEF}\end{bmatrix} \; (= {}_{univ}\begin{bmatrix}\text{+DEF}\end{bmatrix}) \\ \text{RESTIND} \; _{npro}\begin{bmatrix}\text{INDEX } \boxed{1} \; _{ref}\begin{bmatrix}\text{PERSON } \textit{3rd} \\ \text{NUMBER } \textit{sing} \\ \text{GENDER } \textit{neut}\end{bmatrix} \\ \text{RESTR } \left\{ \textit{book}(\boxed{1}) \right\}\end{bmatrix}\end{bmatrix}$$

[62] Or '$\forall(\lambda x\colon \text{book}(x))$' and '$\exists^{*}\lambda x\colon [\text{book}(x) \wedge \forall^{*}\lambda y\colon [\text{book}(y) \supset y = x]\,]$', in GQT notation.

(98) a. $(\forall x|\,\text{book}(x))$

b. $(\exists x|\,\text{book}(x))\,(\forall y|\,\text{book}(y))\,y{=}x$

To separate the NP's logical form – hence the 'generalized quantifier' expression of GQT strictly speaking – from its presupposition, it is sufficient to exploit a partial representation allowed by the HPSG formalism. That is, we can encode the information (98a) through an underspecified version of (97) where the DEF feature is omitted, so as to yield the logical form that "the book" and "every book" have in common. (Likewise, (89a), in § 3.3.1 above, still holds as logical form for "some book", reinterpreting the '∃' notation of the DET value.)

The fact that definite NPs require universal quantification at the level of logical form (as we argued since § 3.2.1) results from the feature co-occurrence restriction specified in **Figure 3.1** by distinguishing two subsorts of *rrt*. While *univ* corresponds to logical ∀ and can (but need not) be specified for [+DEF] information, *free-domain* is only compatible with [−DEF], the specification of those quantifier-SRs whose DET value introduces no presupposition. The case [−DEF] should be glossed 'not marked as definite' (= free from the definiteness constraint) and the readers are warned against equating it with 'indefinite', a label usually employed by modern semanticists to indicate only the ∃ option for items not marked as definite. Since we stick to this terminological usage, the 'indefinite(ness)' concept corresponds to [+EXIS] in our notation, but [−DEF] is much more general in that it also combines with [+UNIV] or [−EXIS].[63] So, it is clear that the value '−' in [−DEF] indicates mere irrelevance of the state represented by the positive feature (whether the state accidentally obtains or not), instead of logical negation as in [−EXIS].[64]

We ensure the intended interpretation of *quant* objects as generalized quantifiers through the following 'translation rule', mapping from feature structures to corresponding expressions of logical form in GQT notation, so as to make explicit the functional application of the DET interpretation to the RESTIND interpretation.

(99) $\begin{bmatrix}\text{DET}\ \boxed{1}\\ \text{RESTIND}\ \boxed{2}\end{bmatrix} \rightsquigarrow \boxed{1}'(\boxed{2}')$

In (99), the prime-bearing version of a given HPSG 'tag', i.e. boxed numeral, stands for some logical expression τ with the same semantic interpretation as the value tagged accordingly on the lefthand side. The rule format [...]$\rightsquigarrow\tau$ is

[63]The alternative terminological usage applying 'indefinite' to all [−DEF] items (including, e.g., *every* and *no* besides *a*, *some*, *many*, etc.) was typical of traditional grammarians and is still found, at times, in the linguistic literature.

[64]Cf. the issue of binarism in generative phonology, where "it is ... arguable that the + and − values of given attributes do not have a unique interpretation" (Durand 1990: p. 74).

resolved as an equation $\boxed{k}' = \tau$, with $\boxed{k}$ tagging the whole feature structure [...] in question.

Note that the translation of semantic feature structures as logical expressions that gets performed by (99), with other analogous rules/equations, is a meta-grammatical means, not a proper aspect of natural language grammars according to HPSG. Therefore, convenient though the logical translations may prove (for clarity's sake, abbreviation purposes, etc.), in principle they are entirely dispensable. On the contrary, HPSG's CONTENT feature structures have a cognitively motivated linguistic status roughly comparable with that of the Logical Form (LF) level in Chomskyan generative grammar (see our previous note 41 for some references). There are also strong differences, of course, since LF is traditionally characterized as a syntactic level under a transformational derivation or equivalent algorithm, whereas we build up the feature-structure representation of logical form in parallel with surface structure, as two sides (meaning and expression) of the same linguistic sign, aiming at a reasonably compositional system.

The logical translation – or corresponding model-theoretic interpretation – of any *quant* object instantiating the lefthand side of (99) gets compositionally constructed from the component features (as they were declared for the *quant* sort in (96)), but 'tuning' the two formalisms in that way would not suffice to ensure compositionality for a natural language expression with internal phrase structure. What allows overall compositionality requirements to be satisfied is indeed the parallelism of syntax with semantic feature structure. The effect can be schematically exemplified as follows for a Noun Phrase like "the book":

(100) $NP' = f(Art', Nom') = Art'(Nom') = \boxed{k}'$ *where* $[_{NP:\boxed{k}}$ Art Nom$]$

In a meta-grammatical format that takes into account annotations of feature structures to phrase structure nodes with a view to extend a kind of equations we have introduced in § 3.2.2.1, (100) means that the translation/interpretation to be compositionally based on the input from the NP's syntactic components (i.e. immediate constituents) must equal the translation/interpretation of $\boxed{k}$. This tag identifies the CONTENT value of the NP node[65], hence a *quant* object analyzed as before by the rule (99), according to our version of HPSG.

Now, we have already explained that the [+DEF] information is a part of S(emantic) R(epresentation) not affecting truth-conditions, so that it does not belong to logical form. While the DET value's translation/interpretation for the purposes of rule (99) will simply ignore the positive or negative specification of DEF, the distiction matters for the part of SR to be interpreted as associated

[65]We apply a standard abbreviating convention of HPSG: "The CONTENT value may also be mentioned in the [NP] abbreviation, in which case it is notated after a colon" (Pollard & Sag 1994: p. 28).

with implicit, presupposed propositions. The sign-based grammar of a natural language can spell out the resulting pragmatic information through a suitable feature structure, as done by Pollard & Sag (1994: pp. 22, 27):

> "the CONTEXT value [– a structure of sort *context* –] contains certain context-dependent linguistic information usually discussed under such rubrics as indexicality, presupposition and/or conventional implicature. ... For the moment we consider a single *context* attribute called BACKGROUND (BACKR), whose value is a set of psoas... Unlike RESTRICTION psoas, ... BACKGROUND psoas are not part of the CONTENT value but should rather be considered as felicity conditions on the utterance context."

Exploiting a standard formalization of HPSG[66], we encode the 'conventional implicature' of linguistic expressions with [+DEF] meaning rather literally, in terms of an implicational constraint on feature structures:

(101) **Definiteness Constraint:**

$$\left[\text{CONTENT}\begin{bmatrix}\text{DET}|\text{+DEF}\\ \text{RESTIND } \boxed{2}\end{bmatrix}\right] \Longrightarrow \left[\text{CTEXT}|\text{BACKR}\left\{...\right\}\cup\left\{\mathit{Def}^{*}(\boxed{2})\right\}\right]$$

The lefthand side of (101) identifies the linguistic objects whose CONTENT is marked as [+DEF] and, as a consequence of that, the righthand side adds the definiteness presupposition to the set value of CONTEXT|BACKGROUND by means of the union operator '∪'. Here we have adopted a more compact logical formulation of the presupposition given before in a rather longwinded format, like (98b) for the NP "the book". By application of the Definiteness Constraint to this example, the presupposition added to BACKR is '$\mathit{Def}^{*}(\lambda x\colon \text{book}(x))$', a formula with a second-order, starred predicate that takes as argument the set term corresponding to the RESTIND value (or 'nominal object') of (97) and is meant to preserve exactly the truth-conditions of the (98b) formula. (Our star notation was introduced for atomic cases of generalized quantifier, e.g. 'John*', in § 3.2.2.1.)

Since the resulting presupposition for a definite description encompasses the familiar existence and uniqueness conditions, its referential effect is to restrict

[66]See, e.g., Pollard & Sag (1987: p. 43): "The symbol '⟹' here denotes a certain binary operation on feature structures. ... if A and B are feature structures, then A ⟹ B is the greatest (i.e. least informative) feature structure whose unification with A is subsumed by B". Another piece of notation displayed in (101) is a 'path', i.e. a finite sequence of feature attributes $\mathcal{F}_1 \mid \mathcal{F}_2 \mid ... \mathcal{F}_n$ such that each non-initial $\mathcal{F}_{i+1}$ (e.g., BACKGROUND) is declared for the sort of objects taken as value of the immediately preceding $\mathcal{F}_i$ (= CONTEXT, or CTEXT, in our example). This path notation is useful to abbreviate the embedding of feature structures when only one feature per structure has to be shown.

the domain D to one and only one individual, a restriction that consequently holds for the range of reference R_Σ too. (Definiteness is a case of ∀-reference, so that $R_\Sigma = D$; v. (91a), § 3.3.2.1 above.) It sounds natural to call the individual in question 'the **referent** of the NP', conforming to traditional terminology, but we see no good reason why the same notion should not be appropriate in cases other than definite NPs. At least generalizing to all NPs in the singular, we assume that every individual which belongs to a set R_Σ intended as range of reference for one such NP (on a given occasion) is taken as referent, a particular entity the speaker refers to.

The fact that the traditional notion of referents is arrived at in RRT by setting a **range** of reference, under more or less flexible constraints, has various advantages. In the first place, the same NP token can be used for simultaneous 'distributive' reference to more than one individual in the same context. It is a phenomenon especially transparent with ∀ determiners in the singular – like English *every* and the closely related form *each*[67] – which "pick out the members of a set ... singly [i.e. as distinct referents], rather than look at them all together" (Leech & Svartvik 1975: p. 50). Since *universal* (=∀) equates the range of reference to the whole domain D, every element of the latter too is taken as referent, thus achieving the result of universal distributive reference (restricted to D, as usual). On the other hand, when R_Σ has no elements, as systematically required for [–EXIST] (=¬∃), we may well say that there is no referent without denying referentiality in a weaker sense, because the empty set is nonetheless envisaged as range of reference.

In the remaining case [+EXIST] (=∃) the range of reference of an indefinite NP in the singular like *a*, or the corresponding reading of *some*, is restricted to a single individual, although the restriction has a different status compared with definite NPs. As we explained in § 3.3.2.1, it is a cardinality constraint of the explicit lexical meaning (not a presupposition) and applies directly to R_Σ while the cardinality of D may well be (and normally is) greater. Our account leads to quite a simple way of treating anaphoric co-references at the level of discourse, as in:

(102) At the end of the lesson, *a girl* was leaving the classroom. John decided to follow *her / the girl* among the crowd.

The antecedent NP, *a girl*, and the anaphor (whether pronoun or definite description) share the same referent $\boldsymbol{r}$ because this individual is the only element of the intended range of reference in both cases. The first sentence introduces $\boldsymbol{r}$ as just one indefinite member of some domain of contextually existing girls

[67]Note that *every*, historically, derives from *everich* = 'ever each'. The semantic and/or pragmatic differences between the modern forms *every* and *each* are subtle (v. Vendler 1967, Leech & Svartvik 1975: § 63, Robin Cooper 1991) and negligible for our current discussion.

(possibly including other girls that were leaving the classroom), but reference becomes definite for the anaphor in the second sentence by presupposing the same range-of-reference set of the antecedent, i.e. $\{\boldsymbol{r}\}$, and equating it with the new D to be adopted as quantification domain.

Of course, coreference is successfully established subject to compatibility with the anaphor's inherent semantic content constraining the domain D. For the descriptive NP *the girl*, the referent must have the property 'girl' expressed by the nominal head, whose denotation gets contextually restricted through coreference in a case like (102). That is, the NP in context means 'the relevant girl previously referred to', with the **uniqueness** condition of its definiteness presupposition formula relativized accordingly, so as to exclude from D any other possible girls of the situation in which the discourse is uttered. By the same token, an anaphoric personal pronoun *her*, interpreted as replacing the definite description in the discourse in question, means 'the relevant feminine individual previously referred to'. In our analysis – a variant of so-called 'E-type' pronouns (in the sense of Evans 1977; 1980) – it's enough to assume that they are [+DEF] and the only difference from descriptive NPs arises from the pronouns' lack of inherent semantic constraints on D besides agreement.

We would like to conclude the discussion of definiteness by explaining how plural instances can be covered. Cf. our quantifier-SR for "the books":

(103)
$$_{quant}\begin{bmatrix} \text{DET } \forall\begin{bmatrix}\text{+DEF}\end{bmatrix} \\ \text{RESTIND } _{npro}\begin{bmatrix} \text{INDEX } \boxed{1}\ _{ref}\begin{bmatrix}\text{PERSON } \textit{3rd} \\ \text{NUMBER } \textit{plur} \\ \text{GENDER } \textit{neut}\end{bmatrix} \\ \text{RESTR } \left\{ \textit{books}(\boxed{1}) \right\} \end{bmatrix} \end{bmatrix}$$

(104) a. $(\forall x |\, \text{books}(x))$

b. $(\exists\, x |\, \text{books}(x))\, (\forall\, y |\, \text{books}(y))\, y \subseteq x$

The *quant* feature structure (103) differs from that of the corresponding singular example "the book" (= (97) above) just because of the plural information found within index and restriction. A language of logic with sufficient expressive power recodes the same information through **variables** and **predicates** assigned to pertinent 'logical types' (in the sense we made clear in § 3.2.2.1), even though our simplified notation for (104) omits explicit typing (by superscripts, say) and exploits the inflection of English to indicate plurality. What matters now is the intended semantic interpretation due to a systematic type-raising whose general implications will be presented in chapter 4: at least for the kind of plural uses exemplified in (103)/(104), the minimal components of denotations are not individuals from the 'universe of discourse' but sets of such individuals.

We can appraise the effect on plural definiteness by paraphrasing the presupposition of "the books" accordingly. Given the inclusion predicate '$\subseteq$' and consistent assignments of set-type values to the variables x and y, (104b) means that a set x of books includes every set y of books (up to the identity of values w.r.t. x and y). Thus, the set x verifying (104b) is the maximal set of individual books available in the relevant context (under a certain world model), i.e. the set whose elements are all and only those individuals. As we informally anticipated in chapter 1, the fact that this set indeed exists and is unique satisfies the definiteness conditions, irrespective of the number of individual elements. But then, since '$\subseteq$' allows decomposition as two disjoint cases, namely identity and proper inclusion, and the former (contrary to the latter) may well hold for individuals besides sets, plural definiteness follows from a straightforward generalization of the 'Russellian' conditions.[68] That is, we are eventually in a position to state the equivalence below – a sort of 'meaning postulate', in the terminology of Carnap (1947)[69] – for the second-order predicate representing definiteness in a compact fashion:

(105) $Def^{*}(\xi)$ *iff*: $(\exists x \mid \xi(x))\,(\forall y \mid \xi(y))\,[y{=}x \vee y{\subset}x]$

Our treatment clarifies why the plural definite article, which in logical form comes down to '$\forall$' binding a variable restricted to sets (v. (104a)), can express universality w.r.t. an arbitrary number of individuals by distributive reference to all members of the sets concerned. It is just the singular number's difference in logical type that confines $\forall$-quantification to a unique individual, as '$\subset$' qua condition for sets is falsified while enforcing its alternative in (105), hence the usual identity condition on individuals.[70] There would be much more to say on the semantics of plural, especially the way it interacts with some predicates so as to allow 'collective' readings whereby predication is not distributed to the individual members of the relevant set (cf. Scha 1981, Hoeksema 1983, Link 1983; 1987, Lønning 1987, etc.), but we can stop here for the purposes of the present discussion.

---

[68]See also Sharvy (1980) for a comparable approach within a partly different semantics.

[69]Alternatively, the part before *iff* could be considered a mere abbreviation, one of the kind known as 'parameterized macro' in computer science. In this case, (105) has a parameter ξ to be instantiated throughout by the nominal-object's set term. E.g., the RESTIND value of (103) instantiates ξ as 'λx: books(x)', which reduces to 'books' by a so-called *λ-conversion* (v. Dowty et al. 1981: pp. 99-100); hence the resulting formula (104b), or equivalent.

[70]In a suitable logic, "the ... symbol '=' can be used to assert the identity of two expressions of any type whatsoever as long as both expressions have the same type" (Dowty et al. 1981: p. 159). We assume the same combinatorial properties for '$\subset$', yet it will always yield *false* when applied to individuals instead of sets.

3.4 Conclusions

This chapter has sketched a basic semantic analysis of determination in terms of the feature-theoretic labels *universal*, [+/− EXIST] and [+/− DEF], which are understood so as to be compatible with model-theoretic interpretations (or corresponding logical translations). Although the notions thus captured look intuitive and should be covered somehow by any semantic theory, our specific proposal for integrating the resulting feature specifications into a version of HPSG's CONTENT structure is obviously not without alternatives. In § 3.3.2.1 we have cursorily mentioned possible variants as regards the universality and existentiality notions, but the most controversial issue is clearly raised by the status of definiteness.

Given the CONTEXT|BACKGROUND side of linguistic 'signs' in HPSG, the occurrence of presuppositional features like [+DEF] within the CONTENT might look unnecessary, even a useless complication. The definiteness presupposition triggered by a certain word, e.g. the definite article, could be added to the set of 'background psoas' through that word's lexical entry, which would directly specify what our Definiteness Constraint (101) has represented on the right-hand side of an implication. For a direct lexical treatment of the kind, the definite article (or other determiner) must have access to the semantic content of the adjacent head, so as to instantiate the particular presupposition accordingly, but an equivalent power is already required for building the NP's generalized quantifier within the lexical entry of the same determiner (as we saw in § 3.3.1). The simplified set-up would dispense with our [+/− DEF] feature and related implicational constraint.

There are nonetheless two or three reasons why we believe that our feature is well-motivated. First, the use of [+DEF] together with the (101) constraint captures a generalization across words (and the phrases thereby projected), avoiding the repetition of the same type of lexical coding for a large number of entries. Actually an 'open class' of lexical entries (of various morpho-syntactic categories) is relevant, insofar as not only definite determiners, but also self-determining definite items of nominal category must be covered, as chapter 5 will show in detail for proper names. Second, [+DEF] does more than triggering the addition of a presuppositional 'psoa' on HPSG's *context* side: the feature explicitly connects the same information with the piece of logical form it derives from and preserves their link while construction of the overall Semantic Representation of the sentence proceeds. To recover that link from the BACKGROUND set alone would be conceivable – by comparing the various parts of the logical form with the elements of the set – but formally more complex, especially considering that one sentence may carry several presuppositions at the same time.

It turns out that the SR notion we envisaged since section 3.2 (also including the 'quantifier-SR' at NP level) allows refinement by distinguishing two representational methods, whose difference – contrary to the difference between logical formulae and feature structures – is not a purely notational matter. We started from the design of an 'SR pair' consisting of the logical form of a given expression $\mathcal{E}$ and its associated presupposition (if any), which one should more technically conceive as a (possibly empty) set of presuppositional formulae introduced at the $\mathcal{E}$ level or inherited from component expressions [71]. On the other hand, a more structured representational design showing the links between presuppositions and respective pieces of logical form, to be called 'SR structure', can be worked out in a natural fashion. Let's say the logical form ℓ is assigned a tree structure that recapitulates its 'derivational history', in such a way that ℓ results as the terminal sequence of the tree and every tree node corresponds to a different subsequence ℓ' of ℓ satisfying conditions of logical well-formedness [72]; then the node may well be added annotations like the logical type of ℓ' (e.g. $<<e, t>, t>$ for a quantifier) and, whenever relevant, the presupposition linked to that specific piece of logical form.

The non-equivalence between 'SR pair' and 'SR structure' is also due to the fact that the presuppositional set in the former version of SR undergoes a so-called 'projection' process whereby a presupposition introduced at some stage or another need not be preserved in the final outcome, for (con)textual reasons that should be clear by now. (See a presentation in section 3.2 above.) On the contrary, the presuppositional information of SR structure is recorded permanently where it belongs as a part of conventional meaning. There is no contradiction between these two versions, since Gazdar (1979) has shown how the notion of 'presupposition' is actually intended in two senses, to be made explicit by labels like '**pre**-supposition' and 'speaker's presupposition'. The **pre**-suppositions are just potential presuppositions conventionally associated with natural language expressions because of the linguistic meaning alone, but they need not always be confirmed in a broader (con)text as actual presuppositions by the speaker.[73] Therefore, SR structure in our system consists precisely of a logical form annotated with information about **pre**-suppositions (among other things), while the presuppositional set in SR pairs is meant to arrive at the speaker's presuppositions via a (con)text-sensitive projection process.

---

[71] Due to the semantic interpretation of a set value as conjunctive formula, which was mentioned for RESTR (in note 51, § 3.3.1), we can nevertheless view the value of BACKGROUND as one implicit proposition paired with the proposition expressed.

[72] Of course the tree root is the node corresponding to the whole ℓ as subsequence of itself (i.e. $\ell' = \ell$).

[73] Although the notion of '**pre**-supposition' is derived from Gazdar (1979), the readers are warned that we don't adopt his entire theory of presuppositions (and other 'implicatures'), which lays itself open to criticism as argued by van der Sandt (1988) and Blok (1993).

The account of SR structure, which was only briefly and informally sketched here in terms of a tree apparatus complementing the standard notation of logicians, lends itself to be converted into the formalism of HPSG so as to yield CONTENT feature structures augmented through presuppositional features[74], as we did in § 3.3.2.2. All of this is indeed consistent with (and, theoretically, provides additional evidence for) our treatment based on the [+DEF] feature, instead of relying just on the BACKGROUND. If we adopt the conceptual refinements proposed in the current section, the *quant* object for definites in HPSG will be meta-grammatically interpreted as a **quantifier-SR structure** where [+DEF] is the annotation that allows one to build up the **pre**-supposition of definiteness in parallel with logical form. It is up to the Definiteness Constraint, the implication (101), to feed the projection process with a BACKGROUND *psoa* of definiteness, which will achieve the speaker's presupposition status when canceling conditions don't apply.

[74]Note that the feature structures are also supplied with sort symbols, essentially corresponding to the logical types envisaged as another source of annotations for the SR structure nodes in tree format. (E.g., <<*e*, *t*>, *t*> is replaced by *quant*, <*e*, *t*> by *nominal-object* qua 'set term', etc.)

Chapter 4

HPSG and the Noun Phrase

4.1 Preamble

If the semantic interpretation of natural language expressions results from application of compositional techniques (as was argued before), the syntactic structures on which it is systematically based must be adequately specified. So this chapter sets out to present in some detail the kind of syntax we rely on, with special reference to a treatment of the Noun Phrase, the structure where determiners are located. More generally, we will examine the syntactic component of the grammatical framework we have assumed since chapter 1, a system of 'interpreted phrase structure grammar' which follows in many respects the **HPSG** (= Head-driven Phrase Structure Grammar) theory by Pollard & Sag (1987; 1994).

Besides the aspects that HPSG has in common with other phrase structure systems (especially the framework by Gazdar et al. 1985), there is some broad resemblance to Chomsky's (1981; 1986) theory of Universal Grammar with 'principles and parameters':

> "in both theories, [syntactic] structure is determined chiefly by the interaction between highly articulated lexical entries and parameterized universal principles of grammatical well-formedness, with ... a handful of highly general and universally available phrase structure (or immediate dominance) schemata. ... At the same time, however, there are great many differences between the two theories, with respect to both global theory architecture and matters of technical detail."
>
> Pollard & Sag (1994: p. 2)

A fundamental difference is due to the fact that transformational operations (see the so-called "Move α"), with contributory conditions on their formulation and application, play an important role in orthodox versions of the Chomskyan framework, whereas phrase structure grammars are non-transformational by definition. Nevertheless, HPSG achieves great expressive power because of its formalism with complex feature structures, whereby constraints are encoded directly in lexical entries and phrase structure rules/schemata or through the statement of sort hierarchies, separate principles, etc.[1] That strategy proved suitable for the semantic component of grammar, in chapter 3, and now it is time to say more on syntactic applications as well.

Section 4.2 is an overview of the theoretical background from which our syntactic component derives, starting from the 'X-bar Theory' of phrase structure schemata in the Chomskyan tradition of generative grammar (while the transformational side of the same tradition is not considered, consistently with the approach adopted here)[2]. Then we move on to more recent developments of phrase structure grammars, such as the separate statement of 'immediate dominance' and 'linear precedence' for syntactic trees, in the wake of Gazdar et al. (1985), and HPSG's radically lexicalist account of subcategorization, which is one of the main contributions by Pollard & Sag (1987; 1994). Section 4.3 takes into account achievements emerging from this scenario and applies them to the NP structure and determination of languages that belong to our coverage. At the same time we gather up the threads of much work started in the previous chapters, not only from a syntactic point of view (so as to complete and refine the NP analysis already motivated in chapter 1), but also as far as the syntax-semantics interface is concerned (accounting for empirical and formal issues raised by the chapters 2-3). Finally, section 4.4 is devoted to some conclusions.

4.2 From X-bar Theory to HPSG

4.2.1 Phrase structure patterns

In early generative grammar (e.g., Chomsky 1957; 1965), the purely phrase-structural, non-transformational part of syntax was a language-specific set of category-specific rules: namely, context-free phrase structure rules rewriting a left-hand side category as a sequence of right-hand side categories. The former represents the mother and the latter its daughters (= immediate constituents) in a 'local tree', i.e. a tree configuration (or labelled bracketing) 'of depth one', in the sense of Gazdar et al. (1985: p. 45). In (106) we state some trivial sample rules (for a language like English), building up phrases – sentences included

[1]Also lexical rules (stating relations across lexical entries) are applied in HPSG, but they were already available in Chomsky's system; cf. Radford (1981: ch. 4).

[2]For phrase structure grammar alternatives to movement transformations, v. Gazdar et al. (1985: ch. 7) and Pollard & Sag (1994: ch. 4-5) in the first place.

– from lexical constituents or other phrases, in a possibly recursive fashion.[3] As usual, in the phrase structure rules an optional constituent gets indicated by enclosing its category between parentheses, whereas alternative categories for a given constituent are vertically listed between braces. (E.g., by these notational conventions rule (106d) turns out to allow ten hypothetical patterns of VP structure, which would require as many rules without optionality and alternation; thus (106d) may well be viewed as an abbreviation standing for all those rules.)

(106) a. S → NP VP
b. NP → (Det) Nom
c. Nom → N (PP)
d. $\mathrm{VP} \rightarrow \mathrm{V}\ (\mathrm{NP})\ (\left\{\begin{matrix}\mathrm{PP}\\ \mathrm{NP}\end{matrix}\right\})\ (\mathrm{S})$
e. PP → P NP

Several objections can be raised against a traditional rule-based approach. To start with, it clearly brings about a lot of redundancy concerning information conveyed by the hierarchical relations between constituents. There is a systematic correspondence between phrasal categories like VP, NP, PP, etc. and the respective lexical categories V, N, P, etc., which coincide with 'parts of speech'. Indeed, the various types of phrases look strictly classifiable according to information projected from the lexicon by means of an obligatory constituent acting as **head** of the construction concerned, but a grammar treating all categories as if they were atomic, indecomposable symbols cannot express the generalization. The correspondences in question remain accidental and nothing would prevent a grammar from including some rule that violates them, e.g. AP → V NP, which "is odd because an adjectival phrase would be expected to contain an adjective. Such rules are not just inappropriate for (say) English; we can confidently predict that they will never be required for any natural language grammar" (P. Bennett 1995: p. 15).

An adequately general, restrictive and non-redundant treatment, however, is available in modern grammatical frameworks:

> "Harris (1946; 1951) proposed that the relation between categories such as V and VP, N and NP, ... could be captured by breaking the ... labels into two components, namely a category type and a phrasal level. This insight was subsequently taken up in the 'X-bar syntax' suggested by Chomsky (1970) and most fully developed in Jackendoff (1977)."
>
> Gazdar et al. (1985: pp. 17-18)

[3] The connection between lexical constituents and corresponding entries in the lexicon was established by rules of 'lexical insertion', which have become totally obsolete in view of subcategorization methods like those that we shall discuss soon.

The typical notation of X-bar Theory justifies its name, because a syntactic variable 'X' ranges over category types (= parts of speech) while phrasal levels are notated by 'bars' (or other superscripts), as in (107)-(108) below.

This approach aims at a handful of very abstract cross-categorial patterns of phrase structure, formally encodable in terms of underspecified, 'schematic' rules, a.k.a. **X-bar schemata**. To exemplify them, we shall start from the classical version by Chomsky (1970; 1981: pp. 48, 51; 1986: pp. 2-3). Using '___' informally as a positional slot for nonhead daughters, the following schema combines any lexical head (i.e. zero-bar X, or also X^0) with its sequence of possible complements and yields an intermediate (i.e. one-bar) projection:

(107) $\bar{X} \rightarrow X$ ___ **Head-Complement Schema**

In another schema, a so-called *specifier* (e.g., determiner) may fill the nonhead slot to combine with an intermediate projection qua phrasal head, yielding a maximal (i.e. two-bar) projection:

(108) $\bar{\bar{X}} \rightarrow$ ___ $\bar{X}$ **Specifier-Head Schema**

Moreover, we can posit X= [+/–N, +/–V] since X-bar theory is usually supplemented by the feature-theoretic analysis of those parts of speech which project phrase structure, hence the 'major' ones in the sense of our first chapter. (Cf. § 4.2.2 below for further discussion.)

The linguistic consequences of (107)-(108) are readily seen. Here is the structure uniformly assigned to maximal phrases through the joint action of the two schemata:

(109) $[_{\bar{\bar{X}}}$ ___ $[_{\bar{X}}$ X ___]]

By appropriately setting the X value, which is shared at all levels, we derive four types of phrases as the [+/–N, +/–V] analysis implies. That is to say, at the maximal level the possible categories are $\bar{\bar{N}}$, $\bar{\bar{V}}$, $\bar{\bar{A}}$ and $\bar{\bar{P}}$ (or N″, V″, A″ and P″, in an equivalent 'prime notation'), where each major part of speech acting as category type is specified as we mentioned in chapter 1. The consequent instantiation of (109) is particularly clear for type [+N, –V] *alias* N:

- the traditional NP corresponds to $\bar{\bar{N}}$;
- some suitable determiner can be the specifier, if any;
- there is a constituent (motivated by empirical syntactic criteria, v. Radford 1981: ch. 3) which was provisionally labelled 'Nom(inal)' since our chapter 1 and now gets formally predicted as the intermediate projection $\bar{N}$;
- a lexical head N subcategorizes for its own complement(s), if any.

Dependents (whether specifiers or complements) may well be missing, but note that a rigid application of the structure (109) to NPs that just consist of a proper name yields the analysis $[_{\bar{\bar{\mathrm{N}}}}\ [_{\bar{\mathrm{N}}}\ \mathrm{N}\,]\,]$, because all bar levels are expected to be present even if they involve vacuous, unary-branching projections. (This can be obviated in more flexible versions of X-bar Theory, to be presented later on.)

The same structural patterns and notions are applicable to categories other than N, essentially as shown for English by Gazdar et al. (1985: ch. 6), building on Jackendoff (1973; 1977). So, let us consider APs and PPs: the X-bar Theory presented here equates them with phrases of category $\bar{\bar{\mathrm{A}}}$ and $\bar{\bar{\mathrm{P}}}$, respectively, and predicts the existence of specifiers and complements for both adjectival and prepositional heads. That prediction is borne out by such evidence as (110); in the analysis, for convenience, we have underwritten **nonhead** constituents according to the function and omitted their phrase structure.

(110) a. $[_{\bar{\bar{\mathrm{A}}}}$ **so** $[_{\bar{\mathrm{A}}}\ [_{\mathrm{A}}$ afraid $]$ **of thunder** $]\,]$
Spec. *Compl.*

b. $[_{\bar{\bar{\mathrm{P}}}}$ **right** $[_{\bar{\mathrm{P}}}\ [_{\mathrm{P}}$ at $]$ **the bottom** $]\,]$
Spec. *Compl.*

Quite controversial is the empirical status of $\bar{\bar{\mathrm{V}}}$, because there are two possible candidates: the traditional VP, arguing from analogy with the other 'XPs', or the whole S, keeping to the familiar idea that sentences are headed by the Verb. At least for the moment, we can follow Pollard & Sag (1994: pp. 37-39) when they adopt a version where $\bar{\bar{\mathrm{V}}}$ corresponds to S and the subject NP acts as the relevant specifier.[4] Then, it turns out that the Specifier-Head Schema generalizes over our previous rules (106a) and (106b) as well as corresponding ones for APs and PPs:

(111) a. AP $\rightarrow$ (Deg) AG

b. PP $\rightarrow$ (AdvP) PG

Likewise, the Head-Complement Schema generalizes over (106c), (106d) and corresponding rules for adjectival and prepositional 'groups'[5]:

(112) a. AG $\rightarrow$ A (PP)

b. PG $\rightarrow$ P NP

[4] This is similar to the approach by Jackendoff (1977), but his maximal number of bar levels was 3 instead of 2.

[5] Cf. also P. Bennett (1995: p. 9): "We can use the term 'group' ... for the constituent consisting of a word and its arguments" occurring as sisters, i.e. the complements; hence the labels 'AG' and 'PG' informally assigned to the $\bar{\mathrm{X}}$ constituents in some category-specific rules. (But note that (112b) with 'PG' is meant to replace the original (106e) with 'PP'.) On the categories 'Deg(ree)' and 'Adv(erb)P' (which is actually understood as abbreviation of 'AP[+ADV]') in (111), see Gazdar et al. (1985: pp. 122-123, 134), among others.

The generalization potential of X-bar Theory goes much beyond structural patterns of a single language. A strong, but plausible working hypothesis can be adopted, claiming that all natural languages must have heads, complements and specifiers, whose hierarchical connections conform to the X-bar schemata we have already provided. On the other hand, it is clear that **linear order** will change according to the languages: e.g., the way the Head-Complement Schema is ordered in (107) above is adequate for English and other languages behaving alike, but not for Japanese, where complements precede the lexical head (including P, which may well cover the Japanese postpositions too)[6]. If one wants to make the X-bar schemata fully universal, they should abstract away from linear order, a result achieved in different fashions depending on the formal tools the grammarian is prepared to apply. At the current stage of our work we find it convenient to draw a format of 'immediate dominance (ID) rules' from the GPSG system by Gazdar et al. (1985: ch. 3).

The ID rule (113)[7], just to give an example at random, replaces the pair (114) of phrase structure (PS) rules, which could respectively deal with clause-initial and postpositive subjects in Italian, say.

(113) S → NP, VP

(114) a. S → NP VP e.g. *Maria è tornata* ('Maria is back')

b. S → VP NP e.g. *è tornata Maria* ('is back Maria')

Thus our single ID rule admits alternative local trees in which a node S immediately dominates a node NP, a node VP and nothing else. Since (113) does not make any claim about the linear order of daughter nodes, two cases in fact are licensed: a local tree in which NP precedes VP (the case corresponding to the conventional PS rule (114a)) and another in reverse order (corresponding to (114b)). By the same token, we can re-express the X-bar schemata in ID format, yielding 'schematic' cross-categorial ID rules, a.k.a. **ID (X-bar) schemata**[8]. That is:

(115) $\bar{X} \rightarrow X, \underset{Compl.}{\_\_\_}$ (instead of (107) above)

(116) $\bar{\bar{X}} \rightarrow \bar{X}, \underset{Spec.}{\_\_\_}$ (instead of (108) above)

[6]See, e.g., Graffi (1994: § 6.2.1). Being independent of linear order, the feature-theoretic definition of the part of speech P remains the same, i.e. [–N, –V], whether the corresponding category label is spelled out as 'Preposition' or 'Postposition' for a given (type of) language.

[7]In accordance with the notation of GPSG, we use comma between two right-hand side categories in an ID rule, meaning their linear order is immaterial. Therefore, the following is nothing but an orthographic variant of the same rule (113): S → VP, NP.

[8]Cf. Pollard & Sag (1994: § 1.5), whose technical characterization of the notion is partly different from the present one and will come into play in our chapter 5.

E.g., if S is $\bar{\bar{\text{V}}}$ with the subject NP in specifier position (as mentioned before), the effects of our category-specific ID rule (113) follow from the ID schema (116) by setting X to [–N, +V] *alias* V.

The question is how to account for the fact that a given language exploits only some of the linear order options theoretically allowed by the universal ID schemata. In one possible approach, these schemata are seen as abstract meta-grammatical generalizations that have to be specified for linear order when they get incorporated into the grammar of a given language.[9] Therefore, the X-bar schemata in ordinary PS rule format from which we started, (107)-(108), would be appropriate for the grammar of English, but derived from the corresponding ID universals by setting their pertinent **parameters** (in a Chomskyan sense) to 'head-initial' if the head is lexical, or 'head-final' if the head is the one-bar projection. An alternative approach, inspired by GPSG (Gazdar et al. 1985: ch. 3) and revised for HPSG purposes (cf. Pollard & Sag 1987: § 7.2), directly applies rules/schemata in ID format within the grammar of a given language, but ensures language-specific linearization by means of few 'linear precedence (LP) statements' constraining the relations between sisters in the local trees that are licensed by the ID component.

Here is a minimal – and relatively informal – LP statement[10], which can interact with the universal ID schemata (115)-(116) to yield the same effects as the PS versions (107)-(108) for a language like English:

(117) *Spec.* $\prec$ *Head* $\prec$ *Compl.*

The LP component of a particular grammar will actually require more or less elaborated language-specific statements depending on how consistent the given language is, compared with the relevant typological generalizations:

> "Hawkins (1982) argues that X-bar theory fares rather poorly in capturing appropriate generalizations in the realm of word order. Note, however, that this is not necessarily a problem for GPSG, [or any other grammatical system] which captures ordering facts in LP-statements, not in conditions on X-bar-based PS-rules. 'Consistent' languages are easier to describe by means of general LP-statements, whereas inconsistent languages need more specific statements."
>
> P. Bennett (1995: p. 32)

[9] We refer to Graffi (1994: § 6.2), among others, for an introductory discussion based on the 'principles and parameters' framework by Chomsky (1981; 1986). The idea is that general principles of Universal Grammar (i.e. the meta-grammar which the particular grammars instantiate) are 'parameterized' insofar as they envisage a limited range of options for language-specific variation.

[10] As in Gazdar et al. (1985: p. 46), 'A $\prec$ B' means 'B cannot appear to the left of A in a local tree', but A and B in our case (117) are functional labels instead of categories.

An example is German, where the head verb follows its sisters in subordinate clauses but the other lexically headed local constructions are not head-final (e.g. there are prepositions, not postpositions).[11] Hence a feature like [+/−MC] used by Uszkoreit (1987: p. 60) to distinguish main and subordinate clauses, as well as verb forms projecting them, and relativize LP statements accordingly. Equivalent constraints may be imposed on two opposite PS versions of the lexically headed schema to be adopted for German in the other approach, yet this means undermining a strictly cross-categorial view of X-bar schemata, as the head-final version would be confined to V[−MC] heads.

Various phenomena confirm the convenience of adopting some kind of ID-LP separation. A case in point is the relatively free occurrence of dependents that are not subject to the same restrictions as complements and specifiers:

> "A sentence may have ... elements ... that are syntactically related to the predicate but are not syntactically restricted by it. These are the adverbial and prepositional modifiers that serve as **adjuncts** of a predicate. ... A predicate imposes neither category nor feature restrictions on its adjuncts, semantic appropriateness being the only requirement that must be satisfied."
>
> Bresnan & Kaplan (1982)

In the following example, adapted from Bresnan (1982b), the optional phrases between parentheses are all adjuncts which 'modify' the verbal predicate acting as the lexical head of the whole sentence:

(118) (**Without interrupting the discussion**) Fred (**deftly**) handed a toy to the baby (*over lunch*) (*at noon*) (**in a restaurant**) (*last Sunday*) (**in Back Bay**)

Indeed, while a certain lexical head dictates the precise number and type of complements it subcategorizes for in a given reading (as already mentioned in chapter 1), the same word can theoretically take any number ≥ 0 of appropriate adjuncts, which "are semantically interpreted as phrasal or clausal operators rather than as predicate arguments" (Bresnan 1982b) and prove easy to multiply even if they fulfil the same semantic function.[12] In (118), see the possible co-occurrence of two adjuncts of Manner, three of *Time* and two of **Location**.

[11]The head verb precedes its sisters in main clauses, if the so-called 'verb second' phenomenon of German is accounted for by combining the leftmost constituent with a phrasal projection of the verb in question. We refer to Bennett & Schmidt (1998) for a review of related treatments.

[12]"In contrast to the grammatical functions which are assigned to predicate arguments, multiple locative, temporal and manner adjuncts can occur in a single clause" (ibid.). On the distinction between adjuncts and arguments and its relevance for the syntax-semantics interface, see also our § 4.3.1.2 below.

Evidence for ID-LP separation is provided by the fact that adjuncts are equally found before the pertinent head (projection), like the manner ones in (118), or after it, like the others in the same example, and often their positions may well change without consequences: cf. "In Back Bay, last Sunday, in a restaurant, Fred deftly handed a toy to the baby over lunch, at noon, without interrupting the discussion".

Although the controversial status of adjuncts inspired a number of alternative treatments in grammatical theories (cf. Jackendoff 1977, Bresnan & Kaplan 1982, Pollard & Sag 1987 and Miller 1991, among others), here we will stick to a recursive structure that has been made very popular by presentations of X-bar syntax in Chomskyan grammar (e.g. Radford 1981: ch. 3, Graffi 1994: pp. 164-166), GPSG (Gazdar et al. 1985: pp. 126, 129) and HPSG (especially Richard Cooper 1990: pp. 70-74, Pollard & Sag 1994: p. 384). The relevant X-bar schema in ID format is:

(119) $X^n \rightarrow X^n, \underset{\textit{Adjunct}}{\bar{\bar{Y}}}$ **Head-Adjunct (ID) Schema**

where the superscript variable n means that mother and head daughter share the same number of 'bars'. That is, "adjuncts are constituents which combine with a constituent of category α to form another constituent of category α" (Richard Cooper 1990: p. 70); this implies a bar-preserving projection in order to yield full categorial identity and allows the schema to recursively apply to its output as many times as given data may require[13]. As far as linear order is concerned, the ID schema (119) would be enough if all adjuncts enjoyed the freedom of those modifying the verb (projections) in English sentences like (118) above, but positional constraints can be enforced in other cases by adding suitable LP statements (ibid., pp. 71-75).

A crucial question that has been left aside so far is how the general phrase structure scenario interacts with the subcategorization requirements implied by the various lexical heads. E.g., nonhead daughters occupying the 'positional slot' in (107) or (115) above are assumed to be subcategorized-for complements, but it is unclear how the (PS or ID) X-bar schema can ensure that a specific head combines with the right number and type of complements. As noticed by Gazdar et al. (1985: pp. 31-32), an example like **I devoured to him that the grass is green* is ungrammatical because the verb *devour* must combine with an obligatory NP object and no other complements, contrary to what happens in the example. Somebody might invoke some purely semantic approach, so as to "let the syntax generate strings in which ... verbs occur with the wrong

[13]Multiple adjuncts are thus captured by recursive application of the schema, each time attaching one and only one (maximal) constituent in *Adjunct* position; optionality results from the fact that the schema itself need not apply at all.

number and type of other constituents in the VP, and use the mechanisms that associate syntactic structures with meanings to eliminate them", but "there is fairly clear evidence that the meaning of a verb does not completely determine its subcategorization" (ibid.). A case in point is actually *devour*, which means *eat voraciously*, or similar, and still cannot occur without direct object, while *eat* can (even if a modifier like *voraciously* is present); this partial difference in the subcategorization properties of the two verbs does not appear to have any semantic motivation.

The need for morpho-syntactic frames of subcategorization systematically arises with PP complements involving semantically vacuous uses of prepositions. That is:

> "prepositions ... which can be regarded as denoting identity functions on NP meanings. ... The phrase that they head has a meaning identical with that of the noun phrase it contains; the preposition adds nothing. ... Consider English indirect objects. We need to be able to guarantee that where a verb like *hand* occurs with a single prepositional phrase sister, then the latter will have *to* as its preposition (because while *She handed it to me* is grammatical, we want to block **She handed it for me*, **She handed it near me*, and so on)."
>
> Gazdar et al. (1985: p. 132)

The lack of any semantic contribution by the preposition *to* in VPs whose head is *hand*, or *give*, etc., looks evident, as these verbs have a so-called 'double object' reading in which the *to*-PP gets replaced by the embedded NP, with a change in linear order but without changing meaning (so that *She handed a toy to the baby* = *She handed the baby a toy*). Besides, the distinction between semantically contentful (uses of) prepositions and vacuous ones is confirmed by contrastive data: the use of *on* with a locative meaning (yielding [+LOC] PPs, in GPSG notation) regularly translates as *su/sopra* in Italian, e.g., but when *on* is required for the obligatory PP complement of *depend*, or *rely*, the translation is dictated by the corresponding Italian verb, hence *da* (literally 'from') for *dipendere*, or *di* (literally 'of') for *fidarsi*.

To enforce the subcategorization restrictions in a GPSG approach like that of Gazdar et al. (1985: pp. 33-35, 132), context-free rewriting rules that introduce a lexical head would be distinguished according to the number and type of complements it subcategorizes for:

> "This can be done in a manner which is at once simple and transparent, by using integers as values of a feature SUBCAT... As far as the lexicon is concerned, these integers are best seen as pointers to the rules which will allow the relevant item to be introduced."
>
> (ibid., p. 33)

Here are some sample rules of the kind:

(120) a. VP → *Head* [SUBCAT *1*] (e.g. *die*)

b. VP → *Head* [SUBCAT *2*], NP (e.g. *devour*)

c. VP → *Head* [SUBCAT *3*], PP[PFORM *on*] (e.g. *rely*)

d. VP → *Head* [SUBCAT *4*], NP, PP[PFORM *to*] (e.g. *hand*)

e. VP → *Head* [SUBCAT *5*], NP, NP (e.g. *spare*)

f. VP → *Head* [SUBCAT *6*], NP, PP[+LOC] (e.g. *put*)

g. VP → *Head* [SUBCAT *7*], S[VFORM *fin*] (e.g. *believe*)

Thus a category-specific rule rewriting 'VP' – like our previous (106d)[14] – gets replaced by quite a few subcategory-specific ones, each keyed to a given SUBCAT value which indicates the subcategorization frame of the verb in a given reading. E.g., only those verbs lexically marked with value *5*, like *spare* (or the double-object reading of *hand*, *give*, etc.), will be accepted in the *Head* position by rule (120e).

Several comments deserve to be made about these and other rules with subcategorization frames based on Gazdar et al. (1985: pp. 247-248) and P. Bennett (1995: § 4.4). First, the same treatment is equally feasible by means of the PS counterparts of such 'lexical' ID rules as the (120), but ID-LP separation allows Gazdar et al. (1985: p. 110) to capture a grammatical generalization of English through the following LP statement:

(121) $\bar{\bar{\mathrm{N}}} \prec \bar{\bar{\mathrm{P}}} \prec \bar{\bar{\mathrm{V}}}$

(i.e., in case of co-occurrence as sisters, NPs precede PPs and both precede clauses). Second, in GPSG the feature SUBCAT is only appropriate for lexical categories and therefore occurs on the *Head* in lexical ID rules[15]; since the ID-LP output is meant as a local tree conforming to X-bar Theory, rules do not redundantly repeat the information that the lexical head projecting a VP is V (where 'VP' is just the *alias* of a verbal projection with suitable number of bars, viz. $\bar{\mathrm{V}}$ in terms of our current assumptions). Third, PPs can be typed according to the prepositions heading them: "we allow the feature PFORM to take particular prepositions as its value, one of them being *to*. We enter *to* as being a lexical item of category P[PFORM *to*]. ... Now any rule that has

[14]Despite its category-specific status, (106d) is clearly not restrictive enough. In fact, that rule would allow a VP like **devoured to him that the grass is green*, as well as many other ungrammatical combinations of verbs with NPs, PPs or Ss.

[15]In the GPSG format of (headed) ID rules by Gazdar et al. (1985: p. 51), there is "a metagrammatical place-holder standing for a largely unspecified category which has the status of head". We have simply equated such a place-holder with the *Head* label spelling out its functional status (cf. the GPSG notation 'H').

to guarantee the presence of the preposition *to* in a prepositional phrase can simply introduce PP [PFORM *to*]" (ibid., p. 132), provided that some feature instantiation mechanism ensures the sharing of PFORM values between PP node and P head.

The feature sharing required for that treatment can simply follow from X-bar schemata, if one develops more formally the notion of a syntactic variable 'X' ranging over [+/−N, +/−V]. Under an HPSG-style analysis of the **parts of speech** which was adopted in chapter 1, there is a sort *prep(osition)* whose feature declaration specifies [−N, −V], but then the introduction of PFORM in the same declaration will equally allow the prepositional form of a lexical head P to be 'passed up' via the schemata, as part of their X value. Here the 'X' of X-bar Theory is indeed tantamount to a notational convention encoding the token-identity of feature structures stated by the **Head Feature Principle** in HPSG: "The HEAD value of any headed phrase is structure-shared with the HEAD value of the head daughter" (Pollard & Sag 1994: p. 34). Thus 'X' can abbreviate a category with the feature [HEAD *major*], for any instantiation of *major* in the sense of the *part-of-speech* hierarchy that we have presented in chapter 1.[16] The mechanism also applies to parts of speech other than P whose declarations introduce features to be shared by head and mother node, e.g. VFORM with values *fin(ite)*, *inf(initive)*, ... for *verb* (= V and its projections); the subcategorization relevance of VFORM was exemplified in rule (120g).

Essentially similar results are achieved by Gazdar et al. (1985) in terms of the formalism of GPSG, which is partly different from its HPSG descendant. E.g., feature structures in GPSG are not sorted and their feature co-occurrence restrictions, "stated as material conditionals or biconditionals[[17],] ... amount to 'meaning postulates' which constrain the possible uses of the features" (ibid., pp. 29-30). The difference that we would like to emphasize now, however, is not merely formal insofar as it affects the substantial linguistic way of modelling subcategorization. The GPSG approach to subcategorization frames has the merit of being formally simple, but lacks generality: it requires a large number of construction-specific rules[18], contrary to the ideal scenario of a single, cross-categorial and possibly universal (ID) X-bar schema for all lexically headed local constructions.

---

[16]Cf. Pollard & Sag's related but not identical category system (ibid., pp. 22-23).

[17]That is, the closest equivalent in HPSG terms is the format of implicational (i.e. conditional) constraints we have touched on in chapter 3. (A biconditional is equivalent to two implicational constraints, which differ from each other only because of the opposite direction of the arrows connecting the same pair of feature structures.)

[18]Note that the rules (120) are only a little part of those required for a reasonable coverage of English VPs. In particular, there are several other subcategories of verbs calling for PPs headed by some semantically vacuous preposition (v. "laugh *at* __", "approve *of* __", etc.).

Like P. Bennett (1995: p. 48), we conclude our discussion on GPSG-style subcategorization with the remark that "some other theories have attempted to retain some of the benefits of the GPSG approach, but to do away with the large set of ID-rules". This can be done by joining in "the general trend within linguistics known as **lexicalism**, which refers to the statement of linguistic phenomena within the lexicon rather than the grammar" (ibid.) if the latter is narrowly understood as repertory of syntactic rules. Whereas X-bar Theory in GPSG mostly boils down to a meta-grammatical generalization underlying the numerous grammar rules actually applied to generate trees, the more lexicalist kind of grammar we will draw from HPSG separates in a modular fashion the grammatical formulation of few (ID) X-bar schemata of phrase structure from the lexical information detailing subcategorization requirements.

4.2.2 Lexical selection of dependents

The HPSG-style solution of the subcategorization problem, following Pollard & Sag (1987; 1994) [19], implies that the SUBCAT feature does not take an atomic value, but a complex one, namely some ordered list. A brief comment should clarify the formal status of such a SUBCAT value in HPSG. The ordered list of elements is conventionally written between angle brackets (instead of the curly brackets used for sets, cf. chapter 3 above), yet this is actually a simplified notation, because Pollard & Sag (1994: p. 19) "have chosen to model nonempty lists as a sort of feature structure – *nelist* – specified for the two attributes FIRST and REST; the empty list is modelled by another sort – *elist* – for which no attribute labels are appropriate". So, $\langle \boxed{1}, \boxed{2}, \boxed{3} \rangle$ (with 'tags' standing for corresponding feature structures as elements of the list) is nothing but the abbreviation of a recursive attribute-value matrix:[20]

(122)
$$ {}_{\textit{nelist}}\begin{bmatrix} \text{FIRST } \boxed{1} \\ \text{REST } {}_{\textit{nelist}}\begin{bmatrix} \text{FIRST } \boxed{2} \\ \text{REST } {}_{\textit{nelist}}\begin{bmatrix} \text{FIRST } \boxed{3} \\ \text{REST } \textit{elist} \end{bmatrix} \end{bmatrix} \end{bmatrix} $$

To begin with, though the SUBCAT is equally relevant for semantic aspects of HPSG to be considered later on, let us confine ourselves to the presentation of a simple syntactic version, which can be straightforwardly adapted to frameworks whose syntax-semantics interface is different from the HPSG one, as done for GPSG by Miller (1991: p. 32):

[19] Cf. also Shieber's (1986: § 3.4.2) sample computational grammar in PATR-II.

[20] One can also define the concatenation of two (possibly empty) lists L and L′, as a list obtained from L by substituting L′ for *elist* (= L itself when this is empty).

> "Each lexical head is assigned as value for SUBCAT the list of categories which it requires as complements. The fact that a single item may allow more than one complement structure will be accounted for by it being assigned more than one SUBCAT list, either by general lexical rules (e.g. for direct transitive verbs, the passive SUBCAT list will be systematically obtained from the active list ...), or on a case by case basis in the lexicon, for unpredictable idiosyncrasies. ... Furthermore, again following the hypotheses of HPSG, verbs subcategorize for their subject, i.e. ... the category of the subject appears in the list of categories that is the value of SUBCAT."

Even if the elements of the list are just syntactic categories as assumed in Miller's version, by now it should be clear that they in turn are not atomic but get decomposed according to a feature-theoretic analysis. In this connection, category types (= parts of speech) and bar levels are supplemented with such attributes as PFORM for the prepositional categories and VFORM for the verbal ones (v. § 4.2.1 above). The CASE of nominal categories is another example of category-specific attribute declared for the corresponding part of speech, so as to be shared by head and mother node as part of the 'X' of X-bar Theory. Hence the following classes of verbs (123), encoding the same subcategorization frames as the previous ID rules (120), with the addition of the subject qua NP marked by *nominative* (= *nmt*) case, instead of *acc(usative)*[21].

(123)
a. V[SUBCAT <NP[CASE *nmt*]>]
b. V[SUBCAT <NP[CASE *nmt*], NP[CASE *acc1*]>]
c. V[SUBCAT <NP[CASE *nmt*], PP[PFORM *on*]>]
d. V[SUBCAT <NP[CASE *nmt*], NP[CASE *acc1*], PP[PFORM *to*]>]
e. V[SUBCAT <NP[CASE *nmt*], NP[CASE *acc1*], NP[CASE *acc2*]>]
f. V[SUBCAT <NP[CASE *nmt*], NP[CASE *acc1*], PP[+LOC]>]
g. V[SUBCAT <NP[CASE *nmt*], S[VFORM *fin*]>]

At least when the lexical head category is V(erb), as in (123), "the ordering of elements on the SUBCAT list corresponds to a version of the traditional obliqueness hierarchy. Thus subjects appear first (leftmost), followed by other complements (if any) in the order primary object, secondary object, then

[21]Note that we distinguish two subsorts of *accusative*, *acc1* and *acc2*, for English NPs occurring as primary and secondary objects, respectively. This distinction, which is bound to the syntactic position (i.e. *acc2* is reserved for the second of two NP objects depending on the same verb), gets neutralized morphologically (so that the form of pronouns will be sensitive to the supersort *acc* only), but can be exploited for linearization purposes as we will show soon.

oblique PP and verbal [(= VP or S)] and/or predicative complements" (Pollard & Sag 1994: p. 24). For convenience, now we exemplify the subcategorization mechanism by considering the syntactic effects on a simple English sentence in which the relative linear order of the phrases subcategorized for by the verb coincides with the obliqueness order, namely "She gave a toy to Kim":

(124) $[_{S}\ [_{\boxed{1}NP}\ \text{she}]\ [_{VP}\ [_{V<\boxed{1},\boxed{2},\boxed{3}>}\ \text{gave}]\ [_{\boxed{2}NP}\ \text{a toy}]\ [_{\boxed{3}PP}\ \text{to Kim}]]]$

Here the tags (= boxed numerals) are meant to show that the head V shares the categories on its SUBCAT list with relevant constituents of the tree (124), i.e. the feature structures thus listed are token-identical with the categories of those constituents. The sharing of information is used to check the appropriateness of the lexical head's subcategory for the syntactic context where it occurs: in our example, the subject "she", the direct object "a toy" and the oblique complement "to Kim" prove compatible with the verb *give*, because they respectively are a nominative NP, an accusative NP (or rather, one that is underspecified for CASE in isolation, but gets the value by sharing [22]) and a PP with preposition form *to*, as required by the SUBCAT of (123d) verbs.

Then the question is how token-identities between SUBCAT list elements and corresponding nodes of a tree are established by means of a phrase structure grammar. This notion implies a strictly 'local' view of grammatical statements, such that the (sub)tree structure they concern cannot exceed a configuration 'of depth 1' (= mother with daughter nodes). An obvious way to satisfy the restriction consists in directly expressing the identities within the PS or ID rewriting rules/schemata which are independently motivated for the pertinent tree structures, though an equally local alternative separating the statement of identities from the rules/schemata proper is possible in HPSG and will be discussed by chapter 5. At any rate, as in typical structures like (124) above the subject NP node and the head V do not belong to the same 'local tree' [23], SUBCAT information about the subject must be passed up to the VP node so as to meet the locality requirement.

Under the most straightforward treatment based on Pollard & Sag (1987; 1994), it is the SUBCAT feature itself that carries the subject-matching element up, while 'discharging' all the others from the list. Let us consider our example again: (a) the verb *give*, which exploits the last two elements of its ternary

[22] Once again (cf. chapter 3 for previous exemplification concerning semantics), we see how additional yet compatible information accrues to a 'partial' feature structure from another one, thanks to the 'unification-based' formalism of HPSG. The feature structure representing the category of "a toy" in isolation lacks any value for CASE or, at most, restricts it to a sort other than *gen* (if English genitive too is treated as a value of CASE) but without specifiying *acc1*, which results from the lexical information of the verb.

[23] The former belongs to the local tree whose mother node is S, the latter to the local tree whose mother node is VP.

SUBCAT list in order to capture the complements "a toy" and "to Kim", is expected to project a VP node with a reduced, unary SUBCAT list <NP[*nmt*]> [24]; (b) therefore, the subject "she" will be captured within the local tree where its NP node belongs, the token-identical list element being discharged by yielding a mother node S with empty SUBCAT list. As a first approximation, the two steps can be assumed to instantiate these SUBCAT-annotated versions of the X-bar schemata in ID format that § 4.2.1 presented:

(125) a. $\bar{X}[\text{SUBCAT}\langle\boxed{k}\rangle] \rightarrow X[\text{SUBCAT}\langle\boxed{k}\,|\,\boxed{1},\ldots\,\boxed{n}\rangle], \boxed{1},\ldots\,\boxed{n}$

Head-Complement (ID) Schema [25]

b. $\bar{\bar{X}}[\text{SUBCAT}\langle\,\rangle] \rightarrow \bar{X}[\text{SUBCAT}\langle\boxed{k}\rangle],\ \boxed{k}$

Head-Specifier (ID) Schema

Due to the unordered righthand side of the schemata, the grammar of a given language must be provided with an adequate LP component too. In particular, granting that all specifiers, not only subjects, correspond to the first element of the SUBCAT list, the functional notions informally assumed for a cross-categorial LP statement of English like *Spec.* ≺ *Head* – a part of our previous (117) – are simply accounted for by reference to the sharing of the only element left on the list:

(126) $\boxed{k} \prec [\text{SUBCAT}\langle\boxed{k}\rangle]$

We can restate the *Head* ≺ *Compl.* part of (117) in a similar fashion:

(127) $[\text{SUBCAT}\langle\boxed{k}\,|\,\ldots\,\boxed{i}\,\ldots\rangle] \prec \boxed{i}$

where $\boxed{i}$ stands for any of the categories that can be captured as complements by the righthand side of (125b). While (131) might be enough for a language like Italian allowing a rather free order of complements after the lexical head, English enforces its rigid order of complements (apart from so-called 'heavy XP shift' phenomena [26]) by means of such LP statements as the (121) introduced before. Another example is:

[24] Note the abbreviation omitting the attribute of an unambiguous feature value, as proposed by Gazdar et al. (1985: p. 23) or Pollard & Sag (1994: p. 28). Indeed we indicate the nominative CASE value by means of *nmt*, instead of *nom*, because the latter label might as well mean *nominal* when the attribute is omitted.

[25] The notation $\langle\boxed{k}\,|\,\textit{list}\rangle$ abbreviates [FIRST $\boxed{k}$, REST *list*], i.e. a list with at least one element, the first, followed by a possibly empty (sub)list. The match between all elements on the latter list and the $n \geq 0$ complements is represented by a semi-formal notation, to be re-expressed more precisely in chapter 5.

[26] E.g., in "John gave to Ellen (for her birthday) *an old book he had bought in the bookstore on 17th Street*", the 'heavy' NP which we have italicized is preceded by some PP(s), but can be treated as leaving a 'gap' in canonical position of object adjacent to the verb. (Cf. Sells 1985: p. 55.)

(128) NP[*acc1*] $\prec$ NP[*acc2*]

which orders secondary (*acc2*) objects after primary (*acc1*) ones.

The SUBCAT approach was criticized by Robert Borsley in a number of papers (e.g., Borsley 1987; 1993), leading to a revision of HPSG that has been eventually accepted by Pollard & Sag (1994: ch. 9). An important reason for the change arises because a single subcategorization list fails to distinguish between a subject/specifier and the first or only subcategorized-for dependent, in case of lexical heads that do not appear to take any subject/specifier. The problem is particularly evident with prepositions:

> "if there is only one complement [on the SUBCAT list of a nonpredicative preposition[27]], then the prepositional object would really be a subject; consequently one might expect that whatever principle orders subjects before verb phrases ... would also order prepositional objects before the prepositions. This is a flaw in standard HPSG: if nonpredicative *on* is lexically specified as [SUBCAT <NP[*acc*]>], then the grammar ... runs the danger of predicting, for example, that (...a) is good and (...b) bad:
>
> (...) a. *Kim depends [Sandy on]
>
> b. Kim depends [on Sandy]".
>
> Pollard & Sag (1994: p. 347)

Indeed the ungrammatical example could be generated by the joint action of the SUBCAT-annotated Head-Specifier (ID) Schema and the corresponding LP statement of English (v. (125b) and (130) above).

Even if the intervention of a real specifier – like *right* in "*right* at the bottom", under the analysis shown before by (110b) – restores the complement status of the embedded NP, the problem is not solved in the frequent case of specifierless PPs. As a matter of fact, it would be utterly implausible to postulate a phonologically unexpressed specifier of prepositions just to enforce correct linearization. We are well aware that the linguistic literature abounds in 'empty' pronominal subjects of clauses (PRO or *pro*, in the Chomskyan notation) and 'Ø' forms of the articles for NPs, but the remark that a solution of the kind cannot be extended to specifiers of other phrases – cf. also APs besides PPs – entitles us to believe that there is evidence for a general alternative. (Note that the cross-categorial character of the schemata and their way of encoding subcategorization in (125) prevent the solution typical of category-specific rules, which would resort to an optional specifier position with head

[27]That is, some preposition projecting a phrase whose function is not predicative. The further issue of predicative PPs and prepositions will be addressed soon.

categories allowed to yield vacuous, unary-branching projections in absence of the specifier.[28])

The use of a phonologically empty constituent as specifier is made superfluous in variants of X-bar Theory like the one adopted by Pollard & Sag (1994: ch. 9), assuming that such examples as "*pictures of Mary* ... are perfectly good X″[, i.e. $\bar{\bar{\text{X}}}$,] even though *pictures* (in this case) does not require a specifier" (ibid., pp. 362-363). In a way reminiscent of Gazdar et al. (1985: p. 50) and Chomsky (1986: pp. 4, 47), the result is achieved by allowing phrase structure configurations in accordance with the X-bar template $\text{X}^j \rightarrow \ldots \text{X}^i \ldots$, for $j \geq i \geq 0$, so that zero-bar X (= X^0) may project $\bar{\bar{\text{X}}}$ directly, skipping the $\bar{\text{X}}$ step if unnecessary.[29] To implement the idea in technical terms consistently with HPSG, up-to-date versions of the theory split the original SUBCAT list into two or more lists qua values of corresponding 'valence' features (a notion loosely borrowed from Tesnière 1959). There are various proposals as regards the exact number and labelling of the attributes concerned or even the methods whereby they constrain phrase structure (cf. Borsley 1987; 1993, Richard Cooper 1991: ch. 3, Pollard & Sag 1994: ch. 9, Allegranza 1998a; 1998b, among others), but for a start we can neglect the debate and exemplify the mechanism by showing how to revise our previous schemata (125) with some pair of valence attributes $\mathcal{F}_1$ vs. $\mathcal{F}_2$.

(129) a. $\text{X}^{\text{P}}[\mathcal{F}_1 \boxed{l}] \rightarrow \text{X}^0[\mathcal{F}_1 \boxed{l}, \mathcal{F}_2 {<} \boxed{1}, \ldots \boxed{n} {>}], \boxed{1}, \ldots \boxed{n}$

b. $\bar{\bar{\text{X}}}[\mathcal{F}_1 {<\,>}] \rightarrow \bar{\text{X}}[\mathcal{F}_1 {<} \boxed{k} {>}], \boxed{k}$

Before we discuss the division of labour between features replacing SUBCAT, it is worth stressing the other syntactic difference from the original system. In the variant version (129a) of the Head-Complement Schema, the X^{P} category labelling the mother "subsumes both of the possibilities X′[, i.e. $\bar{\text{X}}$,] and X″, corresponding to the cases where the X^0 does or does not require a specifier, respectively" (Pollard & Sag 1994: p. 363). That is, the mother category X^{P}

[28] Admittedly, a residual form of unary branching is exploited by Pollard & Sag (1994) in order to turn a complementless lexical head into a phrase, but in that case the status is different because no *ad hoc* additions to the system of schemata are required. Indeed the result follows as an instance from the Head-Complement Schema (v. our version (125a), where the number of possible complements is $n \geq 0$, as we mentioned in note 25 too). The possibility of revising HPSG's X-bar Theory so as to dispense with all vacuous projections will be investigated in chapter 5.

[29] The template states metagrammatical restrictions on the possible structures to be generated through framework-dependent means available to a given grammar (whether rules, schemata, principles, etc.). Another such restriction the template can easily encode is the maximal number of bars $m \geq j$, for $m = 2$ in the most common versions of X-bar Theory. The option of $\bar{\text{X}}$-skipping follows if one does not add the further restriction $j = i + 1$ (but this would be too strong anyway, as also $j = i$ should hold to allow bar-preserving adjuncts; cf. Radford 1981: ch. 3).

is a phrasal projection, but underspecified as to its number of bars, so that the resulting phrase can be accepted as head by the Head-Specifier Schema (= 129b), which enforces the option with one bar, while the alternative qua maximal, two-bar projection is relevant to the occurrence of the same phrase in some dependent (i.e. argument or adjunct) position[30]. The option with two bars gets directly projected by a lexical head (skipping the one-bar level), as allowed by the X-bar template stated above.

Now the difference in subcategorization that intuitively should be established between a complementless verb and a specifierless preposition, in contrast with their uniform SUBCAT treatment, is accounted for by lexically coding the former as $V[\mathcal{F}_1\text{<NP>}, \mathcal{F}_2\text{< >}]$ and the latter as $P[\mathcal{F}_1\text{< >}, \mathcal{F}_2\text{<NP>}]$. In other words, the only NP argument of the lexical head is captured through a valence that differs in the two cases, depending on the parts of speech. The verb's empty $\mathcal{F}_2$ valence is accepted by the Head-Complement Schema, as a particular case of its listing of $n \geq 0$ complements, and the outcome is a unary branching whose mother node preserves the $[\mathcal{F}_1 \boxed{\ell}]$ valence of the daughter. Here it is worth noticing that the tag $\boxed{\ell}$ stands for a whole (variable) list, which might be empty, contrary to what happens in the Head-Specifier Schema, where $[\mathcal{F}_1 \text{<} \boxed{k} \text{>}]$ is a valence with one element $\boxed{k}$ on the list as in the case of the verb. The option of an empty $\mathcal{F}_1$ valence is exploited by the preposition, building a phrase with head-complement structure whose mother node cannot combine with any specifier and then must be a maximal projection (under the pertinent X-bar Theory). Correct linearization follows, if the two attributes replace SUBCAT in the LP statements (130)-(131) offered before:

(130) $\boxed{k} \prec [\mathcal{F}_1 \text{<} \boxed{k} \text{>}]$

(131) $[\mathcal{F}_2 \text{<} \ldots \boxed{i} \ldots \text{>}] \prec \boxed{i}$

It is time to decide which actual attribute labels of the grammar are expected to embody $\mathcal{F}_1$ and $\mathcal{F}_2$, a decision that need not come down to arbitrary conventions inasmuch as one can find different theoretical and even empirical motivations. A rather natural position, adopted by Richard Cooper (1991: ch. 3), would simply exploit the X-bar Theory terminology which we have used in a meta-grammatical fashion so far: hence the attributes SPECIFIER (= SPR[31]), for $\mathcal{F}_1$, and COMPLEMENTS (= COMPS), for $\mathcal{F}_2$. On the other hand, since the

[30] Indeed the adjunct position in the Head-Adjunct Schema (119) of § 4.2.1 was explicitly represented as a two-bar phrase. The same could be done for the complement positions in the Head-Complement Schema, and so on, but that move is made unnecessary by a lexicalist treatment encoding the bar information in the elements occurring on the valence lists of the selecting heads.

[31] An alternative abbreviation found in the HPSG literature is SPEC (see Borsley 1987; 1993, Richard Cooper 1991: ch. 3), but Pollard & Sag (1994) employ it with a different meaning, as we will explain soon.

HPSG treatment of subcategorization develops some general ideas stemming from GPSG, $\mathcal{F}_1$ and $\mathcal{F}_2$ might as well be considered the list-valued counterparts of former GPSG features (and labelled accordingly). It would indeed be tempting to assume that $\mathcal{F}_2$ restores original coverage and scope of SUBCAT in GPSG, being restricted to elements that correspond to complements and are 'discharged' together at the lexical head level. Thus a way of explaining the fact that $\mathcal{F}_2$ did not appear on phrasal categories in our schemata (129) is to identify the feature with SUBCAT in the GPSG sense, appropriate for lexical categories only. Moreover, an alternative interpretation of $\mathcal{F}_1$ could identify this with SUBJ(ECT), because to distinguish phrasal projections (of V) "as to whether they are [SUBJ < >] or [SUBJ <Y″>] ... is much the same as the [+SUBJ] vs. [−SUBJ] distinction in GPSG" (Pollard & Sag 1994: p. 363).

To settle the controversy, we have to go into more details about the linguistic status of the two valence features. Focussing on $\mathcal{F}_2$ first, we can easily find reasons for rejecting purely lexical SUBCAT status, i.e. the GPSG interpretation. There are some generalizations that HPSG's grammatical theory is in a position to capture, provided the valence features behave in a parallel fashion, as their common notion of 'valence' would suggest. In any version of HPSG (cf. Pollard & Sag 1987; 1994), categories – and the constituents belonging to them – are classified according to the '(un)saturation' w.r.t. valences represented by list-valued features: a category C is **saturated** w.r.t. a given valence $\mathcal{F}$ when the $\mathcal{F}$ attribute of C has empty list value (='< >'), or else C is **unsaturated** w.r.t. $\mathcal{F}$. The capacity of a head (category) to capture arguments, in the ways that were shown by the relevant schemata, is due to the head's unsaturation and conforms to the **Valence Principle** of HPSG[32], roughly saying that for each valence feature $\mathcal{F}$ the $\mathcal{F}$ value on the head daughter is the concatenation of the mother's $\mathcal{F}$ value with the list of the elements matching those daughters in the construction that are arguments of the $\mathcal{F}$ kind (if any).

Reverting to our familiar example "She gave a toy to Kim", in the revised HPSG approach a verb like *give* is lexically encoded with the following category inclusive of subcategorization frame:

(132) V[$\mathcal{F}_1$ <NP[*nmt*]>, $\mathcal{F}_2$ <NP[*acc1*], PP[*to*]>]

Since (132) is not lexically saturated for any valence (contrary to verbs with [$\mathcal{F}_2$ < >] like *die*), both valences $\mathcal{F}_1$ and $\mathcal{F}_2$ call for syntactic saturation by tree constituents matching list elements. In our sample sentence, the VP node

[32]In older (a.k.a. 'standard') HPSG, it was called **Subcategorization Principle** and restricted to the only feature SUBCAT (in the HPSG, not GPSG sense), but Pollard & Sag (1994: p. 348) arrive at a generalized **Valence Principle**, which now we state informally as a metagrammatical generalization across X-bar schemata. The issue will deserve more careful discussion in chapter 5.

becomes saturated w.r.t. $\mathcal{F}_2$ by discharging the two elements that correspond to the complements "a toy" and "to Kim", while the $\mathcal{F}_1$ valence is preserved unchanged. The Valence Principle is satisfied in both cases, because the $\mathcal{F}_2$ value on the head verb concatenates the VP's empty $\mathcal{F}_2$ list with the canonical list of the two complements in the construction[33], while the fact that there are no subject daughters within the VP means that the $\mathcal{F}_1$ value on the head verb concatenates the VP's unary $\mathcal{F}_1$ list with the empty list. By the same token, in the local tree where the VP is head the Valence Principle is satisfied so as to yield a fully saturated category S $[\mathcal{F}_1 < >, \mathcal{F}_2 < >]$, i.e. the mother node preserves the saturation w.r.t. $\mathcal{F}_2$ and becomes saturated for $\mathcal{F}_1$ by discharging the element that corresponds to the subject "she".

All of this clearly implies that $\mathcal{F}_2$ cannot be identified with SUBCAT under the GPSG-ish interpretation appropriate for lexical heads only, so that we will follow Richard Cooper (1991: ch. 3) as well as Pollard & Sag (1994: ch. 9) and adopt the attribute label COMPS instead. The decision is also supported by the existence of a different application for SUBCAT in HPSG:

> "it would appear that the use of distinct [valence] features ... obviates the need for a ... SUBCAT feature ... that represents all the selectional requirements of a lexical head within a single list. This is not quite the case, however; for the entire binding theory set forth in Chapter 6 [of Pollard & Sag's cited book] is formulated in terms of the less-oblique-than relation, which in turn is defined in terms of just such a SUBCAT feature."
>
> Pollard & Sag (1994: p. 375)

But then the issue of where to locate that feature arises (ibid., p. 376):

> "Since the satisfaction of valence requirements is now mediated by the [valence] features ..., there is no longer any need for the SUBCAT feature to play any role in this task. Thus we might assume that SUBCAT is a head feature [[34]]: that is, the valence requirements of lexical heads would be reflected also on all their phrasal projections. This would be a highly undesirable result, however, for endowing phrases with such information would made it available for ... nonlocal subcategorizations[, which] are in principle impossible and should be ruled out by a correct theory of the organization of linguistic information... For this reason, ... the SUBCAT feature is appropriate only for words".

[33] Complement daughters can be captured in any order thanks to the ID status of the Head-Complement Schema, but the corresponding elements on the $\mathcal{F}_2$ list get canonically ordered by obliqueness as mentioned before.

[34] Here the notion of 'head feature' (in the sense of the Head Feature Principle which was stated in § 4.2.1) means a feature belonging to the HEAD value.

To sum up, a purely lexical SUBCAT exists in HPSG too, but one that is not restricted to complements and therefore cannot coincide with $\mathcal{F}_2$ anyway.

Let us take advantage of our discussion about SUBCAT in order to exemplify the above-mentioned application to Binding Theory, in a sense reminiscent of Chomsky's (1981) celebrated work in the field, but adapted to HPSG. E.g, consider these coindexation options:

(133) $\textit{John}_1$ believes that $\textit{Bill}_2$ hates $\left\{ \begin{array}{l} \textit{himself}_{2/*1} \\ \textit{him}_{(1)/*2} \\ \textit{Harry}_{*1/*2} \end{array} \right\}$

Since the direct object of the verb *hate* occurs on that verb's SUBCAT list together with the subject *Bill*, which is in a less oblique position (being the first element of the list), the coindexation between the only two list elements – hence the 'binding' of the object to the subject – is obligatory if the object is a reflexive pronoun, like *himself*, and impossible when we replace it with a personal pronoun, like *him*, or a nonpronoun, like the proper name *Harry*. On the other hand, contrary to *himself* and *Harry*, the personal pronoun can optionally be bound by the subject of the verb *believe*, *John*, occurring on a SUBCAT list that does not directly include *him* but the complement clause where *him* is selected. (See Pollard & Sag 1994: §§6.4, 6.8.3.)

As chapter 3 has made clear, the coindexation between NPs gets formalized in HPSG by token identity of their INDEX values belonging to the semantic CONTENT. It follows from this that we must give up a simplifying assumption which was (provisionally) made before: the elements on the SUBCAT list cannot be just syntactic categories, and consequently the same holds for the valence lists it concatenates. A 'sign-based framework', like HPSG, proves actually ideal for extending subcategorization in the appropriate way, since syntactic and semantic information will be gathered up as (two sides of) one linguistic unit, described by a feature structure. The pertinent part of any such 'sign' is a grammatical entity dubbed *synsem* (Pollard & Sag 1994: ch. 1), which combines a CAT(EGORY) with the associated CONTENT but does not include the expression's PHONOLOGY, among other things. Thus, the fact that the elements on the SUBCAT list are 'synsems' allows the lexical entry of a verb like *give* to assign their indices a semantic role:

(134)
$$\left[\begin{array}{l} \text{CAT} \; {}_{\textit{cat}}\!\left[\begin{array}{l} \text{HEAD } \textit{verb} \\ \text{SUBCAT} < \text{NP}[\textit{nmt}]_{\boxed{1}}, \text{NP}[\textit{acc1}]_{\boxed{2}}, \text{PP}[\textit{to}]_{\boxed{3}} > \end{array} \right] \\ \text{CONTENT} \mid \text{NUCLEUS} \; {}_{\textit{give}}\!\left[\begin{array}{l} \text{AGENT } \boxed{1} \\ \text{THEME } \boxed{2} \\ \text{GOAL } \boxed{3} \end{array} \right] \end{array} \right]$$

(While referring back again to our chapter 3 for various notations and notions involved by (134), it is worth pointing out that also the PP has an index, which is part of the CONTENT value entirely inherited from the NP object of the semantically vacuous preposition *to*.)

We finally turn to the $\mathcal{F}_1$ valence and the theoretical alternative between interpretations of the feature as SPECIFIER (abbreviated SPR) or SUBJ(ECT). The latter, GPSG-based interpretation lays itself open to facile criticisms precisely because it is restricted to subjects (with the proviso that such a SUBJECT label be understood according to its traditional meaning in the grammatical field) and therefore does not capture the X-bar Theory generalization that subjects are a particular case of specifiers; above all, how to treat specifiers other than subjects looks unclear. There is more to it than meets the eye, however, since one could try to show that the generalization is spurious, or propose a different and, arguably, better way of expressing it and account for all specifiers. To weigh up the pros and cons in the light of linguistic evidence, now we have to slightly expand on the application of HPSG's SPR feature to non-subject specifiers.

In particular, a characterization of the specifier notion in valence terms as the dependent that some head may select by means of the list-valued feature SPR, discharging it from the list through the Head-Specifier Schema, is relevant to determiners under the assumption that locally, "N′[= $\bar{\text{N}}$ projection]s are the heads of NPs and subcategorize for their determiners" (Pollard & Sag 1994: p. 50). This idea has been exploited in HPSG (after Pollard & Sag 1987: pp. 139-141) to account for the empirical requirement that singular count nouns, as opposed to plural nouns and non-count nouns, obligatorily take an article or another overt determiner with the same distribution, in English (as we mentioned since chapter 1) and other languages. E.g., Netter (1994) provides the following NP data from German, concerning overt vs. Ø- determination with the two nouns *Auto* ('car') and *Wein* ('wine'):

sing.	**plur.**	**sing.**	**plur.**
das Auto	die Autos	*Auto	Autos
der Wein	die Weine	Wein	Weine

The relevant information lends itself to be encoded by lexical entries of HPSG, in the format [SPR $<\mathcal{D}>$] for a singular count noun (where $\mathcal{D}$ abbreviates a 'synsem' object compatible with suitable determiners), or else [SPR $<\mathcal{D}>\vee<>$] (equivalent to [SPR $<(\mathcal{D})>$], where parentheses indicate optionality), and can be passed up to the $\bar{\text{N}}$ node through the Head-Complement Schema if SPR is our $\mathcal{F}_1$.

More generally, SPR is assigned a theoretical role of fundamental importance for the X-bar syntax of revised HPSG. Indeed, unlike the GPSG feature

BAR with numerical values (Gazdar et al. 1985: pp. 22-26), bar levels in HPSG are not primitives of the grammatical system, but get reconstructed by Pollard & Sag (1994: § 9.4.2) in terms of the lexical vs. phrasal distinction combined with the SPR valence. Hence a metagrammatical definition of the X-bar notation by abbreviating conventions like the following:

(135) **X-bar Conventions**

a. $X^0 = X[+\text{LEX}]$

b. $X^P = X[-\text{LEX}, \text{COMPS} < >]$

c. $\bar{X}\ (= X') = X^P[\text{SPR} <\boxed{k}>]$

d. $\bar{\bar{X}}\ (= X'') = X^P[\text{SPR} < >]$

Exploiting a feature [+/−LEX] (originally proposed by Pollard & Sag 1987), (135) defines zero-bar constituents as lexical and all the others as phrasal, the latter being one-bar phrases when they have an element on the SPR list, or two-bar phrases in case of empty SPR list. A related constraint is enforced by our convention b. consistently with the desired interpretation of the Head-Complement Schema: "inasmuch as all phrases will now be [COMPS < >], we ... incorporate this specification into the definition of ... *phrase*" (Pollard & Sag 1994: p. 346).

The question that remains to be answered, then, is whether such a feature SPR, which looks independently motivated on both empirical and theoretical grounds, will cover subjects too. Pollard & Sag (1994: pp. 359-360) have noted how "a purely syntactic difficulty arises from attempting to identify subjects and (traditional[, e.g. determinative]) specifiers as instances of the same grammatical relation... The difficulty is that ... both specifiers and subjects can appear with the same head". The nonverbal (= N, A or P) head of predicative complements showing some specifier – as exemplified by (136) below – is a case in point, because the predicative import makes them additionally carry the head's valence concerning a subject qua 'external argument', so as to allow the copular verb to inherit that valence from the complement and select the actual subject of the sentence. E.g.:

(136) a. **John** is $[_{\text{NP}}$ **an** idiot]
Subj. *Spec.*

b. **She** is $[_{\text{AP}}$ **so** afraid of thunder]
Subj. *Spec.*

c. **The cops** were $[_{\text{PP}}$ **right** around the corner]
Subj. *Spec.*

The readers are reminded that the SPR list is allowed to carry at most one element, a postulate which cannot be withdrawn without messing up the feature-theoretic reconstruction of bar levels in revised HPSG (see (135) and the related discussion above). Thus, according to Pollard & Sag (1994: pp. 360-361) "the most obvious solution to this problem is simply to posit distinct grammatical relations (and therefore distinct valence features) SPR and SUBJ".

Let us draw some conclusions from Pollard & Sag's decision of adopting both SPR and SUBJ as instantiations of $\mathcal{F}_1$ (together with COMPS qua $\mathcal{F}_2$) for the X-bar ID component of HPSG. Both $\mathcal{F}_1$-type features are passed up in the Head-Complement Schema, so that the former version (129a) becomes:

(137) $X^P[\text{SPR}\,\boxed{\ell}, \text{SUBJ}\,\boxed{f}] \rightarrow X^0[\text{SPR}\,\boxed{\ell}, \text{SUBJ}\,\boxed{f}, \text{COMPS} <\boxed{1}, \ldots \boxed{n}>], \boxed{1}, \ldots \boxed{n}$

In the Head-Specifier Schema, while SUBJ is passed up (an information which was not envisaged by (129b)[35]), the element on the SPR list gets discharged to yield $\bar{\bar{X}}$ as mother category:

(138) $\bar{\bar{X}}[\text{SUBJ}\,\boxed{f}] \rightarrow X^P[\text{SUBJ}\,\boxed{f}, \text{SPR}<\boxed{k}>], \boxed{k}$

Finally, the fact that subjects are not treated as specifiers means that Pollard & Sag (1994: p. 362) have to introduce another X-bar schema, the **Head-Subject (ID) Schema**:

(139) $\bar{\bar{X}}[\text{SUBJ}< >] \rightarrow \bar{\bar{X}}[\text{SUBJ}<\boxed{k}>], \boxed{k}$

Note "that gaining its subject does not affect a phrase's bar level (as defined here). For example, both S and VP are X'', differing only as to whether they are [SUBJ < >] or [SUBJ $<Y''>$]" (ibid., p. 363)[36]. There are some comments this account of subjects would deserve, but we postpone them to chapter 5, whereas the Head-Specifier Schema is discussed for our NP analysis in the rest of the current chapter.

4.3 A cross-linguistic NP analysis

Aim of this section is to develop into a proper HPSG treatment the analysis of the Noun Phrase which was started informally in chapter 1 on the basis of English. Evidence from other languages belonging to our coverage, especially Italian (for peculiarities of possessives, 'bare' plurals, etc.) and German (for the so-called 'declension congruence'), will play a crucial role.

[35] At the same time, (138) dispenses with the empty (SPR case of $\mathcal{F}_1$) list specification on the lefthand side of (129b), because it follows from the X-bar Convention (135d) for two-bar projections. Likewise, the fact that the head phrase is a one-bar projection follows from the X-bar Convention (135c) because of the SPR list with one element.

[36] On $\bar{\bar{V}}$, cf. GPSG: "there will be two instantiations of this category: one where [+SUBJ] is instantiated, and one where [−SUBJ] is instantiated. The former gives rise to clauses; the latter to verb phrases" (Gazdar et al. 1985: p. 114).

4.3.1 Determiners as specifiers or adjuncts

4.3.1.1 On multiple determination

A straightforward approach to the syntax-semantics interface of modern phrase structure grammars is adopted by Gazdar et al. (1985) for the GPSG framework, where the syntactic categories of X-bar Theory receive a model-theoretic interpretation in terms of denotation types. Thus, a determiner of GPSG is syntactically treated as a specifier of NPs, the NP being $\bar{\bar{N}}$, and semantically denotes some function from denotations of $\bar{N}$ heads to NP denotations (ibid., cf. pp. 126, 189). That is to say, consistently with the mainstream way of interpreting determiners in the semantics of Montague Grammar (see Montague 1974, Dowty et al. 1981) and Generalized Quantifier Theory (GQT: Barwise & Cooper 1981), which we have presented in chapter 3, a determiner corresponds to a semantic functor of type:

(140) <$\bar{N}$, NP> (= <<*e*, *t*>, <<*e*, *t*>, *t*>>[37])

Here, in a simplified notation by Gazdar et al. (1985: ch. 9-10)[38], the syntactic categories 'NP' and '$\bar{N}$' conventionally stand for the respective **logical types**, namely generalized quantifiers (<<*e*, *t*>, *t*>) and their restriction sets (<*e*, *t*>).

Neglecting some technical, framework-dependent differences as regards the complex structuring of linguistic information to be assumed for handling scope in quantification[39], Pollard & Sag's (1987; 1994) HPSG essentially shares the syntax-semantics correspondence scheme which underlies (140), i.e. the view of a determiner as specifier yielding a generalized quantifier qua NP-level interpretation from the interpretation of the adjacent nominal head. All of this sounds quite reasonable, but unfortunately the logically based picture turns out to be oversimplified if one compares it with the empirical characterization of determiners that we outlined for English in chapter 1 (on the lines of Quirk et al. 1985) and extended to other languages in chapter 2. A problem which has not been seriously addressed by supporters of the received wisdom, in HPSG as much as other frameworks, is how to reconcile (140) with **multiple determination**. We mean the co-occurrence of two, or more, non-coordinated determiners depending on (projections of) the same head noun, whereas some authors seem to take for granted a different manner of understanding the phenomenon.

[37]For convenience, let us consider extensional and not intensional interpretations, so that Montague's primitive types *e* ('elementary entity', a.k.a. *individual*) and *t* ('truth value') will suffice without calling into play possible worlds, contexts, etc.

[38]Ibid., p. 189: "We shall adopt the convention that a category label X denotes [the type] *TYP*(X) when it occurs in an unambiguous context".

[39]Scoping techniques will be taken into account by our chapter 5.

Barwise & Cooper's (1981) GQT system for a fragment of English, e.g., covers article-numeral combinations, as in "*the twenty* books", by interpreting each *the n* like an unanalyzed determiner whose two parts are purely orthographic. Therefore, two series of cardinals are listed in the basic vocabulary of the system – those with an 'inherent prefix' *the* (*the 1*, *the 2*, *the 3*, ...) and those without (*1*, *2*, *3*, ...) – while the stand-alone definite article in the singular is disposed of as a mere abbreviation for *the 1*. Such a treatment is clearly 'ad hoc' and cannot be reasonably extended to more complex combinations ignored by Barwise & Cooper (1981), as in "*the first twenty* books", "(*almost*) *all the twenty* books", "(*almost*) *all the first twenty* books", etc. (For related criticism, cf. also Hoeksema 1983.)

A less simplistic version could aim at treating this phenomenon by means of an adequately complex phrase combining the pertinent items. It would be up to the whole phrase to play the specifier role for the NP and express a semantic determiner of GQT/HPSG, though one that would require a compositionally interpreted internal structure. Hence the issue of how to 'generate' all the possible complex determiners (with their semantic interpretation), which is hinted at – but left open – by Pollard & Sag (1994):

> "In our fragment, we can get by with a small finite number of atomic subsorts of *semdet*. A more complete grammar would require a separate subgrammar for an infinite set of semantic determiners (including, e.g., cardinality determiners for each natural number)."
>
> (ibid., p. 397)

Note that the only case they cite as an example need not be understood in the sense we are focussing on, because it is beyond doubt that an infinite number of genuinely complex cardinals must be generated (and interpreted) by mechanisms already mentioned in chapter 2: affixation and compounding, at the level of morphological word-structure, plus others, such as coordination. But the actual question is whether the 'subgrammar' Pollard and Sag vaguely refer to will yield also complex determiner phrases covering the heterogeneous combinations that fall under our notion of multiple determination.

Even leaving all semantic issues aside, a serious difficulty with the putative 'complex determiner phrase' to be adopted as specifier is its rather uncertain internal syntax, due to the lack of reliable criteria for deciding dependency and phrase-structure relationships between the component expressions. If only binary branching is considered in the first place, a combination of **predeterminer**, **central determiner** and **postdeterminer** (in the terminology we have borrowed from Quirk et al. 1985), as exemplified by "*all the twenty* books", allows a priori 8 alternative analyses, depending on whether the article is attached to the left or to the right and on which lexical head projects the embedded two-word constituent and/or the whole specifier. See below, where we have highlighted candidate lexical heads by capitals:

(141) a. [[ALL the] twenty]
b. [[all THE] twenty]
c. [[ALL the] TWENTY]
d. [[all THE] TWENTY]
e. [all [THE twenty]]
f. [all [the TWENTY]]
g. [ALL [THE twenty]]
h. [ALL [the TWENTY]]

If local trees with more than two daughters (immediate constituents) are not excluded here, there are other three options, depending on the head to be envisaged for the resulting 'flat' three-word phrase:

(142) a. [ALL the twenty]
b. [all THE twenty]
c. [all the TWENTY]

All in all, one would have to investigate 11 possible alternatives, which is still a simplified picture, since it is not obvious that non-heads in *all the twenty* should always play the same dependency role.[40] (E.g., one might imagine that *all* and *twenty* in (141e) be specifier and complement of the article, respectively, but we see no cogent reason why they could not be adjuncts, giving rise to new alternatives.) A rather puzzling situation, considering that standard syntactic criteria for a choice among alternative patterns of dependency and phrase structure do not look very helpful in this case. Indeed, all the three words in the putative determiner phrase *all the twenty* are equally good candidate heads, inasmuch as they can be considered distributionally equivalent to it (cf. the NPs "*all* books", "*the* books", "*twenty* books").

It would be a mistake to believe that a choice among the alternatives in question may result from differences w.r.t. the part-of-speech category of candidate lexical heads. The point is that our discussion of the matter in chapter 1 has shown how the assignment of determiners to parts of speech tends to be controversial and theory-internal, being often dictated or influenced by the linguist's position on the syntactic analysis of constructions within the NP. We do not deem it necessary to review again all the options that we discussed, to see what they would imply for (141)-(142), but one case deserves to be

[40]We are equally neglecting related issues of 'bar' level.

mentioned because of its relevance to our category system. Since that chapter has provided some evidence for the assignment of articles to a part of speech known as 'minor' in that it does not project phrase structure and, by the same token, disallows any dependent, somebody might consider applying the idea so as to exclude all cases in which *the* is assigned the head role in (141)-(142). Of course, the reduction in the number of options would not be sufficient without some criterion for choosing between *all* and *twenty* as co-occurring candidate heads, but at least the proposal solves the head problem for two-word determiner phrases with an article.

The weakness of such an attempt at adapting our conception of the article as minor category to the 'complex determiner phrase' approach to multiple determination, however, is readily seen. Minor status was originally motivated for the article so as to reject the dependency of *all* on *the*, thus avoiding an otherwise unmotivated additional reading for the former word. Indeed, the optimally simple way of treating "*all* (*the*) books", or similar[41], is to exploit always the same reading of *all* as dependent of a nominal projection, whether the central determiner is present or not. But this line of reasoning may well be applied to *the* itself and prevents an extra reading as dependent of *all*, because the optimally simple treatment of "(*all*) *the* books" needs just one reading of *the*, the obvious one as dependent of a nominal projection, whether the predeterminer is present or not. The fact that combinations with further items must be taken into account too – as in the case of *twenty* considered above – increases the danger of adding new readings to some word or another, of course.

Finally, the hypothesis that multiple determination corresponds to a single determiner phrase, acting as specifier, does not only require quite arbitrary decisions concerning its syntactic structure, as well as the introduction of extra readings for some of the co-occurring words, but cannot reasonably handle data showing an interposed qualifying adjective for languages where the phenomenon proves possible. In the following Italian NPs, which mean 'the two famous books of yours$_{sing.}$', a cardinal and a possessive qua post-determiners (cf. § 4.3.1.2 below, for this status of Italian possessives) get shuffled together with a qualifying adjective, actually in any order after the article[42]:

---

[41]The article can be replaced by a central determiner such as a demonstrative or possessive, whose category is 'major' (for reasons already explained in chapter 1), but *all* will not modify it anyway, lacking any reading as dependent of determiners.

[42]The examples (143) are all grammatical and acceptable, modulo appropriate (but not necessarily emphatic) intonation patterns, and the intuitive judgements of Italian speakers here hardly distinguish 'marked' and 'unmarked' orders, or do that rather subjectively. For instance, the author of the present book occasionally finds (143f) slightly less natural (though still acceptable) compared with other options, but the feeling tends to vary from day to day.

(143) a. i tuoi due famosi libri
(lit. 'the your$_{sing.}$ two famous books')
b. i due tuoi famosi libri
(lit. 'the two your$_{sing.}$ famous books')
c. i tuoi famosi due libri
(lit. 'the your$_{sing.}$ famous two books')
d. i due famosi tuoi libri
(lit. 'the two famous your$_{sing.}$ books')
e. i famosi tuoi due libri
(lit. 'the famous your$_{sing.}$ two books')
f. i famosi due tuoi libri
(lit. 'the famous two your$_{sing.}$ books')

The three determination items in each of the examples c.-f. could all be part of the same specifier phrase provided the qualifying adjective were included in that phrase. But this would give rise to implausible dependency relations with the article, numeral or possessive, whereas *famosi*, intuitively, modifies the nominal head: not only in a.-b., also in the last four examples.

The syntactic problems we have mentioned disappear altogether if one adopts a different approach to multiple determination, according to which the attachment of determiners is entirely dictated by the nominal headedness of the NP. That is, assuming binary branching, co-occurring determiners attach directly to the nominal backbone, one at a time, so as to yield a new nominal projection in each case, without combining with each other first[43]. Heuristically, this approach has the advantage of a drastic reduction of alternatives, resulting in just one structural option to be investigated for our previous English example:

(144) [all [the [twenty ___]]]

where '___' is a nominal head slot. If non-binary branching were considered too, other three structures (i.e. [all the [twenty ___]], [all [the twenty ___]] and [all the twenty ___]) would become possible; a strong reduction, nevertheless, would be confirmed, resulting in four options against the 11 allowed by the 'determiner phrase approach'. Anyway, it is the binary version which we will adopt, as maximally restrictive working hypothesis on heuristic grounds.

[43]We are referring to the combinations postulated by the 'complex determiner phrase' approach to multiple determination, but the fact that determiners can be combined in other ways, like coordination and morphological compounding (for complex numerals), has been acknowledged since chapter 1. Our approach is compatible with genuinely complex determiners, like the modified predeterminer and the coordination of numerals in "*almost all* the *twenty or twenty-one* books".

Now it is time to introduce fine-grained distinctions in terms of bar level labelling and related dependency roles. As a first approximation, the following X-bar Theory version of the proposed structural analysis of the Noun Phrase, where NP is $\bar{\bar{N}}$, provides an appealing account of multiple determination:

(145) $[_{NP}\ \alpha/\mathit{Deg.}\ [_{NP}\ \beta\ [_{\bar{N}} \cdots [_{\bar{N}}\ \gamma/\mathit{Qual.}\ [_{\bar{N}} \cdots]]]]]$

α = predeterminer
β = central determiner
γ = postdeterminer

According to standard characterizations of syntactic functions within X-bar Theory (v. section 4.2 above), β in (145) plays the 'specifier' role for the whole NP, i.e. it is the dependent whose attachment changes an intermediate, one-bar projection into a maximal, two-bar one, but both α and γ are 'adjuncts' instead, given their bar-preserving attachments to a maximal and an intermediate projection, respectively. A further difference holds between pre- and post-determiners in that the former are restricted to a single position, which can alternatively be filled by some NP-compatible degree modifier (= *Deg.*), like "quite" or "rather" [44]; on the contrary, recursive $\bar{N}$-level adjunction allows the occurrence of multiple postdeterminers and the interposition of qualifying adjectives (= *Qual.*) in some languages.

The general pattern (145) of NP structure with multiple determination will indeed be parameterized in different ways depending on the (type of) language. English normally appears to be more restrictive than other languages in this connection, because of a constraint proposed by Radford (1997: p. 46): "both determiners and [qualifying] adjectives can be used together to modify a noun, but when they do so, any determiner modifying the noun has to precede any adjective(s) modifying the noun". The language-specific character of such a constraint, stated by Radford on the basis of English only, is proved by the Italian examples we have given in (143), where the article is bound to the left-most position (in those NPs without predeterminer) owing to its specifier role, but the relative order of $\bar{N}$-level adjuncts is free, irrespective of postdeterminer or qualifying modifier status.

Another constraint by the same author looks inadequate even for English: (qualifying) "adjectives can be recursively ... stacked in front of the noun they modify ..., whereas determiners cannot be stacked in this way, in that you can generally only have one determiner (of a given type – e.g. one referential determiner and one quantificational determiner) premodifying a noun" (ibid.). First of all, the constraint relies on a dubious semantic distinction, which is only vaguely sketched by Radford, but apparently must confine reference to

[44] Typical English examples of degree items that have an adnominal and syntactically predeterminer-like function, which were discussed in chapter 1.

'definiteness'[45], while that misconception has been argued against at length in our previous chapters. To make sense out of the distinction, even though we reject his labels, the constraint might be interpreted as saying: at most one determiner that is semantically definite and one that is not can depend on (projections of) the same head noun. But then all cases with three determiners, like "*all the twenty* books", are evident counterexamples. Interestingly, some of the cases apparently excluded by the constraint show the possibility of multiple postdeterminers in different orders for English too, when cardinals and ordinals co-occur, as in "*the first two* pages" (= the very first page and the second) vs. "*the two first* pages" (of distinct books, say).[46]

It may well be that a weaker interpretation of the 'one-determiner-per-type constraint' was actually intended by Radford, whose informal version sounds ambiguous enough to accept other sorts of determiners besides the two he explicitly mentioned. A step in that direction was already taken by Jackendoff (1977: § 5.2.1), e.g., who stated a similar constraint based on three semantic classes, inasmuch as numerals too were distinguished from 'quantificational' determiners (or 'quantifiers' *tout court*, in Jackendoff's terminology). If the constraint were finally made so fine-grained as to allow at most one item for each of the six 'paradigmatic kinds' of determiners we have introduced since chapter 1 – i.e. articles, demonstratives, possessives, quantitatives, cardinals and ordinals – also an example like "*all the first twenty* books" would not be ruled out. Still, there is more to it than meets the eye here, because "*all the many* books (that Mary bought)" is perfectly acceptable, in spite of the two co-occurring quantitative determiners *all* and *many*. Chapter 5 will show how to achieve an empirically adequate (and considerably technical) account of the various co-occurrence restrictions on multiple determination, involving a subtle classification of lexical items.

For the moment, suffice it to say there is an intricate interplay of syntactic and semantic aspects, which cannot be reduced to the oversimplified picture envisaged by the received wisdom in determination matters. Quite relevant in this connection is a consequence of pattern (145) looking somewhat surprising compared with the orthodox GQT notion of determiner. The logical type <$\bar{\text{N}}$,

[45]See how he presents the matter: "referential determiners are determiners like *the / this / that / my* which are used to introduce referring expressions – e.g. an expression like *the car* ... is a referring expression in the sense that it refers to a specific car whose identity is assumed to be known to the hearer" (ibid.).

[46]Note that the equivalent ordinal could be added to the Italian examples (143), making them even more complex, but still acceptable: "i tuoi due famosi *primi* libri" (lit. 'the your two famous first books'), "i *primi* due tuoi famosi libri" (lit. 'the first two your famous books'), etc. Since a predeterminer may well be added too, there is evidence that as much as five determiners – three being postdeterminers – are compatible with (projections of) the same head noun in Italian.

NP> (in the abbreviated notation previously introduced through (140)) turns out to be sufficient but not necessary for determinative status according to our approach, considering that adjuncts whose type is $<\bar{\mathrm{N}}, \bar{\mathrm{N}}>$ ($<<e, t>, <e, t>>$) or $<\mathrm{NP}, \mathrm{NP}>$ ($<<<e, t>, t>, <<e, t>, t>>$) are also allowed to be determiners. The point is that the notion of 'determinative function' we are assuming is referentially based, not just a denotational matter, in the light of a distinction between reference and denotation which is taken for granted here but was argued for at length by chapter 2. In section 4.4 we shall have more to say on the flexible correlation of the determiners' classes with their possible denotation types as emerging from the current discussion.

Getting back to our original issue of how to apply and parameterize the general pattern according to the languages, it is worth noting that predeterminers like *tutti* (= $\mathrm{all}_{plur.}$) and *entrambi* (= both) in Italian, contrary to their English translations, are unable to combine with a common noun (projection) unless a suitable central determiner such as the definite article is interposed: cf. *all* (*the*) *books* and It. *tutti i libri* vs. * *tutti libri*. Somebody might understand this behaviour as a proof that at least in Italian the article takes the predeterminer as dependent and therefore cannot be minor, but we believe the idea to be wrong, because *tutti* does occur without central determiner if the NP is headed by a pronoun: e.g. *tutti noi* ('all [of] us'), *tutti quelli che arriveranno* ('all those who will arrive'). Moreover, the same predeterminer in the singular can be combined directly with a proper name in appropriate contexts, v. *tutta Roma* ('all Rome'), *tutto Picasso* ('all Picasso' = all the work of Picasso). Considering that the embedded pronoun or proper name gets classified as $\bar{\bar{\mathrm{N}}}$ since it may well occur as a full NP on its own, the behaviour of Italian predeterminers is captured by the generalization that they are always $\bar{\bar{\mathrm{N}}}$-level adjuncts but call for a central determiner when the NP is headed by a common noun.

The lack of recursive NP-level adjunctions with multiple predeterminers or interposed non-determinative modifiers, however, seems to counter the adjunct role of predeterminers in (145). There is, in fact, an asymmetry between the pattern's two sides lying before and after the central determiner slot, so that somebody could conclude that a more complex approach, adopting a maximal projection with **three bars**[47], is necessary. In that way, the predeterminer would not be adjunct, but a sort of higher-level specifier changing the two-bar

[47]Cf. Coppen's (1991) analysis of the Dutch NP, which resembles our pattern (145) but applies the more complex system of bar levels. A different instance of that system was originally proposed by Jackendoff (1977), using nonbinary branching: in his treatment, bar-preserving adjunctions do not exist, so that postdeterminers and qualifying adjectives become sisters under the two-bar node, while pre- and central determiners can only occur under the three-bar node.

projection into a three-bar one, this change being what prevents recursion. We will not explore the consequences for HPSG (in terms of features, schemata, etc.), because the purported alternative is actually unwarranted. For one thing, even if the lack of multiple predeterminers were explained by parallelism with the central determiners qua specifiers, the occurrence of non-determinative adjuncts before a predeterminer and between it and the central determiner remains possible in principle under that system, contrary to empirical evidence. On the other hand, there are independent motivations for the asymmetry we remarked, without altering the well-established assumption of a maximally two-bar system stemming from Chomsky (1970).

Let's begin by pointing out that recursive right-adjunction to $\bar{\bar{\mathrm{N}}}$ is actually found if appositive relative clauses or other phrases modifying a whole NP get covered too, as in:

(146) $[_{\bar{\bar{\mathrm{N}}}}$ $[_{\bar{\bar{\mathrm{N}}}}$ $[_{\bar{\bar{\mathrm{N}}}}$ (all) those boys], *the students of theology*], *who make a great fuss about nothing*], ...

What's more, the $\bar{\mathrm{X}}$-skipping approach of HPSG to missing specifiers (in § 4.2.2 above) must presumably entail that a 'bare nominal' NP with some qualifying adjective(s) – which would otherwise adjoin to $\bar{\mathrm{N}}$ – be the result of (possibly recursive) left-adjunction of the adjective(s) to an embedded two-bar phrase without specifier. E.g.:

(147) $[_{\bar{\bar{\mathrm{N}}}}$ *nice* $[_{\bar{\bar{\mathrm{N}}}}$ *new* $[_{\bar{\bar{\mathrm{N}}}}$ pictures (of Mary)]]]

As Netter (1994) noticed when discussing German data like *der gute Wein* (= the good wine) / *guter Wein* (= good wine) / **gute(r) der Wein* (= good the wine), suitable feature information is thus needed to distinguish 'bare nominal' NPs from those with determiner, so as to reject incorrect left-adjunctions of qualifying adjectives to the latter phrases. While deferring a technical discussion to chapter 5, we can safely assume that the same mechanism will prevent the occurrence of such undesired adjuncts before a predeterminer and between it and the central determiner.

Since the grammar is expected to predict that qualifying adjectives cannot interact with predetermination in the way they do with postdetermination in some languages, items occupying the predeterminer slot remain the only potential source of recursive left-adjunctions to $\bar{\mathrm{N}}$. (For all the remaining dependents of a nominal head the problem simply does not arise, inasmuch as they are right-adjoined, or adjoined to a node other than $\bar{\bar{\mathrm{N}}}$, or not considered adjuncts at all.) However, it seems to us that a little change in our original (chapter 1) definition of the three positional classes of determiners offers a simple explanation for the otherwise puzzling adjunction behaviour of predeterminers. If a predeterminer is characterized as the case of determiner that cannot be preceded by any determiner, recursive adjunction is blocked by the predeterminer notion itself – contrary to the postdeterminer notion, which is 'flexibly' characterized as before (= the determiners that can follow but cannot precede determiners of the other two classes). All of this, though admittedly informal at the present stage, will be formally specified within the overall treatment of co-occurrence restrictions on multiple determination to be worked out in due course.

4.3.1.2 Lexical selection of heads

The idea that various determiners fulfil the function of adjuncts calls for an adequate syntactic and semantic analysis of head-adjunct combinations. We will essentially adopt Pollard & Sag's position (1994, p. 55):

> "adjuncts select their heads. This approach has much in common with the analysis of adjuncts in categorial grammar, where it is assumed that adjuncts are functions that take heads as arguments. The basic idea of our analysis is that, in a head-adjunct structure, the content of the mother is token-identical to that of the adjunct... For semantically restrictive adjectives like *red*, the content has a particularly simple form: it is just a nominal object whose index ... coincides with that of the head noun, and whose restriction is the set of psoas obtained by adding to the restrictions imposed by the head noun one further restriction imposed by the adjective itself".[48]

In compliance with HPSG's lexicalism, the selection of the adjacent nominal head (viz. $\bar{\text{N}}$, the only case to be considered for the moment) and the incorporation of its content are performed through the lexical entry of the adjective:

(148)
$$\begin{bmatrix} \text{CAT}\,|\,\text{HEAD}\ \underset{adj}{\begin{bmatrix}\text{MOD } \bar{\text{N}}\text{:} \begin{bmatrix}\text{INDEX } \boxed{1}\\ \text{RESTR } \boxed{2}\end{bmatrix}\end{bmatrix}} \\ \text{CONTENT} \begin{bmatrix}\text{INDEX } \boxed{1} \\ \text{RESTR } \left\{ red(\boxed{1}) \right\} \cup \boxed{2}\end{bmatrix}\end{bmatrix}$$

The syntactic and semantic object, i.e. 'synsem', selected in (148) is the value of MOD(IFIED), an attribute declared appropriate for HEAD, so as to pass it up from the lexical entry via all the phrasal nodes that the adjectival head may happen to project (in APs like "almost *red*", "so terribly *red*", etc.).

We can apply the pertinent selectional relationship in syntactic structures by superimposing it on the X-bar Theory backbone of the Head-Adjunct (ID)

[48] We have already presented in chapter 3 such semantic notions of HPSG as 'nominal object', 'index' and '(restriction) psoa'.

Schema, previously sketched as (119), § 4.2.1. In the usual abbreviated notation, employing X-bar conventions and omitting – entirely or in large part – the path of features[49], we get:

(149) $X^n[\text{VAL}\,\boxed{z}] \rightarrow \boxed{h}X^n[\text{VAL}\,\boxed{z}],\ \bar{\bar{Y}}\,[\text{MOD}\,\boxed{h}]$

The new version states bar-preserving adjunction to any X^n as before, while ensuring that "the MOD value of the adjunct daughter is token-identical to the SYNSEM value of the head daughter" (Pollard & Sag 1994: p. 56). Moreover, the fact that adjunction preserves unchanged all the three valences of the head daughter (i.e. COMPS, SPR and SUBJ) is explicitly formulated in (149) by sharing the VAL(ENCE) value, where they can be assumed to belong.[50] (The valence-preserving character of adjunction conforms to the generalization known as Valence Principle in HPSG: indeed, for each valence $\mathcal{F}$, the head daughter concatenates the mother node's $\mathcal{F}$ list with the empty list, due to the lack of any dependent of the $\mathcal{F}$ kind in the head-adjunct construction. Cf. § 4.2.2 above.)

So far the HPSG treatment of adjuncts could look very different from that of specifiers, the latter being selected by the nominal head – on a par with subjects and complements. Still, a semantic problem arises when the specifier is a determiner and builds up the NP's generalized quantifier in the way we mentioned in chapter 3:

> "How does it come about that ... the RESTIND value ... within the content of the determiner is token-identical to the content of the noun? At first blush it might be thought that this identity could be lexically specified within ... the noun[, exploiting its selection of the determiner]. This will not work, however, since if the head noun were modified (say, by relative clauses or attributive adjectives), the semantic contribution of the modifiers would not be taken into consideration in the content of the determiner... Under present assumptions, it is clear that the determiner must in some sense be able to select its N′ sister, in order to 'have its hands on' the N′ sister's content."
>
> Pollard & Sag (1994: p. 50)

The strategy applied to that end by the two HPSG theorists parallels their MOD approach to adjuncts, inasmuch as the selection of $\bar{N}$ (or N′ in the cited

[49]In the case of [MOD $\boxed{h}$], e.g., we write only the final attribute of the full path:
[SYNSEM|LOCAL|CAT|HEAD|MOD $\boxed{h}$]
whose theoretical motivations are postponed to chapter 5. The tag prefixed to a constituent (like the instance of $\boxed{h}$ prefixed to the head daughter in (149)) stands for the constituent's SYNSEM value though the attribute is omitted, following Pollard & Sag (1994: pp. 362, 384).

[50]See, e.g., Balari & Dini (1998: Intro.): "we introduce the VALENCE attribute, which gathers all *valence* features. This ... feature, although not assumed by most authors, seems appropriate, given ... the split of valence lists".

excerpt) and the incorporation of a 'nominal object' content (which becomes the RESTIND value of the relevant quantifier) are performed through a head feature within the lexical entry of the determiner. A difference from adjuncts is the attribute SPEC(IFIED) adopted for the *synsem*-valued feature in question (ibid., pp. 45, 50-51), as shown by this (partial) lexical representation suitable to the indefinite article:[51]

(150) $\begin{bmatrix} \text{CAT} \mid \underset{minor}{\text{HEAD}} \begin{bmatrix} \text{SPEC } \bar{\text{N}}{:}\boxed{1}\begin{bmatrix}\text{INDEX} \mid \text{NUMBER } sing\end{bmatrix}\end{bmatrix} \\ \underset{quant}{\text{CONTENT}} \begin{bmatrix} \text{DET } \exists \\ \text{RESTIND } \boxed{1} \end{bmatrix} \end{bmatrix}$

To complete such a treatment of specifiers, the SPEC-based selectional relationship is superimposed on the Head-Specifier (ID) Schema:

(151) $\bar{\bar{\text{X}}}[\text{SUBJ}\,\boxed{g}] \rightarrow \boxed{h}\,\text{X}^{\text{P}}[\text{SUBJ}\,\boxed{g},\ \text{SPR}{<}\boxed{k}{>}],\ \boxed{k}\,[\text{SPEC}\,\boxed{h}]$

(cf. our previous version (138), § 4.2.2). But note that the result is a construction in which the nominal head and the determiner mutually select each other (ibid., pp. 50-51, 362-363), yielding a **cyclic** feature structure. (That is, $\boxed{h}$ includes $\boxed{k}$ by virtue of SPR, and $\boxed{k}$ includes $\boxed{h}$ by virtue of SPEC.) This can be criticized from various angles, as also Netter (1994) pointed out. For one thing, cyclic graphs were actually excluded from the original HPSG formalism by Pollard & Sag (1987: p. 37), consistently with the standard assumption that 'directed **acyclic** graphs' (a.k.a. DAGs) are the appropriate kind of data structure for grammatical descriptions in computational linguistics (cf. Gazdar & Mellish 1989: p. 107). And even if computational frameworks allowing cyclic feature structures have been developed in the while (Carpenter 1992), the property at issue is far from being commonly available in natural language processing systems[52].

We believe that general methodological considerations should favour the formally more restrictive (and conceptually easier to grasp) acyclic structures, also considering that the extension of expressive power offered by cyclicity can be proved unnecessary to achieve linguistic adequacy. Linguistically, the *prima facie* appeal of treating SPR on a par with other valences is weakened insofar as also a selection of the head by the specifier must apply, for empirical reasons

[51]The representation (150), where the HEAD value is of sort *minor* instead of Pollard and Sag's *det*, has been adapted to the category system we have been arguing for since chapter 1. Though the article category is minor and therefore cannot head any phrase, the fact that SPEC is declared appropriate for HEAD suits specifiers whose category can take dependents, as in "almost *every*". (Cf. also § 4.4 below.)

[52]E.g., see comments by Van Genabith et al. (1994) on the implementation of HPSG in the ALEP system.

we have made clear. Indeed the novel feature SPEC, rather than SPR, lends itself to enforce morpho-syntactic and semantic constraints relating the two constituents, such as determiner-noun agreement (an example being the constraint in (150) whereby the article $a(n)$ selects a nominal in the singular). It is thus sufficient to provide the specifier with information about which category of heads it can depend on, in order to capture the fact that different categories take different kinds of specifiers, e.g. determinative specifiers for nominal heads and degree specifiers for adjectival heads. This method makes redundant the *synsem* information that SPR could convey in its turn, like $\mathcal{D}$ on the suitable $<\boxed{k}\,\mathcal{D}>$ list of a specifier-selecting noun (cf. § 4.2.2 above). A non-redundant formulation of the list element will just come down to an unadorned tag ('$\boxed{k}$') – which has also the advantage of avoiding the disjunctive analysis disguised by the abbreviation $\mathcal{D}$, inasmuch as determiners in our system belong to various part-of-speech categories.

But then, if the whole information that SPR supplies is reduced to an opposition between two states, the unsaturation represented by '$<\boxed{k}>$' (without further details) and the saturation represented by '$<>$' (the empty list), it seems to us that the valence mechanism based on a list-valued feature and a token-identical *synsem* becomes mostly superfluous in this case. All what is required for SPR purposes is a simple binary feature to distinguish those expressions that need a specifier (whatever) from the others, roughly as proposed in Netter's (1994) approach. Under a system that remains close to Pollard & Sag's (1994: ch. 9) one at least for the moment, we ensure the same selection effect as the subcategorization for a specifier by replacing throughout [SPR $<>$] and [SPR $<\boxed{k}>$] with [+SPR] and [−SPR], respectively, if the Head-Specifier Schema is revised accordingly:

(152) $\bar{\bar{X}}[\text{SUBJ}\,\boxed{g}] \rightarrow \boxed{h}\,\bar{X}[\text{SUBJ}\,\boxed{g}],\ Y^{M}[\text{SPEC}\,\boxed{h}]$

Note that the X-bar Conventions of HPSG which were stated by (135), § 4.2.2, are still assumed here, modulo a systematic change in the SPR value (e.g., '$\bar{X}$' means 'X^{P}[−SPR]' now). In addition, we introduce the $\_\_^{M}$ superscript to indicate that the constituent filling its slot is either a minor category (as necessary for articles and some other specifiers) or a saturated maximal projection of major category (hence $\bar{\bar{Y}}$).[53]

The resulting treatment removes cyclicity from Pollard and Sag's original Head-Specifier Schema, while preserving unchanged the other ID schemata (i.e. the versions (137), (139) and (149) provided before). A problem to be taken into account when we check all the implications of such a simple proposal, however, may arise because of the impossibility of concatenating the SPR

[53]Let's say 'Y^{M}' abbreviates '$Y[\alpha$ LEX, +SPR]', where α is '+' for minor items or '−' for major ones. (But see a more compact definition in chapter 5 below.)

value with those of SUBJ and COMPS, so as to yield the SUBCAT list required for Binding Theory. (We have already mentioned this residual application of SUBCAT in § 4.2.2.) Of course, it would be easy to stipulate that SUBCAT concatenates just SUBJ and COMPS, yet the move appears to be in conflict with data of English, a language where possessive determiners show the behaviour of specifiers and, at the same time, prove relevant to Binding Theory:

(153) $[\textit{Kim and Sandy}]_1 \left\{ \begin{array}{c} \text{met} \\ *\,\text{are} \end{array} \right\} \textit{their}_1$ greatest admirers

The fact that possessives have personal pronoun status w.r.t. Binding Theory explains why the coindexing in (153) is incompatible with the copula, which causes the subject (*synsem*) to occur on the SUBCAT list of the predicative noun "admirers" and precede therein the possessive (*synsem*) acting as determinative specifier (v. Pollard & Sag 1994: pp. 375-376)[54]. But the lack of a suitable SPR value to be covered within SUBCAT makes the specifier exempt from Binding Theory, leaving the ungrammatical example unexplained.

Nevertheless, we don't think the argumentation is enough to falsify our approach, for reasons that should become evident as soon as a few contrastive data will be taken into account. Let us first recall that an important restriction on the co-occurrence of determiners, informally stated for English by Quirk et al. (1985: p. 254), requires the central determiners to be "mutually exclusive with each other". E.g.:

(154) $(*\left\{ \begin{array}{l} \textit{a} \\ \textit{the} \\ \textit{this} \\ \textit{my} \end{array} \right\}) \left\{ \begin{array}{l} \textit{a} \\ \textit{the} \\ \textit{this} \\ \textit{my} \end{array} \right\}$ book

This behaviour of central determiners – which we have related to the single 'specifier' slot of the NP, in the X-bar theoretic analysis (145) – holds across languages, but chapter 2 pointed out language-specific variation as regards the repertory of items involved. To be sure, English possessive determiners share the distribution in question, as shown by (154), whereas Italian possessive determiners don't, and therefore are not central; more precisely, they are postdeterminers, because a central determiner can precede but cannot follow them. Cf. the Italian counterparts of the examples (154):

(155) $(*\left\{ \begin{array}{l} \textit{un} \\ \textit{il} \\ \textit{questo} \\ \textit{mio} \end{array} \right\}) \left\{ \begin{array}{l} \textit{un} \\ \textit{il} \\ \textit{questo} \end{array} \right\}$ (*mio*) libro

[54]The binding of the possessive by the subject – via coindexation – is compatible with a verb like "met", whose non-predicative complement (due to an empty SUBJ valence) prevents the subject from occurring on the SUBCAT list of "admirers".

Interestingly, the distributional behaviour of possessive words lends itself to be connected with their 'part of speech' by supposing they are basically adjectival in Italian, but not in English. The data below should make clear that Italian items of this kind share with qualifying adjectives the whole pattern of occurring as adjuncts after the central determiner position, pre- or post-nominally (v. (156a)-(156b)), and also as predicative complements (v. (156c)).

(156) a. il *mio/vecchio* libro
'THE my book' (= my book) / 'the old book'

b. il libro *mio/vecchio*
'the book MY/OLD' (= the book of mine / the old book)

c. il libro è *mio/vecchio*
'the book is MY(= mine)/old'

d. il *mio/vecchio*
'the $\text{MY}_{sing.}$' (= mine) / 'the old [one]'

To interpret the parallelism in terms of common adjectival status is obviously not a matter of logical necessity, but we deem it quite plausible as empirical generalization (cf. Serianni 1988: p. 228). Indeed possessive words in the Italian grammatical tradition are considered adjectival at least in their 'adnominal' use, which implies the dependence on an overt head noun, while a pronoun reading is introduced to account for their 'independent' use replacing that head (in a way comparable with the 'substantivized double' of qualifying adjectives; v. (156d)) [55].

The syntactic distribution of English possessive words, on the contrary, offers evidence for the generalized pronominal status that was ascribed to them since chapter 1. There are two morphological paradigms of possessives with distinct syntactic functions in English: the series of central determiners *my*, *your*, etc., which is restricted to the specifier function only, and the series of their 'independent' counterparts, *mine*, *yours*, etc., which is used for all other functions of possessives. But the occurrence of Saxon genitive NPs as determinative specifiers of the possessive kind (e.g. in "*the teacher's* book") entitles us to assume that possessive word forms with the same distribution and function – i.e. belonging to the determinative paradigm – act as 'closed-class' substitutes for those NPs and thus are pronouns as much as the forms belonging to the 'independent' paradigm.

Morphology is a potential source of confusion for our analysis, insofar as both English and Italian possessives are morpho-phonologically related to personal pronouns and accordingly inflected w.r.t. the three grammatical persons.

[55] The pronominal reading can be predicative too (cf. Renzi 1988: ch. 13 by P. Cordin), as exemplified in "quel libro è il *mio*" ('that book is the $\text{MY}_{sing.}$'), where the article occurring after the copula shows the NP character of the predicative complement in question.

In English, the traditional view on genitive case already defended and elaborated on in chapter 1 justifies the conclusion that *my*, *your*, *his*, etc. are simply the (determinative) genitive forms of the corresponding personal pronouns *I*, *you*, *he*, etc., but then one could wonder why the Italian possessive adjectives *mio*, *tuo*, *suo*, etc. look equally related to the personal pronouns *io*, *tu*, *esso*, etc. The point is that we have to distinguish two notions of 'pronoun' overlapping only partially. There is a syntactic notion, whereby pronouns are identified with the closed, grammatically fixed class of those words of nominal category (broadly speaking) to be considered 'pro-forms', inasmuch as they substitute for open-class items of the same category such as proper names.[56] At the same time, there is a morphologically based and semantically/pragmatically related notion applying to all items that can be provided with so-called 'pronominal reference', deictic or co-referential, by virtue of their morphological form and under appropriate linguistic and extra-linguistic conditions of use.

The two notions are associated for a characterization of personal pronouns proper and others with similar properties, like the reflexives (*myself*, *yourself*, *himself*, etc., but also the Italian ones *me stesso*, *te stesso*, *se stesso*, etc. – cf. Graffi 1994: p. 62). However, it is only in the syntactic, distributional sense that some notion of pronoun can be applied to the 'independent counterparts' of non-pronominal determiners, as done by traditional grammarians (which we follow in that respect). E.g., quantitative determiners with purely logical meaning turn into form-preserving pronouns, as in the case of *each*, *all* and *both*, or morphologically composite ones, as in the case of *everybody* (from *every*), *someone* (from *some*), *nothing* (from *no*) and the like. Italian possessive determination exemplifies precisely the opposite phenomenon of reference properties typical of a personal pronoun – hence 'pronominal' in a sense – that get morphologically encoded by word forms with adjectival distribution, even if these are not pronominal syntactically.

Since what matters for Binding Theory in HPSG is the semantic/pragmatic notion of *pronoun* represented as a subsort of *nominal-object* (Pollard & Sag 1994: p. 249), it is possible to predict that co-reference properties of English and Italian possessive determiners are the same despite all syntactic differences. The prediction is borne out by the Italian translation of our previous example (153):

(157) $[\textit{Kim e Sandy}]_1 \left\{ \begin{array}{l} \text{incontrarono} \\ *\,\text{sono} \end{array} \right\} \text{i } \textit{loro}_1 \text{ maggiori ammiratori}$

For Italian as much as English, the copula proves incompatible with the co-indexation between subject NP and possessive determiner of the predicative

[56] On nominal pro-forms, v. Jackendoff (1977), Radford (1981) and Miller (1991).

complement, yet (157) raises a theoretical problem because the specifier is the definite article ("i"), whereas the possessive is an adjunct, as should be clear by now[57]. Thus the fact that adjuncts are not selected by any head and therefore do not occur on any SUBCAT list makes Italian possessive determination exempt from Pollard and Sag's version of Binding Theory, irrespective of what sort of values one assumes for SPR. A first conclusion is that our decision of making SPR binary cannot affect binding in Italian, but it seems also reasonable to believe that the same kind of conclusion should carry over to English, or else the parallel behaviour of (153) and (157) would be unexplained. According to the treatment that chapter 5 will present, the relevant information of possessive determiners becomes accessible for Binding Theory through a mechanism that is independent of their specifier or adjunct status across languages.

The restrictive approach adopting a maximally simple, binary SPR and dispensing with cyclicity altogether, as we have advocated, is an empirical hypothesis and indeed might be falsified by other phenomena of some languages, but all the data we are aware of at present appear to corroborate our hypothesis. To provide additional evidence, we are going to discuss the so-called 'declension congruence' in German NPs, which was originally treated by Pollard & Sag (1994: § 2.5.1) through a cyclic account involving the noun's selection of specifiers. That these mechanisms are actually not necessary for handling the phenomenon is proved by the existence of an alternative treatment, due to Netter (1994), where determiners select the nominal sister and not vice versa; yet there is an important difference from the approach to be sketched soon, insofar as we preserve nominal headedness while Netter applies a 'DP Analysis' (see criticism in chapter 1 above).

Both determiners and attributive adjectives can be assigned to two different inflectional paradigms as regards declension in German:

> "Wunderlich (1988) ... treats as strong adjectives those that occur in NPs without determiners, or else combine with weak determiners (e.g. the singular and nonfeminine nominative or singular neuter accusative form *ein*), and as weak adjectives those that combine with strong determiners (e.g. all form of the definite article *der* or all other inflected forms of the determiner *ein*). ... Mixed declension patterns then arise because a determiner like *ein* has a paradigm all of whose singular forms are strong, except for the form *ein* itself".
>
> Pollard & Sag (1994: p. 66)

Cf. these simple examples:

---

[57]For striking evidence that the two cannot be combined into a single phrase acting as the specifier, cf. our sample NPs (143) in § 4.3.1.1 above.

(158) a. $\text{das}_{st.} \left\{ \begin{array}{c} \text{kluge}_{we.} \\ *\,\text{kluges}_{st.} \end{array} \right\}$ Mädchen
'the intelligent girl'

b. $\text{ein}_{we.} \left\{ \begin{array}{c} \text{kluges}_{st.} \\ *\,\text{kluge}_{we.} \end{array} \right\}$ Mädchen
'an intelligent girl'

To get a reasonably adequate grasp of the matter, more complex cases too must be considered, though. First, the same congruence criteria prove relevant for head nouns, because "there are clearly some nouns, such as *Verwandter* [= relative], *Beamter* [= functionary] (not all of which are de-adjectival forms), which show the same inflectional declension classes as adjectives" (Netter 1994). Second, the declension opposition between determiners and attributive adjectives in a given NP construction applies to a single item of the former kind but possibly several of the latter, as it reflects the specifier vs. adjunct distinction (allowing multiple adjuncts, yet only one specifier per noun). Here is an exemplification of both the additional factors to be accounted for:

(159) $\text{der}_{st.}$ $\text{liebe}_{we.}$ $\text{alte}_{we.}$ $\text{Verwandte}_{we.}$
'the dear old relative'

Now, the problem is that determiners and attributive adjectives do not literally combine as sisters (a point we have already made for other languages in § 4.3.1.1) and consequently their 'congruence' must be checked in some indirect fashion. Pollard and Sag's method which we want to avoid specifies the desired declension of the determiner on the SPR (or, originally, SUBCAT) list of the nominal represented within the lexical entry of a suitable adjective, using the MOD feature. Weak adjectives obligatorily select nominals with a strong determiner on the SPR list, whereas strong adjectives select nominals with a weak and, at the same time, optional determiner on that list (so that they can occur in determinerless NPs). Multiple adjectives modifying projections of the same head noun share the information about its specifier, among other things, and therefore agree with each other as regards declension (Pollard & Sag 1994: p. 90).

But interestingly, Pollard and Sag themselves have acknowledged that the specifier's selection of the adjacent nominal via SPEC (which is independently motivated as we mentioned before) and the existence of nouns inflecting for adjective-related declension (as in the previous example (159)) may well be exploited to replace the SPR-based analysis with a straightforward alternative. Assuming the nominal categories to have DECL as a head feature (= feature within the HEAD value) yet to lexically specify it only in few head nouns (like *Verwandter*), both specifiers and adjectival modifiers will specify the DECL value of the adjacent nominal – through the respective features SPEC and MOD

– so as to ensure 'congruence' w.r.t. their morphology (ibid., pp. 372-373). In a particularly simple version of this approach, we assign DECL just binary, *boolean* values[58] (i.e. '+/–' in the notation used since chapter 1) and set the morpho-phonological realizations of word forms consistently with the following correspondences: nouns are [+DECL] if strongly inflected or [–DECL] if weakly inflected; strong attributive adjectives MOD-select a [+DECL] nominal and weak ones a [–DECL] nominal; strong specifiers SPEC-select a [–DECL] nominal and weak ones a [+DECL] nominal.

The noun's DECL value becomes accessible to pertinent dependents (at any level of nominal projection) because of its head feature status, which makes it subject to the generalization known as 'Head Feature Principle' in HPSG (cf. § 4.2.1 above), i.e. the mother-daughter sharing of the 'X' within X-bar schemata. Since SPR does not play any role in giving DECL a value[59], the SPR-based selection of a determiner by the noun can be dispensed with, thus breaking the undesired cyclicity. A remaining issue, such that the subcategorization power Pollard and Sag ascribed to SPR might seem appropriate again (ibid., p. 373), is how to prevent nouns that are weakly inflected, or modified by a weak adjective, from projecting a determinerless NP:

> "In the first case, we can simply say that the weak ... nouns obligatorily select a determiner via the SPR feature. In the second case, the adjective itself can select, via the MOD feature, an N′ head that in turn obligatorily selects a determiner via the SPR feature."

It should be clear that with the solution in the quoted excerpt, all weak nouns – also plural or mass ones – undergo a constraint which applies to singular count nouns irrespective of declension, i.e. the need for a specifier whatever[60]. But then we can equally extend the recoding of this requirement in accordance with our proposal for a binary (instead of *synsem*-valued) version of SPR. By the same token, weak adjectives simply select N′ qua [–SPR] phrasal projection of N.

So far we have explicitly considered only the typical NP structure whose single determiner occupies the specifier slot, but the impact of multiple determination on declension congruence must be addressed as well. An interesting case, exemplified by (160b), is due to the postdeterminer behaviour of cardinal numerals, which may (but need not) co-occur with a preceding determiner in specifier position. Compare:

---

[58] Binarism is possible since mixed declension was resolved into the other two.

[59] Now DECL is not a head feature of determiners, whereas adjectival modifiers could get it by agreement with nouns (even if its presence under MOD looks enough as an input for morphology, just like presence under SPEC in the other case).

[60] Indeed, the correct specifier-nominal combinations are determined via SPEC.

(160) a. zwei$_?$ gute$_{st.}$ Freunde
'two good friends'

b. meine$_{st.}$ zwei$_?$ guten$_{we.}$ Freunde
'my two good friends'

Here the question mark used as subscript means that a numeral, being uninflected, has uncertain declension status, but the solution follows from the kind of treatment under discussion, as Netter (1994) noticed:

> "as far as we can see, the most consistent strain of analysis in that approach would be to assume that *zwei* is marked as weak in both constructions... Since the following adjective has different declensions in the two expressions, one would have to assume that the numeral functions as a [specifier] determiner ... in the first case, whereas it would be a simple modifier showing agreement with the adjective in the second case."

However, data are also compatible with Netter's alternative claim that *zwei* always agrees with the adjective and therefore is strong in (160a). To settle the issue, § 4.3.2 will have to say more on the (syntactic and semantic) function of numerals, among other things.

4.3.2 Plurals between semantics and syntax

In § 4.2.2 we have already explained how HPSG can treat the syntax of those NPs whose head does not call for any specifier, skipping the $\bar{\text{N}}$ level instead of resorting to **empty** determiners or **vacuous**, unary-branching projections from $\bar{\text{N}}$ to $\bar{\bar{\text{N}}}$. Of course, one should also consider what the proposed HPSG treatment implies for the syntax-semantics interface, a question that is quite relevant for the semantic account of plurality, since **bare plurals** – like "(nice) pictures (of Mary)" as a maximal projection – are typical and much debated examples of NPs without specifier. Essentially, two sorts of approaches look available within a logically based, model-theoretic framework:

- in absence of a syntactic structure overtly reflecting the *determiner-restriction* form of a generalized quantifier, one could opt for some non-quantificational analysis of bare plurals as 'argumental terms';

- with a view to preserve a uniform quantificational analysis for all NPs, one could take an appropriate generalized quantifier to be lexically associated with the bare plural head-noun, in much the same way this is done for proper names in Montague Grammar and related work in GQT (a point to be developed in detail by our chapter 5).

To be in a position to assess the alternatives, let us start from a few remarks on the meaning of bare plurals in English, which we are going to compare with data from different languages.

As pointed out by Carlson (1977) and others (e.g. Diesing 1992), not only **existential**, but also **generic** interpretations (in some sense of 'genericity' to be discussed soon) are possible for English bare plurals, depending on various factors, like the occurrence of the NP in subject or object position and the semantic typology of selecting predicates. The genericity involved appears to be predominantly subject-oriented, so that bare plural objects mostly allow the existential interpretation alone, but there are exceptions such as generic bare plural objects of verbs whose semantics implies an 'experiencer' role for the subject, e.g. *like*, *fear*, *hate* or similar. As for bare plural subjects, those selected by a predicate expressing an activity or a temporary state may well allow both interpretations, as in the example (161a)[61], unless extra factors – relating to tense, modality, deixis, etc. – override one of the two, as in (161b), which is only existential. By contrast, any bare plural subject selected by a predicate expressing a permanent or tendentially stable state is only interpreted generically, see examples (162).

(161) a. Firemen are available (in case of need)

b. Carpenter ants destroyed my table

(162) a. Brussels sprouts are unsuitable for eating

b. Opera singers know Italian

No doubt these phenomena call for an adequate account of generic meaning, but practically every theory that was put forward in the field remains somehow controversial. Run-of-the-mill versions of a logical treatment – which are summarily criticized by Bach (1989: pp. 81-82), among others – assume some form of universal quantification covering the whole, contextually unrestricted class of all possible entities of the kind described by the (possibly complex) nominal head in question. Thus, *horses* qua NP would look ambiguous, in isolation, between the same two options of reference a speaker can explicitly distinguish by adding *all*, in its generic use, or *some*; cf. "(*All*) *horses* are mammals" and "(*Some*) *horses* were galloping across the plain". That approach turns out to be simplistic, inasmuch as it is easy to find examples like "Chickens lay eggs", whose generic truth-conditions change if the universal determiner is added.[62] The quantification problem is confirmed by contrastive remarks on French, a

[61] The speaker can refer to a particular group of fireman in a given situation or firemen in general (cf. Diesing 1992: § 2.2.1).

[62] "It is certainly false that all chickens lay eggs; only grown-up hens do" (Bach, ibid.). Likewise, in *Italians make fine forniture*, the VP "is not predicated of all Italians; indeed it is actually predicated of a rather small subset of Italians, viz. the furniture-makers. ...

language that lacks bare plurals and must express the existential vs. generic distinction by overt determiners. The former option corresponds to the partitive article (as we mentioned in chapter 2), while the latter is captured by the plural definite article without universal determiner *tous* (= all), as in the translation (163) of "Students are seldom ill" (de Swart 1991: p. 45).

(163) Les étudiants sont rarement malades
'THE$_{gen.}$ students are seldom ill'

Instead of overcoming such drawbacks through some revised version of the quantificational analysis (with modal operators or non-monotonic inference rules, as argued by Gerstner-Link & Krifka 1993), Carlson's (1977) alternative proposal was to treat bare plurals as terms in argumental position, lacking quantificational force. They are meant to unambiguously denote 'kinds', being up to the semantics of the selecting predicate to determine what the predication is about. So predicates are classified by Carlson according to the compatibility w.r.t. three sorts of entities he postulates in the universe of discourse: **objects** (i.e. the ordinary individuals), **kinds** (of objects), and spatio-temporal **stages** (of both). As for the typology of selecting predicates presented before, only those expressing a permanent or tendentially stable state of individuals – a.k.a. 'individual-level' predicates – apply to objects and their kinds, respectively denoted by proper names as in (164a) and bare plurals as in (165a); genericity results from the latter[63].

(164) a. Fido hates cats
b. Fido is running

(165) a. Dogs hate cats
b. Dogs are running

Those predicates that express a temporary state or activity are 'stage-level' predicates since they apply to particular stages, 'realizations' of the denoted entities at given spatio-temporal coordinates. Our sample action here can be informally paraphrased by saying that *some stage* of an entity $\mathcal{E}$ is running, $\mathcal{E}$ being the object Fido in (164b), or the kind of Dogs in (165b); hence the existential sense of the bare plural.

At first sight, Carlson's approach to bare plurals as kind-denoting terms is fairly appealing, because it gets rid of a seeming ambiguity of the pertinent

[*Finns always do well in ski-jumping competitions*] has an even more limited reference: not to Finns in general but to Finnish ski-jumpers, and only the cream of these, perhaps only two or three individuals" (Chesterman 1991: p. 38).

[63]Note that a kind is ascribed generic properties of its individual objects by so-called 'individual-level' predicates (such as: *hate cats*, *unsuitable for eating*, *know Italian*, etc.), whereas strictly 'kind-level' predicates are only appropriate for the kind in itself and not for the single objects (cf. *Domestic dogs are widespread* vs. **Fido is widespread*).

NP by deriving existential or generic interpretations from the NP's linguistic context. Empirical phenomena that also appear to support his approach are the possibility of anaphoric relations between generic and non-generic NPs and the fact that existentially interpreted bare plurals do not show the scope ambiguities typical of quantified existential NPs. Concerning anaphora, there are examples like:

(166) Mary hates *rabbits* because *they* ruined her garden

where the bare plural is generic (= she hates the whole kind) but the anaphoric pronoun *they* is not (= some rabbits ruined her garden, in specific situations). Under Carlson's system, this would be a case of co-referential NPs with both denoting the same kind (viz. Rabbits), while the respective predicates selecting them make all the difference. Finally, here is an example about the lack of scope ambiguities:

(167) Every boy noticed (*some*) *spiders* in Mary's bed

i.e. the direct object cannot be interpreted with wide scope (implying that every boy noticed the same spiders) if the determiner *some* is not expressed. Argumental status, as postulated by Carlson for the bare plural, would explain why that NP has only the scope corresponding to the syntactic position where it occurs.

A more careful examination of the alleged evidence in support of this theory reveals several drawbacks, however. The first problem arises because of the unexpected ambiguous value of bare plurals in examples like (161a) above, as Diesing (1992: p. 138) pointed out:

> "Carlson assumes that stage-level adjectival predicates such as *available* allow only an existential reading, whereas individual-level adjectival predicates allow only the generic reading. At first glance, the examples in (i) seem to confirm this.
>
> (i) a. Pigs are available (existential only)
>
> b. Pigs are intelligent (generic only)
>
> I think that in fact the generic reading in (i–a) is ruled out pragmatically. Although it is not unreasonable to expect that firemen might have a generic property of being available, in the actual world is quite odd to expect the same of pigs. Thus, the following sentence involving the stage-level predicate *visible* is clearly ambiguous between the existential and generic readings:
>
> (ii) Pigs are visible."

If Carlson's unambiguously kind-denoting terms are kept, the relevant duplication of readings must be somehow imputed to stage-level predicates, so that he has not really avoided an ambiguity but simply exchanged it for another (whose explanation need not be easier than a quantificational one).

Also the argumentation based on anaphoric links is rather dubious, because it apparently relies on some treatment of anaphora copying the semantic content of the antecedent. That is, the previous example (166) could be paraphrased "Mary hates *Rabbits* because *Rabbits* ruined her garden", where *Rabbits* (informally) stands for the kind in accordance with Carlson's approach, while the copying in a naive quantificational account of the generic bare plural would yield "Mary hates *all rabbits* because *all rabbits* ruined her garden", which misses the non-genericity of *they* in the original. Apart from the fact that we have already seen independent reasons for distinguishing the genericity of bare plurals from that of *all*, the wrong paraphrase of the example shows nothing but the well-known inadequacy of any copying treatment of anaphora with quantificational antecedents. Their content equally disallows the copying in case of an ordinary anaphoric link to an existential NP, as in "Mary noticed (*some*) *rabbits* in her garden because *they* ...", where a paraphrase of *they* as *some rabbits* would not guarantee co-reference with the antecedent. Whatever treatment of anaphora one is going to adopt on the basis of a quantificational analysis, it will have to deal with 'semantic asymmetries' between antecedent and pronoun that go well beyond the problem of genericity.

Above all, Carlson's theory meets with serious difficulties (pointed out by Allegranza 1998a;b) if one tries to apply it to Italian, a language where bare plurals are possible under stylistic constraints (Renzi 1988)[64], but not interpretable generically. Since the only acceptable interpretation of Italian bare plurals is existential, those occurring in our literal translations (168) of the respective English examples (161) are assigned unambiguously that reading (even in the case (168a) without tense restrictions). By the same token, the examples (169) sound mostly inacceptable to Italian speakers, lacking the genericity of their English counterparts (162) and therefore the only interpretation theoretically compatible with the selecting predicates.[65]

(168) a. Vigili del fuoco sono disponibili in caso di bisogno

b. Formiche rodilegno hanno distrutto la mia tavola

(169) a. ?? Cavoletti di Bruxelles sono immangiabili

b. ?? Cantanti d'opera sanno l'italiano

[64] Italian bare plurals are preferable as objects or postverbal subjects, but the preverbal subject position is possible too (especially in case of a bare plural with modifier), though stylistically marked as more literary/formal.

[65] The lack of genericity for Italian bare plurals is confirmed by the object NPs of verbs with an 'experiencer' subject, as in: ?? *Lei odia biscotti al cioccolato* ('She hates chocolate cookies').

In Italian, like French, the plural definite article must be added in order to restore a generic interpretation when other factors don't oppose: v. *I vigili del fuoco sono disponibili in caso di bisogno* ('THE$_{gen.}$ firemen are available in case of need'), *I cavoletti di Bruxelles sono immangiabili* ('THE$_{gen.}$ Brussels sprouts are unsuitable for eating'), *I cantanti d'opera sanno l'italiano* ('THE$_{gen.}$ opera singers know Italian').

Under Carlson's putative explanation of the existential vs. generic dualism for constructions with bare plurals, Italian predicates would mysteriously lack a predication option available to the corresponding English predicates, although the former obviously express temporary or permanent states of affairs just like the latter. On the other hand, an approach retaining his analysis for English, while accounting for the lack of genericity of the acceptable Italian bare plurals by dealing with them as (implicitly) quantified existential NPs, would make the prediction that they should differ from their English counterparts in allowing scope ambiguities. But Italian bare plurals behave just like English ones in this respect[66], e.g. (170) is interpreted consistently with what was said about its counterpart (167):

(170) Ogni ragazzo notò (*alcuni*) *ragni* nel letto di Maria

If Italian bare plurals are treated quantificationally so as to explain their exclusive existential reading, they also require some quantificational account of their exclusive narrow scope – and it is not clear why the same should not be available for English, thus offering in general an alternative to the treatment of bare plurals as argumental terms.

It is well known that wide scope, in fact, is not equally possible with all quantified NPs, as these can be classified along a preference scale according to their determiners' tendency towards wide or narrow scope (cf. Ioup 1975). Therefore, as proposed by Diesing (1992: p. 64), one could simply extend the scale by classifying implicitly quantified plural NPs as tending towards the narrowest scope. An extreme case indeed, but not so inherently different from explicitly quantified cases whose narrow scope reading is strongly preferred – see, e.g., "Every boy noticed (*quite*) *a few* spiders in Mary's bed". In this work, we have to leave aside the issue of a preference-based system of lexical, structural or contextual constraints on quantifier scoping[67], but we believe what has been said so far is enough to show that the putative evidence in favour

[66]Informally, Renzi (1988) assigns Italian bare plurals a non-specific indefinite interpretation, which is accounted for by narrow-scope existential quantification in standard logic. Cf. Longobardi (1994): "They receive an indefinite interpretation corresponding to an existential quantifier unspecified for number and taking the narrowest possible scope".

[67]We refer to Moran & Pereira (1992) for a review of the empirical preferences, as well as a technical proposal of scoping algorithm, building on previous literature.

of Carlson's (1977) approach to bare plurals as kind-denoting argumental terms is rather weak, actually unconvincing.

In other publications (Allegranza 1998a; b) we have developed a treatment of bare plurals for the syntax-semantics interface of HPSG, assuming suitable generalized quantifiers and allowing for language-specific variation as regards presence or lack of generic import [68]. The idea is that the plural noun's lexical entry carries a quantificational content as suggested before, so as to be supplied with NP-level interpretation 'by default', but any adnominal modifiers which the noun can take – as in *nice new pictures* (v. (147), § 4.3.1.1 above) – must functionally apply to the adjacent nominal head and yield an 'updated' version of the original quantifier. Thus, since restrictive qualifying adjectives have no inherent quantificational force, they will just preserve the 'default' DET value of the quantifier, while updating its restriction (= RESTR value) consistently with the semantic analysis of modification in HPSG. (See the technique we have already exemplified at $\bar{\text{N}}$-level in (148), § 4.3.1.2.) In case of determiners the scenario looks less clear, though. Typical is the problem of an NP-initial cardinal determiner, which is seen as specifier with quantificational force in some approaches or as modifier of a bare plural in others, so that it is worth discussing how to choose between the two hypotheses according to the intuitive semantic interpretation and syntactic behaviour of such expressions.

Let us first recall that the treatment of cardinals as indefinite determiners with inherent existential force – e.g., '$\underset{7}{\exists}$' meaning (informally) *there are at least* 7 – is insufficient for the analysis of natural language, because cardinals occur also in NPs that are differently quantified by some preceding determiner(s), as in (*almost all*) *the seven books*, where determination is universal and definite. In § 4.3.1.1, we have already said that these combinations were not adequately treated within GQT by Barwise & Cooper (1981). Of course, one could claim that such a criticism need not affect the status of cardinals when they are used as the only determiners in NP-initial position, dismissing the other use as a very different (and, in a narrow view of determination, actually non-determinative) reading of the same words. Still, if some treatment will prove able to generalize over the two uses of cardinals through a single reading, or at least a simple way of deriving one of two closely related readings from the other, the result will be more adequate in the light of methodological standards of empirical science.

The broad sense of 'determiner' adopted since the beginning of our work is compatible with a line of research where cardinal determiners are argued to be adjectival modifiers, as an alternative to the orthodox GQT-based view of

[68] Here we remain agnostic w.r.t. the precise status and representation of genericity within the quantificational system (cf. Chierchia 1982, Bach 1989: ch. 6, Diesing 1992, Gerstner-Link & Krifka 1993, etc., for various proposals).

cardinal meaning. To put it very simply, making clear the intended parallelism with (extensional) qualifying adjectives applied for restrictive modification, the idea is to interpret a cardinal as **intersective**. We mean that the combination of the cardinal with a nominal head results semantically in a 'set term' (= HPSG's *nominal-object*) denoting the intersection between the set denoted by the head and the set introduced by the modifier, essentially in the same way this is done for a relevant set of red entities by the qualifying adjective *red* (whose lexical entry was sketched as (148) in § 4.3.1.2)[69]. Different versions of the approach arise in relation to different characterizations of the input sets according to the semantics of plurality, which will be discussed here slightly more accurately than in previous chapters.

For a start, let us say that in the classical interpretation stemming from work by M. Bennett (1974), Hoeksema (1983), etc., a common noun or complex nominal with the same distribution/function denotes a set of individuals in the singular, but a set of sets of individuals in the plural. Attuning the adjectival interpretation accordingly[70], a set term corresponding to *seven books* will denote a set of sets of 7 books, namely the intersection between (i) the set of sets that have exactly 7 individuals and (ii) the set of sets of books that is denoted by *books*. In the alternative provided by 'mereological' systems *à la* Link (1983; 1987) or Ojeda (1981; 1983), where the universe of discourse contains also non-atomic individuals constructed as 'sums' of atomic ones, the denotations of plural expressions would be revised so that the relevant intersection would yield the set of all 'sums' of 7 atomic books. We can neglect the model-theoretic, ontological difference (referring the reader to the relevant literature), insofar as it does not have representational consequences for our grammar's semantic component.

A classical set-based system indeed looks enough for interpreting our HPSG representations, like the *nominal-object* (171) to be lexically assigned to the cardinal *seven* in a way quite conform to the treatment of restrictive adjectival modifiers by Pollard & Sag (1994: § 1.9). In essence, it's the same representa-

[69]The set union '∪' in (148), or some comparable entry of cardinal to be presented soon, does not contradict the intersective status of extensional modifiers, because sets of representations and not denotations are meant to be unioned at the level of grammatical formalism. The result can be logically translated into a conjunctive formula (as we mentioned in chapter 3), where the interpretation of conjunction corresponds to the intersection of relevant denotations according to the standard equivalence between propositional logic and Boole's algebra.

[70]In principle, the set introduced by the adjective – e.g., for the cardinal *seven*, (i) below in the text – could be assigned as denotation to that modifier, but HPSG modifies the nominal information within the adjective's lexical entry, so that the appropriate adjectival denotation is actually a function yielding the intersection set from the denotation of the nominal head.

tional strategy applied for the analysis of Greek numerals by Kolliakou (1996), even if she takes for granted a mereological interpretation.

(171)
$$\begin{bmatrix} \text{INDEX } \boxed{1} \begin{bmatrix} \text{NUMBER } \textit{plur} \end{bmatrix} \\ \text{RESTR} \left\{ \textit{card}7(\boxed{1}) \right\} \cup \boxed{2} \end{bmatrix}$$

Compared with the CONTENT value of our previous example (148), the *red*($\boxed{1}$) restriction has been simply replaced by *card*7($\boxed{1}$), whose notation abbreviates (a feature structure expressing) the cardinality constraint Card($\boxed{1}$)=7 on whatever set of individuals the plural index $\boxed{1}$ may refer to. In both examples, the other tag $\boxed{2}$ stands for restrictions to be incorporated from the nominal head, as usual.

Once the *nominal-object* content in question gets fully specified by means of the adjective-$\bar{\text{N}}$ combination, it must be embedded into some feature structure of sort *quant(ifier)* in order to yield the interpretation of a Noun Phrase, as was made clear since chapter 3. Our options for the HPSG quantifiers embedding the *n(on)pro(noun)* nominal object due to the combination "seven books" can be displayed as follows:

(172)
$$\begin{bmatrix} \text{DET } \begin{bmatrix} +/-\text{DEF} \end{bmatrix} \vee \begin{bmatrix} +/-\text{EXIS} \end{bmatrix} \\ \text{RESTIND } \begin{bmatrix} \text{INDEX } \boxed{1} \begin{bmatrix} \text{PERSON } \textit{3rd} \\ \text{NUMBER } \textit{plur} \\ \text{GENDER } \textit{neut} \end{bmatrix}_{\textit{ref}} \\ \text{RESTR} \left\{ \textit{card}7(\boxed{1}),\ \textit{books}(\boxed{1}) \right\} \end{bmatrix}_{\textit{npro}} \end{bmatrix}_{\textit{quant}}$$

The extra information carried by the DET values typically lends itself to be specified by a further determiner preceding the cardinal. A frequent case is due to the article making reference definite and therefore *universal*, i.e. ∀[+DEF] [71], as in the NP "*the* seven books". Clearly the article can be replaced by another definite determiner, as in "*these/my* seven books", but also such cases with a [− DEF] determiner as "*all/any/no* seven books" are possible; cf. Link (1987) for pertinent remarks.

There are various technical issues that would require discussion in order to work out an adequate account of quantification for **sets**, upgrading GQT to plural generalized quantifiers. We refer at least to the revision of logical types to be outlined in section 4.4, whereas chapter 3 already touched on the

[71] See chapter 3 above for these and other feature specifications, their referential interpretation and related co-occurrence restrictions.

interaction with definiteness. What matters here, for completing the picture provided by our HPSG quantifier pattern (172), is the fact that in the [− DEF] case specifying [+EXIS] we get the existential interpretation of "*seven* books" qua full NP, with *seven* as the only determiner. That is to say, if a property ξ – expressed by some verb (phrase) – is predicated of the NP's reference, ξ is meant to be satisfied by **at least one set** $\mathcal{S}$ of books whose cardinality fulfils the constraint Card($\mathcal{S}$)=7. But then, assuming that the predication of ξ be 'distributed' to the individual elements of $\mathcal{S}$ qua particular referents ($\mathcal{S}$ being the 'range of reference', in a sense that should be well-known after our discussion in chapters 2-3), the effect of quantification over sets in this case becomes the same as quantifying over individuals, so that ξ be satisfied by at least 7 books.

Thus, a simple method for generalizing over the uses of a cardinal, with or without preceding determiner(s), appears to be at hand. If we assume a corresponding pair of readings, they prove so closely related that a proper part of the existential reading's CONTENT – the RESTIND value – is identical to the other reading's CONTENT. To express this generalization HPSG could resort to some **lexical rule**, the same kind of formal tool which was applied in chapter 1 for deriving pronominal counterparts of determiners, as an alternative to 'empty' head nouns. Now a lexical rule strategy avoids the 'empty' determiners that would act as specifiers conveying quantificational meaning in absence of overt ones, if cardinals were assigned only the non-quantificational reading (as done by Link 1987, among others).

There is an evident parallelism with qualifying adjectives, given the *quant*-type CONTENT they are assigned – by 'quantifier updating' – when modifying bare plurals as noticed before. Hence a possible common format for the lexical entries of both qualifying and cardinal adjectives in the reading at issue:

(173)
$$\left[\begin{array}{ll} \text{CAT}\,|\,\text{HEAD} & {}_{adj}\left[\text{MOD }\bar{\bar{\text{N}}}: \left[\begin{array}{ll}\text{DET }\boxed{3} & \\ \text{RESTIND} & \left[\begin{array}{l}\text{INDEX }\boxed{1}\\ \text{RESTR }\boxed{2}\end{array}\right]\end{array}\right]\right] \\ \text{CONTENT} & {}_{quant}\left[\begin{array}{ll}\text{DET }\boxed{3} & \\ \text{RESTIND} & \left[\begin{array}{l}\text{INDEX }\boxed{1}\\ \text{RESTR }\left\{\psi(\boxed{1})\right\}\cup\boxed{2}\end{array}\right]\end{array}\right]\end{array}\right]$$

In (173) the meta-variable ψ will be instantiated as *red* or *card*7, say, while the adjective in question just preserves other values as they arise from the $\bar{\bar{\text{N}}}$ head selected via MOD. Since one of them is the DET value $\boxed{3}$, which is existential (= [+EXIS]) in the relevant interpretation of bare plurals, the corresponding reading of a cardinal determiner n would follow by treating n as an adjectival modifier in NP-initial position. An adjunct of bare plurals, preserving their 'default' quantificational force in the same way qualifying adjectives do.

The parallelism seems to be corroborated by Hoeksema's (1983) remark that "numeral-noun combinations may have a generic reading, just like ordinary bare plurals" (with or without qualifying adjectives). He indeed provides clear generic examples such as *Three cars are more expensive than two*; likewise, (174), the result of adding a cardinal to the bare plural subject of our previous example (161a), is interpretable equally well as an existential statement about some situation in which twenty specific firemen are available, or a generic statement relative to the cardinality of any set of firemen that is expected to be available (although its individual members may vary on different occasions) [72].

(174) Twenty firemen are available in case of need

This potential ambiguity of NPs introduced by cardinals, which is also acknowledged by Link (1987), can be resolved in one way or the other thanks to factors already mentioned for bare plurals. Compare:

(175) a. Three men lifted the piano

b. Three men can lift the piano

where the past tense makes (175a) existential and the modalized present tense of (175b) sounds preferably generic.

A problem arises, however, because the expected correspondence between permanent-state (or similar) predicates and lack of existential interpretation for bare plural subjects is not confirmed by the examples with cardinals. E.g., (176) allows the existential interpretation, which is actually preferential.[73]

(176) Two opera singers know Italian

The problem becomes even worse if one considers a language where bare plurals lack the generic interpretation. In Italian, if a cardinal is added to what used to be an existential bare plural and no overriding factors intervene, the NP allows also the generic interpretation: cf. the unambiguously existential (168a) above and the ambiguous translation of (174), "Venti vigili del fuoco sono disponibili

[72]There are various degrees of genericity, to be accounted for by different sorts of modality according to Gerstner-Link & Krifka (1993). E.g., the 'analytic truth' *Bachelors are unmarried* (linguistic necessity) conveys a stronger genericity than *Three kiwis were sold for one dollar last week* (pragmatically restricted modality), and the intended generic sense of (174) is closer to the latter kind of examples.

[73]Though a generic interpretation can be recovered in those contexts where the sentence – uttered with appropriate stress on the verb – expresses a 'law-like' reply to any doubt/question as to whether a couple of opera singers knows Italian.

in caso di bisogno". By the same token, what used to be an inacceptable bare plural (v. (169b) above) becomes existentially or generically interpretable (as in "Due cantanti d'opera sanno l'italiano", which translates (176) with the same effects as to ambiguity and preference). But then the easiest solution is to assume that the ambiguity in examples introduced by cardinals arises from these determiners as their inherent quantificational force and is not a matter of bare plural interpretation.

Moreover, there is syntactic evidence that a cardinal in Italian NPs without preceding determiner, e.g. *due libri* ('two books'), is not an adjunct, but rather a specifier, thus rejecting a bare plural analysis for the pertinent NP. The point is that examples of the kind become ungrammatical if the cardinal is preceded by some qualifying adjective:

(177) (* famosi) due libri

Sample NPs like *i famosi due libri* ('the famous two books') – or also (143e)-(143f) in § 4.3.1.1 above – show that there is nothing wrong with a qualifying adjective preceding a cardinal within the NP, at least in Italian. On the other hand, a qualifying adjective may well introduce a bare plural NP, in Italian as much as in English (*famosi libri / famous books*). But the ungrammaticality of (177) with qualifying adjective is explained, if we accept that the cardinal can be either an adjunct or a specifier and becomes specifier in absence of any preceding determiner which fills this slot.

Concretely, given the analysis:

(178) $[_{\mathrm{NP}}$ due $[_{\bar{\mathrm{N}}}$ libri]]

our problem case becomes:

(179) $[_{\mathrm{NP}}$ famosi $[_{\mathrm{NP}}$ due $[_{\bar{\mathrm{N}}}$ libri]]]

so that its ungrammaticality follows from the same mechanism called for when the cardinal is superseded by another determiner acting as specifier, like the article (**famosi i libri*); cf. again § 4.3.1.1. It is then sufficient to require that cardinals always combine with an embedded $\bar{\mathrm{N}}$, irrespective of the number of bars of the resulting projection, to rule out a bare plural analysis (= 180a) and ensure that the only remaining alternative is (180b), a nominal that must combine with some specifier in order to yield a full NP.

(180) a. $[_{\mathrm{NP}}$ famosi $[_{\mathrm{NP}}$ due $[_{\mathrm{NP}}$ libri]]]
b. $[_{\bar{\mathrm{N}}}$ famosi $[_{\bar{\mathrm{N}}}$ due $[_{\bar{\mathrm{N}}}$ libri]]]

A lexical conclusion, to be discussed in section 4.4, is that the cardinal reading for specifier usage turns out to instantiate the following entry format (with appropriate $\boxed{3}$ and ψ values) instead of our previous (173):

(181)
$$\left[\begin{array}{l} \text{CAT}\,|\,\text{HEAD}\ {}_{adj}\!\left[\text{SPEC } \bar{\text{N}}{:}\left[\begin{array}{l}\text{INDEX } \boxed{1}\\ \text{RESTR } \boxed{2}\end{array}\right]\right] \\ \\ \text{CONTENT}\ {}_{quant}\!\left[\begin{array}{l}\text{DET } \boxed{3}\\ \text{RESTIND}\left[\begin{array}{l}\text{INDEX } \boxed{1}\\ \text{RESTR } \left\{\psi(\boxed{1})\right\}\cup\boxed{2}\end{array}\right]\end{array}\right]\end{array}\right]$$

The picture emerging from the current discussion is consistent with (our revised version of) a solution *à la* Pollard & Sag (1994: § 9.4.4) for the problem of 'declension congruence' raised by uninflected numerals in German. If the NP-initial cardinal of an example like (160a) – which we have commented on in § 4.3.1.2 – is the specifier, its declension must be weak by contrast with the strong inflection of a subsequent adjectival modifier: hence "zwei$_{we./*st.}$ gute$_{st.}$ Freunde". The alternative making *zwei* agree in strong declension is ruled out under the congruence constraints stated in § 4.3.1.2[74], because the result would be a bare plural NP where the cardinal too acts as modifier and cross-linguistically we have offered independent reasons for excluding that option. It is worth noting that the recognition of specifier and modifier readings, which is just theoretic for the numeral proper, can be seen as reflected by the different inflections of *beide*, a semantically related quantitative item:

(182) a. beide$_{st.}$ lieben$_{we.}$ Verwandten$_{we.}$
'both dear relatives'

b. meine$_{st.}$ beiden$_{we.}$ lieben$_{we.}$ Verwandten$_{we.}$
'my both dear relatives'

4.4 Conclusions

This chapter has answered a major question that was left open in the previous part of the book: what is the precise grammatical status of the dependence linking determiners to the nominal head according to their 'positional class'

[74] As we have cursorily mentioned therein, there is another way of accounting for declension congruence data, if one follows Netter (1994): "uniflected determiners ... are underspecified with respect to the declension feature in the lexicon, ... receive their value either from a governing head or through the specification of the root node, and ... pass it on to their complements". Since Netter adopts (a variant of) the DP Hypothesis and stipulates that the DP's root node is always specified as strong, in *zwei gute Freunde* the numeral qua 'functional head' of the DP would share that value and pass it on to *gute Freunde* qua complement, with consequent declension agreement. Chapter 1 has already provided general arguments against the DP Hypothesis, Netter's version included.

(in the sense we have assumed since chapter 1). The result is a version of the HPSG (and formerly, GPSG) approach to X-bar syntax and its semantic interpretation, revised in such a way as to assign determiners to the following types:

- specifiers of the NP (i.e. $\bar{\bar{\mathrm{N}}}$), interpreted as $<\bar{\mathrm{N}}, \mathrm{NP}>$ functors;
- NP-level adjuncts, interpreted as $<\mathrm{NP}, \mathrm{NP}>$ functors;
- $\bar{\mathrm{N}}$-level adjuncts, interpreted as $<\bar{\mathrm{N}}, \bar{\mathrm{N}}>$ functors.

Thus the case of multiple determination where determiners of all positional classes co-occur is accounted for in compliance with the pattern (145) of § 4.3.1.1 above, treating the predeterminer as NP-level adjunct, the central determiner as specifier and the postdeterminer(s) as $\bar{\mathrm{N}}$-level adjunct(s). In addition, § 4.3.2 has shown that at least cardinal postdeterminers are ambiguous between two types, being raised to the role of specifier in absence of any other determiner playing it for the given NP. We could then introduce a 'parameterized' type notation and say that cardinals are $<\bar{\mathrm{N}}, \mathrm{N}^k>$ functors, with k standing for 1 or 2 bars so as to yield corresponding types by alternative instantiations.

The very understanding of '$\bar{\mathrm{N}}$' and 'NP' qua denotational types of the corresponding syntactic categories (in the notation which we have drawn from Gazdar et al. 1985) indeed requires some parameterization anyway, inasmuch as the semantics of plurality involves quantification over sets. If we take the familiar conventions $\bar{\mathrm{N}} = \mathrm{VP} = <e, t>$ and $\mathrm{NP} = <\mathrm{VP}, \mathrm{S}> = <<e, t>, t>$ based on Montague's primitive types e and t[75], the problem is that his characterization of e as the type of standard individuals holds in the singular only. To cover the plural in accordance with the treatment that was suggested in chapter 2 and has been further discussed in § 4.3.2, we assume a broader interpretation of the notion of 'elementary entity' which e stands for: depending on whether the universe of such entities is made up of individuals or sets of individuals, we distinguish the respective types e_0 and e_1. It's easy to parameterize conventions accordingly, hence $\bar{\mathrm{N}}_u = \mathrm{VP}_u = <e_u, t>$ and $\mathrm{NP}_u = <\mathrm{VP}_u, \mathrm{S}> = <<e_u, t>, t>$,

[75]Readers are reminded that the notations – as well as the pertinent semantic notions – taken for granted here were explained in chapter 3 and/or § 4.3.1.1 (v. also note 37). The identity of logical type for the categories $\bar{\mathrm{N}}$ and VP, since both translate as set terms in the logical language, allows their use as abbreviations of $<e, t>$ depending on the syntactic context (but a different interpretation of VP is discussed by Gazdar et al. 1985: pp. 189-199). In classical Montague Grammar, the respective categories with that type are CN (mnemonic for 'Common Noun') and IV (mnemonic for 'Intransitive Verb'); cf. Montague (1973), M. Bennett (1974) and the introductory presentation by Dowty et al. (1981: pp. 182-184, 187-189).

for the same u value = 0 or 1.[76] However, since this parameterization extends systematically to the various types of functors – e.g., specifier determiners will become $<\bar{\mathrm{N}}_u, \mathrm{NP}_u>$ functors – we can consider it implicit in the older notation, if appropriately reinterpreted, and drop all subscripts when there is no danger of confusion.

A non-trivial consequence of our classification of determiners is the fact that only specifier ones have a type setting them apart, compared with qualifying adjectives. The latter are attributively applied as $<\bar{\mathrm{N}}, \bar{\mathrm{N}}>$ or (when modifying bare nominals) <NP, NP> functors[77], their logical types being the same as those for the adjunct readings of post-determiners and pre-determiners. Not a surprising connection, as the items belonging to these positional classes too have been argued to be adjectives since chapter 1, and so the task becomes how to represent the semantic difference between the two kinds of adjectival modifiers, determinative vs. qualifying. Even though in both cases the meaning within a relevant lexical entry will be structured in the same formal fashion, i.e. $\{\psi(\boxed{1})\} \cup \boxed{2}$ (where the tags stand for index and restrictions coming from the adjacent nominal head), the specific ψ contribution of that word has to differ according to its semantic (e.g., determinative) status. Then, ψ can be some precise cardinality constraint, like *card*7, or a vague one, as in the case of *many*, but also *poss*, for possessives, or the δ of a demonstrative (cf. chapter 2 above).

To conclude the current presentation, let us consider a possible difficulty concerning the way of applying our broad notion of Adjective to postdeterminers like the cardinals, which prove ambiguous between specifier and adjunct readings. Pollard & Sag's (1994) part-of-speech system for HPSG makes a distinction between two mutually exclusive (super)sorts – *functional* and *substantive*[78] – whose declarations introduce the features SPEC and MOD, respectively; but since that system classifies *adjective* as a subsort of *substantive*, adjectives would always lack SPEC, with consequent exclusion of the specifier role for them. We could adapt our treatment to the purported distinction if

[76] Thus a generalized quantifier $<<e_u, t>, t>$ is characterized as set of sets of elementary entities, whether individuals (in the singular) or sets of individuals (in the plural). This notion of 'elementary entities' can be replaced by the non-standard notion of individuals covering both atomic ones and their mereological 'sums', if one adopts Link's (1987) way of introducing plurality into GQT, or equivalent.

[77] That is, attributive qualifying adjectives in our parameterized type notation are $<\mathrm{N}^k, \mathrm{N}^k>$ functors (which implicitly means $<\mathrm{N}^k{}_u, \mathrm{N}^k{}_u>$, to be more precise).

[78] They use the label *substantive* in a sense that is not synonymous with 'noun' or 'nominal' as in traditional grammar, but much broader, covering the four parts of speech we classify as *major* (cf. Pollard & Sag 1994: p. 22). On the other hand, their *functional* label covers also the determiners acknowledged to project possibly complex phrase structure (ibid., § 9.4.3) and thus differs from *minor* in our sense.

the lexical rule that relates the specifier and the adjunct readings of a cardinal (cf. § 4.3.2 above) were assumed to change part of speech too, besides selectional and semantic aspects. Still, the theory-internal distinction between functional and substantive parts of speech adopted by Pollard and Sag looks rather dubious[79], nor have they tried to provide it with any independent empirical motivation, and thus we feel free to follow a different approach.

Technically, the features SPEC and MOD can be made available for all sorts of morpho-syntactic category by introducing both from the root of the *part-of-speech* sort hierarchy that was proposed in chapter 1. Their possible values will equally be *synsem* or *none*[80], extending the technique already necessary for handling MOD in Pollard and Sag's original work: "Substantives that are not adjuncts are assumed to be [MOD *none*]. It follows that substantive words whose phrasal projections may or may not be adjuncts must have both [MOD *none*] and [MOD XP] entries (for suitable XP)" (ibid., p. 398). In our hierarchy, where no distinction between *substantive* and *functional* holds and the main branches are *major* and *minor*, these inherit MOD and SPEC from the supersort *part-of-speech* and pass that information on to the subsorts for particular parts of speech, which can set one or the other of the two features as *none*-valued whenever appropriate. E.g., *verb* appears to require [SPEC *none*], because the projections of verbs may well be adjuncts (as in the case of relative clauses), but not specifiers.[81]

If *minor* parts of speech were disallowed in adjunct position, as we assumed for the version of the Head-Adjunct (ID) Schema presented before (see (149), § 4.3.1.2), they would not need any feature MOD; then one could introduce it directly from the *major* node of the hierarchy. However, complementizers are arguably minor adjuncts (effecting bar-preserving attachment to S nodes as maximal projections)[82], so that it seems MOD must be also available for *minor* and subsorts thereof. The consequent treatment of a minor category that only occurs in specifier position, e.g. articles, requires the feature declaration [MOD *none*, SPEC *synsem*]. Moreover, in view of parts of speech admitting both MOD and SPEC uses, we must ensure that a *synsem* value for one of the two features implies *none* for the other, a constraint that lends itself to be enforced in the pertinent schemata:

[79] It is vaguely reminiscent of other lexical dichotomies commonly found in the literature, like function words vs. content ones, closed classes vs. open ones, minor categories vs. major ones (see previous note 78), but it does not fit exactly any.

[80] In the simple format of feature declarations by 'appropriateness conditions' (v. Pollard & Sag 1994: p. 395, as well as Schmidt 1998 for introductory discussion), the desidered result is readily achieved through an arbitrary sort label with subsorts *synsem* and *none*.

[81] Since subjects and complements do not select heads, they must receive [MOD *none*, SPEC *none*] from any selecting head, lexically encoding the information via its valence lists.

[82] But cf. a more careful account to be offered in chapter 5.

(183) a. $\bar{\bar{X}}[\mathrm{SUBJ}\,\boxed{g}] \rightarrow \boxed{h}\,\bar{X}[\mathrm{SUBJ}\,\boxed{g}],\ Y^{M}[\mathrm{SPEC}\,\boxed{h},\ \mathrm{MOD}\ \mathit{none}]$
Head-Specifier (ID) Schema

b. $X^{n}[\mathrm{VAL}\,\boxed{z}] \rightarrow \boxed{h}\,X^{n}[\mathrm{VAL}\,\boxed{z}],\ Y^{M}[\mathrm{MOD}\,\boxed{h},\ \mathrm{SPEC}\ \mathit{none}]$
Head-Adjunct (ID) Schema

Note that minor adjuncts now are covered, since (183b) too replaces $\bar{\bar{Y}}$ with the notation Y^{M}, which § 4.3.1.2 introduced in order to indicate a constituent that can be either a maximal projection or a minor word. The striking parallelism of the two schemata (183) will lead to a more general approach in chapter 5, yet for the moment we can be content with these results.

Our departure from Pollard and Sag's original way of linking SPEC and MOD to the morpho-syntactic category system makes it possible for the specifier reading of cardinals to be lexically assigned the same major part of speech as the adjunct reading, namely *adjective*, as was done by (181), § 4.3.2. Such a sharing satisfies criteria of conceptual economy plausibly implying that the differences between (related) readings of a given word – hence the changes to be stated through some lexical rule – come down to the strictly necessary. A (partial) change in syntactic and semantic function like the one we ascertained for cardinals need not require a change in part of speech, lacking independent empirical evidence. After all, functional differences between attributive adjuncts and predicative complements are normally not considered sufficient to restrict the Adjective part of speech to only one of the two functions, and we see no good reason why a radically divergent approach should apply to the distinction between attributive adjuncts and specifiers.[83] On the contrary, if cardinal determiners preserve adjectival status, we avoid the problem of finding an alternative part of speech for the specifier reading in our system, where dubious morpho-syntactic categories of specifiers such as 'Det(erminer)' and 'Q(uantifier)' are rejected (cf. chapter 1 above).

[83]The fact that just a proper subclass of adjectives can be specifiers is not a good reason, inasmuch as there are also adjectives disallowing either attributive or predicative use (cf. Pollard & Sag 1987: pp. 64-65). Moreover, the specifier-compatible subclass of adjectives covers other kinds of determiners besides cardinals.

Chapter 5

Extended Formal Treatment

5.1 Preamble

Aim of the present chapter – which is hinted at by its title – is to extend the formal treatment we have been gradually working out in the precedent part of this book. Following HPSG standards [1], we shall extend the use of sorted feature structures to the representation of phrase-structural relationships of immediate dominance and syntactic dependency, so as to allow formalization of pertinent principles P_1, ... P_n of 'universal grammar' (UG). As proposed by Pollard & Sag (1987: p. 44):

> "each language is subject to the constraints imposed by universal grammar. ... In addition, each language makes available a different set of options for what counts as a lexical sign and what counts as a phrasal sign, i.e. each language has its own lexicon and grammar rules [as well as a number m of language-specific principles [2]]. Thus, if L_1, ... L_p correspond to the lexical signs of English and R_1, ... R_q to its grammar rules, then a theory of English takes the form ...
>
> $$\text{English} = P_1 \wedge ... \wedge P_{n+m} \wedge (L_1 \vee ... \vee L_p \vee R_1 \vee ... \vee R_q)$$
>
> That is, a linguistic object is an English sign token just in case **(i)** either it instantiates one of the lexical signs or it instantiates one of the grammar rules, and **(ii)** it satisfies all the universal and English-specific grammatical principles."

The resulting grammar turns out to be an 'overall constraint' on the feature structures representing linguistic objects, which gathers more specialized constraints by means of logical connectives.

In such a completely **feature-theoretic** approach to grammatical theory, developed by Pollard & Sag (1987; 1994) for their HPSG, constituency can be

---

[1] But the formal approach can be traced backed to the 'functional unification grammar' by M. Kay (1979; 1984; 1985).

[2] The idea of constraints that are formally (like) principles though not universal (cf. also Pollard & Sag 1994: p. 31) will be explained soon.

represented through the attribute DAUGHTERS (DTRS), whose presence identifies a sign as being 'phrasal'. This fact is captured in the sort hierarchy, where *sign* has only two subsorts, *word* and *phrase* (v. Pollard & Sag 1994: p. 31)[3], and the feature declaration for the latter introduces the attribute DTRS. The purpose of DTRS is to display the immediate constituency of a relevant sign, i.e. what is immediately dominated by the mother node in the phrase structure forming the sign itself. Unlike traditional phrase structure grammars, HPSG separates immediate dominance (a.k.a. ID) from linear precedence (a.k.a. LP), exploiting the inherently unordered status of feature structures. E.g., if the value of DTRS is a feature structure with two attributes, taking as respective values a head daughter and a subject daughter, the DTRS feature structure as such leaves unspecified the relative linear order of the two constituents.

An important consequence of the unconventional, innovatory account of phrase structure in a feature-theoretic ID format is the ease with which one can formalize grammatical generalizations across syntactic constructions by means of implicational constraints on feature structures. E.g., the universally valid constraint enforcing token-identity of the respective HEAD values between mother node and head daughter for any headed phrase (as we informally anticipated in chapter 4), or **Head Feature Principle**, resorts to the head's explicit identification via HEAD-DTR, one of the attributes of DTRS feature structures. Formally:

(184) **Head Feature Principle** (HFP):

$$\begin{bmatrix}\text{DTRS } \textit{headed-structure}\end{bmatrix} \Longrightarrow \begin{bmatrix}\text{SYNSEM} \mid \text{LOC} \mid \text{CAT} \mid \text{HEAD } \boxed{1} \\ \text{DTRS} \mid \text{HEAD-DTR} \mid \text{SYNSEM} \mid \text{LOC} \mid \text{CAT} \mid \text{HEAD } \boxed{1}\end{bmatrix}$$

(Cf. Pollard & Sag 1987: p. 43; 1994: p. 399.)

In (184), the token-identity at issue is represented on the right-hand side of the implication symbol ('$\Longrightarrow$'), so as to logically follow from satisfaction of the left-hand side. That is, if a given linguistic object α is a headed phrase (this being what [DTRS *headed-structure*] means[4]), then α must satisfy also the right-hand side of our constraint. Since '$\Longrightarrow$' is nothing but a feature-theoretic application of the conditional connective of propositional logic, those linguistic objects that do not satisfy the condition of being headed phrases (= the antecedent of the conditional) nevertheless vacuously confirm the HFP as a whole; it is the reason why principles jointly hold for all signs covered by a grammar and therefore are connected by logical conjunction (v. above).

[3]Or, respectively, *lexical-sign* and *phrasal-sign*, in an older labelling (v. Pollard & Sag 1987: p. 39).

[4]See § 5.2.1 below for a presentation of *headed-structure* and its attributes.

A language-specific principle does not differ from a universal one as far as formalization is concerned, adopting the same implicational format, yet there is an empirical difference in that the validity of the former principle is confined to the signs of some particular language(s), i.e. the principle belongs to the corresponding language-specific grammar(s) but not to UG.

While this distinction between language-specific and universal principles has its merits especially in terms of clarity and simplicity, it is worth noticing that Pollard & Sag (1994: p. 31) "do not rule out as a possible long-term goal the elimination of language-specific principles ... in favour of 'parametrized' universal principles". A case in which a parametrization of the kind has been tentatively assumed by the two HPSG theorists arises because of their **Constituent Order Principle**, under a treatment of surface order that exploits the syntax-phonology interface. In a nutshell, the phonological string to be computed qua PHONOLOGY value of a phrase is a function of the phrase's DTRS value:

(185) **Constituent Order Principle** (COP):

$$_{phrase}\Big[\;\Big] \Longrightarrow \begin{bmatrix}\text{PHONOLOGY } \textbf{order-constituents}(\boxed{1}) \\ \text{DAUGHTERS } \boxed{1}\end{bmatrix}$$

The principle as formulated in (185) is part of UG, but comes down to a 'black box' whose effects on linear precedence can be made language-specific insofar as "the precise statement of COP requires an explicit definition of the function *order-constituents*" (Pollard & Sag 1987: p. 170). The definition for a particular language actually embodies the whole 'LP component' of the corresponding grammar:

> "We then define **order-constituents** to be that function whose value is the disjunction of all permutations (of the PHONOLOGY values of the daughters) which are consistent with all of the LP constraints [for the given language]."
>
> (ibid.)

Here we need not take up a definite position concerning the COP, or some straightforward alternative whereby every single 'LP statement' (in the sense of our previous chapter 4) would be directly reformulated as language-specific principle[5]. Indeed – like much other HPSG work – we shall simply take for

[5]Informally: "An example of an English-specific principle is the constraint that if X is a phrasal sign whose head-daughter is a lexical sign Y, then Y linearly precedes any of X's complement daughters. (This principle clearly does not apply ... to Japanese, where the head occurs phrase-finally.)" (Pollard & Sag 1987: p. 43). The constraint, which is overtly implicational and could be formalized accordingly, conveys the same linguistic information on English that can be abbreviated as in $H^0 \prec$ *Compl.* (where H^0 = lexical head) using the LP statement notation.

granted the availability of an apt LP component, however formalized, and focus on the ID component alone. By doing so, section 5.2 will complete both the presentation of Pollard & Sag's (1994) system of '(X-bar) ID schemata' and the revision of that system which were started in chapter 4. At the same time, consistently with the main topic of our book, the resulting version of HPSG syntax will be applied to determination, formally reworking an account of *pre-*, *central* and *post-determiners* outlined less technically in preceding chapters. To complete the sign-based modelling of relevant linguistic facts, with special reference to such issues as quantifier scope, indexicality and naming, section 5.3 will carry out a formalization of the **syntax-semantics interface** exploiting HPSG's feature structures and lexicalism. By way of conclusions, the chapter ends with a brief summary in section 5.4.

5.2 The syntactic framework

5.2.1 Phrase structure constraints in HPSG

For all the cases of phrase structure concretely treated by Pollard & Sag (1994), the attribute DTRS we presented in the Preamble takes a value of sort *headed-structure* (*head-struc*)[6], so that the phrase thus analyzed (or 'headed phrase') is always projected by a head daughter. The various subsorts of *head-struc*, which introduce further daughters, account for corresponding patterns of headed structure. A subset of those eventually adopted by Pollard and Sag (ibid., p. 391) is sufficient for the coverage of our previous chapter 4:

- *head-subject-structure* (*head-subj-struc*)
- *head-complement-structure* (*head-comp-struc*)
- *head-specifier-structure* (*head-spr-struc*)
- *head-adjunct-structure* (*head-adj-struc*)

Some other subsorts, which we neglect here (but cf. also § 5.2.2 below), may well turn out to be necessary for special cases of headed structure, a plausible example being the *head-filler-structure* applied in the treatment of non-local filler-gap dependencies by Pollard & Sag (1994: ch. 4).

[6]To be more precise, DTRS is declared with values of sort *constituent-structure* (*con-struc*) and Pollard and Sag "leave open the question of what subsorts of *con-struc* exist other than *head-struc*" (ibid., p. 397). They just mention coordinate structures as a possible example of non-headed constructions, but see Gazdar et al. (1985: ch. 8) for a different approach, implying that coordination is multiply headed.

The partition of *head-struc* into subsorts, to be supplied with their appropriate feature declarations, aims at a characterization of non-head daughters according to their syntactic function as dependents of the structure's head, indicated by the attribute HEAD-DTR. Drawing the other pertinent attributes from Pollard & Sag (1994: ch. 9), non-head constituents in headed structures are indicated through SUBJ-DTR, for subjects, COMP-DTRS, for complements, SPR-DTR, for specifiers, and ADJ-DTR, for adjuncts (a.k.a. modifiers). In the original version, the first three of such functions of non-heads (that is, excluding adjuncts) are those assumed to involve subcategorization: a sign thus classified saturates a corresponding 'valence' (= subcategorization requirement) of the head it depends on. Chapter 4 has already presented how this can be done in the projection from head to mother by means of three *list*-valued VALENCE features, SUBJ, COMPS and SPR, in such a way that each element on the list of one of the features is discharged from that list when a corresponding sign occurs as non-head daughter with the intended grammatical function.

The HPSG approach to the formalization of syntactic dependency relations, however, has been revised inasmuch as only SUBJ and COMPS are *list*-valued VALENCE features for us. As we have argued in the same chapter, the feature SPR can be assumed to be *boolean*-valued (i.e. binary) without loss and the resulting system avoids the ciclicity of Pollard and Sag's original while keeping to the same view of X-bar Theory.[7] We recall how Pollard & Sag (1994: p. 362) defined bar projections by combining the *word* vs. *phrase* sort distinction with the SPR saturation degree: words are X^0 (null projections) irrespective of the saturation degree; phrases with [SPR<[...]>] are $\bar{X}$ (intermediate projections); phrases with [SPR<>] are $\bar{\bar{X}}$ (maximal projections). In essence, the same kind of definition can be maintained for the revision we propose, though replacing [SPR<[...]>] and [SPR<>] with [−SPR] and [+SPR], respectively. Hence the following restatement of the **X-bar Conventions** which were formulated in chapter 4 by means of the older [+/−LEX] encoding of the word vs. phrase distinction:

	subsort of *sign*	SPR value
X^0	*word*	*boolean*
X^P	*phrase*	*boolean*
$\bar{X}$ (= X′)	*phrase*	−
$\bar{\bar{X}}$ (= X″)	*phrase*	+

Moreover, it is worth noting that in the X-bar Theory system *à la* Pollard & Sag (1994: ch. 9), where the notion of *phrase* (= X^P) covers intermediate and maximal projections, every phrase is [COMPS<>], but not every [COMPS<>]

[7] The binary SPR is also comparable to Netter's (1994) feature FCOMPL, encoding what he calls the 'functional (in)completeness' of signs.

sign is a phrase. The only unary branching, or 'vacuous' projection, in the sense of Bennett & Schmidt (1998), is due precisely to the case of some [COMPS<>] word to be structurally projected into a phrase (like the VP consisting of a complementless verb). All other instances of *head-struc* which do not combine at least two daughters – e.g., vacuous projection from $\bar{N}$ to $\bar{\bar{N}}$ in a specifierless NP – are avoided, because X^0 may project $\bar{\bar{X}}$ directly, skipping any intermediate $\bar{X}$ node if unnecessary (v. chapter 4 above). This is achieved because the [SPR<>] or, in our variant, [+SPR] information is shared between a suitable *word*-type head and the immediately dominating *phrase* node, so as to make the latter a maximal projection by virtue of the HPSG definition of bar levels previously discussed. We further develop the approach hereafter, dispensing with the residual case of unary branching.

Informally, let us assume that even if every X^0 is a terminal node of the phrase structure, the opposite need not hold, i.e. we take categories of any bar level to be legitimate as terminal nodes. For instance[8]:

(186) $[_S [_{NP} [_{Art}$ a $] [_{\bar{N}}$ woman $]] [_{VP} [_V$ loves $] [_{NP}$ Bill $]]]$

is not shorthand for the version with unary-branching projections:

(187) $[_S [_{NP} [_{Art}$ a $] [_{\bar{N}} [_N$ woman $]]] [_{VP} [_V$ loves $] [_{NP} [_{\bar{N}} [_N$ Bill $]]]]]$

but a well-formed terminated phrase structure in its own right, while (187) is ruled out. Under this revised system (cf. also Allegranza 1998b, Bennett & Schmidt 1998), specifierless NPs are terminal nodes in case of an 'unadorned' noun, like the proper name *Bill* in (186). They remain direct projections of N^0, as mentioned before, in case of a noun with complement(s); v. the NP "*pictures* of Mary".

Such a novel version of X-bar Theory can be easily formalized through few adjustements of HPSG's phrase structure component, whose 'ID schemata' actually are feature structures that our chapter 4 introduced in abridged form, using an (extended) X-bar notation. Pollard & Sag (1994: ch. 9) take the ID schemata to be in one-to-one correspondence with the subsorts of *head-struc*, so that each structural pattern thus encoded licenses 'headed' phrases with a DTRS value of the respective (sub)sort. Before going into feature-theoretic details, suffice it to say that the Head-Complement Schema, in particular, is responsible for the vacuous projections found in the original HPSG, because the head is allowed to combine with a list of $n \geq 0$ complements. Our pertinent revision of the X-bar Theory system, then, can be carried out inasmuch as **(a)** we prevent the application of the Head-Complement Schema to any structure

[8]Focussing on the noun phrase (with $\bar{\bar{N}}$ abbreviated as NP as usual), in the examples we omit for convenience the X-bar analysis of non-nominal categories.

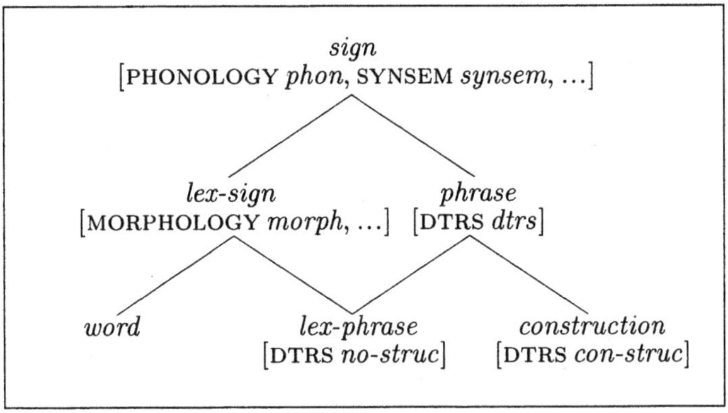

Figure 5.1: Sign Hierarchy

with a *word*-type head but an empty list of complements and **(b)** we manage to compensate for the excluded unary branching thanks to a daughterless phrase in the phrase structure tree.

The simplest way of achieving the result **(a)** is to restrict the COMP-DTRS value in a *head-complement-structure* to a non-empty list (*nelist*). As regards **(b)**, the solution that we put forward consists in adopting a more structured classification of signs, where the sort *sign* is 'partitioned' (= subclassified into immediate subsorts) by *lex(ical)-sign* and *phrase*, with further partitions such that the immediate subsorts of *lex-sign* are (*pure-*)*word* and *lex(ical)-phrase*, those of *phrase* are *lex-phrase* and *construction*. Hence the sort hierarchy of **Figure 5.1**, displaying feature declarations too: e.g., every *sign* has at least the attributes PHONOLOGY (see the Preamble) and SYNSEM (for syntactic and semantic information, as we discussed in chapter 4).

The (abbreviated) label *word* stands for null projections – i.e. constituents with 'zero bars' – as before, but now it is just referred to 'pure words' as a particular case of lexical signs. That is, a broader sort *lex-sign* (whose label we borrowed from Pollard & Sag 1987) is envisaged for all signs that are terminal constituents of the syntax and possible input/output of lexical rules; then also a MORPHOLOGY feature with relevant morphological information pertains to these signs (cf. Krieger & Nerbonne 1993). On the other hand, even though *phrase* is always the sort of non-null (intermediate or maximal) projections, we distinguish between a phrase grouping at least two constituents, which is called *construction*, and a lexical sign acting as phrase because of the ban on all unary-branching projections. The Sign Hierarchy shown by **Figure 5.1** is not tree-shaped, but a more general kind of 'directed acyclic graph', in which two (or more) sorts have a common immediate subsort, enduring 'multiple inheritance' of their features accordingly[9]; here the option is exploited in the case of *lex-phrase*, subsort of *lex-sign* and *phrase*.

Thus, whereas the 'pure words' do not form a phrase on their own, terminal constituents with more than zero bars are allowed as lexical (instead of constructional) phrases, which inherit *lex-sign* features (of morphology, etc.) together with the *phrase* attribute DTRS, although they set it to a value that does not introduce any daughter[10]. Since all phrases specify [COMPS<>] according to Pollard and Sag (see above), we can directly encode as *word* all lexical signs with non-empty COMPS list, so that these will never be available for the alternative sort *lex-phrase.* Not all signs which are 'pure words' in our sense must have a non-empty COMPS list, however. Within the framework we have been developing since chapter 1, there are *minor* parts of speech – such as articles and complementizers – to be understood as words that cannot project bar levels (see also Gazdar et al. 1985: p. 25), and now they are lexically encoded as *word*-type signs with [COMPS<>]. The list restriction makes them unsuitable as heads, as desired, by virtue of the previously cited revision **(a)** of the Head-Complement Schema.

On the other hand, candidate non-constructional phrases could be lexically underspecified as *lex-sign*, resulting in ambiguity between the pure *word* use and the *lex-phrase* use. Let us give an example relevant for NP analysis: the [COMPS<>, −SPR] noun "horse" occurs as *word* in N N compounds like "horse race", "horse laugh", "horse guards", etc., whereas it is a *lex-phrase* ready to combine with some specifier (hence $\bar{\mathrm{N}}$) when occurring in the syntactic head position of NPs. Neglecting here the case of compounding as a matter of (recursive) word structure to be arguably treated within the MORPHOLOGY part of signs, the same lexical item will be accepted by phrase structure schemata insofar as it is compatible with the *phrase* slot in a construction, yielding a *lex-phrase* from *lex-sign.*

We finally turn to the system of sorts and constraints related to the DTRS value of those phrases that are constructional and, in particular, headed. The feature declaration for the sort *headed-structure* is:

[9]By 'multiple inheritance' we mean inheritance from (at least) two sorts, neither of which dominates the other, and the subsort they have in common is introduced within a single hierarchy graph, under Carpenter's (1992) 'feature logic' and its restrictions. In the present work, Carpenter-style hierarchies should prove enough to meet our (relatively modest) classificatory requirements, but see Pollard & Sag (1987: § 8.1) and Erbach (1994) for a more powerful formalism, where multiple inheritance results from simultaneous cross-classification in multiple hierarchies. (Introductory discussions of inheritance and its linguistic applications are offered by Markantonatou & Sadler 1998 as well as Schmidt 1998.)

[10]The label *no-struc(ture)* – a sort/value without any features, to be discussed further in § 5.2.2 – is conventionally employed, as per **Figure 5.1**. From the same diagram one can see the other slight refinement implied in DTRS declarations: we introduce this attribute with values of sort *dtrs*, to be specified as *con-struc* (from Pollard & Sag 1994) or *no-struc*.

(188)
$$\left[\begin{array}{l}\text{HEAD-DTR } \textit{sign} \\ \text{SUBJ-DTR } \textit{list}(\textit{phrase}) \\ \text{COMP-DTRS } \textit{list}(\textit{phrase})\end{array}\right]_{\textit{head-struc}}$$

This means that some features representing daughters with a certain function are already introduced for *head-struc*, unlike others, which will be only declared w.r.t. the specific subsort they characterize (e.g., ADJ-DTR for *head-adj-struc*). Unsurprisingly, the declaration of HEAD-DTR concerns the supersort level, since any headed structure needs a head by definition. The features that (188) shows take values whose sorts can be made more specific at lower levels of the hierarchy for headed structures: the HEAD-DTR value becomes *word* in *head-comps-struc*, for instance, whereas it is just declared as *sign* in general. By the same token, the value of each feature $\mathcal{F}$-DTR(S) corresponding to a valence feature $\mathcal{F}$ – i.e., SUBJ or COMPS, in our approach – will be specified as the empty list (*elist*) for those subsorts of *head-struc* where that kind of daughter is absent.[11]

As we have mentioned before, HPSG employs the subsorts of *head-struc* to achieve X-bar/ID schemata in a completely feature-theoretic format, the outcome being shown below in (189)-(190) for two of those resulting from our previous chapter 4 (with few simplifications to be commented on soon). In each case, we shall first provide the version using an X-bar notation and then turn it into a feature-theoretic version consisting of two complementary parts, where a. is the declaration for the subsort of *head-struc* classifying the DTRS value of any phrase the feature structure b. may represent. The actual grammatical status of this b. part appears open to different solutions, considering that the same feature structure could occur among the R_1, ... R_q disjuncts specifying phrasal sign options for a given language, in the approach which was cited by § 5.1, or alternatively could be the right-hand side of an implicational constraint on [DTRS *head-$\mathcal{F}$-struc*] (with some *head-$\mathcal{F}$-struc* subsort of *head-struc*). While the former solution makes b. a language-specific 'grammar rule' in the sense of Pollard & Sag (1987), the latter formally sets up a 'principle'[12] (whether universal or language-specific). We can safely ignore the issue for our present purposes.

(189) $X^P[\text{SPR}\,\boxed{1},\ \text{SUBJ}\,\boxed{2}] \rightarrow H^0[\text{SPR}\,\boxed{1},\ \text{SUBJ}\,\boxed{2},\ \text{COMPS} <\boxed{k_1}, \ldots \boxed{k_n}>],$
$\boxed{k_1}, \ldots \boxed{k_n}$ (for $n \geq 1$)

[11]The reason why $\mathcal{F}$-DTR(S) in those cases is not simply omitted will be clarified soon when considering HPSG's **Valence Principle**.

[12]In a variant by Pollard & Sag (1994: p. 38), instead of separate implicational constraints for the different subsorts of *head-struc*, there is just one: the so-called 'ID Principle', with [DTRS *head-struc*] as left-hand side of the implication and a disjunctive right-hand side covering the full range of b. options for headed phrases.

a.

$$_{\textit{head-comp-struc}}\begin{bmatrix}\text{HEAD-DTR } \textit{word}\\ \text{SUBJ-DTR } \textit{elist}\\ \text{COMP-DTRS } \textit{nelist}\end{bmatrix}$$

b.

$$\begin{bmatrix}\text{SYNSEM}\,|\,\text{LOC}\,|\,\text{CAT} & \begin{bmatrix}\text{SPR } \boxed{1}\\ \text{VAL}\,|\,\text{SUBJ } \boxed{2}\end{bmatrix}\\ \text{DTRS} & \begin{bmatrix}\text{H-DTR}\,|\,\text{SYNS}\,|\,\text{LOC}\,|\,\text{CAT} & \begin{bmatrix}\text{SPR } \boxed{1}\\ \text{VAL} & \begin{bmatrix}\text{SUBJ } \boxed{2}\\ \text{COMPS} < \boxed{k_1}, \ldots \boxed{k_n} >\end{bmatrix}\end{bmatrix}\\ \text{COMP-DTRS} < \begin{bmatrix}\text{SYNSEM } \boxed{k_1}\end{bmatrix}, \ldots \begin{bmatrix}\text{SYNSEM } \boxed{k_n}\end{bmatrix} > & \end{bmatrix}\end{bmatrix}$$

(190) $\bar{\bar{\text{X}}}[\text{SUBJ} < >] \rightarrow \bar{\bar{\text{H}}}[\text{SUBJ} < \boxed{1} >],\ \boxed{1}$

a.

$$_{\textit{head-subj-struc}}\begin{bmatrix}\text{HEAD-DTR } \textit{phrase}\\ \text{COMP-DTRS } \textit{elist}\end{bmatrix}$$

b.

$$\begin{bmatrix}\text{SYNSEM}\,|\,\text{LOC}\,|\,\text{CAT} & \begin{bmatrix}+\text{SPR}\\ \text{VAL}\,|\,\text{SUBJ} < >\end{bmatrix}\\ \text{DTRS} & \begin{bmatrix}\text{H-DTR}\,|\,\text{SYNSEM}\,|\,\text{LOC}\,|\,\text{CAT} & \begin{bmatrix}+\text{SPR}\\ \text{VAL}\,|\,\text{SUBJ} < \boxed{1} >\end{bmatrix}\\ \text{SUBJ-DTR} < \begin{bmatrix}\text{SYNSEM } \boxed{1}\end{bmatrix} > & \end{bmatrix}\end{bmatrix}$$

Some commentary on the foregoing schemata may help the reader to grasp them better. Here we need not say much about the abridged version using 'rewriting rules' in X-bar format, because the differences from what was proposed in chapter 4 are minimal. The Head Feature Principle (184), § 5.1, makes it unnecessary to redundantly repeat the X information sharing between mother and head, so that the 'X' in the latter position of each schema is replaced with a less informative 'H' notation (from Gazdar et al. 1985), which indicates the head function but not the concomitant sharing. Another piece of information omitted from the schemata is the requirement of complement-saturation for phrases, since Pollard & Sag (1994: p. 346) suggest that "we might incorporate this specification into the definition of the sort *phrase*". By 'definition' they cannot simply mean its feature declaration, which is limited to an attribute-sort format of 'appropriateness conditions' disallowing paths (ibid., p. 395)[13], but the desired specification could be enforced via an implicational constraint on *phrase*:

(191) **Complement-Saturation Constraint** (CSC):

$$_{phrase}\Big[\ \Big] \Longrightarrow \Big[\text{SYNSEM} \,|\, \text{LOC} \,|\, \text{CAT} \,|\, \text{VAL} \,|\, \text{COMPS} < > \Big]$$

If one takes into account the CSC effect of adding [COMPS<>] to the mother node of the structures licensed by the Head-Complement Schema (189), among others, its parallelism with the Head-Subject Schema (190) becomes evident. In both cases, the $\mathcal{F}$ characterizing the *head-$\mathcal{F}$-struc* at issue corresponds to a valence feature, whose list value on the head daughter consists of elements that are token-identical with the SYNSEM values of the respective elements on the $\mathcal{F}$-DTR(S) list in that phrase, while the $\mathcal{F}$ list for the mother is empty. In plain words, the head's argumental dependents with syntactic function $\mathcal{F}$ saturate the pertinent valence, causing the same list to discharge all elements in the projection from head to mother. So, schema (190) looks simpler than the other because exactly one subject is envisaged, contrary to the $n \geq 1$ complements simultaneously allowed by (189).

As we noticed since chapter 4, the parallelism under consideration is not accidental, but follows from a comprehensive generalization due to Pollard & Sag (1994: p. 348), the **Valence Principle**: "In a headed phrase, for each valence feature $\mathcal{F}$, the $\mathcal{F}$ value of the head daughter is the concatenation of the phrase's $\mathcal{F}$ value with the list of SYNSEM values of the $\mathcal{F}$-DTR(S) value". Stated in this fashion, it can be literally viewed as a higher-level, meta-grammatical generalization, which the different versions of HPSG somehow conform to (irrespective of their actual number and repertory of $\mathcal{F}$ features)[14], whereas no direct formalization with a variable ranging over attributes is available at the grammatical level applying the standard HPSG formalism by Pollard & Sag (1987: ch. 2). However, the expressive power of that formalism is sufficient for a grammar-internal version of the principle specifying the attributes in question and using well-defined functions to operate on lists. In our case:

(192) **Valence Principle**:

$$\Big[\text{DTRS } \textit{head-struc}\Big] \Longrightarrow$$

[13]Cf. Schmidt (1998): "One could simulate the effect of paths defining types [= sorts] by introducing a great number of artificial subtypes in systems with appropriateness conditions. ... However, such type systems are completely unintuitive and they become completely unmaintainable as soon as the type system becomes big enough". If this hypothetical strategy were applied in spite of all, *phrase* would imply *elist* for COMPS through corresponding subsort distinctions introduced for each attribute of the relevant path starting from SYNSEM.

[14]Also the Subcategorization Principle, adopted by Pollard & Sag (1994: p. 34) before they introduced the Valence Principle, can be considered a particular case of the latter (in meta-grammatical terms), namely the version with SUBCAT as the only valence feature.

$$\begin{bmatrix} \text{SYNSEM}\,|\,\text{LOC}\,|\,\text{CAT}\,|\,\text{VAL} \begin{bmatrix}\text{SUBJ } \boxed{1} \\ \text{COMPS } \boxed{2}\end{bmatrix} \\ \text{DTRS} \begin{bmatrix} \text{H-DTR}\,|\,\text{SYNSEM}\,|\,\text{LOC}\,|\,\text{CAT}\,|\,\text{VAL} \begin{bmatrix} \text{SUBJ } \boxed{1}\oplus\boxed{3} \\ \text{COMPS } \boxed{2}\oplus\boxed{4}\end{bmatrix} \\ \text{SUBJ-DTR } \boxed{5} \\ \text{COMP-DTRS } \boxed{6} \end{bmatrix} \end{bmatrix}$$

where: $\boxed{3} = \textbf{synsem-list}(\boxed{5})$ and $\boxed{4} = \textbf{synsem-list}(\boxed{6})$

Here '$\oplus$' is the concatenation function – an ordinary list-theoretic tool – and **synsem-list** is a function yielding as output the list of SYNSEM values that corresponds to the input list of signs [15].

There are actually several alternative ways of encoding a Valence Principle, depending on related linguistic assumptions and the formal machinery at the linguist's disposal. (E.g., at worst, one could make a disjunction of all possible cases [16], relying on the plausible assumption that each valence list allows only few elements, i.e. at most one subject and two or three complements.) Anyhow, what really matters for us is the fact that once a version of the principle qua separate implicational constraint is adopted in the grammar, a drastic simplification of X-bar/ID schemata follows. All the references to valence features, hence SUBJ and COMPS (unlike SPR, which does not express a true valence in our work), will disappear from the various schemata. Indeed the Valence Principle does not only discharge SUBJ or COMPS elements in the corresponding structures, but also performs the percolation of an unchanged valence $\mathcal{F}$ from head to mother – preserving the relative degree of (un)saturation – in each case in which no dependent that $\mathcal{F}$ could select occurs within the local construction concerned. Such an effect results from concatenation between the $\mathcal{F}$ value on the mother and the empty list assigned to $\mathcal{F}$-DTR(S) by feature declaration in the subsorts of *head-struc* lacking any daughter with that function.

To exemplify the simplification of our schemata in view of (192) or another equivalent statement of the Valence Principle, let us just look at the Head-Subject Schema (190), whose version in X-bar notation might be consequently revised as follows:

---

[15]Definition: **synsem-list**(<>) = <> and, for L = [FIRST|SYNSEM $\boxed{1}$, REST $\boxed{2}$], **synsem-list**(L) = [FIRST $\boxed{1}$, REST **synsem-list**($\boxed{2}$)]. Note that in (192) we have followed Richard Cooper's (1990: p. 25) convention of attaching functional equations to feature structures through an annotation part introduced by "where", but this is just for notational convenience, since the same functions could have been used directly in the feature structure positions where they have to yield their output (as done by Pollard & Sag 1987).

[16]Preferably encoding correspondences through a compact notation like that of so-called 'distributed disjunctions', in the sense of Krieger & Nerbonne (1993).

(193) $\bar{\bar{\bar{\mathrm{X}}}} \rightarrow \bar{\bar{\bar{\mathrm{H}}}}$, *Subject*

By expanding the abbreviations in (193) – the usual ones plus *Subject*, standing for a daughter which the function is assigned to – we get the feature structure (194), i.e. a [+SPR] phrase with DTRS value of sort *head-subj-struc*, such that ***i)*** the HEAD-DTR is a [+SPR] phrase, ***ii)*** the COMP-DTRS list is empty and ***iii)*** the SUBJ-DTR list has exactly one element[17].

(194)
$$\left[\begin{array}{ll} \text{SYNSEM}\,|\,\text{LOC}\,|\,\text{CAT}\,|\,{+}\text{SPR} & \\ \text{DAUGHTERS} & {}_{\textit{head-subj-struc}}\left[\begin{array}{l} \text{HEAD-DTR} \;{}_{\textit{phrase}}\left[\text{SYNSEM}\,|\,\text{LOC}\,|\,\text{CAT}\,|\,{+}\text{SPR}\right] \\ \text{COMP-DTRS } \textit{elist} \\ \text{SUBJ-DTR} < [...] > \end{array}\right] \end{array}\right]$$

Our grammar, however, deduces (194) – hence the Head-Subject Schema – from two simpler postulates, viz. the feature declaration a. for *head-subj-struc* and the feature structure b. representing phrases with a DTRS value of that sort. While a. remains the same as in (190), b. becomes (195), which is all what is left of its more complex predecessor (190b).

(195)
$$\left[\begin{array}{ll} \text{SYNSEM}\,|\,\text{LOC}\,|\,\text{CAT}\,|\,{+}\text{SPR} & \\ \text{DAUGHTERS} & \left[\begin{array}{l} \text{HEAD-DTR}\,|\,\text{SYNSEM}\,|\,\text{LOC}\,|\,\text{CAT}\,|\,{+}\text{SPR} \\ \text{SUBJ-DTR} < [...] > \end{array}\right] \end{array}\right]$$

Similar considerations hold for the Head-Complement Schema and readers can verify by themselves how the way it was formulated in (189) gets simplified omitting all references to valence features (but see also § 5.2.2 below). Finally, the simplification due to the Valence Principle has a more limited impact on remaining cases of X-bar/ID schemata, because they do not change the head's valences. Thus, both values of valence features percolate unchanged between head and mother, as an effect of the principle, without stating pertinent token-identities in the Head-Specifier Schema and the Head-Adjunct Schema as we did in chapter 4. Apart from that[18], the two schemata with non-argumental dependents remain relatively complex, given various technical details which deserve a specific discussion, aiming at simpler assumptions. It is indeed the topic we are going to expand on hereafter.

[17]The information is displayed by the SUBJ-DTR value in (194) as much as it was in (190), but now a completely unspecified element occurs on the list, <[...]> being just a notational variant of an ordinary feature structure using FIRST and REST attributes (cf. chapter 4 above). One should define an equivalent subsort of *nelist*, *singleton-list* with [REST *elist*], if the constraint on SUBJ-DTR were anticipated in the feature declaration for *head-subj-struc*.

[18]Plus the concomitant effect of applying the Head Feature Principle, of course.

5.2.2 Functors for a 'construction theory'

The idea that sort hierarchies – with their feature inheritance – apply also to the phrase structure of syntactic constructions, leading to what may well be called HPSG's Construction Theory[19], opens up a range of possibilities that are precluded by a traditional formulation of phrase structure grammar in terms of rewriting rules (or equivalent). However 'schematic', cross-categorial, cross-linguistic, etc. these rules could be, it is clear that they are mutually exclusive and impervious to broader grammatical generalizations (to be distinguished from generalizations in meta-grammatical theorizing which lack a direct implementation as grammar-internal statements). On the contrary, a hierarchical system of sorts with related feature declarations and implicational constraints does not have the same limitations. The consequent simplification of phrase structure (or rather, ID) schemata has already been exemplified in § 5.2.1, introducing such fundamental constraints on the feature structures of sort *headed-structure* as Pollard and Sag's Head Feature Principle and Valence Principle (the latter in a slightly adapted version). But so far, we have not really exploited the full potential of a construction-theoretic sort hierarchy.

To start with, there is no reason why one should stick to a 'flat' hierarchy of headed structures, where terminal – a.k.a. 'maximal' – sorts are just the immediate subsorts of *head-struc* (as assumed by Pollard & Sag 1994: p. 391). Hierarchically intermediate sorts can be introduced, so as to capture further generalizations avoiding redundancies at the most specific level. This method turns out to be especially useful for the sorts *head-spr-struc* and *head-adj-struc*, whose respective feature declarations (196) and (197) are largely similar.

(196)
$${}_{\textit{head-spr-struc}}\begin{bmatrix}\text{HEAD-DTR } \textit{phrase}\\ \text{SUBJ-DTR } \textit{elist}\\ \text{COMP-DTRS } \textit{elist}\\ \text{SPR-DTR } \textit{sign}\end{bmatrix}$$

(197)
$${}_{\textit{head-adj-struc}}\begin{bmatrix}\text{HEAD-DTR } \textit{phrase}\\ \text{SUBJ-DTR } \textit{elist}\\ \text{COMP-DTRS } \textit{elist}\\ \text{ADJ-DTR } \textit{sign}\end{bmatrix}$$

At least the information [HEAD-DTR *phrase*, SUBJ-DTR *elist*, COMP-DTRS *elist*] could follow by inheritance from (the feature declaration for) a common super-

[19] In a sense explicitly reminiscent of the Construction Grammar framework by Fillmore & Kay (1995) and Goldberg (1995). Cf. also construction-based versions of HPSG as developed by Sag (1997), Ginzburg & Sag (2001) and other ongoing attempts at integrating the two frameworks.

sort to be interposed between *head-struc* and the two sorts of structure with non-argumental dependents.

Before proceeding, it seems appropriate to make a brief comment on the linguistic import of the shared information at issue. Whereas the rationale behind the empty lists for argumental dependents should be clear by now, readers might wonder why the HEAD-DTR value has been restricted to *phrase* in head-adjunct structures, besides head-specifier ones. The most general X-bar Theory view of adjuncts actually allows their bar-preserving attachment to any projection level, both phrasal and 'null' (v. Graffi 1994: pp. 165-166, Sadler & Arnold 1994 and other references therein). Postnominal adjectives preceding all complements of the noun, as in the Italian examples (198), are plausible candidates for the role of adjuncts that yield N^0 from N^0.

(198) a. Il fratello maggiore di Maria
'the brother ELDER of Maria'
(= Maria's elder brother)

b. La distruzione brutale della città
'the distruction BRUTAL of the town'
(= the brutal distruction of the town)

This idea looks compatible with the Head-Adjunct Schema in X-bar notation which was proposed by chapter 4, insofar as mother and head are just assigned the same n bars for any $n = 0/1/2$. But the translation from X-bar notation proper to feature structures of a system where '$\rightarrow$' (the rewriting instruction) becomes [DTRS *con-struc*] – in Pollard & Sag's (1994) original HPSG as much as our variant [20] – implies building a *phrase*; thus its head too must be *phrase* in order to satisfy the adjunction pattern.

Here a theoretic problem is to avoid blurring dependency notions embodied in X-bar syntax. If a head-adjunct structure were allowed a ('pure') *word* as HEAD-DTR value, the X-bar Conventions of HPSG, identifying that sort of signs with X^0 and the *phrase* sort with $X^{n \geq 1}$, would make the resulting phrase not bar-preserving, contrary to the standard characterization of 'adjunct' [21]. What's more, it would not be sufficient to alter the Head-Adjunct Schema, because another typical tenet of X-bar Theory is that all complements combine with X^0 (a.k.a. *word*); hence the HEAD-DTR position in a head-complement structure cannot be occupied by any *phrase*, irrespective of how this may have been built by a certain schema. Presumably, a solution consistent with the present framework will be based on the following assumptions:

[20] Cf. the Sign Hierarchy in our previous **Figure 5.1**.

[21] The usefulness of keeping to the standard X-bar theoretic characterization will be particularly evident when we will show how to replace the ADJ-DTR attribute with a more general one.

- every $[_{X^0} \ldots X^0 \ldots]$ pattern – for (198)-type adjectival attachments[22], but also N N compounds, etc. – is, by definition, a (recursive) *word* structure, not a syntactic *construction*, and therefore must be treated in the MORPHOLOGY component (in the sense of § 5.2.1 above);

- the bar-preserving character of syntactic adjuncts is not abandoned, yet made more restrictive, implying they always modify some head positively supplied with bars to be preserved, not a bar-less one.

Reverting to the subsort of *head-struc* that can be introduced with a view to group head-specifier and head-adjunct structures together, the declaration (199) reflects the approach to be adopted for our work (but originally proposed in Allegranza 1994a).

(199)

$$\begin{bmatrix} \text{HEAD-DTR } \textit{phrase} \\ \text{SUBJ-DTR } \textit{elist} \\ \text{COMP-DTRS } \textit{elist} \\ \text{FUN-DTR } \textit{sign} \end{bmatrix}_{\textit{head-fun-struc}}$$

The *head-functor-structure* (*head-fun-struc*) is called that way because the two actual daughters it consists of (besides the empty lists for subject and complement daughters) are the phrasal head and a 'functor', in a relevant sense. By 'functor' we mean the constituent which selects its sister(s) in a construction, both syntactically and semantically, as done by the head in case of argumental dependents, but *head-fun-struc* is meant to cover all constructions where the selecting constituent is the (non-argumental) dependent, not the head.

Neglecting semantic aspects for the moment (cf. section 5.3 below), the 'functor' role that is not taken on by the head becomes syntactically explicit through FUNCTOR-DAUGHTER (FUN-DTR), an unconventional feature of our HPSG system[23]. Its fundamental purpose is to generalize over 'specifier' and 'adjunct'[24], two notions that so far were mostly treated as proposed by Pollard & Sag (1994: ch. 9). Corresponding primitives of the DTRS representation, i.e.

[22]The postnominal case in question is identified for structural reasons, but see Liberman & Sprout (1992) for various criteria that would allow to distinguish A N compounds (to be treated at the X^0-level) from the ordinary syntactic (i.e. phrase-level) adjunctions of prenominal adjectives. (Cf. a related discussion in Sadler & Arnold 1994.)

[23]Reape (1994) used the same attribute label to cover both head and non-head functors within a rather different version of HPSG. Work that is much closer to our approach (and in fact includes explicit references to it) has been carried out by Frank Van Eynde in a number of papers (cf. especially Van Eynde 1998b), but there are also divergences: he essentially rejects bar levels and the classical distinction between adjuncts and specifiers; moreover, the use of an explicit FUNCTOR-DAUGHTER attribute has been abandoned in recent papers by the same author (like Van Eynde 2004; 2006).

[24]But see also the remarks on 'marker' below.

SPR-DTR and ADJ-DTR, were used, obscuring the strong resemblance those two kinds of non-head bear to each other in that both select the head of a binary structure by token-identity of some feature value with the SYNSEM value of the head. Other technical differences were actually added to the distinct SPR-DTR and ADJ-DTR in Pollard and Sag's own analysis: specifiers select the head via SPEC, a feature assigned only to 'functional' parts of speech, whereas adjuncts do the same via MOD, a feature assigned only to 'substantive' parts of speech; moreover, adjuncts select the head but are not selected, unlike specifiers, which are simultaneously selected by subcategorization. In the revision our chapter 4 has already motivated, however, there is no such distinction of 'functional' and 'substantive', so that SPEC and MOD are potentially available for all parts of speech, and the head's selection of the SYNSEM value of specifiers (resulting in a cyclic feature structure) is rejected.

At the same time, we do not mean there is no difference between specifiers and adjuncts; rather, the distinction turns out to follow from independent properties. In a way reminiscent of versions of Categorial Grammar where the two syntactic roles are distinguished by adding suitable features to categories (see Bouma 1988), the proposed notion of 'functor' is subclassified so as to allow two corresponding effects on the mother node projected by the selected head:

specifiers are functors yielding $\bar{\bar{X}}$ from $\bar{X}$, i.e. they trigger the SPR value change from the selected head (with [–SPR]) to the projected mother node (with [+SPR]);

adjuncts are bar-preserving functors, yielding $\bar{X}$ from $\bar{X}$, or $\bar{\bar{X}}$ from $\bar{\bar{X}}$, i.e. they let the SPR value percolate unchanged between selected head and projected mother node.

A side-effect of this characterization is to formally support the HPSG position distinguishing subjects from specifiers, which was motivated on more empirical grounds in our chapter 4. Irrespective of the phrase structure configuration where subjects occur, the fact that they are clearly not functors – as indeed they do not select the head – precludes the function of specifiers. By the same token, subjects cannot be adjuncts either, even though they combine with a maximal projection heading another maximal projection (as in Pollard & Sag 1994: pp. 362-363); a subject is simply a bar-preserving argument, just like a complement is a bar-changing argument (combined with X^0 to yield X^P).

dependents:	**functors**	**arguments**
changing bars:	specifiers	complements
preserving bars:	adjuncts	subjects

To achieve the desired results, a functor is assigned a couple of apt features of HEAD. In particular, HEAD-SLOT supersedes SPEC and MOD and takes on their selection task, making no difference between the functions of specifier or adjunct. The new attribute is meant to be appropriate for all parts of speech, but accepts values of sort *synsem* or *none*[25], the latter being the alternative to *synsem* for those items that are not and do not project head-selecting functors. We also need some attribute whose value encodes the effects of the functor on the mother node projected by the selected head, so as to induce the distinction between specifiers and adjuncts accordingly. Contrary to a Categorial Grammar, where the whole mother category is the syntactic output of the functor (cf. again Bouma 1988), most information accrues to that category directly from the head through the Head Feature Principle and the Valence Principle, in the head-driven approach of HPSG. It is up to the functor to convey such other information as the mother's SPR value (and consequent bar levels), but also the 'marking' of an S node according to the complementizer.

Reference is made here to the treatment of complementized clauses (finite like "*that*/*whether* John leaves", or infinitive like "*for* John to leave"[26]) developed by Pollard & Sag (1994: pp. 45-46), exploiting a technical notion of 'markers':

> "complementizers ... are a subspecies of *markers*. A marker, so called because it formally *marks* the constituent in which it occurs, combines with another element that heads that constituent. ... Although markers are not heads, we assume that they resemble heads inasmuch as they select the phrases that they mark; for example, *that* selects S [*fin* ∨ *base*] while *for* selects S [*inf*]."

However, we need not postulate any extra part-of-speech category of *marker* words, with a special syntactic function (MARKER-DTR) and no phrasal projection, as Pollard and Sag do. This 'marker' notion, in our view, is a hybrid which collapses two different properties – being 'minor' and marking – and at the same time involves an unmotivated restriction of their range of application.[27] Several kinds of *minor* words exist, under the category system we have proposed since chapter 1, and the traditional part of speech Complementizer is naturally treated as one of them. Its syntactic dependency role is just that

[25]More precisely, we declare HEAD-SLOT with values of sort *head-slot* (instead of a clumsier label *synsem-or-none*), partitioned by the subsorts *synsem* and *none*.

[26]As we have cursorily mentioned in chapter 4, V and its projections (including S) share the head feature VFORM, whose possible values – at least for a language like English – are *fin(ite)*, *inf(initive)*, *base* (= uninflected tensed forms), etc. (See Pollard & Sag 1987: p. 60; 1994: p. 396).

[27]For partly related criticism, cf. also Van Eynde (1994; 1998b) and other work by the same author.

of a head-selecting functor whose occurrence at a beginning of a clause gets recorded ('marked') by some feature on the resulting S node.

In the revised HPSG we are working out, the property of marking given nodes becomes potentially applicable by head-selecting functors in general and therefore we need a more general marking mechanism, compared with the one originally envisaged by Pollard & Sag (1994). So, let us assume an attribute MARKER, appropriate for the HEAD value, and an attribute MARKED, appropriate for the CATEGORY value, and assign values of the same sort *marking* to both; the mother node a selected head projects can be marked by making its MARKED value token-identical to the functor's MARKER value. But then the desired result of conveying the SPR value of the mother node from the functor may as well be achieved via that token-identity, if SPR is introduced by the feature declaration for *marked*, an immediate subsort of *marking*. (The other subsort partitioning *marking* is *unmarked*, which can be the MARKER value at least for those items that are not and do not project head-selecting functors.) Hence this feature geometry for CATEGORY values with SPR embedded one step deeper than before:

(200)
$$
{}_{category}\left[\begin{array}{ll}
\text{HEAD}_{\,p\text{-}o\text{-}s} & \left[\begin{array}{l}\text{MARKER } \textit{marking}\\ \text{HEAD-SLOT } \textit{head-slot}\end{array}\right]\\
\text{MARKED}_{\,marked} & \left[\text{SPR } \textit{boolean}\right]\\
\text{VALENCE}_{\,valence} & \left[\begin{array}{l}\text{SUBJ } \textit{list (synsem)}\\ \text{COMPS } \textit{list (synsem)}\end{array}\right]
\end{array}\right]
$$

The reason for using two attributes, viz. MARKER and MARKED, instead of the single MARKING by Pollard & Sag (1994), is that our functors, unlike their 'markers', can have phrase structure. Lexically encoded, the marking power of a word heading a functor phrase must be percolated up to the root node of the same phrase (so as to become accessible within the construction to be marked) and the natural, most straightforward way of effecting such a percolation is to make it follow from the independently motivated Head Feature Principle. Once some feature (declared) appropriate for the HEAD value is used as 'marking tool' of a functor, however, the same feature cannot record the relevant information on a node α to be marked by means of the functor, or else the HFP would cause the sharing of the same marking between α and the selected head projecting that node. Clearly this would be absurd, because the point of marking is precisely to distinguish α from its head in some respect(s). Moreover, the use of a single MARKING attribute can be shown to be inadequate for our purposes even if it is declared at the *category* level, without exploiting the HFP for percolation inside the functor.

At first sight, an alternative percolation mechanism might be seen as part of Pollard and Sag's **Marking Principle** (ibid., p. 45):

> "In a headed phrase, the MARKING value coincides with that of the marker daughter [= the functor for us,] if there is one, and with that of the head daughter otherwise."

The part enforcing token-identity of MARKING value between mother and head (in absence of any non-vacuous marking by a head-selecting marker) was originally meant to percolate *unmarked*, as "the default value ... borne by words other than markers" (ibid.). Now, one could also imagine the same mechanism applied inside a marking functor with internal phrase structure, so as to percolate a MARKING value of sort *marked* (i.e. not vacuous or default) up to the functor's root, where it becomes accessible to the rest of the Marking Principle. This strategy would work only if no marking functors could include others marking them in a different way, but the phenomenon actually exists to control the attachment of adverbial dependents, as in "(***almost*) *almost* every". Finally, without the distinction between MARKED|SPR value, relevant for determining the bars of the node where it occurs, and MARKER|SPR value, whose information is referred to another node, a phrasal functor would be forced to share the (possibly non-maximal) bar number of the marked mother node, altering X-bar syntax.[28]

It's time to show the principle whereby a functor applies in phrases with *head-functor-structure*, marking them and selecting their head:

(201) **Functor Application Principle** (FAP, partial version)

$$\begin{bmatrix}\text{DTRS } \textit{head-fun-struc}\end{bmatrix} \Longrightarrow$$

$$\begin{bmatrix} \text{SYNSEM} \mid \text{LOC} \mid \text{CAT} \mid \text{MARKED } \boxed{1} \\ \text{DTRS} \begin{bmatrix} \text{FUN-DTR} \mid \text{SYNS} \mid \text{LOC} \mid \text{CAT} \;{}_{\textit{satcat}}\begin{bmatrix} \text{MARKED} \mid +\text{SPR} \\ \text{HEAD} \begin{bmatrix} \text{MARKER } \boxed{1} \\ \text{H-SLOT } \boxed{2} \end{bmatrix} \end{bmatrix} \\ \text{HEAD-DTR} \mid \text{SYNSEM } \boxed{2} \end{bmatrix} \end{bmatrix}$$

This **Functor Application Principle**, whose complete version includes a purely semantic aspect to be added in § 5.3.1, is reminiscent of the 'application rule' of (non-directional) categorial grammars:

[28]X-bar Theory systems with similar properties have been occasionally proposed (v. Chomsky & Lasnik 1993, Sadler & Arnold 1994), but we will not investigate them. We stick to the traditional idea that Bennett (1995: p. 18) summarizes by saying that "nodes off the [head's] projection path must be either maximal projections or minor categories", irrespective of the bar level they attach to.

> "an expression of category A/B ... combines with an expression of category B to give an expression of category A. The notation is consciously chosen to suggest a kind of algebraic cancellation operation ... and the result is that the specification of what categories combine with what others is implicit in the categorial labels themselves."
>
> Dowty et al. (1981: p. 182)

The evolution of categorial grammars – following Lambek (1958) – has led to directional systems in which the application of a functor category can cancel to the right or to the left, depending on the orientation of the categorial slash operator ('/' or '\'), and application rules etc. are doubled accordingly. On the contrary, our FAP remains non-directional (as in the early categorial grammar by Ajdukiewicz 1935), since HPSG does not mix immediate dominance and linear precedence, but the coverage of the principle is restricted to head-selecting functors. Indeed HPSG traditionally includes also a complementary principle, which works as an 'application rule' for head functors selecting their arguments: the Valence Principle already presented in § 5.2.1.

Looking at (201) more closely, our implicational HPSG formulation of the FAP is a constraint on all phrases with a FUNCTOR-DAUGHTER, irrespective of its status as for **major** or **minor** category and **adjunct** or **specifier** function. In view of the former distinction, the FUN-DTR value was simply required to be a *sign* by (199), feature declaration of *head-fun-struc*, and therefore the FAP allows both words and phrases as functors, provided they are fully saturated w.r.t. the valence lists and do not call for any specifier. These conditions are equally satisfied by a word with *minor* category (like article, complementizer, etc.) or a **saturated maximal projection** in case of *major* category, so that they correspond to the abbreviated notation 'Y^{M}' – meaning '$\bar{\bar{Y}}$ or minor Y' – which chapter 4 introduced for the X-bar versions of Head-Specifier Schema and Head-Adjunct Schema. The feature structure version offered in (201) has rendered 'Y^{M}' as a CATEGORY value of sort *satcat*, whose feature declaration [VALENCE *saturated*] implies empty lists for both valence features COMPS and SUBJ; the same category is also specified [+SPR] so as to exclude intermediate projections. All of this, instead of being repeated in two schemata, is now stated once in the FAP (with the only difference that [+SPR] is a MARKED value).

Concerning the other distinction which the FAP generalizes over, namely adjuncts vs. specifiers, it ultimately depends on the input and output values a given functor bears in connection with SPR. By 'input' for that purpose we mean the MARKED|SPR value of the selected head, accessible through the functor's HEAD-SLOT; by 'output', the value of MARKER|SPR the functor shares with the MARKED|SPR on the mother node of the resulting construction. Thus, a specifier functor produces a change in SPR value by taking '–' as input and yielding '+' as output, whereas an adjunct functor implies the identity of input and output SPR values. We assume that the two options be explicitly distinguished in our Construction Theory by means of corresponding constraints on *head-spr-struc* and *head-adj-struc*, the subsorts of *head-fun-struc*. This exhaustive partition accounts for the lack of any functor changing SPR value from input '+' to output '–', an option to be excluded because of the X-bar Conventions which would read it as decreasing (instead of augmenting or preserving) the number of bars in the projection from head to mother.[29]

To sum up, our Functor Application Principle takes on the kind of information that Head-Specifier Schema and Head-Adjunct Schema were forced to encode redundantly, inasmuch as they employed the respective pairs of features SPR-DTR plus SPEC and ADJ-DTR plus MOD. The fact that we have stated the pertinent generalization via a separate implicational constraint, then, will allow us to successfully complete the programme of formulating all X-bar/ID schemata in a simplified and maximally 'schematic' fashion. Furthermore, the FAP itself extends to all head-selecting functors a marking potential like the one Pollard & Sag (1994) reserved for the putative part of speech *marker*, assigned to the special role of MARKER-DTR; now both are dispensed with, and so are the related *head-marker-structure* and Head-Marker Schema. What is left of Pollard and Sag's original Marking Principle (v. above) corresponds to the part saying that heads mark the mother node – at least vacuously, i.e. for *unmarked* – when no other marking item occurs in the same construction. It is such a head-driven marking that in our system enforces token-identity between the MARKED|SPR values of mother and head, for phrases with head-complement or head-subject structures.[30] Hence the implicational constraint (202), in which these two sorts of structure are grouped together by means of a common supersort *head-argument-structure* (*head-arg-struc*), the alternative to *head-fun-struc*.

---

[29]The explicit exclusion of the undesired, theoretically meaningless option is a difference from our previous work in the field (Allegranza 1998a;b), where *head-fun-struc* did not have subsorts and essentially the same constraint as the FAP was considered an X-bar/ID schema, called **Head-Functor Schema**. The older system is equivalent to the new one as regards description of empirical data, granting that only legitimate combinations of input and output SPR values be allowed in the lexical (head) entries of functors, but the fact remains accidental and unexplained insofar as nothing in the grammar forbids the excluded option. Even if there are other possible ways of stating such a restriction grammatically, the construction-theoretic way we have chosen looks appealing because of its elegance; hence the status of our FAP gets neatly distinguished from X-bar/ID schemata, the former being a more complex type of constraint.

[30]According to Pollard & Sag (1994: ch. 9), the sharing of SPR values between mother and head nodes would follow from application of the Valence Principle in specifierless constructions, but SPR is not a (list-valued) valence feature for us.

(202) $\begin{bmatrix}\text{DTRS } \textit{head-arg-struc}\end{bmatrix} \Longrightarrow$

$$\begin{bmatrix}\text{SYNSEM}\,|\,\text{LOC}\,|\,\text{CAT}\,|\,\text{MARKED } \boxed{1} \\ \text{DTRS}\,|\,\text{HEAD-DTR}\,|\,\text{SYNSEM}\,|\,\text{LOC}\,|\,\text{CAT}\,|\,\text{MARKED } \boxed{1}\end{bmatrix}$$

If subjects are treated as mentioned before, i.e. they combine with an $\bar{\bar{\text{X}}}$ node and preserve the same number of bars on the mother node of the construction, the result can be simply achieved by adding the information [+SPR] to one of the two nodes in the Head-Subject Schema; thus (202) will ensure sharing with the other node. We may well adopt a more flexible approach, however, dropping the [+SPR] restriction so as to make it possible for a subject to combine with some maximal or intermediate projection. This solution has an advantage over the former treatment: we are finally able to find specifiers for (clauses projected by) verbs[31], since complementizers become eligible for that role. That is, in a grammar where subject attachment was reserved for maximal projections, a preceding complementizer could only preserve the same number of bars, acting as (minor) adjunct, but now subjects occur in both configurations exemplified by (203), a complementizer being the specifier when the subject fits the intermediate projection.

(203) a. $[_{\bar{\bar{\text{V}}}}$ **that** $[_{\bar{\text{V}}}$ $[_{\text{NP}}$ **John** $]$ $[_{\bar{\text{V}}}$ left $]]]$
Spec. *Subj.*

b. $[_{\bar{\bar{\text{V}}}}$ $[_{\text{NP}}$ **John** $]$ $[_{\bar{\bar{\text{V}}}}$ left $]]$
Subj.

Owing to the revised, more flexible account of subjects, our Head-Subject Schema will be simplified further. Compared with the version we eventually formulated as the feature structure (194) in § 5.2.1, there is no need for any reference to SPR in the schema itself, since its token-identity of value between mother and head follows from the separate constraint (202) and equally allows '+' or '−' depending on the linguistic context. More generally, we can gather up the threads of the original discussion on X-bar/ID schemata by providing the final versions (204)-(207) hereafter, in both the abridged format as 'rewriting rules' and an entirely feature-theoretic HPSG format. Concerning the latter, every **Head-$\mathcal{F}$-Schema** whose dependent daughter(s) must fulfil the function $\mathcal{F}$ is resolved into two components, as in the older versions (189)-(190) of § 5.2.1: the feature declaration a. for its *head-$\mathcal{F}$-struc*, plus a feature structure b. representing any phrase with DTRS value of that sort.

This distinction between a. and b. implies that the full schemata are not postulated as such, but deduced as theorems from postulates which can have more general import. Indeed, if $\mathcal{F}$ is a case of functor, hence adjunct or specifier, the feature declaration for the respective sorts is identical, being inherited

[31] By now it should be clear why subjects are not such specifiers.

from their supersort *head-fun-struc*. Thus a. in the case in question is just the same as (199) above, while the alternative subsorts inheriting the declaration are justified by a phrase-level (hence b.) alternative between adjunct and specifier effects w.r.t. SPR. The opposite situation, in which a schema-specific declaration a. is combined with some more general feature structure b., underlies the Head-Complement Schema insofar as the [COMPS<>] generalization for phrases can be achieved thereby dispensing with the Complement-Saturation Constraint we stated in (191). That is, there are two cases: once [COMPS<>] is found on the phrasal node α of a head-complement construction, the Valence Principle ensures that any further projection of α by another schema must preserve the saturated COMPS; but α with [COMPS<>] may well be a daughterless *lex-phrase* of **Figure 5.1**, according to the system we adopted in § 5.2.1. Thus (204b) generalizes DTRS as *compsat-struc*, partitioned by *head-comp-struc* and the sort *no-struc* for 'lexical phrases' (cf. again **Figure 5.1**).

(204) **Head-Complement Schema**:

$$X^{P}[\text{COMPS} < >] \rightarrow H^{0}, \underbrace{\boxed{k_1}, \dots \boxed{k_n}}_{\textit{Comps}} \quad (\text{for } n \geq 1)$$

a. $\begin{bmatrix} \text{HEAD-DTR } \textit{word} \\ \text{SUBJ-DTR } \textit{elist} \\ \text{COMP-DTRS } \textit{nelist} \end{bmatrix}_{\textit{head-comp-struc}}$

b. $\begin{bmatrix} \text{SYNSEM} \mid \text{LOC} \mid \text{CAT} \mid \text{VALENCE} \mid \text{COMPS} < > \\ \text{DAUGHTERS } \textit{compsat-struc } (= \textit{head-comp-struc} \vee \textit{no-struc}) \end{bmatrix}$

(205) **Head-Subject Schema**:

$$X^{P} \rightarrow H^{P}, \textit{Subject}$$

a. $\begin{bmatrix} \text{HEAD-DTR } \textit{phrase} \\ \text{COMP-DTRS } \textit{elist} \end{bmatrix}_{\textit{head-subj-struc}}$

b. $\begin{bmatrix} \text{DAUGHTERS} \mid \text{SUBJ-DTR} <[\dots]> \end{bmatrix}$

(206) **Head-Specifier Schema**:

$$\bar{\bar{X}} \rightarrow \bar{H}, \textit{Functor}$$

a. $\begin{bmatrix} \text{HEAD-DTR } \textit{phrase} \\ \text{SUBJ-DTR } \textit{elist} \\ \text{COMP-DTRS } \textit{elist} \\ \text{FUN-DTR } \textit{sign} \end{bmatrix}_{\textit{head-spr-struc}} \quad (= \textit{head-spr-struc} \wedge (199))$

b. $\begin{bmatrix} \text{SYNSEM} \mid \text{LOC} \mid \text{CAT} \mid \text{MARKED} \mid +\text{SPR} \\ \text{DTRS } \begin{bmatrix} \text{H-DTR} \mid \text{SYNSEM} \mid \text{LOC} \mid \text{CAT} \mid \text{MARKED} \mid -\text{SPR} \end{bmatrix}_{\textit{head-spr-struc}} \end{bmatrix}$

(207) **Head-Adjunct Schema:**
$X^n \rightarrow H^n$, *Functor*

a. $$\textit{head-adj-struc}\begin{bmatrix} \text{HEAD-DTR } \textit{phrase} \\ \text{SUBJ-DTR } \textit{elist} \\ \text{COMP-DTRS } \textit{elist} \\ \text{FUN-DTR } \textit{sign} \end{bmatrix} \quad (= \textit{head-adj-struc} \wedge (199))$$

b. $$\begin{bmatrix} \text{SYNSEM} \,|\, \text{LOC} \,|\, \text{CAT} \,|\, \text{MARKED} \,|\, \text{SPR } \boxed{1} \\ \text{DTRS } {}_{\textit{head-adj-struc}}\begin{bmatrix} \text{H-DTR} \,|\, \text{SYNSEM} \,|\, \text{LOC} \,|\, \text{CAT} \,|\, \text{MARKED} \,|\, \text{SPR } \boxed{1} \end{bmatrix} \end{bmatrix}$$

5.2.3 The marking system of determination

In the revision of HPSG that we have proposed above, there is no separate class of 'markers' assumed as primitive by the DTRS component and/or as part of speech (pace Pollard & Sag 1994: pp. 45-46). On the other hand, the property of marking instead of the head becomes potentially available to head-selecting functors in general. Here we want to argue that this is not only appropriate for X-bar Theory formalization (as discussed in § 5.2.2 above), but also specifically motivated by empirical evidence concerning determination. A pertinent issue was already touched on cursorily in chapter 4: namely, the marking of NP nodes to indicate whether they allow the adjunction of a qualifying adjectival modifier through a further NP projection, as in $[_{NP}$ *Adj.* $[_{NP} \ldots]]$. E.g., data of English and other languages (v. Netter 1994 on German) show that in case of a bare plural the adjunction is possible, whereas it is not if the input NP is provided with a specifier. However, the distinction cannot be made just in terms of SPR, as also bare plurals are marked [+SPR]. Our conclusion is that an additional dimension of marking is called for, causing determiners which play the specifier role to mark the resulting NP node differently from bare plural heads.

Another problem is raised by postdeterminers: even if a language allows them to co-occur more or less freely in a given NP (as chapter 4 has shown especially for Italian), that behaviour is barred when they belong to the same 'paradigmatic kind' in our sense, like **cardinals**. For items of the same kind that are individually distinct, as in **the five three books*, it would be tempting to appeal to an extra-grammatical explanation by semantic inconsistency (of numeral information, in the case under discussion), yet the solution does not apply to repetitions of the same item, as in **the three three books*. Indeed, we must remind that all numerals of these examples work as 'intersective modifiers' in the way we explained in chapter 4. If T is the set of ternary sets (sets with cardinality 3) and B is the set of sets of books, then T∩B=I but also

T∩I=I, i.e. the intersection with T can be freely iterated without changing the result, which is always the set of ternary sets of books. (The same line of reasoning holds for a 'mereological' account, where T, B and I are corresponding sets of 'sums' of atomic books.)

At first sight, a solution would seem to be available exploiting the semantic representations provided by the grammar, as distinguished from their model-theoretic interpretation. Thus, a cardinal determiner could enforce the HEAD-SLOT constraint that no *psoa* representation of any cardinality condition may belong to the RESTR set in the adjacent head's *nominal-object* (cf. previous chapters for all the relevant notions). The idea is formally implementable by annotating the lexical entry of the cardinal with a set-theoretic constraint on feature structures that negates the membership relation at issue, but we free ourselves from going into details since the approach proves linguistically inadequate. There is a problem due to such adjectives as *alleged*, *fake*, *false*, etc., which apply non-intersective modification to the nominal head:

> "for the simple reason that *alleged* Xs need not be Xs ..., the lexical entry of an adjective need not specify a restriction set that the modified nominal's restriction set is part of. Rather, the lexical entry for an adjective like *alleged* may embed the ... [latter] set as an argument of the *alleged* relation".
>
> Pollard & Sag (1994: p. 331)

It follows that the above-mentioned set-theoretic constraint imposed by a cardinal on the $\bar{\mathrm{N}}$ phrase it combines with may well be bypassed if this nominal is introduced by a non-intersective adjective, because the cardinality condition of a second cardinal possibly embedded into the same phrase will not belong to the RESTR set to be checked, being internal to the argument of the non-intersective relation.[32]

Moreover, the inadequacy of any purely semantic check on the co-occurrence of postdeterminers is confirmed when they are **possessives**, as in examples from Italian. Chapter 2 pointed out how possessive meaning – corresponding to the abstract *poss* relation, in Pollard & Sag (1994: § 1.8) – is compatible but not necessarily associated with a determinative function; indeed it may be expressed by PPs, covering the same options as possessive determiners for the instantiation of *poss* according to the pragmatic context (ownership, authorship, inclusion, etc.). Common possessive status, however, does not prevent determinative and prepositional expressions from co-occurring as exemplified

[32] E.g., *i falsi quaranta ladroni* ('the false forty bandits'), Italian NP with a non-intersective adjective preceding a cardinal, is fine, but becomes ungrammatical if *falsi* is also preceded by a cardinal (**i quaranta falsi quaranta ladroni*).

by the following Italian NP, where we assume the first person to be the owner and Moravia the author [33].

(208) i miei libri di Moravia
'THE MY books OF (= by) Moravia'

Considering that all examples derived from this NP by replacing the PP with a (pre- or post-nominal) 3rd-person possessive determiner are ungrammatical (cf. **i suoi miei libri*, **i miei suoi libri*, **i miei libri suoi*), it should be clear that some suitable constraint is needed but not one that bans adnominal co-occurrence of semantically possessive expressions as such [34], otherwise (208) would be discarded too.

If we look at the possessive determiners of a language like English (or, in Romance, French), the problem w.r.t. co-occurrence disappears because of the specifier status making them mutually exclusive, on a par with the other determiners we assigned to the 'central' positional class. Although that syntactic constraint does not apply to possessive postdeterminers qua adjuncts [35], a comparable solution suggests itself inasmuch as the change of SPR value bounding specifier attachment turns out to be just a particular case of 'marking' within our version of HPSG. Thus we assume there are features specific to the marking of nominal projections, so that the mutual exclusion of determiners when these are adjuncts belonging to the same paradigmatic kind can be accounted for in terms of a corresponding feature value change. A relevant determiner marks the nominal mother node for some feature value v, while demanding that the adjacent nominal head be marked for a value incompatible with v. (E.g., in the simplest opposition, '+' is v and '–' the other value.)

We are going to exemplify the proposed approach by presenting a technically refined set-up of the tentative marking system designed for Italian determination in previous work of ours (Allegranza 1998a); the system will be also commented in a contrastive fashion, with special reference to the differences

[33]The assumption guarantees that the co-occurrence in (208) does not violate a uniqueness constraint on the particular 'role slot' the referent of some possessive can be assigned to, as a result of interaction between the lexical meaning of the modified noun and the instantiation of *poss* in context. Resorting to a cognitive, AI notion of 'frame' *à la* Minsky (1975), which is broader than that of syntactic subcategorization, the frame of *book(s)* will envisage a slot for the owner role as much as a slot for the author role (among others) and both can be filled through possessive expressions depending on the noun, yet apparently not more than one such expression per slot.

[34]On the other hand, to introduce subsorts of *poss* like *det-poss* vs. *pp-poss* and relativize the co-occurrence constraint accordingly would have the undesired effect of mixing the semantic relation with heterogenous information found elsewhere in the grammar (as it is especially evident for the syntactic category PP).

[35]It is indeed the article which acts as specifier for the Italian example (208), not the possessive determiner. (This issue was already discussed in chapter 4.)

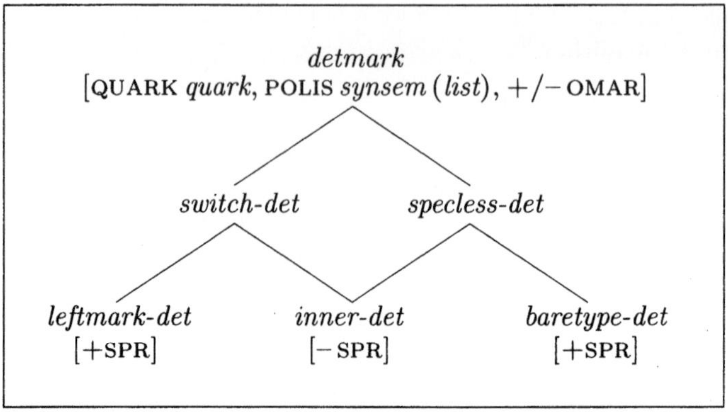

Figure 5.2: Determination Marking Hierarchy

that its English counterpart would imply. In the first place, however, let us recall that § 5.2.2 adopted Pollard & Sag's (1994) sort *marking*, partitioned by *marked* and *unmarked*, but in addition the feature SPR was declared for the former subsort:

(209) $_{marked}\left[\text{SPR } \textit{boolean}\right]$

From (209), it follows that all subsorts of *marked* inherit the feature, possibly specified positively or negatively. This is shown by the sort hierarchy in **Figure 5.2**, whose root *detmark* we take as the immediate subsort of *marked* which introduces determination marking:

What the three terminal node labels – a.k.a. 'maximal sorts' – of the hierarchy represent for the purposes of linguistic analysis is readily summarized:

- *leftmark-det* labels those [+SPR] nominal projections that cannot be modified by a qualifying adjective on their left;
- *inner-det* labels all [−SPR] nominal projections (i.e. we mean that these can only occur inside some broader nominal construction, ultimately a suitable NP, since they call for an external specifier);
- *baretype-det* labels bare plurals and the other [+SPR] nominals that do not fall under the *leftmark-det* sort.

It is worth noticing that all nominal constructions marked *inner-det* or *baretype-det* cannot include any specifier attached to their projection path, because the former sort of nominals is still in need of a specifier and the latter covers (some) 'bare nominals' only. The generalization is captured by *specless-det*, a common supersort of the two maximal sorts in question, interposed between them and *detmark* as in **Figure 5.2**. There is also an alternative immediate subsort of *detmark*, *switch-det*, which acts as common supersort of *leftmark-det* and *inner-det*[36]; then it can be used when one wants to leave the SPR value unspecified while excluding *baretype-det*.

At the same time, *detmark* introduces three attributes by feature declaration, allowing us to state co-occurrence restrictions on so-called 'paradigmatic kinds' of determiners. In view of the fact that six such kinds were considered since the beginning of the present work, we could theoretically expect as many attributes, but in practice this will prove unnecessary (at least as far as our language coverage is concerned), for reasons to be made clear soon. The attribute labels introduced through **Figure 5.2**, viz. QUARK, POLIS and OMAR, are meant to abbreviate the periphrases 'quantitative and cardinal marking', 'possessive (pronoun) list' and 'ordinal marking', respectively. A broad discussion will indeed explain the possible ranges of QUARK and POLIS values and why they are not simply *boolean*, unlike OMAR values.

Sorts and attributes of the determination marking system are also relevant for nominal categories that are not marked by any determiner, as in the case of lexically specified marking for 'self-determining' nouns and pronouns. (A related terminological comment can be made about the actual sense of our *det* found in **Figure 5.2** sorts: the abbreviation stands for *determination*, broadly speaking, rather than *determiner*.) Moreover, NP-internal adjuncts other than the determinative ones are involved in determination marking, at least by preserving unchanged the MARKED value of the selected nominal heads, i.e. passing it up the phrase structure tree. In the rest of this section, we shall present first and foremost the marking effects of determiners, but self-determining heads and non-determinative adjuncts will be touched on as well.

The following pairs of feature structure descriptions, where i. is a MARKER value and ii. a HEAD-SLOT|LOC|CAT|MARKED value, show how HEAD information about marking gets lexically encoded by some kinds of determiners to be discussed now. As we see in (210)-(212), the pertinent kinds specify a particular QUARK value via i., marking accordingly the nominal mother node which the determiner is attached to. The same kinds, being those of determiners other than ordinals and possessives, preserve unchanged whatever OMAR and POLIS values are captured through ii. from the selected nominal head and thus share them with i. in the way stated here as the separate constraint (213).

(210) **Quantitative determiners**:
i. $\left[\text{QUARK}\ qdet\right]$ ii. $\left[\text{QUARK} \neg\ qdet\right]$
(to be specified further depending on the positional class)

[36]On the other hand, *inner-det* gets involved as common immediate subsort of *switch-det* and *specless-det*, a formal possibility that was already applied in **Figure 5.1** of § 5.2.1.

(211) **Articles and demonstrative determiners:**

i. $_{\textit{leftmark-det}}\begin{bmatrix}\text{QUARK } \textit{nil}\end{bmatrix}$ ii. *inner-det*

(212) **Cardinal postdeterminers:**

i. $_{\textit{switch-det}}\begin{bmatrix}\text{QUARK } \textit{cardet}\end{bmatrix}$ ii. $_{\textit{inner-det}}\begin{bmatrix}\text{QUARK } \textit{nil}\end{bmatrix}$

(213) **For all determiners other than ordinals and possessives:**

i. $\begin{bmatrix}\text{OMAR } \boxed{1}\text{, POLIS } \boxed{2}\end{bmatrix}$ ii. $\begin{bmatrix}\text{OMAR } \boxed{1}\text{, POLIS } \boxed{2}\end{bmatrix}$

Let us have a closer look at our marking constraints for the various kinds of determiners, starting from the quantitative one. In order to hold for quantitatives irrespective of their differences in positional class as pre-, central or post- determiners, (210) is underspecified: it simply states that any quantitative determiner attached to a nominal mother node marks this as *qdet* and prevents the selected nominal head from being marked the same. If *quark*, the root sort of QUARK values, has only three maximal subsorts, viz. *qdet*, *cardet* and *nil*, the constraint ¬ *qdet* in (210) is equivalent to the disjunction of *cardet* and *nil*[37], but in most cases the alternative disappears insofar as a given quantitative item enforces the stronger condition that the selected constituent be marked *nil*. Above all, for each quantitative determiner entry the sort labels of our feature structures i. and ii. must be lexically assigned by choosing subsorts of *detmark* consistent with the intended positional class.

There is no doubt about the choice in case of a central determiner, owing to its **specifier** status: the consequent change of SPR value from '–' to '+', going up the nominal projection path, implies that the sorts of ii. and i. be *inner-det* and *leftmark-det*, respectively. The former is in fact the only subsort of *detmark* with [–SPR], whereas *baretype-det* would yield [+SPR] but differs from *leftmark-det* because an instance of *specless-det*, by definition, cannot be the marking effect of specifiers. In short, a quantitative central determiner will be just treated like any other determiner belonging to the same positional class, apart from the difference in QUARK values which shows up through a comparison with (211) above. The lexical coding of articles and demonstratives accounts for their specifier role while making them compatible with precedent or subsequent quantitatives, since these are allowed by (211) thanks to the *nil* marking in i. and the lack of any ii. constraint on the QUARK value of the selected nominal.

Turning to quantitative determiners that fall under a non-central positional class, those with postdeterminer behaviour tend to parallel cardinal numerals, so that the syntactic treatment chapter 4 sketched for the cardinals can be

[37]Another equivalent solution could replace the logical (negative or disjunctive) constraint with an 'intermediate' subsort of *quark* – call it *notqdet* – partitioned by *cardet* and *nil*.

easily extended here. To sum up, in both cases a postdeterminer works as (a) adjunct to $\bar{N}$ or (b) specifier, depending on whether the specifier slot is already filled by a central determiner or not. The part (a) of this treatment appears well-established, inasmuch as a central determiner must be the specifier and therefore its presence precludes the specifier role for any co-occurring determiner, but part (b) is more delicate. The postdeterminer's role-switching in absence of a central determiner might look unnecessary, an alternative treatment being possible in principle by keeping the adjunct role and changing the level of attachment, which would become $\bar{\bar{N}}$ within a specifierless NP. Since the alternative way of handling the case in which the central determiner is missing will be applied to other kinds of postdeterminers as we are going to show soon, it is clear that the decision to adopt the role-switching solution for cardinal and quantitative postdeterminers requires justification.

In chapter 4, we have indeed offered semantic and morpho-syntactic evidence supporting our approach to cardinals. Especially relevant for the current discussion is a syntactic phenomenon of Italian: adjectival modifiers of some nominal category can precede a cardinal determiner, provided a central determiner precedes them as well. (We refer again to the same chapter for data.) That **co-occurrence restriction** is readily explained – as an instance of the independently motivated constraint which prevents pertinent adjectives from modifying NPs with specifier – if one assumes that the cardinal itself occupies the specifier position when no central determiner does. We find comparable (although more limited and subtle) evidence by looking at Italian quantitative postdeterminers, e.g. *molti* ('many'). The idea that these tend to behave like cardinals is confirmed by examples where a possessive adjective occurs as preceding adnominal modifier:

(214) $\left\{\begin{array}{c} i \\ *\emptyset \end{array}\right\}$ miei $\left\{\begin{array}{c} venti \\ molti \end{array}\right\}$ libri
'the (vs. $*\,\emptyset$) MY *twenty/many* books'

Yet a difference arises because quantitatives prove always incompatible with preceding qualifying adjectives, whether a central determiner in specifier position is present or not:

(215) $\left\{\begin{array}{c} i \\ *\emptyset \end{array}\right\}$ famosi $\left\{\begin{array}{c} venti \\ *molti \end{array}\right\}$ libri
'the (vs. $*\,\emptyset$) famous *twenty/*many* books'

We have an easy way to deal with all of this by marking. Let us first assume that only the QUARK values in i. make a difference between (212) qua lexical coding of cardinals and its counterpart for quantitative postdeterminers. That is, the two kinds of determiners are respectively *cardet* and *qdet* markers (the latter sort of marking being dictated by (210) for all quantitatives), but in both cases the syntactic behaviour as role-switching postdeterminers results from the sorts of the i. and ii. feature structures. Generally speaking, the marking mechanism allows our HPSG to substantiate a notion of 'switches' yielding $\bar{\bar{X}}$ or $\bar{X}$ from $\bar{X}$, i.e. functors whose lexical encoding does not settle the MARKER|SPR value, so that they can be specifiers in one type of syntactic context and $\bar{X}$-level adjuncts in another. The desired underspecification effect is achieved for a determiner by labelling i. with the non-maximal sort *switch-det*, as in (212). However, the interaction with other adnominal functors depends on their marking constraints too, like the following for qualifying adjectives used as prenominal modifiers:

(216) i. [1] ii. [1] $_{specless\text{-}det}$[QUARK ¬ *qdet*]

Here the information displayed in (216) – exploiting the same pair format which was applied to determiners – exemplifies rather well how an adnominal functor without determinative meaning standardly contributes to marking of nominal projections. The tag '[1]' means that i. and ii. share the whole feature structure, with consequent identity of marking between their corresponding (mother and head) nominal nodes. Since SPR is part of that sharing, the given functor necessarily has an adjunct role, whether attached to $\bar{\bar{X}}$ or $\bar{X}$ according to the SPR value to be instantiated. On the other hand, the same item may well imply or forbid that the selected head be marked in a certain way (this being just one among various properties which are commonly relevant to selection, v. part of speech, agreement, etc.). In the case of (216ii)[38], there are two such constraints: the sort *specless-det* excludes *leftmark-det*, hence all the NPs with a specifier; the QUARK value is constrained through ¬ *qdet* (or equivalent), so as to reject also the *specless-det* nominals marked by quantitative determination. The latter constraint can be strengthened as [QUARK *nil*] for qualifying adjectives of languages that extend the same incompatibility to cardinal determination (cf. Link 1985 on English).

A further positional class remains to be addressed by the current survey of determination, namely predeterminers. In Italian, as chapter 4 argued on the basis of empirical evidence that we do not repeat now, they are $\bar{\bar{N}}$-level adjuncts which precede a suitable central determiner if the head thus selected is not a pronoun or proper name. Given the marking output of central determiners in (211i), our labelling system captures the predeterminer behaviour of a co-occurring quantitative item – as in: "*tutti* i possibili libri" (= all the possible books) – through the assignment of sort *leftmark-det* to both feature structures i. and ii. of the underspecified constraint pair (210). That is, the predeterminer

[38]Actually, nothing would change here if the constraints were expressed on the (216i) side, due to the token-identity [1], but nonetheless it is appropriate to discuss them w.r.t. the feature path value directly responsible for head selection in any functor-head combination.

modifies some nominal head incompatible with a qualifying adjectival modifier in the same preceding position and preserves this restriction for the resulting projection: **possibili* (*tutti*) *i libri*. Yet the conflicting QUARK values of i. and ii. in (210) make the predeterminers mutually exclusive, in Italian as much as in English: *tutti* (**entrambi*) *quei libri*, *all* (**both*) *those books*; *entrambi* (**tutti*) *quei libri*, *both* (**all*) *those books*.

To complete the Italian system, let us add the following assumptions: (A) the bare nominal NPs that a predeterminer can modify, i.e. proper names and personal or demonstrative pronouns, are inherently marked as *leftmark-det* and indeed reject modification by a qualifying adjective to their left[39]; (B) for all quantitatives, predeterminers included, the constraint on the (210ii) QUARK value, ¬ *qdet*, is instantiated as *nil*. In English, though, predeterminers differ from Italian ones in their behaviour because a nominal constituent without central determiner need not consist of some proper name or suitable pronoun in order to combine with the predeterminer, see "*all* books". A particular case of such language-specific combinations arises when a cardinal determiner begins the nominal sister selected by *all*, as in "*all* three books". Then, assumption (B) does not apply to *all*, which allows *cardet* as another possible instance of ¬ *qdet*, but the situation is less clear as regards the implications of (A) for English.

It could be tempting to treat English predeterminers as the reverse type of 'switches', compared with the postdeterminative one discussed before. We mean that they would yield $\bar{\bar{\bar{X}}}$ from $\bar{\bar{\bar{X}}}$ or $\bar{X}$, being $\bar{\bar{\bar{X}}}$-level adjuncts in the former syntactic context and specifiers in the latter; so, functors whose lexical encoding does not settle the selected head's MARKED|SPR value. The desired underspecification would result from labelling the (210ii) feature structure with *switch-det* qua 'non-maximal sort', while keeping to the assumption (A) already adopted for Italian. In the analysis in question, e.g., the common noun heading "*all* (the) books" is marked *inner-det*, [−SPR] instance of *switch-det*, irrespective of the presence or absence of the central determiner, and therefore in neither case the predeterminer modifies a bare nominal NP. Elegant though this treatment may look, it also creates problems of empirical adequacy which turn out to support an alternative analysis, as we are going to argue.

A major problem is raised by examples like "all three books", due to the match between the predeterminer's feature structure ii. selecting the nominal

[39]The assumption is language-specific, in view of examples like "little John", "beautiful Austria", etc., which are possible in English as NPs with nonrestrictive modification (Kathol 1999), whereas they are not in Italian. Both languages allow examples irrelevant here because they are not NPs, but a special type of clauses whereby the adjective is predicated of the subsequent noun or pronoun, as in "poor thing", "lucky you", etc. Cf. the NP in "*poor Elvis* did not make a good end" and the clause in "*poor Elvis*, he did not make a good end".

head and the cardinal's feature structure i. whereby the same nominal constituent gets marked. Since both feature structures are lexically underspecified as *switch-det* (and their QUARK values have been made compatible by dropping the assumption (B) in English), a **spurious ambiguity** results, i.e. the given example yields two different syntactic trees which do not seem to make any sensible difference for the interpretation. In one tree *switch-det* is instantiated by *inner-det*, hence the predeterminer is specifier and the cardinal an adjunct to $\bar{\text{N}}$:

(217) $[_{\text{NP}}$ all $[_{\bar{\text{N}}}$ three $[_{\bar{\text{N}}}$ books $]]]$

In the other tree, *switch-det* is instantiated by *leftmark-det*, hence the cardinal becomes specifier and the predeterminer an adjunct to NP:

(218) $[_{\text{NP}}$ all $[_{\text{NP}}$ three $[_{\bar{\text{N}}}$ books $]]]$

A plausible solution, to be adopted in our work, gives up the idea that predeterminers can play the specifier role and consequently avoids the spurious ambiguity, (218) being chosen as the only analysis for "all three books". It follows that also the corresponding example without cardinal determiner (or any other item in specifier position), viz. "all books", must be analyzed by preserving the role of NP-level adjunct for the predeterminer; but this implies that our previous assumption (A) does not hold in English[40]. That is, an English predeterminer may well modify a bare nominal NP consisting of a common noun, or some specifierless projection thereof, compatible with prenominal qualifying adjectives. To capture the intended coverage of selected NPs – which excludes *inner-det* but allows *leftmark-det* and *baretype-det* – the (210ii) feature structure of the predeterminer is lexically assigned [+SPR] and no sort label more specific than *detmark*.

It's time to complete the present review of the marking properties of determiners by addressing two paradigmatic kinds that we have left aside so far: ordinals and possessives. In Italian they can be considered postdeterminers whose syntactic behaviour closely resembles that of qualifying adjectives because of the exclusive role as adjuncts, attached to $\bar{\bar{\text{X}}}$ or $\bar{\text{X}}$ depending on the SPR value they preserve. Such a theoretical status is empirically corroborated by data showing that possessive or ordinal postdeterminers cannot occupy the specifier position of NPs:

(219) $\left\{ \begin{array}{c} \textit{il} \\ *\emptyset \end{array} \right\} \left\{ \begin{array}{c} \textit{mio} \\ \textit{primo} \end{array} \right\}$ libro
'the (vs. $*\,\emptyset$) MY/*first* book'

[40]A related difference of English concerns proper names as note 39 mentioned.

(See also (214), for a previous example, as well as Allegranza 1998a, for an explanation of seeming exceptions.) Moreover, there is evidence that postdeterminers of the two kinds, in appropriate contexts, modify bare plurals, given the compatibility with preceding qualifying adjectives.[41] E.g.:

Inquietanti loro notizie ebbero larga diffusione ('worrying news of theirs had broad propagation'),

Conoscerai carissimi miei amici ('you will know dearest friends of mine'),

Malinconici ultimi fuochi ardevano nella pianura ('melancholy last fires burned in the plane'),

Giungono promettenti primi segnali di pace ('there arrive promising first signals of peace').

We refer back to chapter 4 for more discussion on the distributional parallelism with qualifying adjectives, which characterizes the postdeterminers in question as a typical subclass of the category Adjective. Their difference from the qualifying subclass is essentially a semantic matter, but has a morpho-syntactic correspondence in marking terms through the change of OMAR value, for ordinals, and POLIS value, for possessives. Therefore, they will preserve the value of all marking features other than the one which concerns the respective determination kind, as stated in (220)-(221), and not the full i. = ii. marking like qualifying adjectives (cf. (216) above).

(220) **Ordinal postdeterminers**:

i. $_{specless\text{-}det}\left[+\text{OMAR, QUARK }\boxed{1}\text{, POLIS }\boxed{2}\text{, SPR }\boxed{3}\right]$

ii. $_{specless\text{-}det}\left[-\text{OMAR, QUARK }\boxed{1}\text{, POLIS }\boxed{2}\text{, SPR }\boxed{3}\right]$

(221) **Possessive postdeterminers**:

i. $_{specless\text{-}det}\left[\text{POLIS} < >\text{, QUARK }\boxed{1}\text{, OMAR }\boxed{2}\text{, SPR }\boxed{3}\right]$

ii. $_{specless\text{-}det}\left[\text{POLIS} < [...] >\text{, QUARK }\boxed{1}\text{, OMAR }\boxed{2}\text{, SPR }\boxed{3}\right]$

While the feature value change w.r.t. ordinal marking exemplifies the simplest binary opposition, '+' vs. '–', more has to be said about possessives in order to motivate the status of POLIS as a list-valued feature. Re-setting the POLIS value from a singleton list, in ii., to the empty list, in i., ensures that possessive determiners cannot co-occur (as dependents on projections of the same head noun), but obviously the feature must have an additional function justifying why it is not simply *boolean*-valued like OMAR. Only the additional function indeed motivates POLIS in English and other languages (French, e.g.), where possessive determiners belong to the central positional class:

[41] Cf. the different behaviour of cardinal and quantitative postdeterminers discussed before.

(222) **Possessive central determiners:**

i. $${}_{\textit{leftmark-det}}\left[\text{POLIS} < >,\ \text{OMAR}\ \boxed{1},\ \text{QUARK}\ \textit{nil}\right]$$

ii. $${}_{\textit{inner-det}}\left[\text{POLIS} < [\ldots] >,\ \text{OMAR}\ \boxed{1}\right]$$

In (222), the effect of blocking co-occurrence is already achieved by the different sortal labelling of i. and ii., with consequent change of SPR value, resulting in the role of specifier. By the same token, there is no particular marking distinguishing the paradigmatic kind of such other central determiners as articles and demonstratives; hence the lexical encoding we provided in (211).

The function that POLIS fulfils in any language (of our coverage, at least) is to make possessive determiners relevant for HPSG's SUBCAT-based Binding Theory, irrespective of the specifier or adjunct role they play. Now the problem chapter 4 noticed in this connection is solved, since the SUBCAT list in the lexical entries of nouns concatenates the POLIS value between the SUBJ and COMPS values, in the same obliquity position that Pollard & Sag (1994: p. 375) assigned to their SPR value qua list of *synsem* objects. See the concatenation represented together with selection and marking properties of an ordinary head noun:

(223)
$${}_{\textit{cat}}\left[\begin{array}{l}
\text{HEAD}_{\textit{noun}}\left[\begin{array}{l}\text{HEAD-SLOT}\ \textit{none}\\ \text{MARKER}\ \textit{unmarked}\end{array}\right]\\
\text{MARKED}\left[\begin{array}{l}-\text{QUARK}\\ -\text{OMAR}\\ \text{POLIS}\ \boxed{2}\end{array}\right]\\
\text{VALENCE}\left[\begin{array}{l}\text{SUBJ}\ \boxed{1}\\ \text{COMPS}\ \boxed{3}\end{array}\right]\\
\text{SUBCAT}\ \boxed{1}\oplus\boxed{2}\oplus\boxed{3}
\end{array}\right]$$

In case of selection by a possessive determiner used as adjunct (in Italian) or specifier (in English), the head noun's POLIS value, which is lexically undetermined in the entry of the noun, becomes instantiated according to the determiner's HEAD-SLOT, as an effect of the Functor Application Principle we stated in § 5.2.2. It is up to the lexical entry of the possessive – given (221) or (222) above – to supply some suitable *synsem* object on the MARKED|POLIS list [42], while 'discharging' that element because of the empty list for MARKER|POLIS. On the other hand, the SUBJ and COMPS valences of external heads will require any NP they subcategorize for to be [MARKED|POLIS $< >$], thus ensuring

[42] See Allegranza (1998a) for a more precise characterization of the object (cf. also Allegranza 1998b, on semantic aspects involved).

that NPs without possessive determiner receive the empty POLIS list 'by default'. No matter how the POLIS value is determined, it will be transmitted unchanged from the mother node to the head daughter in each local nominal construction lacking a possessive determiner; this result is enforced by non-possessive functors (as we did in (213), (216) and (220)) or else follows from the head-driven marking constraint (202) on constructions with *head-arg-struc* (v. § 5.2.2 again).

5.3 On the syntax-semantics interface

5.3.1 A lexicalist account of quantifier scope

To refine and complete (to a reasonable extent) the HPSG treatment of quantification outlined in chapter 3, we still have to settle a fundamental issue which was touched on but left open therein. The problem for a phrase structure grammar, where semantic interpretation must be based on surface syntactic structures without any transformation-like operation attuning them to the semantic representations[43], is how to tackle **quantifier scope ambiguity**. See an example in (224), whose alternative interpretations are formally represented by the respective 'logical translations' according to (a notational variant of) Generalized Quantifier Theory:

(224) $[_{\mathrm{S}}\,[_{\mathrm{NP}_1}$ *every* pilot $]\,[_{\mathrm{VP}}$ admires $[_{\mathrm{NP}_2}$ *some* hostess $]]]$

a. $(\forall x |\, \mathrm{pilot}(x))\,(\exists\, x |\, \mathrm{hostess}(x))\,\mathrm{admires}(x, y)$
'every pilot admires a possibly different hostess'

b. $(\exists\, x |\, \mathrm{hostess}(x))\,(\forall x |\, \mathrm{pilot}(x))\,\mathrm{admires}(x, y)$
'there is some hostess that every pilot admires'

Due to the existential NP's ambiguity in logical scope, this sentence has both a narrow-scope reading (224a) as 'compositional logical form', strictly speaking, and a wide-scope reading (224b), clearly involving a violation of compositionality as regards the correspondence between logical translation (or its model-theoretic interpretation) and surface syntax.

Whereas earlier work about the semantic component of HPSG just ignored such ambiguities (cf. Pollard & Sag 1987: ch. 4), the standard system developed by Pollard & Sag (1994) draws upon Robin Cooper's (1983) revision

[43]Like the Quantifier Rule by May (1977), within Chomsky's transformational framework. But similar considerations apply to the non-concatenative operations on strings for 'quantifying-in' *à la* Montague (1973), which is equivalent to the transformation of 'NP-lowering' (in the sense of Robin Cooper 1983: pp. 38-39) under a more standard grammatical formulation.

of Montague Grammar, because **quantifier storage** is applied to deal with quantificational scope:

> "If we think of ... the semantics as working from the bottom of the tree (where the words are) to the top, the storage technique involves putting an NP interpretation on ice for a while until you have interpreted enough of the tree to represent the scope you want to give the NP. At that point you may take the NP-interpretation out of storage and quantify it in."
>
> Robin Cooper (1983: p. 55)

Thus the problem of creating additional wide-scope readings is solved through an extended notion of semantic interpretation, which appends a possibly empty 'store' of relevant semantic objects to the ordinary interpretation of each given tree node. The notion of compositionality is also extended accordingly, any local construction's mother node being assigned its 'interpretation-cum-store' – ICS henceforth – as a function of the ICS of the daughters. That is, two degrees of compositionality hold here: a strict one, for compositional logical form interpretation, and a weaker, extended one, for ICS as a whole.

Just like ordinary interpretation, ICS – hence the store it carries – need not be directly assigned to syntactic nodes as Robin Cooper has done using model-theoretic techniques, but may well interpret (and be consequently represented by) suitable 'semantic representations' that the grammar associates with the same nodes, in a compositionality-preserving fashion. Under the sign-based system of HPSG, where semantic representations and corresponding syntactic categories are encoded in parallel as (parts of overall) feature structures, the quantifier store is represented by a feature QSTORE whose value is a set of *quant* objects (i.e. feature structure descriptions of generalized quantifiers, already presented in chapter 3) [44]. Then, storage-based quantifying consists of a feature computation process, subdivided into three phases according to Pollard & Sag (1994):

> "All quantifiers 'start out in storage' [at the lexical level] ..., are inherited by successively larger phrases ..., and are 'retrieved' at an appropriate higher level of structure, whose CONTENT value will be a quantified psoa."
>
> (ibid., p. 319)

More precisely, in the first phase a quantifier that corresponds to (some version of the GQT interpretation of) a given NP is stored as the only element

[44] Robin Cooper (1983: ch. 3) did not store quantifiers alone, but – in essence – pairs made up of (i) a quantifier and (ii) a token of the variable to be bound by the λ-binder of the set-term the quantifier eventually applies to. Bit (ii) is avoided by using the revised notational and binding conventions for generalized quantifiers without explicit λ-binders, as in HPSG-style logical translations (interpreted as done by our chapter 3).

of the QSTORE set value within the lexical head entry of a determiner, the NP's specifier. In the second phase all quantifiers are transmitted up the syntactic structure according to a constraint, the **Quantifier Inheritance Principle** (QIP), which prescribes that the QSTORE value on a mother node is the union of the QSTORE values on the daughter nodes less those quantifiers that are retrieved in a list as value of the mother's RETRIEVED feature (ibid., pp. 48, 322-323). The scope of quantifiers depends on the node they are retrieved at and on their relative position in the list (in case of more than one quantifier retrieved at the same node), so that the RETRIEVED value is exploited by another constraint – the **Scope Principle** (ibid., p. 323) – to ensure that the retrieved quantifiers be added to a scope-preserving QUANTS list within the CONTENT of the relevant node. The result of this third phase (= retrieval/scoping) is a feature structure of sort *psoa* with the attributes QUANTS and NUCLEUS, their values being a possibly empty list of *quant* objects and a *qfpsoa* (quantifier-free psoa), respectively.[45] E.g., for (224) above, if Q_1 corresponds to NP_1 and Q_2 to NP_2:

(225)
$$
{}_{psoa}\begin{bmatrix} \text{QUANTS} < Q_1, Q_2 > \vee < Q_2, Q_1 > \\ \text{NUCLEUS} \; {}_{qfpsoa}\begin{bmatrix} \text{RELATION } \textit{admire} \\ \text{EXPERIENCER } \boxed{1} \\ \text{THEME } \boxed{2} \end{bmatrix} \end{bmatrix}
$$

Storage-based quantifying as formulated in Pollard & Sag's (1994) HPSG clearly prevents a simple approach in which the mother node of any headed phrase would share the CONTENT of a daughter acting as the 'semantic head', i.e. either the syntactic head daughter or some sister which takes over that semantic function whenever appropriate[46]. Hence the need for a disjunctive **Content Principle** (ibid., p. 322):

> "In a headed phrase,
>
> **(Case 1)** if the semantic head's CONTENT value is of sort *psoa*, then its NUCLEUS is token-identical to the NUCLEUS of the mother;
>
> **(Case 2)** otherwise, the CONTENT of the semantic head is token-identical to the CONTENT of the mother."

[45] By doing so we remove a simplification adopted since chapter 3, insofar as all sample 'psoas' were treated as non-quantified without showing the additional layer of structure due to the NUCLEUS and QUANTS attributes. (The latter will actually take an empty-list value in the non-quantified case.)

[46] The only instance of semantic head other than the syntactic head is the adjunct in the original (ibid., p. 322), whereas our version will be generalized to any head-selecting functor.

The rest of the mother node's *psoa* in Case 1 is specified by the Scope Principle already mentioned, which says that "the QUANTS value is the concatenation of the RETRIEVED value with the QUANTS value of the semantic head" (p. 323). The three principles for the syntax-semantics interface of HPSG (QIP, Content P. and Scope P.) can be collectively referred to as the **Semantics Principle** and also merged into a single 'prose' statement as Pollard and Sag eventually did (ibid.), without actual gain in generality.

Despite its considerable technical complexity, the 'trine' Semantics Principle (however worded) fails to adequately predict empirical data, for reasons which have been pointed out by various authors. In the first place, spurious ambiguities arise when retrieval of a given quantifier at distinct phrasal nodes does not make any difference of scope, repeating the same reading. E.g., the narrow-scope reading (224a) of our previous example "every pilot admires some hostess" would be produced twice, retrieving the quantifier of "some hostess" ($= Q_2$, in *psoa* (225)) at both the VP node and the S node. If our example occurs preceded by *that* qua semantically vacuous complementizer, so as to form a subordinate clause, the further S node thus projected allows retrieval again, this time extending spurious ambiguity to the wide-scope reading (224b) as well. One could try to tackle the problem by restricting retrieval to a particular class of phrasal nodes, the obvious candidates being those S nodes that do not head further projections, but we can show there is more to it than meets the eye.

As Huang (1982: § 4.1.1) originally argued criticizing May (1977: ch. 2), any treatment which entails that only the S node attracts quantifier scope in the following examples would miss their a. reading, where the restriction of a quantifier corresponding to the subject NP includes a second quantifier, corresponding to the most embedded NP.

(226) $[_{S} [_{NP_1}$ *some* congressman $[_{PP}$ in $[_{NP_2}$ *every* committee$]]] [_{VP} \ldots]]$

a. $(\exists x |\, \text{congressman}(x) \wedge (\forall y |\, \text{committee}(y))\, \text{in}(x, y))\ \text{VP}'$
'some congressman who is in every committee...'

b. $(\forall y |\, \text{committee}(y))\, (\exists x |\, \text{congressman}(x) \wedge \text{in}(x, y))\ \text{VP}'$
'in every committee there is a possibly different congressman such that...'

(227) $[_{S} [_{NP_1}$ *every* patient $[_{PP}$ with $[_{NP_2}$ *a* mental disease$]]] [_{VP} \ldots]]$

a. $(\forall x |\, \text{patient}(x) \wedge (\exists y |\, \text{mental}(y) \wedge \text{disease}(y))\, \text{with}(x, y))\ \text{VP}'$
'every patient with a possibly different mental disease...'

b. $(\exists y |\, \text{mental}(y) \wedge \text{disease}(y))\, (\forall x |\, \text{patient}(x) \wedge \text{with}(x, y))\ \text{VP}'$
'there is a mental disease such that every patient with it...'

The more or less acceptable status of one of these two reading options compared with the other depends on the interaction between lexical choices and pragmatic factors[47]; at the same time, there is no good reason for assuming a grammar generates exclusively the reading which does not preserve surface scope relations, viz. b. (the 'inversely linked reading', in May's terminology). Hence the plausible conclusion that in examples like (226)-(227), NP_2 may well be interpreted as taking quantificational scope within NP_1. But now, a problem for standard HPSG (noticed but not solved by Pollard & Yoo 1998) arises because one could not simply extend the repertory of possible retrieval nodes to $\bar{N}$ or adnominal PP[48], the CONTENT value of both phrases being a *nominal-object*, not a *psoa* as the Semantics Principle requires.

Another class of quantifier scope phenomena causing HPSG to miss some legitimate readings of sentences was cursorily acknowledged by Pollard & Sag (1994: p. 328). Because of 'quantifier inheritance' according to (the QIP part of) the Semantics Principle, retrieval is restricted to phrasal nodes that in the tree dominate the terminal node (and lexical entry) whereby the quantifier to be retrieved was originally introduced into store. Therefore, a quantifier interpreting the subject of a 'raising verb', like *appears* in (228), is wrongly prevented from taking scope at the level of the complement clause, i.e. within the predication scope of that verb, thus missing the possible b. reading of the sentence.

(228) A unicorn appears to be approaching

a. 'there is a unicorn that appears to be approaching'

b. 'it appears that a unicorn is approaching'

(Intuitively, a., the reading in which surface scope is preserved, implies an allegedly existent unicorn, contrary to the other reading, where the unicorn's existence itself could be appearance.)

A number of partly different solutions may well prove theoretically available for the various scope-related problems we have mentioned, if one considers these separately, but here our aim is to solve all of them together by means of a drastic lexicalization of mechanisms originally embodied by the Semantics Principle of standard HPSG. In particular, we begin by making the following changes:

[47]E.g., if "town" replaces "committee" in (226), the a. reading becomes unlikely, since it seems to imply ubiquity, whereas simultaneous membership in different committees is obviously possible in the real world under appropriate conditions.

[48]Our logical representations (226a) and (227a) imply PP-level quantifier scope as the most straightforward account of NP_2, but logically equivalent formulae can be constructed with scope shifted to the $\bar{N}$-level of NP_1 (cf. Huang, ibid.).

A) As proposed by Manning et al. (1996), the only retrieval nodes for quantifiers are lexical, not mothers in syntactic constructions. To introduce RETRIEVED, which used to be a general attribute of the sort *sign* according to Pollard & Sag (1994: ch. 8, App.), we can consequently shift its declaration to the subsort *lex-sign* in the Sign Hierarchy (cf. our **Figure 5.1**, § 5.2.1 above).

B) Lexical entries have access to the quantifier store of the phrases they select through SUBJ, COMPS or HEAD-SLOT, since we locate the QSTORE feature within the *synsem* objects. As observed by Pollard & Yoo (1998), who adopt a similar approach, "there was never actually any particular motivation for considering QSTORE a feature of signs" (that is, introduced by the feature declaration for the sort *sign*) in the way Pollard and Sag did (ibid.).

C) The QSTORE value on a mother node is just inherited from the 'semantic head', defined as the FUNCTOR-DAUGHTER if any, the HEAD-DAUGHTER (= syntactic head) otherwise. So, quantifiers from other daughters in the same construction must be collected within the lexical entry that instantiates or projects the semantic head, yielding the complementary sets of elements for the entry's QSTORE and RETRIEVED values. Since quantifier inheritance has been made fully store-preserving, it comes down to the sharing of QSTORE value between mother and semantic head.

D) Finally, lexical retrieval implies that there is no need for Case 1 of the Content (part of the Semantics) Principle, the CONTENT of the semantic head being always token-identical to the CONTENT of the mother. The quantifiers retrieved by a given lexical entry are added to the scope-preserving QUANTS list of a *psoa* specified in that entry's CONTENT, but not necessarily coincident with it.

Before we give some examples that should make clear the typology of lexical cases relevant to this novel version of the quantifier storage system, let's see what conclusions follow in general for the Semantics Principle qua constraint on syntactic constructions, not lexical entries. Comparing the points **C)** and **D)**, it turns out that there is a complete parallelism between CONTENT and QSTORE as regards the way their values are 'passed up' to the mother node. We are able to capture the generalization without stating two distinct token-identities, insofar as SEM(ANTIC-)HEAD, instead of CONTENT, is declared for *local* and the latter attribute gets embedded one level deeper together with QSTORE. The resulting, final feature geometry for SYNSEM values, displayed in (229), allows us to state a revised version of the Semantics Principle: in a headed phrase, the SEMHEAD value (on the mother node) is token-identical to the SEMHEAD value of the semantic head.

(229)
$$
{}_{synsem}\begin{bmatrix} \text{LOCAL} & {}_{local}\begin{bmatrix} \text{CATEGORY } \textit{category} \\ \text{SEMHEAD } {}_{semhead}\begin{bmatrix} \text{CONTENT } \textit{content} \\ \text{QSTORE } \textit{set (quant)} \end{bmatrix} \\ \text{CONTEXT } \textit{context} \end{bmatrix} \\ \text{NONLOCAL } \textit{nonlocal} & \end{bmatrix}
$$

From a sufficiently abstract, meta-grammatical point of view, the revised Semantics Principle – which could be dubbed 'Semantic Head Principle' – seems faithfully modelled on the Head Feature Principle of syntax (v. (184) in § 5.1 above). Indeed the SEMHEAD feature we have introduced is to the semantic head as the HEAD feature mentioned by the HFP is to the syntactic head, both features being shared between the mother node and a daughter playing the respective head role. Yet an important difference arises as soon as one considers how that role is formalized within the DTRS component of HPSG. While the attribute HEAD-DTR univocally identifies the syntactic head, we know that the semantic head is the syntactic head in constructions which combine it with some argument(s), or else a daughter selecting the syntactic head and identified here as FUNCTOR-DTR (but the same remark holds for ADJUNCT-DTR in Pollard & Sag 1994). Even if our revision achieves a considerable simplification of the Semantics Principle compared with the complexity of the original[49], the residual disjunction, due to two cases of semantic head, may look like an imperfect generalization.

The best set-up for the present variant of HPSG, however, avoids raising such a problem, because no separate Semantics Principle (or Semantic Head Principle) is actually required. The disjunction the putative principle involves corresponds to an independently motivated, construction-theoretic distinction – already introduced by § 5.2.2 – between *head-fun-struc* and *head-arg-struc*, the immediate subsorts of *head-struc*. These are subject to their respective constraints (201), a.k.a. Functor Application Principle (FAP), and (202), i.e. the remnant of what used to be the Marking Principle. Thus, it is enough that both constraints be added the SEMHEAD token-identity that proves suitable to the given type of constructions, depending on which daughter acts as semantic head. The results are (230), complete (syntactic and semantic) version of the FAP, and (231), which we label **Unselected Head Principle** since it covers the class of constructions whose (syntactic and semantic) head is not selected by any sister.

[49] Note that whenever the semantic head notion is applied in Pollard and Sag's prose statement, a duplication of cases results, interacting with other distinctions they envisage. In particular, what they call 'Case 1' and 'Case 2' – in the Content Principle – turn out to be four cases because of the semantic head alternation.

(230) **Functor Application Principle** (FAP, complete version)

$$\begin{bmatrix}\text{DTRS } \textit{head-fun-struc}\end{bmatrix} \Longrightarrow$$

$$\begin{bmatrix} \text{SYNSEM}\,|\,\text{LOC} & \begin{bmatrix}\text{SEMHEAD } \boxed{1}\\ \text{CAT}\,|\,\text{MARKED } \boxed{2}\end{bmatrix} \\ \text{DTRS} & \begin{bmatrix} \text{FUN-DTR}\,|\,\text{SYNS}\,|\,\text{LOC} & \begin{bmatrix} \text{SEMHEAD } \boxed{1} \\ \text{CAT} \; {}_{\textit{satcat}}\begin{bmatrix} \text{MARKED}\,|\,\text{+SPR} \\ \text{HEAD} \begin{bmatrix}\text{MARKER } \boxed{2} \\ \text{H-SLOT } \boxed{3}\end{bmatrix}\end{bmatrix}\end{bmatrix} \\ \text{HEAD-DTR}\,|\,\text{SYNSEM } \boxed{3} & \end{bmatrix}\end{bmatrix}$$

(231) **Unselected Head Principle** (UHP)

$$\begin{bmatrix}\text{DTRS } \textit{head-arg-struc}\end{bmatrix} \Longrightarrow$$

$$\begin{bmatrix} \text{SYNSEM}\,|\,\text{LOC} \begin{bmatrix}\text{SEMHEAD } \boxed{1}\\ \text{CAT}\,|\,\text{MARKED } \boxed{2}\end{bmatrix} \\ \text{DTRS}\,|\,\text{HEAD-DTR}\,|\,\text{SYNSEM}\,|\,\text{LOC} \begin{bmatrix}\text{SEMHEAD } \boxed{1}\\ \text{CAT}\,|\,\text{MARKED } \boxed{2}\end{bmatrix}\end{bmatrix}$$

Having simplified or, eventually, dropped the separate 'Semantics Principle' constraint on headed phrases, all operations relating to the collection, retrieval and scoping of quantifiers are recoded at the lexical level, as informally summarized before in A) - D). For a formalization of our treatment, we draw from Pollard & Yoo (1998) the idea of the attribute POOL used "to keep track of an explicit set of QSTORE values from which a certain subset is retrieved". Given the radically lexicalist approach advocated here, which differs from theirs in this and other respects, POOL is introduced by the declaration for *lex-sign* (on a par with RETRIEVED, cf. A) above). Thus, as per (232), we lexically restrict the constraint implying that "the set of elements in the RETRIEVED value will form a subset R of P, [the POOL value,] and the QSTORE value will be ... the set difference between P and R" (ibid.).

(232) **Quantifier Retrieval Constraint** (QRC)

$$\textit{lex-sign}\begin{bmatrix}\;\end{bmatrix} \Longrightarrow \begin{bmatrix}\text{POOL } \boxed{1} \\ \text{RETRIEVED } \boxed{2} \\ \text{SYNSEM}\,|\,\text{LOC}\,|\,\text{SEMHEAD}\,|\,\text{QSTORE } \boxed{1} - \boxed{3}\end{bmatrix}$$

$$\text{where: } \boxed{1} \supseteq \boxed{3} = \textbf{set-of}(\boxed{2})$$

In the annotated feature structure (232), a long dash '—' indicates the set difference function, an ordinary set-theoretic tool, and **set-of** a function applying to a given list so as to yield the (unordered) set of the elements occurring on that list.

While the **Quantifier Retrieval Constraint** captures a generalized, formally invariable part of the lexical process we are dealing with, it is up to the idiosyncratic encoding of lexical entries to specify how input quantifiers are collected by the POOL and how retrieved quantifiers are introduced into the CONTENT. Such a lexical variation is not without regularities, of course, and comes down to a relatively limited typology of cases, which we are going to illustrate at least in part. For the sake of concreteness, the discussion will mainly focus on the linguistic and logical examples given before, showing that our treatment solves the problems they raised.

To start with, the quantificational ambiguity of our example (224), namely "Every pilot admires some hostess", is correctly predicted by this lexical entry representation for the verb:

(233)
$$
\begin{bmatrix}
\text{SYNS}\,|\,\text{LOC} & \begin{bmatrix}
\text{CAT} & \begin{bmatrix}
\text{HEAD } \textit{verb} & \\
\text{VALENCE} & \begin{bmatrix}
\text{SUBJ} <\text{NP}_{\boxed{1}}:[\text{QST}\,\boxed{3}]> \\
\text{COMPS} <\text{NP}_{\boxed{2}}:[\text{QST}\,\boxed{4}]>
\end{bmatrix}
\end{bmatrix} \\
\text{SEMHEAD}\,|\,\text{CONT} & \textit{psoa}\begin{bmatrix}
\text{QUANTS } \boxed{5} & \\
\text{NUCLEUS} & \textit{qfpsoa}\begin{bmatrix}
\text{REL } \textit{admire} \\
\text{EXPER } \boxed{1} \\
\text{THEME } \boxed{2}
\end{bmatrix}
\end{bmatrix}
\end{bmatrix} \\
\text{POOL } \boxed{3}\cup\boxed{4} & \\
\text{RETRIEVED } \boxed{5} &
\end{bmatrix}
$$

It is the ordinary case of lexical head whose POOL value collects (by set union) the stored quantifiers of all arguments – here the subject and one complement. At the same time, the entry's CONTENT is a *psoa* with QUANTS value token-identical to the resulting RETRIEVED list of quantifiers. Assuming that our sample sentence is not embedded into any other, the verb *admires* is the only possible retrieval site for the two quantifiers available on the respective NP nodes through QSTORE features. Then, by QRC application [50], the verb's own QSTORE value is the empty set and there are exactly two alternative ways in which the quantifiers can be retrieved, yielding the corresponding scope orders as we represented in (225). Each reading is generated just once, without the

[50] The entry representation (233), like others to follow, does not display the part of information we stated separately through the constraint (232). Moreover, a lot of other lexical information – phonology, morphology, etc. – is obviously omitted as irrelevant here but would be explicitly displayed in a full encoding of the entry.

additional, spurious ambiguities that would arise from retrieval on phrasal nodes of syntactic constructions.

What happens at the phrasal level, in a simple example like "Every pilot admires some hostess", should also be clear by now. Since that sentence combines the verb with a complement and the resulting VP with the subject, both constructions being [DTRS *head-arg-struc*], the CONTENT of the verb is passed up to the S node (via the VP node) by the SEMHEAD token-identity in our Unselected Head Principle. (The same holds for the verb's empty QSTORE.) But the sentence includes other two constructions, the NPs, and CONTENT and QSTORE features in this case follow from application of the FAP, because the phrases in question are constructed by combining a determiner qua functor with the nominal head it selects.

Here is the format of the determiner's lexical entry [51], exemplifying the DET value for *some*:

(234)
$$\begin{bmatrix} \text{SYNSEM}\,|\,\text{LOC} \begin{bmatrix} \text{CAT} \begin{bmatrix} \text{HEAD} \; {}_{adj}\!\begin{bmatrix} \text{MARKER} \begin{bmatrix}\text{QUARK } \mathit{qdet} \\ +\text{SPR}\end{bmatrix} \\ \text{H-SLOT } \bar{\text{N}}: \begin{bmatrix}\text{CONT } \boxed{1} \\ \text{QST } \boxed{2}\end{bmatrix}\end{bmatrix} \\ \text{VALENCE } \mathit{saturated} \end{bmatrix} \\ \text{SEMHEAD}\,|\,\text{CONT } \boxed{3} \begin{bmatrix}\text{DET } \exists \\ \text{RESTIND } \boxed{1}\end{bmatrix}\end{bmatrix} \\ \text{POOL } \boxed{2} \cup \{\boxed{3}\} \\ \text{RETRIEVED} < > \end{bmatrix}$$

The contribution of the determiner to quantifying mechanisms remains essentially the same as in Pollard & Sag (1994: pp. 49-50), so that the quantifier corresponding to the NP projection of $\bar{\text{N}}$, the selected nominal head, is composed as the entry's CONTENT value and introduced 'into store' within the same lexical sign. A technical difference of our system implies that the quantifier be collected by POOL first, leaving to the separate, general QRC the task of feeding QSTORE as the only option compatible with the empty RETRIEVED list in (234).

The lexical entry of a determiner at the beginning of some NP_1 can collect and store other quantifiers besides that of its CONTENT, due to the embedding

[51] More precisely, the item thereby represented is (the lexical head of) a central determiner – hence a specifier – with quantitative adjectival category, as the CAT value shows. In particular, we refer back to § 5.2.3 for MARKER information.

of one or more NP_2 inside NP_1. A previously discussed kind of examples gives rise precisely to that situation in their so-called **inversely linked reading**, like (226b), for "some congressman in every committee (approved the idea)", and (227b), for "every patient with a mental disease (looks worrying)". The quantifier corresponding to NP_2 will be subsequently collected, retrieved and scoped in the relevant way through the verb whereby NP_1 is selected. However, we already know that the technically hard reading of the given examples turns out to be the one preserving surface scope, which involves quantifier retrieval within NP_1 (v. again (226a) and (227a)). The lexicalist method adopted here tackles the problem through the prepositional entry taking NP_2 as complement and heading the adnominal modifier attached to the NP_1 projection path:

$$(235)\quad \begin{bmatrix} \text{SYNS}\,|\,\text{LOC} & \begin{bmatrix} \text{CAT} & \begin{bmatrix} \text{HEAD} & \begin{bmatrix}\text{H-SLOT}\ \bar{\text{N}}_{\boxed{1}}:\begin{bmatrix}\text{CONT}\,|\,\text{RESTR}\ \boxed{6}\\ \text{QST}\ \boxed{3}\end{bmatrix}\end{bmatrix} \\ \quad \textit{prep} & \\ \text{VALENCE} & \begin{bmatrix}\text{SUBJ} < > \\ \text{COMPS} <\text{NP}_{\boxed{2}}:[\text{QST}\ \boxed{4}]>\end{bmatrix}\end{bmatrix} \\ \text{SEMH}\,|\,\text{CONT} & \begin{bmatrix}\text{INDEX}\ \boxed{1}\\ \text{RESTR}\ \left\{\begin{bmatrix}\text{QUANTS}\ \boxed{5}\\ \text{NUCL}\ \textit{in}\,(\boxed{1},\boxed{2})\end{bmatrix}\right\}\cup\boxed{6}\end{bmatrix}\end{bmatrix}\\ \text{POOL}\ \boxed{3}\cup\boxed{4} & \\ \text{RETRIEVED}\ \boxed{5} & \end{bmatrix}$$

The pertinent entry of preposition P – e.g. *in*, as per (235) – is endowed with a *nominal-object* CONTENT value[52], but quantifier retrieval has been made entry-specific in this system, thus allowing the quantifier of NP_2 (if retrieved) to be correctly inserted into the RESTRICTION-level *psoa* that P for its part contributes to the aforesaid CONTENT.[53]

[52] Readers are reminded that the adjunct phrase syntactically and semantically headed by the preposition acts as semantic head of the resulting $\bar{\text{N}}$ construction, whose CONTENT value sort is *nominal-object*. The same P obviously requires also entries for other uses/readings (e.g., heading an adverbial rather than adnominal PP) and its sort of CONTENT changes accordingly; cf. Pollard & Sag (1994: p. 57).

[53] When the P entry (235) selects some $\bar{\text{N}}$ head whose QSTORE set $\boxed{3}$ is not empty, also quantifiers from that set could theoretically be retrieved in $\boxed{5}$, but the result would make it impossible to bind corresponding variables within $\boxed{6}$. Those wrong cases of scope get discarded, if 'open formulae' are banned (as § 5.3.2 will argue). Otherwise, one may well prevent the undesired retrieval by annotating the entry with a condition saying that the intersection between the nominal head's QSTORE set and the set of retrieved quantifiers is empty: $(\boxed{3} \cap \textbf{set-of}(\boxed{5})) = \emptyset$.

The treatment we advocate solves also the last problem mentioned before, namely how quantificational scope of the **raised** subject in such constructions as "A unicorn appears to be approaching" can be narrower than surface scope, making the sentence ambiguous (cf. the two reading paraphrases in (228)). Since our solution of the problem is essentially as proposed by Pollard & Yoo (1998), *mutatis mutandis* [54], we assume that the lexical entry for a raising verb does not collect the subject's QSTORE set from the SUBJ valence of the verb itself:

(236)
$$\left[\begin{array}{l} \text{SYNS}\,|\,\text{LOC} \left[\begin{array}{l} \text{CAT} \left[\begin{array}{l}\text{HEAD } \textit{verb} \\ \text{VAL} \left[\begin{array}{l} \text{SUBJ} \boxed{1} \langle \text{NP} \rangle \\ \text{COMPS} \langle \text{VP}\left[\text{SUBJ} \boxed{1}\right] : \left[\begin{array}{l}\text{CONT} \boxed{2} \\ \text{QST} \boxed{3}\end{array}\right] \rangle \end{array}\right]\end{array}\right] \\ \text{SEMHEAD}\,|\,\text{CONT} \left[\begin{array}{l}\text{QUANTS } \boxed{5} \\ \text{NUCLEUS } \textit{appear}\,(\boxed{2})\end{array}\right]\end{array}\right] \\ \text{POOL } \boxed{3} \\ \text{RETRIEVED } \boxed{5}\end{array}\right]$$

To understand what's going on in the entry, we must recall the purely lexicalist, non-transformational analysis of raising by Pollard & Sag (1994: § 3.5):

> "in the case of raising verbs, the entire SYNSEM value of the subject of the VP complement is structure shared with that of another subcategorized for dependent (the subject in ... [(236)]). It follows from this that the SYNSEM value of the raising controller, i.e. the NP standardly considered to have been raised, need not be specified, since that information will be provided by the unexpressed subject of the complement. ... Raising controllers, on the other hand, are ... assigned no semantic role in the CONTENT of the raising verb."
>
> (ibid., pp. 136, 138)

The consequence for our version of quantifier storage is that the verb *approach*, pivotal for the VP complement in the example, has access to the 'synsem' of

[54] A major difference of their version arises insofar as they remain closer to Pollard & Sag (1994: p. 328), who guessed "a reformulation of the Semantics Principle ... wherein more quantifier scoping options are available than are permitted by the mechanism of retrieval at phrase-structural nodes". The result is a hybrid system adding lexical retrieval to the phrase-structural retrieval of standard HPSG, so that the problem with raising constructions is solved but not the others we have treated too; in particular, spurious ambiguities are increased. Pollard & Yoo (1998) extend their treatment to *wh*-phrases interpreted as quantifiers, but this status is controversial and alternatives have been developed (cf. Ginzburg & Sag 2001).

the raised subject, collects the corresponding quantifier and decides whether to retrieve it locally (yielding the narrow scope, not existentially committed reading) or let the store pass it up again (as in the wide scope, existentially committed reading)[55].

5.3.2 The proper treatment of proper names

5.3.2.1 Problems with individual terms

The treatment of proper names w.r.t. semantics (as well as pragmatics) is one of the fields where Pollard and Sag's work in HPSG differs more from the mainstream of PTQ (Montague 1973) and GQT (Barwise & Cooper 1981). Essentially, the two HPSG theorists elaborate on the traditional idea "that the semantic content of a proper noun is just the individual named by the proper noun (i.e. similar to an individual constant in standard logic)" (Pollard & Sag 1987: p. 96). For instance, "the semantic contribution of a token use of *Kim* is that the utterance which contains it has something to do with the individual Kim. This is obviously an oversimplification, for *Kim* can be used to talk about **different** individuals depending on the circumstances of the utterance" (ibid., pp. 83-84).

Before presenting the actual solution eventually adopted by Pollard & Sag (1994), it seems indeed appropriate to discuss a problem that individual constants – qua individual terms with constant denotation – give rise to, once the context-dependence of their interpretation is seriously taken into account. The denotational status of a constant of that type becomes uncertain if we abandon the simplified modelling of some fixed world and context and expand the model definition to cover not only a 'universe of discourse' and an interpretation function, but also a set of 'Indices' corresponding to (the variation of) possible worlds/contexts[56], as in Montague's (1968; 1970a) formal pragmatics and intensional logic. There are two opposite ways of interpreting an individual constant τ in a model indexed for possible worlds/contexts:

- as a 'rigid designator', τ denotes the same individual at every Index (but this denotation, unlike that of a logical constant, can vary from model to model in an arbitrary fashion);

- as a 'non-rigid designator', τ denotes an individual which can vary from Index to Index (but this denotation, unlike that of a variable, meets the requirement of being constant at a given Index).

[55]In the latter reading, then, (236) retrieves the quantifier collecting it from VP.

[56]To distinguish them from 'NP indices' in the referential sense explained before, we will conventionally use the upper case initial.

Without indulging in technical details and philosophical arguments concerning the notion of a rigid designator (cf. Thomason 1967, Kripke 1972, Putnam 1975, among others), suffice it to cite a strong reason that prevents us from applying rigid interpretations to an individual constant employed for logical form representation in natural language analysis. If no such τ can be used for more than one individual within the same model, every proper name of English must be disambiguated by as many individual constants as there are individuals bearing that name in the extralinguistic world(s) to be modelled. So, imagine the language is interpreted w.r.t. a model where 237 individuals (who need not co-exist at the same Index) are named *John*: out of context, a very simple and linguistically unambiguous sentence like "John is tall" will be translated by 237 alternative logical forms, whose only difference from each other is due to the individual constant τ.[57] Moreover, to avoid building into the linguistic system any arbitrary restriction on the number of possible namesakes, one should supply an infinite number of pertinent constants, but then infinitely many logical forms would result for the same sentence – which is tantamount to a *reductio ad absurdum* of the approach at issue.[58]

Since in natural language a proper name can be re-used for different individuals, this behaviour might seem to be adequately captured by a non-rigid designator. E.g., at a given Index the constant 'John' would denote the only individual that in the relevant world/context is associated with the name *John* by virtue of some social convention (whether official or informal). Changing the Index, the denotation could change too as a consequence of differences in the repertory of existing individuals and their names. But obviously there are also situations without any individual named *John*, as well as others where namesakes co-exist making the use of *John* ambiguous. In such cases, the individual constant is comparable to an improper definite description and should be treated in the way chapter 3 mentioned for the descriptive individual terms *à la* Frege-Strawson: the denotation is undefined at all the Indices involving

[57] One could imagine escaping the proliferation of alternative readings thanks to a context-sensitive translation process, whereby the natural language sentence (with its morpho-syntactic analysis) should be deterministically assigned the only logical translation reflecting the reading appropriate in a given context. That solution remains wishful thinking without an adequate knowledge of the contextual mechanisms involved, but even if it were available we would object to any unmodular approach skipping a methodologically well-motivated level of representation that must be devoted to the purely linguistic, conventional meaning of sentences, to the exclusion of context-dependent aspects of 'meaning in a broad sense'.

[58] Here the problem is not to ensure the potential availability of an infinite repertory of constants, because one can generate it, say, by attaching different numerical subscripts to an invariant body. Still, the infinite proliferation of logical forms for a single sentence is barred by their grammatical status (which we have motivated since chapter 3), given a hardly disputable constraint: the grammar of a natural language must provide every well-formed sentence of that language with a complete and finite description out of context.

a violation of existence or uniqueness. And that clearly makes the non-rigid interpretation untenable for an approach based on standard two-valued logic, disallowing truth-value gaps, etc., like ours.

Interestingly, under Pollard and Sag's HPSG the problem with individual constants is bypassed interpreting proper names like another kind of individual terms from logical languages, viz. variables. Insofar as 'NP indices' in HPSG work as logical variables (cf. chapter 3 again), the logical form for a sentence (237a) would be (237b), by instantiation of the argument positions through the respective indices $\boxed{1}$ and $\boxed{2}$ of the two NPs. (Here, as usual, $\boxed{i}$ = 'x_i' neglecting agreement information.)

(237) a. *Sandy*$_{\boxed{1}}$ admires *Kim*$_{\boxed{2}}$

b. admires(x_1, x_2)

Of course, there is more to it than meets the eye, because all naming information is missing, as Pollard & Sag (1987: p. 103) acknowledge:

> " $\boxed{1}$ can only be anchored to an individual named *Sandy* and $\boxed{2}$ can only be anchored to an individual named *Kim*. These facts are relevant to the semantic interpretation of the entire sentence, but somehow this information has gotten lost in the shuffle: they do not appear anywhere in the description of the semantic content of the sentence itself.[59] What is required is some means of keeping track of information about variables (such as restrictions on what they can be anchored to ...) that makes it available at the sentence level."

Quite a few technical details in this connection have undergone changes, depending on different versions of HPSG, but the starting point for our comments will be the standard (1994) framework as before. Thus the means of 'anchoring' the index/variable of some proper name to an individual bearing that name – say, John – is "the presupposition that the referent of a use of the name *John* be ... identifiable in the utterance context by means of the name *John*" (Pollard & Sag 1994: p. 27). Technically, the presupposition is represented as a 'psoa' feature structure like (238), to be added to the BACKGROUND part of CONTEXT already touched on in our chapter 3.[60]

(238)
$$_{naming}\begin{bmatrix}\text{BEARER } \boxed{1} \\ \text{NAME } \textit{John}\end{bmatrix}$$

[59]Even if the NPs show the information locally, it is not passed on to (237b).

[60]Although we actually give an instance of *qfpsoa* (cf. Pollard and Sag, ibid.), the ordinary abbreviation is meant to apply, assuming (238) as the NUCLEUS value of a *psoa* with empty QUANTS list (v. also our previous note 45). Since presuppositions may well involve quantification, the BACKGROUND value must be a set of (possibly quantified) *psoa* objects proper.

What Pollard and Sag's solution has in common with our approach to **Semantic Representation** (SR) – in the sense clarified in the same chapter – is the idea that the SR is made up of two complementary components, a logical form and a presuppositional aspect, allowing the HPSG system to shift to the latter component some information that other approaches would try to treat in terms of logical form alone. In the case at issue, the shift ensures that a variable as logical form of a proper name can freely vary its denotation while being pragmatically constrained by the related presupposition, which discards all contexts where the denoted individual is not named appropriately. It is up to some 'presupposition projection' mechanism (*à la* Karttunen 1973, or Karttunen & Peters 1979) to keep track of the naming information at the sentence level by inheritance of the pertinent 'BACKGROUND psoa' – e.g. (238) – from the NP level. (Pollard & Sag 1994: § 8.4.1.)

Let us now illustrate the reasons why we will not resort to such a treatment of proper names, appealing though it may look at first sight. First of all, the classical methods of model-theoretic interpretation our work relies on should be altered with "a proviso for default existential interpretation of free variables" (as Heim 1990 summarizes a relevant aspect of DRT[61]). By doing so, **open** formulae like (237b) above would express a complete proposition, whose evaluation w.r.t. truth or falsity – in each given model/world/context – generalizes over assignments of values to variables, on a par with corresponding **closed** formulae. We prefer to stick to the familiar, mainstream approach stemming from logical work by Frege, Russell and others, according to which an open formula expresses a so-called 'propositional function': that is, a whole class of propositions just distinguished from each other because of the alternative values that each free variable is assigned. For the purposes of natural language interpretation, open formulae are only a step in the building of larger formulae, where free variables become bound, because the logical form of a (well-formed) independent sentence must be closed to get one complete proposition[62].

[61]The Discourse Representation Theory developed by Hans Kamp (see Kamp 1981, Kamp & Reyle 1993), but cf. also Heim's (1982) File Change Semantics. Pollard & Sag's version of Situation Semantics appears to make compatible assumptions in this respect.

[62]Or equivalent, in case of a non-declarative sentence. Closure can be generalized to approaches where 'interrogatives', 'imperatives', and the like, are envisaged as semantic objects other than true-or-false propositions. Admittedly, the semantic object expressed by a *wh*-question could be considered a propositional function (as proposed, e.g., by Searle 1969: § 2.4), but this is certainly not the only solution found in the literature. An influential line of research – stemming from Polish logic and standardly followed by linguistic work on the Chomskyan level of Logical Form – treats wh-interrogatives too as closed formulae. That is, "Ajdukiewicz described questions as consisting of a sentential matrix (a sentence with one or more of its components replaced by variables) preceded by an interrogative operator... The interrogative operator plays a similar role to that played by a quantifier in that it binds the free variables of the sentential matrix" (Hiz 1978: Intro.). Our closure requirement

A second, crucial reason for rejecting Pollard and Sag's account of the logical form of proper names has to do with the effects on the compositionality of a syntax-semantics interface. In this connection, the two atomic kinds of individual terms – i.e. constants and variables – show the same behaviour, so that henceforth our argumentation can apply to both. (For convenience, then, we shall informally use proper name labels as logical translations of either kind; let's say 'John' may mean an individual constant, or some individual variable restricted by the presupposition (238) as mentioned before.) The following discussion will argue that only at the cost of missing an important generalization the individual terms traslating proper names are compatible with compositional logical forms of sentences.

The sample sentence "*Sandy* admires *Kim*" (= 237a) may well be assigned a compositional logical form in which verb and VP translate as set terms [63], but NPs as individual terms. It is enough to apply the former terms to the latter, exploiting compatibility of their respective logical types $<e, t>$ and e, in such a way that the formula (239) results. This is equivalent to 'admires(Sandy, Kim)', which can be derived through appropriate **λ-conversions** [64] (cf. Dowty et al. 1981: pp. 99-100).

(239) $[\lambda x\colon [\lambda y\colon \text{admires}(x, y)\,](\text{Kim})\,](\text{Sandy})$

However, it is clear that (239) instantiates the new compositional schemata (240b) and (241b), not those for S and VP constructions involving quantification, which were already stated in chapter 3 and get revised as (240a) and (241a) here.[65]

(240) a. $S' = f(NP', VP') = NP'(VP')$ *where* $[_S \underset{[+Q]}{NP}\ VP]$

b. $S' = f(NP', VP') = VP'(NP')$ *where* $[_S \underset{[-Q]}{NP}\ VP]$

(241) a. $VP' = f(V', NP') = \lambda x\colon NP'(V'_x)$ *where* $[_{VP}\ V \underset{[+Q]}{NP}\ ]$

b. $VP' = f(V', NP') = \lambda x\colon V'_x(NP')$ *where* $[_{VP}\ V \underset{[-Q]}{NP}\ ]$

---

is also satisfied if the binding is some form of 'λ-abstraction' without quantification, as in Groenendijk & Stokhof (1984) or, for Situation Semantics, Ginzburg & Sag (2001).

[63]The set-denoting expressions formed by 'λ-binding' (a.k.a. 'abstraction'), in the original GQT language that was presented by chapter 3.

[64]Since two λ-bindings are involved, the derivation proceeds in two steps. The first yields an intermediate formula, '$[\lambda x\colon \text{admires}(x, \text{Kim})\,](\text{Sandy})$', moving 'Kim' so as to replace the bound variable 'y' (and omitting the corresponding λ-binder); the second step relates 'Sandy' to 'x' in the same fashion.

[65]We refer back to the same chapter for an explanation of the schematism and relevant notational conventions.

We see that these schemata have been made conditional upon the value chosen for an hypothetical feature of the NP constituent of the pertinent constructions. If [+/− Q] is assigned to nominal categories, broadly speaking (i.e. [+N, −V] categories in the notation defined ever since chapter 1), so as to be specified positively for the cases which require quantificational interpretation and negatively for the others, proper names included, it turns out that no proper name can fill the subject position of (240a) or the object position of (241a), due to the presence of [+Q] therein. Focussing on the S construction (but the VP one is similar, *mutatis mutandis*), we must consider that the original schema in chapter 3 was expected to hold for NP-VP clauses in general, whereas now an extra schema (240b) is needed to interpret those with proper names (or other possible [− Q] NPs) in such a way that the VP interpretation functionally applies to the subject NP interpretation, and not vice versa.

The missing generalization has an obvious impact on the syntax-semantics interface of a grammar, though in technically variant forms depending on the framework. A system of rule-to-rule correspondence between syntax and semantics, as in Gazdar's (1982) phrase structure grammar (on a par with Montague Grammar, v. PTQ and Dowty et al. 1981: ch. 8), would have to double a syntactic rule like 'S → NP VP' or similar, so as to additionally specify the Q value which picks out the corresponding semantic rule, even if that duplication is not necessary from the viewpoint of syntax. Assuming such a framework as HPSG, instead, our equational schemata (240) etc. are just meta-grammatical reconstructions of compositional semantic effects of the grammar, not implying correspondences between two different kinds of rules, because the grammar is not rule-based, but 'constraint-based' and 'lexicalist'. Nonetheless, essentially the same problem persists, causing a duplication – or equivalent disjunction – w.r.t. constraints typically built into rich lexical entries.

The arguments of *admire*, in any logical form HPSG may assign to (237a) above, e.g., are constrained by accessing their respective indices via the verb's **subcategorization frame** $\langle NP_{\boxed{1}}, NP_{\boxed{2}} \rangle$, as discussed before[66]; yet the usual abbreviated notation '$NP_{\boxed{i}}$' disguises the path (of attributes) to be followed for that purpose. If the CONTENT value of a given NP is of sort *quant*, the remaining path is RESTIND|INDEX, but a non-quantificational treatment of proper names, changing the path for them (at least in part), would cause within feature structures the duplication/disjunction which was mentioned. An alternative that looks equally undesirable was adopted by Pollard & Sag (1987: § 4.4), adding vacuous structure to the non-quantificational CONTENT value – called *referential-object* – just in order to normalize its shape. The only

[66]Cf. the lexical entry (233), § 5.3.1, where the frame at issue (corresponding to the whole SUBCAT value) is split according to the valences SUBJ and COMPS, a fact we have clarified since chapter 4.

difference between that sort of object and *quant* was the presence of DET in the latter, so as to access the index via the same path in all NPs, but this solution is quite *ad hoc*. As noticed by Richard Cooper (1990: p. 138), "it seems that the need to model referential objects and quantifiers by feature structures which are subsorts of a common sort leads to unnecessary complications in the case of referential objects. In short, it seems strange that it is necessary to embed the [restricted] index one level deep in the feature structure modelling a referential object".[67]

Pollard & Sag (1994) bypass the problem under discussion, insofar as they have eventually opted for a uniform analysis generalizing to all NPs the sort of CONTENT compatible with their account of proper names, at the expense of compositionality. That is:

> "on this analysis a quantificational NP's CONTENT value is of the same sort as that of a nonquantificational NP ..., namely *nominal-object* (i.e. an index together with a restriction on that index). In fact the CONTENT value of *every book* will be precisely the same as that of ... *book*."
> (ibid., p. 48)

Thus the path to be followed within the CONTENT value of any NP in order to access its index can become uniformly INDEX, but the fundamental insight that the CONTENT of quantificational NPs combining a determiner with a nominal head results compositionally from the two constituents gets lost.

In standard HPSG, the quantifier obtained by determiner-nominal combination is not made the CONTENT of the whole NP as one would expect, but only 'stored' through the determiner itself. Pollard & Sag (1994: pp. 47-48) seem to claim independent motivation for that shift because the storage mechanism allows a treatment of quantifier scope ambiguities, neglected in earlier HPSG work (cf. Pollard & Sag 1987: ch. 4), but we see no good reason why storage should not coexist with a compositional account of NP interpretation. If one adopts the version proposed in § 5.3.1 above, the determiner acting as specifier of a given NP is also its semantic head, being a case of 'functor-daughter'; thus the quantifier instantiated as CONTENT value of the determiner[68] (and stored accordingly) turns out to be token-identical with the CONTENT value of the NP. Pollard and Sag's alternative view that specifiers are not semantic heads (contrary to adjuncts) implies that the CONTENT value of the NP is token-identical with that of the $\bar{N}$ head and therefore uniformly

[67]The embedding of *qfpsoa* into a *psoa* without quantifiers is the precedent that might be cited in support of an additional layer of structure, yet the comparison does not work for at least two reasons. First, *qfpsoa* and *psoa* represent semantic objects of the same logical type, unlike a quantifier and its non-quantificational alternative; second, the list-valued status of QUANTS formally justifies the existence of a case with empty list.

[68]For an example, see the entry representation (234) we provided in § 5.3.1.

non-quantificational, yet the reasons are theory-internal as already mentioned. Since we give up any treatment of proper names as individual terms and follow PTQ/GQT in this respect, the CONTENT of all NPs will be assigned to the sort *quant*.

5.3.2.2 Naming, quantification and indexicality

It is time to discuss what Semantic Representation should receive a sentence which differs from the canonical example "*The king of France* is bald" just because some proper name – *John*, e.g. – occurs instead of the definite description. Such alternative NPs being equally definite, the same analysis *à la* Russell (1905), pragmatically revised as we have argued in chapter 3, can be adapted to the case with proper name. As a first approximation, then, let us represent the linguistic meaning of "*John* is bald" through the following pair:

(242) a. $(\forall x|\, x = \text{John})\, \text{bald}(x)$

b. $(\exists x|\, x = \text{John})\, (\forall x|\, x = \text{John})\, y = x$

That is, both the logical form a. and the associated presupposition b. are modelled on the corresponding formulae of the SR (243) for Russell's original example[69], granting that the property of being John replaces the property of being king of France.

(243) a. $(\forall x|\, \text{king}(x, \text{France}))\, \text{bald}(x)$

b. $(\exists x|\, \text{king}(x, \text{France}))\, (\forall x|\, \text{king}(x, \text{France}))\, y = x$

As already noticed in chapter 3 (following Barwise & Cooper 1981), the individual property can be represented through identity with an unambiguous constant of the individual term type, though we simply write it like the English proper name for notational convenience. The presupposition (242b) just makes explicit those denotational requirements the constant is expected to fulfil: its correspondence to one and only one individual (in a particular model/world/context). On the other hand, § 5.3.2.1 has shown why individual constants, irrespective of their interpretation as 'rigid' or 'non-rigid' designators, are unsuitable for the semantic treatment of proper names in natural language analysis, and the same argumentations hold if a constant of that type is part of the quantifier assigned to a proper name. For a quantificational analysis to work, we must give up the assumption that the property of being a certain individual, linguistically identified by some proper name, be

[69]As usual at this stage of our work, we resort to the λ-free notational variant of GQT formulae. Furthermore, for the sake of uniformity, generalized quantifiers are used in the presupposition too.

logically represented via identity with an individual constant. We will represent the property through a predicate instead, adapting to our framework the unconventional treatment of proper names sketched by Kamp & Reyle (1993: § 3.3). So, the semantic representation (242) for "John is bald" changes into the following:

(244) a. $(\forall x |\, \mathrm{John}(x))\, \mathrm{bald}(x)$

b. $(\exists\, x |\, \mathrm{John}(x))\, (\forall x |\, \mathrm{John}(x))\, y = x$

The denotation of the predicate 'John', i.e. the extension of the property thus represented, partly resembles the denotation of the original individual constant under a **non-rigid interpretation**, because both vary from Index to Index according to the repertory of existing individuals and their names. The advantage of a single logical translation for the proper name, which was the main reason for a non-rigid individual designator, is therefore preserved by using the predicate. However, the predicate denotation is a possibly empty set which need not be restricted to one individual per Index, so that no problem of denotation arises in contexts violating existence or uniqueness: the definiteness requirements are only captured by the presupposition (244b), with the usual pragmatic consequences in cases of violation. This version of our treatment of proper names is made completely consistent with a clear-cut distinction between logical form and presupposition (the two different sides of a 'semantic representation'), just like what happens with definite descriptions, whereas in the former version the presupposition came down to an explicit formulation of requirements that were already built into the model-theoretic interpretation of the individual constant qua piece of logical form.

As things are, the meaning of common nouns and that of proper names turn out to be closer than expected. A common noun, in logical semantics, gets standardly interpreted as a predicate of individuals, which GQT takes as pivotal for the **restriction** part of a generalized quantifier interpreting the NP thereby projected. It is also the task to be fulfilled by the predicate we introduce for a proper name, though the name itself occurs as a whole NP and contributes the remaining information of the NP-level quantifier accordingly. What's more, even a distinction in terms of 'part vs. whole' need not always hold, since there are common nouns that occur as complete NPs and have been assumed to express corresponding quantifiers in our chapter 4 (see the treatment of 'bare plurals'). By the same token, a few examples can show that proper names must be allowed a derivative reading which calls for adnominal dependents in order to form a complete NP.

We draw on Chesterman (1991) as regards English and "note that proper nouns can take *the* in some contexts: when the noun is plural (*the Himalayas*), or when a singular noun has a restrictive modifier" (p. 54), as in "I like *the*

London that the tourists see" (p. 16)[70]. The parallelism with common nouns is reinforced by the fact that in other uses discussed by the same author the determiner need not be definite: "It seems that any ... singular proper noun can take *a* if an appropriate context is found" (p. 44), as in "He described *a Finland I had never experienced*", or "There was *a Tom Jones* on the phone for you" (p. 7). Indeed we could go on constructing acceptable examples with any kind of determiners: "*Every Freddie I knew* was from Boston", "*Some Paul or other* is at the door", "*Few Robinsons* live there" etc. There is a constraint of English normally disallowing the definite article with a singular proper name that lacks restrictive modification (**the John*)[71], but even this does not hold for (some dialects of) other languages, like German (v. *der Hans*) or Spanish (v. *el Juan*), as already noticed by Barwise & Cooper (1981).

To sum up, the semantic distinction between common and proper nouns is not really a matter of logical type, insofar as both may well be interpreted ('translated') as a generalized quantifier Q or a restriction predicate P, according to the given noun's reading. Being a necessary part of the appropriate Q, P is associated with the noun in any case, so that the most general difference between the two kinds of nominal words can be plausibly traced back to their respective predicates. As a first approximation, the 'associated predicate' (in the intended sense, which holds irrespective of the noun's logical type) seems to provide common nouns with some **descriptive content**, unlike proper names. Here the terminology intuitively bears on the fundamental linguistic purpose of describing the extralinguistic world in terms of properties (or relations) that occur in it and are conceptualized through suitable expressions, common nouns being indeed a case in point. On the other hand, proper names resemble personal pronouns in this respect, since both lack any inherent descriptive content (for reasons to be clarified in the rest of the current section).

The predicate associated with a common noun is interpreted by a property (or relation) whose truthful ascription to a certain individual (or n-tuple of individuals) depends on the state of the world that is meant to be described. Under a Montague-style reconstruction of the pertinent 'intension' *à la* Carnap (1947), the predicate can be assigned a function from Indices of 'world states' to appropriate extensions: i.e. the function that yields, for each given Index, the possibly empty set of (n-tuples of) individuals which is denoted by the

[70] Restrictive modifiers are typically rejected by a determinerless proper noun (**London that the tourists see in a hurry ...*), contrary to appositive, non-restrictive ones (*London, which the tourists see in a hurry, ...*). We refer back to note 39, in § 5.2.3, for examples with prenominal non-restrictive modifiers.

[71] One can find few exceptions, such as the names of rivers, seas, and the like (v. Chesterman 1991: pp. 54, 86); e.g., *the (River) Thames*. Cf. also Leech & Svartvik (1975: p. 279) for more examples.

predicate at that Index. But to make the idea of **world states** more precise, their Indices turn out to distinguish two sets of primitives as components.

For one thing, we take for granted some non-empty set of **possible worlds**, in a sense accounting for the (Leibnitzian) intuition that the notions of 'necessity' and 'possibility' respectively correspond to truth in *every* and *some* possible world[72]. There are – say – counterfactual worlds as opposed to a world singled out as the 'actual' one, worlds compatible with somebody's knowledge, belief or imagination, worlds in which somebody acts ethically or legally, etc., so as to relativize necessity and possibility accordingly. The temporal dimension of world state descriptions must be treated too, however, because "many, if not most, sentences of natural languages may be now true, now false, as circumstances in the world change" (Dowty et al. 1980: p. 112). Hence also an infinite number of **moments in time**, or similar[73], qua second set of relevant primitives:

> "Thus we can think of our 'semantic space' as expanded to two dimensions. We have, as it were, differing worlds as we move along one axis and differing times as we move on the other axis. Any particular point on this plane can be metaphorically thought of as being a pair of *co-ordinates* <**w**, **t**> ...; that is, as a point whose location is determined by which world [**w**] it is in ... and by what time [**t**] it is".
>
> (ibid., p. 131)

The analysis of Indices into coordinates, as envisaged by Montague (1968; 1970a) for Formal Pragmatics and Intensional Logic (and then applied to the semantics of PTQ), need not only reflect such a notion of world states to be described, though. In model-theoretic systems like those that he and others have developed (cf. Lewis 1970), the original mono- or bi-dimensional Indices feeding the intensions are expanded to n-dimensional ones, where the additional coordinates of the n-tuple capture factors of the utterance context that provide denotations for 'deictically anchored' items of various sorts. If the third coordinate of any Index **j** = <**w**, **t**, **s**, ...> corresponds to the speaker, e.g., then the denotation of a distinguished individual constant approximating to the 1st person singular pronoun ("I" in English) is the value **s** of **j**'s third coordinate. Likewise, if **j**'s fourth coordinate value corresponds to the hearer intentionally addressed by the speaker (a.k.a. the 'addressee'), for every Index **j** = <**w**, **t**, **s**, **h**, ...> the denotation of a distinguished individual constant approximating

[72]The approach of 'possible-world semantics' has become a standard after its successful interpretation of various systems of modal logic (Kripke 1963).

[73]In the present context, we can simply neglect the technical issue as to whether **intervals** should be taken as temporal primitives instead of mere 'points in time' (a.k.a. *moments*, or *instants*). For related treatments, see Dowty (1979), Kamp & Reyle (1993) and Van Eynde (1998a), among others.

to the 2nd person singular pronoun ("tu" in French, Italian or Spanish) is **h**. Further coordinates may be added in order to handle deictic 3rd person pronouns, demonstrative determiners and their pronominal counterparts, locative adverbs such as "here", "there", "nearby", etc.

The definitive coordinate list for Indices in natural language is an open issue, since various authors tend to add or subtract coordinates according to their views on specific phenomena. E.g., consider those approaches to time that treat moments (or other temporal primitives) as elements of the universe of discourse, so as to let them be explicitly denoted, quantified over, etc. by the ordinary logical means available for individuals. If n-ary predicates originally interpreted w.r.t. $<\mathbf{w},\mathbf{t}>$ pairs are added one argument position reserved to **t**-denoting terms, they become n+1-ary predicates interpreted w.r.t. the coordinate **w** qua only aspect of 'world states' to be kept within the Indices. Thus the temporal adverb in a sentence of the form "Always p", say, can translate as universal quantifier, binding the variable over times that fills the extra argument position of some predicate(s) inside p, and the whole sentence is true in a given world **w** iff p is true at every time in **w**. An important line of research has shown how logical techniques of the kind allow the treatment of linguistic expressions of time – including tenses, as modelled after Reichenbach (1947) – without the temporal modality operators of Montague's system.[74]

But our aim is not to argue for or against any of the two methods. On the one hand, we shall continue to ignore temporal information in all logical formulae and feature structures, leaving the readers free to supplement our semantic representation with the time machinery they prefer. On the other hand, we wish to point out that even if the world-state coordinate of time – corresponding to a Reichenbachian notion of 'event time' – is dispensed with by resorting to extended predicates and explicit quantification over moments, or similar, nevertheless an Index must have some time coordinate(s) for contextual reasons. Just to touch on a simple example, "present tense sentences (in one of their most common uses in English) are understood to describe the state of the world that obtains concurrent with the time of utterance" (Dowty et al. 1981: p. 112); this contextual dependence suggests an **utterance time coordinate**[75], supplying a value $\mathbf{u}_t$ linked to the temporal argument of predicates that translate deictic present tense forms of verbs. The 'utterance time' as such is not a component of the described world states, its different role being evident for tenses whereby it does not overlap (but follows or precedes) the 'event time'.

[74]For discussion of linguistic phenomena that seem to favour alternatives to the modality-based interpretation of tense, v. Partee (1984) and Robin Cooper (1987).

[75]The same as Reichenbach's (1947) 'speech time'. He also envisaged a '(temporal) point of reference' (or 'reference time'), which might require yet another coordinate within Indices.

Reverting to the original subject of our discussion, we are allowed to conclude that the 'descriptive predicates' are those whose extension under a model-theoretic system with Indices depends on world-state coordinates, hence at least the possible world one (plus a coordinate for the event time if this is not treated differently, as mentioned). By the same token, we shall indeed call 'non-descriptive' those predicates whose extension is independent of any world-state coordinate, being exclusively assigned through some coordinate of Indices which reflects a factor of the context of utterance rather than the state of the world to be described. Given a deictic pronoun that in traditional versions of Index-based semantics would be interpreted as an individual constant denoting the relevant contextual coordinate value, now we can make the interpretation fit our uniform account of NPs through an appropriate generalized quantifier, restricted by a non-descriptive predicate with extension depending on the same coordinate.

The SR (made up of logical form and presupposition) for a sentence like *I am bald*, e.g., is modelled on the Russellian example (243) above so as to capture the definiteness of the personal pronoun, while changing restriction according to its 'associated predicate':

(245) a. $(\forall x|\,\mathrm{I}(x))\,\mathrm{bald}(x)$

b. $(\exists\, x|\,\mathrm{I}(x))\,(\forall x|\,\mathrm{I}(x))\,y = x$

Compared with descriptive predicates like 'bald', 'king', etc., 'I' has a different model-theoretic status, due to the dependence of its extension on the **speaker coordinate** qua factor of the utterance context. Such a deictic non-descriptive predicate is true of a given individual **a** *iff* **a** is the speaker in the (current) context of utterance[76], irrespective of what **a** may independently be/do in the world state under description. Once a particular speaker is appointed, the Montague-style intension (= function from n-dimensional Indices) of the predicate 'I' yields the same denoted set across all relevant worlds and their temporal states: the set whose only element coincides with that speaker, satisfying the definiteness presupposition carried by the pronoun[77]. So, 'I' works as predicate-type equivalent of a rigid designator relatively to any given class

[76]Hence the difference from a descriptive predicate translating the word *speaker* of ordinary English, which is true of any individual being a speaker in the described world state. The speaker (coordinate) notion relevant for the **metalanguage** of a context-bound interpretation system like this is subject to constraints that do not hold for the ordinary reading of the English word. Whereas the ordinary reading – and therefore the corresponding predicate 'speaker' in some (informally spelled out) logical language – looks roughly paraphrasable as 'one who says something', the metalinguistic sense of *speaker* used for our interpretation of 'I' entails a much more specific paraphrase: roughly, 'the individual saying what is being interpreted as current utterance'.

[77]That is, the usual existence and uniqueness conditions, as per (244b).

of Indices which share the same speaker, even though it has a non-rigid interpretation as regards Indices with different speakers.

A very similar account is available for the non-descriptive status of a proper name and the context-dependence of its usage in reference, supposing the extensions of the associated predicate (e.g. 'John') depend on another coordinate of the utterance context, in such a way that a rigid interpretation is achieved relatively to any given class of Indices which share the same value for that coordinate. The solution, borrowed from Lewis (1970), allows us to reconcile our quantificational treatment of proper names with the influential position that they must be rigid designators:

> "One of the reasons for this position involves the explanation of how people can use names to 'refer' to individuals they do not know personally and cannot identify by first-hand knowledge, e.g. the name *Frege*. This so-called **causal theory of proper names** holds that we simply intend to refer, with such a name, to the individual other speakers have traditionally referred to by this name. Thus our 'reference' to such individuals ... really depends on a causal chain of other speakers' use of the same name, a chain that ultimately goes back to a dubbing of the actual person with this name".[78]
>
> Dowty et al. (1980: p. 171)

In typical versions of the 'causal theory' (see Kripke 1972), the proper name itself is interpreted as an individual constant with invariant denotation/extension for all possible worlds and times, its trivial meaning/intension (if any) being just a constant function. By now it should be clear why we are replacing a linguistically oversimplified approach of the kind with a more elaborate version, which allows a proper name to receive a type of semantic representation independently motivated for (definite) NPs and avoids proliferating alternative translations of that name as unambiguous individual constants.

Let us then provide the Indices with a **naming coordinate** (a.k.a. *causal-history-of-acquisition-of-names coordinate*[79]), whose value will determine the extensions of pertinent non-descriptive predicates like 'John', 'Frege', etc. Although the same mechanism could be applied to corresponding individual con-

[78]The process was informally exemplified as follows by Kripke (1972): "Someone, let's say ... [the famous physicist Richard Feynman], is born; his parents call him by a certain name. They talk about him to their friends. Other people meet him. Through various sorts of talk the name is spread from link to link as if by a chain. A speaker who is on the far end of this chain, who has heard about ... Richard Feynman, in the market place or elsewhere, may be referring to Richard Feynman ... even though he can't identify him uniquely". In fact, what matters here for definite reference through proper names or other NPs is just the **presupposition** of a unique referent, not an additional requirement of actual identification, *pace* Searle (1969: ch. 4).

[79]In the more accurate but unwieldy terminology by Lewis (1970).

stants instead, predicates have the already mentioned advantage of denoting a set which may well be empty (in case of names without referent in that context) or contain more than one element (in case of contextually 'co-existent' namesakes)[80]. But on normal conditions of successful communication, the predicate associated with a proper name denotes a unary set. E.g., at any Index where the naming coordinate makes 'John' denote $\{\mathbf{a}\}$, 'John(x)' is true – relative to an assignment of values to logical variables – *iff* the individual assigned to x belongs to $\{\mathbf{a}\}$ (so that $x = \mathbf{a}$), irrespective of other coordinates of the same Index. From a pragmatic point of view, the individual in the unary set denotation is just the one the speaker intends to refer to (on the given occasion) through the name which is being uttered and interpreted, conforming with the causal chain that has led to the speaker's association between name and referent.[81]

Now, a feature structure encoding for this account of proper names proves quite straightforward, exploiting the CONTEXT representation available in standard HPSG. Next to BACKGROUND (cf. our previous § 5.3.2.1), Pollard & Sag (1994) "add a second *context* attribute called CONTEXTUAL-INDICES (C-INDS), which represents information about various indexical coordinates" (p. 27). Since the detailed repertory of attributes standing for those coordinates remains open (ibid., p. 398), we feel free to introduce also an attribute NAMING among others:

(246)
$$\begin{bmatrix} \text{BACKGROUND } \textit{set (psoa)} \\ \text{C-INDICES} \begin{bmatrix} \text{SPEAKER } \boxed{s} \\ \text{ADDRESSEE } \boxed{h} \\ \text{UTTERANCE-TIME } \boxed{u_t} \\ \text{NAMING } \boxed{n} \\ \vdots \end{bmatrix}_{\textit{c-inds}} \end{bmatrix}_{\textit{context}}$$

Here is the lexical representation for a sample proper name (whose encoding of definiteness was motivated in chapter 3), linking the associated predicate with the coordinate value at issue:

[80] We refer back to the discussion in § 5.3.2.1.

[81] Of course, some cases of 'chain' are shorter than others, to the point that the speaker can also coincide with the person responsible for the initial bestowal of the name (whether official or informal like a nickname) on the individual referred to. Cf. again Kripke (1972): "When the name is 'passed from link to link', the receiver of the name must ... intend when he learns it to use it with the same reference as the man from whom he heard it. If I hear the name 'Napoleon' and decide it would be a nice name for my pet aarvark, I do not satisfy this condition". On the other hand, the aarvark's owner can actually initiate a new causal chain, e.g., by saying "Do you like Napoleon?" while pointing to the pet.

(247)
$$\begin{bmatrix} \text{SEMH}\,|\,\text{CONT} & \begin{bmatrix} \text{DET} & \forall\begin{bmatrix}\text{+DEF}\end{bmatrix} \\ \text{RESTIND} & {}_{npro}\begin{bmatrix} \text{INDEX} & \boxed{1}\; {}_{ref}\begin{bmatrix}\text{NUMBER } \textit{sing} \\ \text{PERSON } \textit{3rd}\end{bmatrix} \\ \text{RESTR} & \left\{ \begin{bmatrix} \text{QUANTS} <> \\ \text{NUCLEUS } \textit{john}\,(\boxed{1}) \end{bmatrix} \right\} \end{bmatrix} \end{bmatrix} \\ \text{CONTEXT}\,|\,\text{C-INDICES}\,|\,\text{NAMING } \boxed{1} & \end{bmatrix}$$

The treatment of contextual dependence thereby applied implies that the values of *c-inds* attributes are typically 'referential indices' in the technical sense of HPSG (being of sort *index* and, more specifically, *ref*)[82], so as to allow their structure-sharing with suitable CONTENT-internal features. Generally speaking, it is the approach proposed by Pollard & Sag (1994: p. 335): "A deictic expression might be defined as one that identifies some part of its content with some part of its context. For example, the first person pronoun *I* ... identifies indices as shown in [(248)]", which retains the essence of the original though we have adapted the CONTENT to our quantificational account of NPs.

(248)
$$\begin{bmatrix} \text{SEMH}\,|\,\text{CONT} & \begin{bmatrix} \text{DET} & \forall\begin{bmatrix}\text{+DEF}\end{bmatrix} \\ \text{RESTIND} & {}_{ppro}\begin{bmatrix} \text{INDEX} & \boxed{1}\; {}_{ref}\begin{bmatrix}\text{NUMBER } \textit{sing} \\ \text{PERSON } \textit{1st}\end{bmatrix} \\ \text{RESTR} & \{\} \end{bmatrix} \end{bmatrix} \\ \text{CONTEXT}\,|\,\text{C-INDICES}\,|\,\text{SPEAKER } \boxed{1} & \end{bmatrix}$$

To fully understand the representation, we recall that the INDEX value logically translates as a variable ${x^{\tau}}_i$ with sortal restriction τ based on agreement information. The effect of τ on semantic interpretation can be considered equivalent to that of '$\tau(x_i)$', the formula predicating τ of the unrestricted version of the same variable; thus 'λx_i: $[\tau(x_i) \wedge \psi]$' corresponds to the set term derived from a formula ψ by binding ${x^{\tau}}_i$. In a case like (248), no ψ translates the empty RESTR value, but a set term 'λx_i: $[\tau(x_i)]$' results as translation of the RESTIND value (Allegranza & Mazzini 2000: p. 227), τ being the pronoun's associated predicate 'I'.

[82]Since contextual coordinates of model-theoretical 'Indices' (with upper case initial) are systematically related to relevant tokens of 'indices' in the other sense, the **contextual index** notion in HPSG may well apply to a single coordinate instead of a whole n-tuple. Whether all such indices are *referential* or some other subsort of *index* is needed for temporal coordinates is a question we will not address here.

5.4 Conclusions

This volume has developed a comprehensive treatment of determiners within the Noun Phrase, accounting for their rich variety as regards distributional behaviour, category features, dependency relations and semantic contribution. A broad descriptive characterization, covering articles as well as the cardinal, demonstrative, ordinal, possessive and quantitative kinds of other determiners, was presented since chapter 1 and illustrated by means of multilingual data especially in chapter 2. Under the grammatical system the current chapter has formalized in detail, the mother node of a determiner-nominal construction receives syntactic information from both constituents, being projected by the nominal head but also 'marked' consistently with the above-mentioned (paradigmatic) kind and/or the positional class of the determiner. In that way, the co-occurrence restrictions on determiners of each given language can be stated by adequately setting few feature values within relevant lexical entries.

The novel approach goes well beyond language-specific considerations, supporting a revision of Head-driven Phrase Structure Grammar that gives due prominence to the notion of 'functor' for head-selecting dependents, so as to enhance the lexicalist, non-configurational view of X-bar Theory by Pollard & Sag (1994: ch. 9). According to the version of HPSG we have proposed, the bar level of a nominal construction with some determiner qua functor daughter and, concomitantly, the specifier or adjunct role of that daughter follow from lexically based values transmitted between the functor and the construction's mother node. It has been shown how this system considerably simplifies the repertory of X-bar/ID schemata which emerged from previous discussion in our chapter 4, without resorting to cyclic feature structures for the treatment of specifiers or abandoning a traditional assumption of nominal headedness of the NP.

As regards semantic aspects, NP interpretation has been modelled quantificationally by drawing on standard logical approaches, which were gradually introduced starting from chapters 2-3. In the current chapter, the quantificational import of determiners, but also of nominal heads, has been addressed in relation to HPSG's syntax-semantics interface, extending and revising a 'quantifier storage' technique so as to achieve radically lexicalist solutions for problems of quantifier scope not adequately treated by previous versions of the framework. We have completed our account of meaning by investigating some connections to the pragmatic dimension of pertinent signs, with special reference to such self-determining definite NPs as proper names and personal pronouns.

Bibliography

Abeillé, A., D. Godard, P. Miller and I. Sag (1998) "French Bounded Dependencies", in Balari & Dini (1998).

Abney, S. (1987) *The English Noun Phrase in Its Sentential Aspect.* PhD thesis, MIT (Cambridge Mass.).

Ajdukiewicz, K. (1935) "Die syntaktische Konnexität", *Studia Philosophica*, 13, pp. 1-27.

Allegranza, V. (1986) "Sulla nozione di 'quantificazione ristretta' in logica e nella teoria grammaticale", *Rivista di Grammatica Generativa*, vol. of year 1983 (published in 1986), 8, pp. 3-84.

Allegranza, V. (1998a) "Determiners as Functors: NP Structure in Italian", in Balari & Dini (1998).

Allegranza, V. (1998b) "Determination and Quantification", in Van Eynde & Schmidt (1998).

Allegranza, V., and G. Mazzini (2000) *Linguistica generativa e grammatiche a unificazione.* Torino: Paravia.

Alston, W. (1964) *Philosophy of Language.* Englewood Cliffs: Prentice-Hall.

Anderson, J. (1971) *The Grammar of Case: Towards a Localistic Theory.* Cambridge: Cambridge University Press.

Anderson, J. (1977) *On Case Grammar.* London: Croom Helm.

Atlas, J. D. (1977) "Negation, Ambiguity and Presupposition", *Linguistics and Philosophy*, 4, pp. 321-336.

Austin, J. (1962) *How to Do Things with Words.* Oxford: Clarendon Press.

Bach, E. (1989) *Informal Lectures on Formal Semantics.* New York: SUNY Press.

Badia, T. (1998) "Prepositions in Catalan", in Balari & Dini (1998).

Badia, T., and C. Colominas (1998), "Predicate-Argument Structure", in Van Eynde & Schmidt (1998).

Balari, S., and L. Dini (eds.) (1998) *Romance in HPSG.* Stanford: CSLI Publications.

Barbu, A.-M. (1999) "Romanian determiners: order and classification", unpublished manuscript, Research Institute for Informatics, Romania.

Barwise, J., and Robin Cooper (1981) "Generalized quantifiers and natural language", *Linguistics and Philosophy*, 4, pp. 159-219.

Barwise, J., and J. Perry (1983) *Situations and Attitudes.* Cambridge Mass.: MIT Press.

Bennett, M. (1974) *Some Extensions of a Montague Fragment of English.* PhD thesis, UCLA.

Bennett, P. (1993) "The interaction of syntax and morphology in machine translation", in Van Eynde (ed.) *Linguistic Issues in Machine Translation.* London: Pinter.

Bennett, P. (1995) *A Course in Generalized Phrase Structure Grammar.* London: University College of London Press.

Bennett, P., and P. Schmidt (1998) "Phrase Structure", in Van Eynde & Schmidt (1998).

Blok, P. (1993) *The Interpretation of Focus. An Epistemic Approach to Pragmatics*, vol. 6 of *Groningen Dissertations in Linguistics.* PhD thesis, University of Groningen.

Blok, P. (1995) "From Structured Meanings to Formal Pragmatics", in Van Eynde & Allegranza (1995).

Borsley, R. (1989) "Phrase Structure Grammar and the Barriers Conception of Clause Structure", *Linguistics*, 27, pp. 843-863.

Borsley, R. (1993) "Heads in Head-driven Phrase Structure Grammar", in G. Corbett, N. Fraser and S. Mc Glashan (eds.), *Heads in Grammatical Theory.* Cambridge: Cambridge University Press.

Bosch, P., and B. Geurts (1990) "Processing definite NPs", *Rivista di Linguistica*, 2 (1), pp. 177-199.

Bouma, G. (1988) "Modifiers and specifiers in categorial unification grammar", *Linguistics*, 26, pp. 21-46.

Branco, A., and F. Costa (2006) "Noun Ellipsis Without Empty Categories", paper presented at the 13th International Conference on Head-Driven Phrase Structure Grammar (HPSG 2006), Varna, Bulgaria.

Bredsdorff, E. (1956) *Danish. An Elementary Grammar and Reader.* Cambridge: Cambridge University Press.

Bresnan, J. (1973) "Syntax of the Comparative Clause Construction in English", *Linguistic Inquiry*, 4 (3), pp. 275-343.

Bresnan, J. (ed.) (1982a) *The Mental Representation of Grammatical Relations.* Cambridge Mass.: MIT Press.

Bresnan, J. (1982b) "Poliadicity", in Bresnan (1982a).

Bresnan, J. (1982c) "Control and Complementation", in Bresnan (1982a).

Bresnan, J., and R. Kaplan (1982) "Introduction: Grammars as Mental Representations of Language", in Bresnan (1982a).

Bunt, H. (1984) "The Resolution of Quantificational Ambiguity in the Tendum System", in *Proceedings of Coling '84*, Stanford University, California.

Burton-Roberts, N. (1981) "Review of J. Hawkins, *Definiteness and indefiniteness*", *Language*, 57 (1), pp. 191-196.

Carlson, G. (1982) *Reference to Kinds in English.* PhD thesis, University of Massachusetts (Amherst).

Carnap, R. (1947) *Meaning and Necessity.* Chicago: University of Chicago Press. (Reprint with appendices in 1956.)

Carpenter, B. (1992) *The Logic of Typed Feature Structures.* Cambridge: Cambridge University Press.

Chesterman, A. (1991) *On definiteness: A study with special reference to English and Finnish.* Cambridge: Cambridge University Press.

Chierchia, G. (1985) "Formal Semantics and the Grammar of Predication", *Linguistic Inquiry*, 16, pp. 417-443.

Chierchia, G. (1997) *Semantica.* Bologna: Il Mulino.

Chomsky, N. (1957) *Syntactic Structures.* The Hague: Mouton.

Chomsky, N. (1965) *Aspects of the Theory of Syntax*. Cambridge Mass.: MIT Press.

Chomsky, N. (1970) "Remarks on Nominalization", in R. Jacobs and P. Rosenbaum (eds.) *Readings in English Tranformational Grammar*. Waltham Mass.: Ginn.

Chomsky, N. (1975) "Questions of form and interpretation", *Linguistic Analysis*, 1, pp. 75-109.

Chomsky, N. (1976) "Conditions on Rules of Grammar", *Linguistic Analysis*, 2, pp. 303-351.

Chomsky, N. (1977) "On *wh*-movement", in P. S. Culicover, T. Wasow and A. Akmajian (eds.) *Formal Syntax*. New York: Academic Press.

Chomsky, N. (1981) *Lectures on Government and Binding*. Dordrecht: Foris.

Chomsky, N. (1986) *Barriers*. Cambridge Mass.: MIT Press.

Chomsky, N. (1995) *The Minimalist Program*. Cambridge Mass.: MIT Press.

Chomsky, N., and H. Lasnik (1993) "Principles and Parameters Theory", in Jacobs et al. (1993).

Church, A. (1951) "The need for abstract entities in semantic analysis", in *Proceedings of the American Academy of Arts and Sciences*, vol. 80. Englewood Cliffs: Prentice-Hall.

Cinque, G. (1991) *Teoria linguistica e sintassi italiana*. Bologna: Il Mulino.

Cooper, Richard (1990) *Classification-based Phrase Structure Grammar: An Extended Revised Version of HPSG*. PhD thesis, University of Edinburgh.

Cooper, Robin (1983) *Quantification and Syntactic Theory*. Dordrecht: Reidel.

Cooper, Robin (1987) "Preliminaries to the Treatment of Generalized Quantifiers and Plurals", in Gärdenfors (1987).

Cooper, Robin (1991) "Three Lectures on Situation Theoretic Grammar", in M. Filgueiras, L. Damas, N. Moreira and A. P. Tomas (eds.) *Natural Language Processing. Proceedings of EAIA 90*, vol. 476 of *Lecture Notes in Artificial Intelligence*. Berlin: Springer.

Coppen, P. A. (1991) *Specifying the Noun Phrase*. Amsterdam: Thesis Publishers.

Croft, W. (1990) *Typology and Universals*. Cambridge: Cambridge University Press.

Cruse, D. (1980) "Review of J. Hawkins, *Definiteness and indefiniteness*", *Journal of Linguistics*, 16 (2), pp. 308-316.

Davidson, D. (1967) "The Logical Form of Action Sentences", in N. Rescher (ed.) *The Logic of Decision and Action*. Pittsburgh: University of Pittsburgh Press.

Diesing, M. (1992) *Indefinites*. Cambridge Mass.: MIT Press.

Dowty, D. (1979) *Word Meaning and Montague Grammar*. Dordrecht: Reidel.

Dowty, D. (1989) "On the Semantic Content of the Notion of Theta Role", in G. Chierchia, B. Partee and R. Turner (eds.) *Properties, Types and Meaning*. Dordrecht: Kluwer.

Dowty, D., R. Wall and S. Peters (1981) *Introduction to Montague Semantics*. Dordrecht: Reidel.

Drijkoningen, F. (1993) "Movement theory and the DP-hypothesis", *Linguistics*, 31, pp. 813-853.

Durand, J. (1990) *Generative and Non-Linear Phonology*. London: Longman.

Eco, U. (1997) *Kant e l'ornitorinco*. Milano: Bompiani.

Erbach, D. (1994) "Multidimensional Inheritance", *Research Report CLAUS*, 18, University of Saarbrücken.

Evans, G. (1977) "Pronouns, Quantifiers and Relative Clauses", *Canadian Journal of Philosophy*, 7, pp. 467-536.

Evans, G. (1980) "Pronouns", *Linguistic Inquiry*, 11, pp. 337-362.

Fillmore, C. (1968) "The Case for Case", in E. Bach and R. Harms (eds.) *Universals in Linguistic Theory*. New York: Holt, Rinehart and Winston.

Fillmore, C., and P. Kay (1995) *Construction Grammar*. Stanford: CSLI Publications.

Flickinger, D., and J. Nerbonne (1992) "Inheritance and complementation: A case study of *easy* adjectives and related nouns", *Computational Linguistics*, 18, pp. 269-309.

Frege, G. (1879) *Begriffsschrift. Eine der arithmetischen nachgebildete Formelsprache des reinen Denkens*. Halle.

Frege, G. (1892) "Über Sinn und Bedeutung", *Zeitschrift für Philosophie und philosophische Kritik*, 100, pp. 25-50.

Gärdenfors, P. (ed.) (1987) *Generalized Quantifiers*. Dordrecht: Reidel.

Gazdar, G. (1979) *Pragmatics: Implicature, Presupposition and Logical Form*. New York: Academic Press.

Gazdar, G. (1981a) "Unbounded Dependencies and Coordinate Structures", *Linguistic Inquiry*, 12, pp. 155-184.

Gazdar, G. (1981b) "A Phrase Structure Syntax for Comparative Clauses", in T. Hoekstra, H. van der Hulst and M. Moortgat (eds.) *Lexical Grammar*. Dordrecht: Foris.

Gazdar, G. (1982) "Phrase Structure Grammar", in P. Jacobsen and G. Pullum (eds.) *The Nature of Syntactic Representation*. Dordrecht: Reidel.

Gazdar, G., E. Klein, G. Pullum and I. Sag (1985) *Generalized Phrase Structure Grammar*. Oxford: Basil Blackwell.

Gazdar, G., and C. Mellish (1989) *Natural Language Processing in Prolog*. Reading Mass.: Addison-Wesley.

Gazdar, G., G. Pullum and I. Sag (1982) "Auxiliaries and Related Phenomena in a Restricted Theory of Grammar", *Language*, 58, pp. 591-638.

Gerstner-Link, C., and M. Krifka (1993) "Genericity", in Jacobs et al. (1993).

Ginzburg, J., and I. Sag (2001) *Interrogative Investigations: The Form, Meaning and Use of English Interrogatives*. Stanford: CSLI Publications.

Goldberg, A. (1995) *Constructions - A Construction Grammar Approach to Argument Structure*. Chicago: University of Chicago Press.

Graffi, G. (1994) *Sintassi*. Bologna: Il Mulino.

Grice, P. (1967) *Logic and Conversation*, The William James Lectures, Harvard University; partly published in P. Cole and J. L. Morgan (eds.) (1975) *Speech Acts*, vol. 3 of *Syntax and Semantics*. New York: Academic Press.

Groenendijk, J., T. Jansen and M. Stokhof (eds.) (1981) *Formal Methods in the Study of Language*. Amsterdam: Mathematisch Centrum. (Reprinted as vol. 2 of *GRASS Series*. Dordrecht: Foris, 1994.)

Groenendijk, J., and M. Stokhof (1984) *Studies on the semantics of questions and the pragmatics of answers*. PhD thesis, University of Amsterdam.

Groenendijk, J., and M. Stokhof (1990) "Dynamic Montague Grammar", in L. Kálmán and L. Pólos (eds.) *Papers from the Second Symposium on Logic and Language*. Budapest: Akedémiai Kiadó.

Groenendijk, J., and M. Stokhof (1991) "Dynamic Predicate Logic", *Linguistics and Philosophy*, 14, pp. 39-100.

Haiman, J. (1985) *Natural Syntax*. Cambridge: Cambridge University Press.

Halliday, M.A.K. (1967/68) "Notes on transitivity and theme in English", *Journal of Linguistics*, 3 (1), pp. 37-81; 3 (2), pp. 119-244; 4 (2), pp. 179-215.

Halliday, M.A.K., and R. Hasan (1976) *Cohesion in English*. London: Longman.

Hawkins, J. (1978) *Definiteness and indefiniteness. A study in reference and grammaticality prediction*. London: Croom Helm.

Hawkins, J. (1982) "Cross-category harmony, X-bar and the predictions of markedness", *Journal of Linguistics*, 18, pp. 1-35.

Heim, I. (1982) *The Semantics of Definite and Indefinite Noun Phrases*. PhD thesis, University of Massachusetts (Amherst).

Heim, I. (1983) "On the Projection Problem for Presuppositions", in M. Barlow, D. Flickinger and M. Westcoat (eds.) *Proceedings of WCCFL II*, Stanford. (Reprinted in S. Davis, ed., *Pragmatics - a Reader*. Oxford: Oxford University Press, 1991.)

Heim, I. (1990) "E-Type Pronouns and Donkey Anaphora", *Linguistics and Philosophy*, 13, pp. 137-178.

Hellan, L. (1986) "The Headedness of NPs in Norwegian", in P. Muysken and H. van Riemsdijk (eds.) *Features and Projections*. Dordecht: Foris.

Hewson, J. (1991) "Determiners as heads", *Cognitive Linguistics*, 2 (4), pp. 317-337.

Hiz, H. (ed.) (1978) *Questions*, Dordrecht, Reidel.

Hjelmslev, L. (1943) *Omkring sprogtheoriens grunlæggelse*. Copenaghen: Munksgaard. (English translation as *Prolegomena to a Theory of Language*. Madison: University of Wisconsin Press, 1961.)

Hoeksema, J. (1983) "Plurality and Conjunction", in A. ter Meulen (ed.) *Studies in Model-theoretic Semantics*, vol. 1 of *GRASS Series*. Dordrecht: Foris.

Horn, L. (1989) *A Natural History of Negation*. Cambridge: Cambridge University Press.

Hornstein, N. (1984) "Interpreting Quantification in Natural Language", *Synthese*, 59, pp. 117-150.

Huang, J. (1982) *Grammatical Relations in Chinese*. PhD thesis, MIT (Cambridge Mass.).

Hudson, R. (1987) "Zwicky on heads", *Journal of Linguistics*, 23, pp. 109-132.

Hudson, R. (1990) *English Word Grammar*. Oxford: Basil Blackwell.

Ioup, G. (1975) *The Treatment of Quantifier Scope in Transformational Grammar*. PhD thesis, CUNY Graduate Center (New York).

Jackendoff, R. (1972) *Semantic Interpretation in Generative Grammar*. Cambridge Mass.: MIT Press.

Jackendoff, R. (1973) "The base rules for prepositional phrases", in S. Anderson and P. Kiparsky (eds.) *A Festschrift for Morris Halle*. New York: Holt, Rinehart and Winston.

Jackendoff, R. (1977) *X'-Syntax: A Study of Phrase Structure*. Cambridge Mass.: MIT Press.

Jackendoff, R. (1983) *Semantics and Cognition*. Cambridge Mass.: MIT Press.

Jacobs, J., A. von Stechow, W. Sternefeld and T. Vennemann (eds.) (1993) *Syntax: An International Handbook of Contemporary Research*. Berlin: W. de Gruyter.

James, C. (1980) *Contrastive analysis*. London: Longman.

Jansen, S. (1978) *Lingua danese. Elementi strutturali.* Roma/Copenaghen: Bulzoni Editore, Akademisk Forlag.

Kamp, J. (1975) "Two theories about adjectives", in E. Keenan (ed.) *Formal Semantics of Natural Language.* Cambridge: Cambridge University Press.

Kamp, J. (1981) "A Theory of Truth and Semantic Representation", in Groenendijk et al. (1981).

Kamp, J., and U. Reyle (1993) *From discourse to logic.* Dordrecht: Kluwer.

Kartunnen, L. (1969) "Discourse referents", paper presented at the International Conference on Computational Linguistics (Coling), Sånga-Säby/Stockholm; published in J. Mc Cawley (ed.) (1976) *Notes from the linguistic underground*, vol. 7 of *Syntax and Semantics.* New York: Academic Press.

Kartunnen, L. (1973) "Presuppositions of compound sentences", *Linguistic Inquiry*, 4, pp. 169-193.

Kartunnen, L., and S. Peters (1979) "Conventional implicature", in C.-K. Oh and D. Dinneen (eds.) *Presupposition*, vol. 11 of *Syntax and Semantics.* New York: Academic Press.

Kathol, A. (1999) "Restrictive Modification and Polycategorial NPs in English", in G. Bouma, E. Hinrichs, G.-J. Kruijff and R. Oehrle (eds.) *Constraints and Resources in Natural Language Syntax and Semantics.* Stanford University, California.

Katz, J. (1972) *Semantic Theory.* New York: Harper & Row.

Katz, J., and J. Fodor (1963) "The structure of a semantic theory", *Language*, 39, pp. 170-210.

Katz, J., and P. Postal (1964) *An Integrated Theory of Linguistic Descriptions.* Cambridge Mass.: MIT Press.

Kay, M. (1979) "Functional Grammar", in *Proceedings of the 5th Annual Meeting of the Berkeley Linguistic Society.*

Kay, M. (1984) "Functional Unification Grammar: A Formalism for Machine Translation", *Proceedings of Coling '84*, Stanford University, California.

Kay, M. (1985) "Parsing in Functional Unification Grammar", in D. Dowty, L. Kartunnen and A. Zwicky (eds.), *Natural Language Parsing.* Cambridge: Cambridge University Press.

Kneale, W., and M. Kneale (1962) *The Development of Logic.* Oxford: Clarendon Press.

Kolliakou, D. (1996) "Definiteness and the Make-up of Nominal Categories", in C. Grover and E. Vallduví (eds.) *Studies in HPSG*, vol. 12 of *Edinburgh Working Papers in Cognitive Science.* University of Edinburgh.

Krieger, H.-U., and J. Nerbonne (1993) "Feature-based Inheritance Networks for Computational Lexicons", in T. Briscoe, A. Copestake and V. De Paiva (eds.), *Inheritance, Defaults and the Lexicon.* Cambridge: Cambridge University Press.

Kripke, S. (1963) "Semantical considerations on modal logic", *Acta Philosophica Fennica*, 16, pp. 83-94.

Kripke, S. (1972) "Naming and Necessity", in G. Harman and D. Davidson (eds.), *Semantics of Natural Language.* Dordrecht: Reidel.

Krzeszowski, T. P. (1984) "Tertium comparationis", in J. Fisiak (ed.), *Contrastive linguistics. Prospects and problems.* Berlin: Mouton.

Labov, W. (1973) "The Boundaries of Words and their Meanings", in Ch.-J. Bailey and R. Shuy (eds.), *New Ways of Analyzing Variation in English.* Washington D.C.: Georgetown University Press.

Lambek, J. (1958) "The Mathematics of Sentence Structure", *American Mathematical Monthly*, 65, pp. 154-170.

Landman, F. (1991) *Structures for Semantics.* Dordrecht: Kluwer.

Lasnik, H. (1972) *Analyses of Negation in English.* PhD thesis, MIT (Cambridge Mass.).

Leech, G., and J. Svartvik (1975) *A Communicative Grammar of English.* London: Longman.

Levinson, S. (1983) *Pragmatics.* Cambridge: Cambridge University Press.

Lewis, D. (1970) "General semantics", *Synthese*, 22, pp. 18-67.

Liberman, M., and R. Sprout (1992) "The stress and structure of modified noun phrases in English", in I. Sag and A. Szabolcsi (eds.), *Lexical Matters.* Chicago: University of Chicago Press.

Link, G. (1983) "The Logical Analysis of Plurals and Mass Terms: A Lattice-theoretical Approach", in R. Baeuerle, C. Schwarze and A. von Stechow (eds.) *Meaning, Use and Interpretation of Language.* Berlin: W. de Gruyter.

Link, G. (1987) "Generalized Quantifiers and Plurals", in Gärdenfors (1987).

Longobardi, G. (1994) "Reference and Proper Names: A theory of N-Movement in Syntax and Logical Form", *Linguistic Inquiry*, 25 (4), pp. 609-665.

Lønning, J. T. (1987) "Collective Readings of Definite and Indefinite Noun Phrases", in Gärdenfors (1987).

Lyons, C. (1980) "The meaning of the English definite article", in J. van der Auwera (ed.), *The semantics of determiners.* London: Croom Helm.

Lyons, C. (1986) "The syntax of English genitive constructions", *Journal of Linguistics*, 22, pp. 123-143.

Lyons, J. (1968) *Introduction to Theoretical Linguistics.* Cambridge: Cambridge University Press.

Manning, C., I. Sag and M. Iida (1996) "The Lexical Integrity of Japanese Causatives", in T. Gunji (ed.) *Studies Based on the Universality of Constraint-Based Phrase Structure Grammars*, Graduate School of Language and Culture, Osaka University.

Marconi, D. (1997) *Lexical Competence.* Cambridge Mass.: MIT Press.

Markantonatou, S., and L. Sadler (1998) "Lexical Generalizations", in Van Eynde & Schmidt (1998).

Martin J. (1987) *Elements of Formal Semantics.* New York: Academic Press.

May, R. (1977) *The Grammar of Quantification.* PhD thesis, MIT (Cambridge Mass.).

May, R. (1985) *Logical Form: Its Structure and Derivation.* Cambridge Mass.: MIT Press.

Milewski, T. (1970) "Voraussetzungen einer typologischen Sprachwissenschaft", *Linguistics*, 59, pp. 64-107.

Miller, P. (1991) *Clitics and Constituents in Phrase Structure Grammar.* PhD thesis, University of Utrecht.

Miller, P., and I. Sag (1995) "Une Analyse Lexicaliste des Affixes Pronominaux en Français", *Revue Québécoise de Linguistique*, 24 (1), pp. 135-171.

Minsky, M. (1975) "A Framework for Representing Knowledge", in P. Winston (ed.), *The Psychology of Computer Vision.* New York: McGraw Hill.

Monachesi, P. (1995) *A grammar of Italian clitics.* PhD thesis, University of Tilburg.

Monachesi, P. (1998) "Decomposing Italian clitics", in Balari and Dini (1998).

Montague, R. (1968) "Pragmatics", in R. Klibansky (ed.) *Contemporary Philosophy.* Florence: La Nuova Italia Editrice. (Reprinted in Montague 1974.)

Montague, R. (1970a) "Pragmatics and Intensional Logic", *Synthese*, 22, pp. 68-94. (Reprinted in Montague 1974.)

Montague, R. (1970b) "English as a formal language", in B. Visentini (ed.) *Linguaggi nella società e nella tecnica.* Milan: Edizioni di Comunità. (Reprinted in Montague 1974.)

Montague, R. (1970c) "Universal Grammar", *Theoria*, 36, pp. 373-398. (Reprinted in Montague 1974.)

Montague, R. (1973) "The Proper Treatment of Quantification in Ordinary English", in J. Hintikka, J. Moravcsik and P. Suppes (eds.) *Approaches to Natural Languages.* Dordrecht: Reidel. (Reprinted in Montague 1974.)

Montague, R. (1974) *Formal Philosophy: Selected Papers*, edited by R. Thomason. New Haven: Yale University Press.

Moore, R. (1981) "Problems in logical form", in *Proceedings of the 19th Annual Meeting of the ACL.*

Morris, C. (1938) *Foundations of the Theory of Signs.* Chicago: Chicago University Press.

Nerbonne, J., M. Iida and W. Ladusaw (1998) "Running on empty: Null heads in head-driven grammar", in J. Fee and K. Hunt (eds.) *Proceedings of the Eight Annual West Coast Conference on Formal Linguistics.* CSLI (Stanford).

Nerbonne, J., and T. Mullen (2000) "Null-Headed Nominals in German and English", in F. Van Eynde, I. Schuurman and N. Schelkens (eds.), *Computational Linguistics in the Netherlands, Selected Papers from the 9th CLIN Meeting.* Amsterdam: Rodopi.

Nerbonne, J., K. Netter and C. Pollard (eds.) (1994) *German in HPSG.* Stanford: CSLI Publications.

Netter, K. (1994) "Towards a Theory of Functional Heads: German Nominal Phrases", in Nerbonne et al. (1994).

Nichols, J. (1988) "On alienable and inalienable possession", in W. Shipley (ed.), *In Honor of Mary Haas.* Berlin: Mouton de Gruyter.

Ojeda, A. (1991) "Definite Descriptions and Definite Generics", *Linguistics and Philosophy*, 14 (4), pp. 367-397.

Ojeda, A. (1993) *Linguistic Individuals.* Stanford: CSLI Publications.

Parsons, T. (1995) "Thematic Relations and Arguments", *Linguistic Inquiry*, 26, pp. 635-662.

Partee, B. (1976) "Some transformational extensions of Montague grammar", in Partee, B. (ed.) *Montague Grammar.* New York: Academic Press.

Partee, B. (1984) "Nominal and Temporal Anaphora", *Linguistics and Philosophy*, 7, pp. 243-286.

Payne, J. (1993) "The headedness of noun phrases: slaying the nominal hydra", in G. Corbett, N. Fraser and S. Mc Glashan (eds.) *Heads in grammatical theory.* Cambridge: Cambridge University Press.

Pelletier, F., and Schubert L. (1989) "Mass expressions", in D. Gabbay and F. Guenthner (eds.) *Handbook of Philosophical Logic. Volume IV.* Dordrecht: Reidel.

Pinkal, M. (1986) "Definite Noun Phrases and the Semantics of Discourse", in *Proceedings of Coling '86*, University of Bonn.

Plank, F., and E. Moravcsik (1996) "The Maltese article: Language-particulars and universals", *Rivista di linguistica*, 8 (1), pp. 183-212.

Pollard, C., and I. Sag (1987) *Information-based Syntax and Semantics.* Stanford: CSLI Publications.

Pollard, C., and I. Sag (1994) *Head-driven Phrase Structure Grammar.* Stanford: CSLI Publications; Chicago: Chicago University Press.

Pollard, C., and E. J. Yoo (1998) "A Unified Theory of Scope for Quantifiers and *Wh*-Phrases", *Journal of Linguistics*, 34, pp. 415–445.

Putnam, H. (1975) *Mind, Language and Reality*, vol. 2 of *Philosophical Papers.* Cambridge: Cambridge University Press.

Quine, W. V. O. (1959) *Methods of Logic.* New York: Henry Holt.

Quirk, R., S. Greenbaum, G. Leech and J. Svartvik (1985) *A Comprehensive Grammar of the English Language.* London: Longman.

Radford, A. (1981) *Transformational Syntax. A Student's Guide to Chomsky's Extended Standard Theory.* Cambridge: Cambridge University Press.

Radford, A. (1997) *Syntactic theory and the structure of English. A minimalist approach.* Cambridge: Cambridge University Press.

Reape, M. (1994) "Domain Union and Word Order Variation in German", in Nerbonne et al. (1994).

Reichenbach, H. (1947) *Elements of Symbolic Logic.* Berkeley: University of California Press.

Renzi, L. (1988) "L'articolo", ch. 7 of L. Renzi (ed.), *Grande grammatica italiana di consultazione.* Bologna: Il Mulino.

Robins, R. (1967) *A Short History of Linguistics.* London: Longman.

Rosch, E. (1973) "Natural categories", *Cognitive Psychology*, 4, pp. 328-350.

Ross, J. (1967) *Constraints on Variables in Syntax.* PhD thesis, MIT (Cambridge Mass.); published as *Infinite Syntax!* (Norwood N. J.: Ablex, 1986).

Russell, B. (1905) "On denoting", *Mind*, 14, pp. 479-493.

Sadler, L., and D. Arnold (1994) "Pronominal adjectives and the phrasal/lexical distinction", *Journal of Linguistics*, 30, pp. 187-226.

Sag, I. (1997) "English Relative Clause Constructions", *Journal of Linguistics*, 33, pp. 431-484.

Saussure, F. de (1916) *Cours de linguistique générale*, edited by C. Bally and A. Sechehaye. Paris: Payot.

Scha, R. (1981) "Distributive, collective and cumulative quantification", in J. Groenendijk et al. (1981).

Schmidt, P. (1998) "Formal Assumptions", in Van Eynde & Schmidt (1998).

Searle, J. (1958) "Proper Names", *Mind*, 67, pp. 166-173.

Searle, J. (1968) "Austin on Locutionary and Illocutionary Acts", *The Philosophical Review*, 77, pp. 405-424.

Searle, J. (1969) *Speech Acts: An Essay in the Philosophy of Language.* Cambridge: Cambridge University Press.

Searle, J. (1975) "A Taxonomy of Illocutionary Acts", in K. Gunderson (ed.) *Language, Mind and Knowledge*, vol. 7 of *Minnesota Studies in the Philosophy of Science*. Minneapolis: University of Minnesota Press.

Seiler, H. (1983) *Possession*. Tübingen: Gunter Narr.

Sharvy, R. (1980) "A more general theory of definite descriptions", *Philosophical Review*, 89, pp. 607-624.

Shieber, S. (1986) *An Introduction to Unification-Based Approaches to Grammar*. Stanford: CSLI Publications.

Smith, C. (1964) "Determiners and Relative Clauses in a Generative Grammar of English", *Language*, 40 (1), pp. 37-52.

Stalnaker, R. (1970) "Pragmatics", *Synthese*, 22, pp. 272-289.

Stalnaker, R. (1974) "Pragmatic presuppositions", in M. Munitz and P. Unger (eds.) *Semantics and Philosophy*. New York: New York University Press.

Stehl, T. (1988) "Les concepts de *continuum* et de *gradatum* dans la linguistique variationnelle", in D. Kremer (ed.) *Actes du XVIII Congrès International de Linguistique et de Philologie Romanes*. Tübingen: Niemeyer.

Steiner, E., P. Schmidt and C. Zelinsky-Wibbelt (eds.) (1988) *From Syntax to Semantics: Insights from Machine Translation*. London: Pinter.

Strawson, P. (1950) "On referring", *Mind*, 59, pp. 320-344.

Strawson, P. (1952) *Introduction to Logical Theory*. London: Methuen.

Szabolsci, A. (1983) "The possessor that ran away from home", *The Linguistic Review*, 3, pp. 89-102.

Tarski, A. (1936) "Der Wahrheitsbegriff in den formalisierten Sprachen", *Studia Philosophica*, 1, pp. 261-405.

Tesnière, L. (1959) *Eléments de syntaxe structurale*. Paris: Klincksieck.

Thomason, R. (1967) "Modal Logic and Metaphysics", in K. Lambert (ed.) *The Logical Way of Doing Things*. New Haven: Yale University Press.

Uszkoreit, H. (1987) *Word order and constituent structure in German*. Stanford: CSLI Publications.

Van der Sandt, R. A. (1988) *Context and Presupposition*. London: Croom Helm.

Vanderveken, D. (1991a) *Meaning and Speech Acts – Vol. I: Principles of Language Use*. Cambridge: Cambridge University Press.

Vanderveken, D. (1991b) *Meaning and Speech Acts – Vol. II: Formal Semantics of Success and Satisfaction*. Cambridge: Cambridge University Press.

Van Eijck, J. (1988) "Quantification", *Technical Report CCSRC*, 7, Cambridge Computer Science Research Centre (SRI International), Cambridge.

Van Eijck, J., and H. Alshawi (1992) "Logical Forms", ch. 2 of H. Alshawi (ed.) *The Core Language Engine*. Cambridge Mass.: MIT Press.

Van Eynde, F. (1994) *Auxiliaries and Verbal Affixes: A monostratal cross-linguistic analysis*. University of Leuven.

Van Eynde, F. (1998a) "Tense, Aspect and Negation", in Van Eynde & Schmidt (1998).

Van Eynde, F. (1998b) "The Immediate Dominance Schemata of HPSG", in P.-A. Coppen, H. Van Halteren and L. Teunissen (eds.), *Computational Linguistics in the Netherlands, Selected Papers from the 8th CLIN Meeting*. Amsterdam: Rodopi.

Van Eynde, F. (2004) "Minor Adpositions in Dutch", *Journal of Comparative Germanic Linguistics*, 7, pp. 1-58.

Van Eynde, F. (2006) "NP-internal agreement and the structure of the noun phrase", *Journal of Linguistics*, 42, pp. 139-186.

Van Eynde, F., and V. Allegranza (eds.) (1995) *Semantics and Discourse: A NLP Perspective*, vol. 9 of *Studies in Machine Traslation and Natural Language Processing*. Luxembourg: Office for Official Publications of the European Commission.

Van Eynde, F., and P. Schmidt (eds.) (1998) *Linguistic Specifications for Typed Feature Structure Formalisms*, vol. 10 of *Studies in Machine Traslation and Natural Language Processing*. Luxembourg: Office for Official Publications of the European Commission.

Van Fraassen, B. C. (1968) "Presupposition, Implication and Self-Reference", *Journal of Philosophy*, 65, pp. 136-152.

Vendler, Z. (1967) "Each and Every, Any and All", in Z. Vendler, *Linguistics in Philosophy*. Ithaca: Cornell University Press.

Wechsler, S., and L. Zlatić (2003) *The Many Faces of Agreement*. Stanford: CSLI Publications.

Winhart, H. (1997) "Die Nominalphrase in einem HPSG-Fragment des Deutschen", in E. Hinrichs, W. Meurers, F. Richter, M. Seiler and H. Winhart, *Ein HPSG-Fragment des Deutschen. Teil I: Theorie*, vol. 95 of *Arbeitspapiere des SFB 340*. University of Tübingen.

Wittgenstein, L. (1921) *Tractatus logico-philosophicus*. London: Kegan Paul.

Wittgenstein, L. (1953) *Philosophische Untersuchungen*, edited by G. E. M. Anscombe and R. Rhees. Oxford: Blackwell.

Wunderlich, D. (1988) "Einige Bemerkungen über Kongruenz", manuscript, Heinrich Heine Universität.

Zadeh, L. (1965) "Fuzzy sets", *Information and Control*, 8, pp. 338-353.

Zelinsky-Wibbelt, C. (1988) "The transfer of quantifiers in a multilingual machine translation system", in Steiner et al. (1988).

Zimmerman, H.-J. (1985) *Fuzzy set theory – and its applications*. Hingham: Kluwer-Nijhoff.

Zwarts, F. (1983) "Determiners: A Relational Perspective", in A. ter Meulen (ed.) *Studies in Modeltheoretic Semantics*. Dordrecht: Foris.

Zwicky, A. (1987) "Suppressing the Zs", *Journal of Linguistics*, 23, pp. 133-148.

Sabest
Saarbrücker Beiträge zur Sprach- und Translationswissenschaft

Fachrichtung Angewandte Sprachwissenschaft
sowie Übersetzen und Dolmetschen
der Universität des Saarlandes

Alberto Gil – Johann Haller – Erich Steiner
(Hrsg.)

Band 1 Alberto Gil / Johann Haller / Erich Steiner / Heidrun Gerzymisch-Arbogast (Hrsg.): Modelle der Translation. Grundlagen für Methodik, Bewertung, Computermodellierung. 1999.

Band 2 Uwe Reinke: Translation Memories. Systeme – Konzepte – Linguistische Optimierung. 2004.

Band 3 Stella Neumann: Textsorten und Übersetzen. Eine Korpusanalyse englischer und deutscher Reiseführer. 2003.

Band 4 Erich Steiner: Translated Texts: Properties, Variants, Evaluations. 2004.

Band 5 Sisay Fissaha Adafre: Adding Amharic to a Unification-Based Machine Translation System. An Experiment. 2004.

Band 6 Tinka Reichmann: Satzspaltung und Informationsstruktur im Portugiesischen und im Deutschen. Ein Beitrag zur Kontrastiven Linguistik und Übersetzungswissenschaft. 2005.

Band 7 María Jesús Barsanti Vigo: Análisis paremiológico de *El Quijote* de Cervantes en la versión de Ludwig Tieck. 2005.

Band 8 Christoph Rösener: Die Stecknadel im Heuhaufen. Natürlichsprachlicher Zugang zu Volltextdatenbanken. 2005.

Band 9 Fadia Sami Sauerwein: Dolmetschen bei polizeilichen Vernehmungen und grenzpolizeilichen Einreisebefragungen. Eine explorative translationswissenschaftliche Untersuchung zum Community Interpreting. 2006.

Band 10 Rosario Herrero: La metáfora : revisión histórica y descripción lingüística. 2006.

Band 11 Ursula Wienen: Zur Übersetzbarkeit markierter Kohäsionsformen. Eine funktionale Studie zum Kontinuum von Spaltadverbialen und Spaltkonnektoren im Spanischen, Französischen und Deutschen. 2006.

Band 12 María José Corvo Sánchez: Los libros de lenguas de Juan Ángel de Zumaran. La obra de un maestro e intérprete de lenguas español entre los alemanes del siglo XVII. 2007.

Band 13 Vahram Atayan: Makrostrukturen der Argumentation im Deutschen, Französischen und Italienischen. Mit einem Vorwort von Oswald Ducrot. 2006.

Band 14 Alberto Gil / Ursula Wienen (Hrsg.): Multiperspektivische Fragestellungen der Translation in der Romania. Hommage an Wolfram Wilss zu seinem 80. Geburtstag. 2007.

Band 15 Anja Rütten: Informations- und Wissensmanagement im Konferenzdolmetschen. 2007.

Band 16 Valerio Allegranza: The Signs of Determination. Constraint-Based Modelling Across Languages. 2007.

www.peterlang.de

Peter Lang · Internationaler Verlag der Wissenschaften

Moritz Neugebauer

Constraint-Based Acoustic Modelling

Frankfurt am Main, Berlin, Bern, Bruxelles, New York, Oxford, Wien, 2007.
215 pp., num. fig. and tab.
Computer Studies in Language and Speech.
Edited by Wolfgang Hess and Winfried Lenders. Vol. 10
ISBN 978-3-631-56076-1 · pb. € 39.–*

This book is concerned with the automatic generation of inheritance hierarchies for the level below the phoneme and their application in acoustic modelling for automatic speech recognition. Over the last decade, computational phonology has adopted the typed feature structure representation formalism while paying little attention to subphonetic feature structures. Similarly, paradigmatic phonological knowledge used in acoustic modelling does usually not go beyond phonological feature bundles. Here, the discrepancy between hierarchically-structured lexica, as they are promoted in computational phonology and the flat-structured feature bundles common in acoustic modelling, is addressed in a powerful framework for solving combinatorial problems, i.e. constraint programming.

Contents: Knowledge Representation in Constraint-Based Grammar Formalisms · Subphonetic Acoustic Modelling · Constraint Programming, Appropriateness and Inheritance · Experimental Evaluation